STUDIES IN ROMANCE LANGUAGES: 32
John E. Keller, *Editor*

FREDERICK A. DE ARMAS

THE RETURN OF ASTRAEA

AN ASTRAL-IMPERIAL MYTH IN CALDERÓN

THE UNIVERSITY PRESS OF KENTUCKY

*Publication of this book has been assisted by a grant
from the Program for Cultural Cooperation
Between Spain's Ministry of Culture and
North American Universities.*

Library of Congress Cataloging-in-Publication Data

De Armas, Frederick Alfred.
   The return of Astraea.

   (Studies in Romance languages ; 32)
   Bibliography: p.
   Includes index.
   1. Calderón de la Barca, Pedro, 1660–1681—
Characters—Astraea.   2. Calderón de la Barca, Pedro,
1600–1681—Knowledge—Folklore, mythology.   3. Astraea
(Greek deity) in literature.   I. Title.   II. Series.
PQ6314.A8D4   1986   862'.3   86–7758
ISBN 0-8131-1570-1

Contents

Preface

HAVING SURVIVED THE CHRISTIAN MIDDLE AGES, the Greek and Roman gods flourished during the Renaissance. Certain mythographers following Euhemerus's example sought to explain the celestial pantheon by interpreting it as the vestige of historical episodes which had been distorted through time, while others viewed pagan myths as expressions of philosophical and theological questions. For the Renaissance Platonists, the pagan mysteries shed light on many Christian concepts. Indeed, some ancient poets were thought to be divinely inspired to foretell Christian mysteries such as the birth of Christ. In these varied and at times contradictory ways, the gods permeated the works of Christian writers in the Renaissance. Such attitudes still prevailed during the seventeenth century, and can certainly be encountered in the *comedias* of the Spanish Golden Age.

In my previous analysis of aspects of feminism and fantasy in the drama of the seventeenth century, I considered that the recurring plot that I labeled the "Invisible Mistress" could not properly be understood unless seen in terms of the Cupid and Psyche myth. Such plays as Lope de Vega's *La viuda valenciana*, Tirso de Molina's *La celosa de sí misma*, and Calderón's *La dama duende* contain a mythical substructure derived from a reversal of the Cupid and Psyche story. Having analyzed the unique manifestation of this myth in the *comedias de capa y espada*, I then turned to the historical and philosophical dramas in an attempt to find a counterpart to Psyche, a counterpart I hoped would be a mythological woman at the basis of a different type of play.

Reviewing the explanations given by the British school of *Calderonistas* regarding the two plots that coalesce in *La vida es sueño*, I found that in spite of their keen observations and insightful arguments justifying unity, I was still concerned by what appeared to be a breakdown in the tone of the work caused by the intrusion of Rosaura into the main action. This was particularly evident to me in several scenes in the second act where Rosaura is involved in a situation reminiscent of a *capa y espada* play. Rosaura does not appear to have a unifying function at this point. The discovery of a possible solution to this problem brought me in contact with the figure that informs the present book. Rosaura takes the name of Astraea in the palace. According to ancient myth, the goddess Astraea was the last of the immortals to leave earth with the decline of the ages. Her return would signal the advent of a new epoch. Could Segismundo's transformation be the result of the guidance of Rosaura as Astraea? Could Rosaura-Astraea's "fall" into Poland at the beginning of the *comedia* be interpreted as the "fall" of the zodiacal sign Astraea-Virgo from the sky and thus a prophecy of future harmony?

My purpose in writing this book on Astraea is twofold: first, to bring to light the pervasiveness of this myth in early Spanish literature, a topic that has been neglected by most critics; second, to show Astraea's significance in Calderón's *comedias*. The goddess adopts many guises in the Spanish playwright's works. She is an imperial goddess, leading men to become ideal rulers of themselves and their people, or she can appear trapped by politicians who wish to exploit her. Astraea can also be interpreted as a pagan mystery that simultaneously conceals and reveals universal truth, or she might represent divine providence, leading mankind through turmoil to a brighter future. As the astrological sign Virgo or Libra, the goddess can highlight occult forces and correspondences. In all of the works by Calderón in which Astraea takes part, she is also paradoxically depicted in terms of a frail woman who nonetheless takes the goddess's name and thus participates in her divine nature. In the many astounding metamorphoses of this woman who resembles the goddess, Calderón never emphasizes the allegoric or prophetic tradition that transforms her into a Christian image. The messianic interpretation of Virgil's *Fourth Eclogue*, where Astraea and the child are considered to be Mary and Jesus, although a most popular motif, is not to be found in these *comedias*. The Catholic Calderón delights in the universal representation of humanity's longing to reach harmony and perfection, an ideal expressed in the archetypal golden age over which Astraea reigns. A pagan myth has not only survived, but even seems to assume political and philosophical authority in these plays.

The present book is divided into ten chapters. The first two constitute an introductory section, tracing the myth of Astraea from its beginnings in Greek astronomy and literature to Calderón's time. This material is not presented as a comprehensive history. It merely highlights the historical significance of the goddess. The pages on

Spanish literature are intended to encourage further research on this broad but little studied topic. The remaining eight chapters treat Calderón's *comedias* dealing with Astraea. The following plays are considered: *La gran Cenobia* (chapter 3); *La puente de Mantible* and *Yerros de naturaleza y aciertos de la fortuna* (chapter 4); *La vida es sueño* (chapters 4, 5, 6); *La hija del aire*, *El mayor encanto, amor*, and *Los tres mayores prodigios* (chapter 7); *El privilegio de las mujeres* and *Las armas de la hermosura* (chapter 8); *El golfo de las sirenas*, *Ni amor se libra de amor*, and *Los tres afectos de amor* (chapter 9); and *El monstruo de los jardines* (chapter 10).

Portions of chapter four are based on my introductory essay on the myth of Astraea: "The Return of Astraea: An Astral-Imperial Myth in Calderón's *La vida es sueño*," in *Calderón at the Tercentenary: Comparative Views*, ed. Wendell M. Aycock and Sydney P. Cravens (Lubbock: Texas Tech Press, 1982), pp. 135-59. The discussion of *La gloria de Niquea* in chapter three is taken from "Villamediana's *La gloria de Niquea*: An Alchemical Masque," *JHP* 8 (1984), 209–31. Chapter five is a revised and expanded version of my article "The Serpent Star: Dream and Horoscope in Calderón's *La vida es sueño*," *FMLS* 19 (1983), 208-23. I would like to thank Texas Tech Press and the editors of *FMLS* and *JHP* for allowing me to include this material.

In the five years that I have spent working on this project, I have received many suggestions from other *comediantes* and much encouragement from colleagues and friends. My colleagues Margaret Parker and Timothy Ambrose have been most helpful. The Text Processing Center of the College of Arts and Sciences at L.S.U. has facilitated my research and the typing of the manuscript. To my friends at M.I.U., Fairfield, Rhoda Orme-Johnson, Silvine Marbury, and Steve Benjamin, I owe a debt of gratitude for providing an environment suitable to carry out this research. I would also like to thank Pedro Campa, Michael McGaha, and Geoffrey Voght, who have made available to me useful information on the Astraea myth. Shirley Whitaker has providentially pointed to manuscripts, pamphlets, and books at a time when I needed them. Everett W. Hesse has given me many valuable suggestions and provided much needed encouragement. Daniel L. Heiple has shared with me his impressive knowledge and insights on Golden Age verse, and has pointed out several instances where Astraea appears among the poets. Finally, I would like to thank Louisiana State University for granting me a sabbatical leave in the spring of 1982 to work on *The Return of Astraea*.

CHAPTER ONE

Astraea Returns: Genesis

OBSERVING THE EARLY EVENING SKY during the spring months, astrologers of ancient Greece and Rome would have been struck by a bright blue-white star shining with unrivaled splendor in the south-eastern corner of the heavens. The stargazers labeled her *spica*, mark-ing the ear of wheat that the zodiacal sign Virgo holds in her left hand. The Asiatic Greek astronomer Hipparchus compared his own observations of the distance of *spica* from the equinox with measure-ments made by Timocharis 160 years before and thus discovered the annual lag of the heavens known as the precession of the equinoxes.[1] According to Copernicus's more accurate calculations, in 2,160 years the sun traverses a complete zodiacal sign. Thus, while today one would encounter the sun in Pisces during the vernal equinox, in the two millennia before Christ an astronomer would have located it in Aries. The complete cycle, called the Great or Platonic Year,[2] lasts approximately 25,920 of our earthly years. When the revolution is complete, Aries will again meet the sun at the March equinox. It is fitting that Hipparchus's observations of the sign Virgo gave rise to the notion of the precession of the equinoxes, since both Virgo and the Platonic Year are associated with the cosmogonic cycle of crea-tion, destruction, and re-creation: the end of the Great Year was viewed by the ancients as a signal of the destruction of the world, while the return of Astraea (Virgo) was equated with re-creation or the return of the golden age.

The discovery of the precession of the equinoxes was but one of Hipparchus's many achievements. He was also well known in an-tiquity for his *Commentary on the Phaenomena of Eudoxus and Aratus*, which contains many corrections of faulty or incomplete astronomical observations found in Aratus's poem, including the location of *spica*.[3] The precession of the equinoxes and the autumnal constellation as

1

perceived by astronomer and poet thus seem to be inextricably inter-related.

Three Greek poets of the fourth and third centuries B.C. were crucial in cataloguing myths related to planets and constellations.[4] Aratus is the most important since, according to A. Bouché-Leclerq, "On sait qu'Aratus . . . a fixé pour toujours l'iconographie stellaire."[5] This poet is responsible for the description and dissemination of the myth of the just virgin in Virgo, the maiden Astraea. The *Phaenomena* describes the first three ages of man and the deterioration of conditions from the first and ideal golden age. In the first epoch, Justice *(Dike)* was queen, abiding on earth and granting her golden race their every desire. During the silver age, *Dike*'s voice became fainter, since she had withdrawn to the remoteness of the hills. Even the highest promontory became contaminated with cruelty and injustice during the bronze age, so that the maiden goddess of justice "Soared up to heaven, selecting this abode, / Whence yet at night she shows herself to men."[6] The goddess was transformed into the constellation Virgo, reminding the inhabitants of earth that justice and chastity no longer dwelt in the sublunary realm. Humanity must realize that Justice "is no longer ours for the taking . . . we must struggle to reach with our minds to the stars."[7] According to Renato Poggioli, this sense of loss is most clearly depicted as the pastoral dream. He explains that the primeval innocence and happiness of the golden age, of which Astraea is a clear reminder, represents the genesis of the pastoral ideal expressed in literature since Theocritus.[8] Thus, from its very beginnings the myth of Astraea is accompanied by several related concepts that make it adaptable to different literary genres; emphasis may be placed on the pastoral dream or on the corruption of man, on the golden age or the apocalyptic vision.

Perhaps it was the open-endedness of the myth which made Aratus's poem one of the more popular works of classical antiquity.[9] The myth of Justice-Virgo is by far the most developed in the poem, and its notion of a return to the beginnings of time is echoed throughout the astrological portion of the work. William Sale claims that Aratus "is filling the sky not just with life, but with gigantic men and frightening animals."[10] This naive poetic vision of a living sky replete with dreams and nightmares also recalls the sentimental qualities of Arcadia and Hesiod's golden race. Yet in sky images such as Virgo-Justice humanity visualizes not only its own sentimental past, but also the divine order of the universe. By reading the language of stars, Aratus deciphers the mysteries of existence in terms of myths which in turn are expressions of the inner self. Aratus's stars thus reveal to an age of magical belief in heavenly correspondences the longing of men as woven in the celestial tapestry by the gods. Leonard Barkan, speaking of man as a microcosm, explains that "man is the crucial and central term in the astral cosmos, and since all the bodies in the cosmos influence all the others, man must contain within him the distillation of the whole astral system."[11] *Dike*'s departure from earth then corresponds to man's own disregard for justice.

The significance of the *Phaenomena* as a catalogue of astral myths and as the *locus classicus* for the notion of Justice-Virgo's departure from earth after the moral decline of the human race should be balanced by an appreciation of Aratus's debt to Hesiod, who included in the *Works and Days* a lengthy discussion of the ages of man and a description of *Dike*, albeit devoid of her astral connotations. Indeed, Hesiod's presentation of this goddess includes many details not found in Aratus: "Justice herself is a young maiden. She is Zeus's daughter, and seemly, and respected by all the gods of Olympos. When any man uses force on her by false impeachment she goes and sits at the feet of Zeus Kronion, her father, and cries out on the wicked purpose of men, so that their people must pay for the profligacy of their rulers."[12]

Hesiod's *Dike* is a mediator between man and the gods. She remains among men and pleads with Jupiter (Zeus) for the punishment of those who undermine her justice. Pietro Pucci notes that what most characterizes the goddess or concept is "the peacefulness of its attitude."[13] Justice never counteracts evil by force, and is thus "dragged perforce" by unjust men.[14] Since Justice will not do battle, she strives to persuade. Indeed, in Hesiod's poem Justice is presented in an analogical relationship to truth. The *Works and Days* is constructed around a series of oppositions. Where *hybris* prevails and where crooked *basileis*, like hawks, speak the language of falsehood, men will be treated by Zeus as though they lived in "the final and worst age of man."[15] Hesiod expresses here his belief that there could be an epoch worse than the present age. Force alone would prevail in the future sixth age of falsehood, as it does in the cities of the iron age that reject justice. In contradistinction to this negative vision, Hesiod relates *Dike* to the persuasive poet whose weak but truthful song is that of the nightingale. If the poet is allowed to sing, Zeus will grant the inhabitants of places where justice prevails blessings akin to those of the golden age, which was characterized by peace and abundance. The men of the golden race lived like gods and were finally overcome by sleep, turning into supernatural beings. They were succeeded by four progressively inferior ages.

As can be seen, much of the *Phaenomena* is already contained in the *Works and Days*. Both works present justice as a young maiden and both discuss the ages of man. Yet there are some major differences. Aratus's work constitutes a revision of Hesiod's concepts through the perspective of Stoicism. The *Phaenomena* places more emphasis on ethics and the relationship between the ascent of art and civilization and the descent of man's moral fiber. Civilization, according to Aratus and the Stoics, corrupts man since it creates a lack of harmony with nature. The inventions of the civilized world, such as the sword and the ship, are emblems of the fall. While Aratus emphasizes the lost ideal in the virtues of the zodiacal goddess, Hesiod points to Pandora and claims that *Elpis* (Hope), the goddess or *daimon* who remains on earth after Pandora's jar is opened, is a bad companion to man since she encourages him to remain idle.

Following Hesiod's *Works and Days*, Aratus's *Phaenomena*, and Hipparchus's *Commentary*, the association of Justice with the golden age and her escape from earth to become a zodiacal sign became commonplaces in Greek and Roman literatures. The description of the golden age in the first book of Ovid's *Metamorphoses* is perhaps the best known. Harry Levin emphasizes that it was Ovid who "crystallized it into a *topos*, who realigned its traditional elements in the grandly rhetorical set-piece that would be imitated, plagiarized, distorted and metamorphosed into so many shapes."[16] Ovid commences his account with a description of the golden age ruled by Saturn when truth, harmony, and distributive justice prevailed. Nature's gifts to man in this land of perpetual spring are represented by the holm-oak, bearer of honey and the acorn, the staple of later Arcadian diet. There is no need for trade in this bountiful environment; the ship, as in Aratus, is the invention of a lesser age.

In the *Metamorphoses*, the dethroning of Saturn signals the arrival of the silver age. Jupiter replaces the continuous spring with the four seasons. Ovid ascribes Aratus's and Horace's notion that man must till the earth to this second age. Further deterioration in man as well as in his relationship with nature occurs during the bronze age. Hesiod's age of heroes is eliminated by Ovid, who codifies the number of ages as four. Speaking of the fourth Ovidian age, Levin asserts that "the Ovidian iron age is the golden age in reverse, as adumbrated in the companion piece and harking back to the original premises. Now, every crime breaks out; shame, truth and faith take flight; into their places steal the vices, fraud, malice, treason and wicked love of gain."[17] Ovid's only direct reference to the myth of Astraea occurs when he remarks that the star-maiden is the last of the immortals to leave this topsy-turvy world. But not even heaven is safe, since the giants resolve to attack Olympus at this time.

Classical mythographers and astrological writers added further identifications and genealogies to the zodiacal sign Virgo. Little purpose would be served by exploring this confusing maze of attributions, which present Virgo under the guise of Atargatis, the Syrian goddess worshipped at Carthage, or even as the Egyptian goddess Isis.[18] Three examples will suffice. Manilius in his *Astronomica*, a treatise that rivaled in popularity Ptolemy's *Tetrabiblos* during the Renaissance, states that "at her rising, Erigone, who reigned with justice over a bygone age and fled when it fell into sinful ways, bestows high eminence by bestowing supreme power."[19] By identifying justice (Astraea) and Virgo with Erigone, Manilius associates a second popular myth with this sign of the zodiac. Erigone was the daughter of Icarius who hanged herself after the death of her father.

Germanicus, a contemporary of Manilius, composed an adaptation of Aratus's *Phaenomena* which, together with the translations by Cicero and Avienius, was to become the *Aratea*. Although Germanicus's work reveals in places the influence of Manilius, the episode of the Virgin follows the Greek original closely. According to André Le Boeuffle, Augustus built a temple to Justice in Rome in 13 B.C., and he notes a number of passages in Germanicus that may refer to this new cult. For Germanicus, Virgo should be worshipped as Justice.[20]

The third writer, Hyginus, is probably of a much later period. Borrowing from Eratosthenes, Aratus, and others, he composed the *Poetica Astronomica*, summarizing many of the catasterisms (transformations of persons and objects into constellations). His statements under the heading of the Virgin provide an adequate summation of classical learning on this matter: "Hesiod calls her the daugher of Jove and Themis. Aratus says that she is thought to be the daughter of Astraeus and Aurora, who lived at the time of the Golden Age of men and was their leader. . . . Others call her Fortune—others, Ceres, and they dispute the more about her because her head is dimly seen. Some have called her Erigone . . . others call her a daughter of Apollo by Chrysothemis, an infant, named Parthenos. Because she died young, she was put by Apollo among the constellations."[21]

Much more important than any of these works is Virgil's *Fourth Eclogue*, often called the Messianic Eclogue. This piece differs radically from Virgil's other nine eclogues in both tone and content as Michael C. J. Putnam notes: "The first line strikes with a boldness unparalleled in the *Eclogues* thus far. . . . This is no humble shepherd craving divine influence, but an equal of the goddess of song, a

prophet ready to sing something beyond either Theocritus or the eclogues composed most closely under his spell."[22] The bulk of the
prophecy is contained in verses 4-10: "Now is come the last age of
the song of Cumae; the great line of the centuries begins anew. Now
the Virgin returns, the reign of Saturn returns; now a new generation
descends from heaven on high. Only do thou, pure Lucina, smile on
the birth of a child, under whom the iron brood shall first cease, and
a golden race spring up throughout the world! Thine own Apollo
now is king!" (vol. 1, p. 29).[23]

In just a few verses, a pessimistic view of history that looks back
to the beginning of time for mankind's happy state in an ideal society
upheld by nature has been infused with new hope through a prophecy of renewal. The early age, best remembered by evoking the figures of Virgo and Saturn, is returning. A boy is now being born who
will lead mankind to a new earthly paradise. This prophecy, placed
in the midst of eclogues that are intended to evoke a sentimental
yearning for past tranquility, certainly constitutes an apparently extraneous and surprising element. The *Fourth Eclogue* goes on to trace
the growth of the child, equating his development with the unfolding
of the new age. This shepherd-king will have to engage in the martial
arts in order to succeed in the creation of a new golden age. Traces of
ancient error will require the skills of a new Achilles to lay siege to
yet another Troy. These martial concerns are somewhat reminiscent
of Hesiod's heroic age. In the end, the new golden generation will
live in harmony, enjoying nature's many gifts without the need for
wars, toil, or suffering. These modern shepherds will live in an environment reminiscent of Arcadia, a land that permeates Virgil's *Eclogues* and his *Georgics*.[24]

The *Fourth Eclogue* is thus a tour de force that harmonizes a number of conflicting elements. In the words of Putnam, Virgil's purpose
has been to "unite pastoral and epic verse, to freshen the secluded,
quiet waters of pastoral with the mainstream of life at large, of history
and the progress of civilization."[25] For others, such as Eleanor Winsor
Leach, the *renovatio* is not an outward one. She relates the new generation with the *gens aurea* in Plato's *Republic*. Here, the metals of the
different ages are related to the tempers of the soul. For Leach, the
Eclogue deals with inner development: "As an offspring of the gods
the child seems to stand for the organizing spirit of the new age. His
life will be synonymous with the perfection of human society. By this
token, we may identify the child as a manifestation of the Jungian
archetype of the divine child: a figure that represents man's longing
for, and confidence in, an idealized better self."[26]

Virgil's fusion of the epic and the pastoral, of prophecy and primitive ideal, was not allowed to remain within the realm of literature. The historical identity of the child and the implications of the prophecy became a matter of heated discussion over the centuries. Frances Yates, who has studied the myth of Astraea in England during the sixteenth century, rightly affirms of the prophecy, "Those are words which have never been forgotten in the history of the West."[27]

The child is not clearly identified. Some speculate that the allusion is to Asinius Pollio, the consul to whom the poem was dedicated in the year 40 B.C.; others associate the *Eclogue* with the Pact of Brindisium sealed that same year by the marriage of Mark Antony and Octavian's sister, Octavia. Cleopatra's son, Alexander Helios, later recognized by Mark Antony, has been proposed as a candidate. Finally, there are those who believe that Virgil was writing about the child Scribonia was expecting in 40 B.C. Her marriage to Octavian assured that if she had a son he would be heir to the empire. Her hopes were dashed when the child turned out to be a girl. Divorce soon followed. Virgil never divulged the identity of the child, and we should follow Putnam's advice that "it is equally precarious—and unnecessary—to measure the qualifications of one candidate or another to be the boy in question, if indeed a real child is meant in the first place."[28]

Virgil refers to the notion of the golden age in at least two other texts. In the *Georgics* II, he claims that Rome was derived from the race ruled by Saturn, adding that his kingship included the frugal Sabines (vol. 1, p. 153). The *Georgics* also presents a contrast between city and country life, between the peaceful countryside and the wars and seafaring that characterize civilization. Justice (Astraea) herself, we are told, lived among the peasants before leaving earth (vol. 1, p. 149). If the *Fourth Eclogue* fails to pinpoint a historical figure as responsible for *renovatio*, such is not the case in the sixth book of the *Aeneid*, where Virgil returns to the subject of the golden age. As in the *Fourth Eclogue*, we are in the presence of the mysterious Cumaean Sybil, who is now accompanying Aeneas in his journey through Hades. Anchises serves as prophet, predicting that the age of Saturn will return under the rule of Augustus Caesar (vol. 1, p. 561). This text links the golden age and thus Astraea with the idea of empire associated with Augustus. As with Germanicus's translation of the *Phaenomena*, we find myth and history interconnected through allusion to Rome's ruler. In Virgil, the key reason for identifying Augustus as the new Saturn is the emperor's success in maintaining peace and tranquility at home and abroad. The *pax romana* will be equated, from this moment on, with the distributive justice found in the first age and represented by our goddess, to whom Augustus, as noted by Germanicus, will dedicate a temple of Justice. The sixth book of the *Aeneid* is then of importance in the development of our myth since Astraea here becomes an imperial virgin, paradoxically associated with the cult of *pax*.

The question remains why Virgil was so concerned with the return of a golden age. The first and obvious answer is that he lived in a period of civil wars when the breakdown of justice and order made the golden age a most attractive dream. A more intriguing and satisfying hypothesis may be found in Mircea Eliade's explanation of the myth of the eternal return. Eliade argues that one of the striking characteristics of archaic or traditional societies is "their revolt against concrete, historical time, their nostalgia for a periodic return to the mythical time of the beginning of things." For these societies historical events per se are meaningless and a part of chaos. They are transcended through imitation of an archetype by repeating the acts of gods and heroes. History is transformed into something cyclic and sacred; every year is a repetition of the cosmogonic act, the passing from chaos to cosmos through the act of creation. Moreover, a new era begins not only with every new year, but also with every new reign and every child's birth: "For the cosmos and man are regenerated ceaselessly by all kinds of means."[29] Regeneration annuls past time and thus abolishes profane history.

One of Eliade's examples is particularly suited for our purpose. From the moment of its foundation, Rome was destined for destruction and regeneration. The city would only last a certain number of years, a "mystic" number which could be computed by utilizing the number twelve, as revealed by Romulus's vision of twelve birds, be they eagles or vultures.[30] In writing the *Fourth Eclogue* and the *Aeneid*, Virgil was well aware of the possible fate of Rome. Prophecies of the city's fall were at times related to a more general cosmogonic cycle. Cicero, whose interest in the Astraea myth is evinced by his translation of Aratus's *Phaenomena*, alludes to the cosmogonic cycle and its relationship to Rome's history in *Scipio's Dream*. Speaking of fame, he contends that it is difficult to have it last a solar year, an infinitesimal amount of time when compared to the Great Year. A cosmic cycle began with the death of Romulus. It is far from complete during Cicero's lifetime: "As, long ago, the sun seemed to be failing and going out when Romulus' soul reached these very regions, so at the time when it will be eclipsed again in the very same quarter, and at the same season, and when all constellations and planets have been returned to their former position, then you may consider the year complete; indeed, you may be sure that not a twentieth part of that year has yet elapsed."[31] Macrobius's commentary on *Scipio's Dream*, a work that preserved and popularized these conceptions during the Middle Ages, contains a lengthy discussion of the Great Year. In Macrobius's interpretation, the duration of this cycle is unrelated to the precession of the equinoxes since it lasts fifteen thousand years and it is signaled by a solar eclipse.[32]

The inevitability of the fall of a state had been linked to the universal cosmogonic cycle as early as Plato. This relationship can be perceived in the description of the fall of the ideal state in the *Republic*. When children are born at a time that signifies the "worse quality" of births, they will be unable to act as righteously as their parents and will thus precipitate the decline of the state. The "geometric number" is somehow related to the "perfect number" that describes the duration of the universe.[33] Plato's prediction is similar to those of Cicero and Macrobius, but while Macrobius speaks of a Great Year of 15,000 years, Plato's Year consists of 36,000 solar years, the same number involved in the precession of equinoxes according to Ptolemy's faulty calculations.

The specific concern with the fall of a state is often related to the universal cycle of creation, maintenance, and dissolution which can be traced back to the Indian concept of the *yuga*.[34] According to Eliade, the most popular cyclic system in classical antiquity was postulated by a contemporary of Aratus, the Chaldean priest Berossus. His *Babyloniaca* "popularized the Chaldean doctrine of the 'Great Year' in a form that spread through the entire Hellenic world (where it later passed to the Romans and Byzantines).[35] Berossus's notions are strikingly similar to Plato's. In the *Politicus*, for example, Plato states that cycles and consequent cosmic catastrophes are derived from the twofold motion of the universe. Kronos (Saturn) rules the forward motion which unfolds a harmonious golden age. The backward motion is characterized by disharmony and ends in catastrophe, only to be followed by a new golden age. In the *Timaeus* Plato states that the meeting of all planets signals the end of the Great Year. Compare Seneca's description of Berossus's system: "Berosos, who translated Belus, says that these catastrophes occur with the movements of the planets. Indeed, he is so certain that he assigns a date for the conflagration and the deluge. For earthly things will burn, he contends, when all the planets which now maintain different orbits come together in the sign of Cancer, and are so arranged in the same path that a straight line can pass through the spheres of all of them.

The deluge will occur when the same group of planets meets in the sign of Capricorn. The solstice is caused by Cancer, winter by Capricorn; they are signs of great power since they are the turning-points in the very change of the year" (*Naturales Quaestiones*, vol. 1, p. 287).[36]

This cyclic view was incorporated by the Romans into their own conception of the *magnus annus*, which was at times related to the rise and fall of their city. The Stoics in particular held that the universe is eternal, but is periodically destroyed and renewed *(metacosmesis)*. Destruction, be it by water (flood) or by fire (from Heraclitus's elemental fire that burns the universe in an *ekpyrosis*), is followed by a golden age. Viewed from the perspective of the cyclic theory of history and the myth of the eternal return, Virgil's *Fourth Eclogue* appears much less enigmatic. The *renovatio* of mankind to be accomplished through the birth of a divinely appointed child is related to the concepts accepted by Stoicism. These theories deal with the cosmos, but at the same time center their attention on Rome. The presence of Apollo in Virgil's *Eclogue* may serve to reassure the Romans that the sun's fire has beneficial uses only. The *Aeneid* also indicates to Virgil's contemporaries that the Augustan golden age has become a reality without the need for previous *ekpyrosis*.

The Augustan golden age was not long-lived, and Seneca noted its metamorphosis into a veritable iron age. This Stoic philosopher was a native of Cordoba, Spain, and thus became a favorite writer of later Spanish authors. Moving to Rome, he became Nero's tutor, and eventually his principal civil adviser. For the first five years Seneca was able to lead Nero to wise and moderate government. Soon, however, the Stoic philosopher became a witness to Nero's tyranny. In the end, he became a victim of the emperor's passions, which he had tried to subdue through Stoic doctrine. Witnessing the excesses of the emperors who followed Augustus, Seneca could not accept Virgil's hope for the empire but felt that this decline would soon lead to the destruction of the world through the elements of fire or water. His vision of the threatening flood is rather lengthy and detailed. For example: "Neither walls nor towers will protect anyone. Temples will not help worshippers, nor will the heights of cities help refugees, since the wave will anticipate the fugitives and sweep them down from the very citadels. The destructive forces will rush together, some from the west, some from the east. A single day will bury the human race; all that the long indulgence of fortune has cultivated, all that it has lifted to eminence above the rest, all that is noble and beautiful, even the kingdoms of great nations—fortune will send all down to ruin at the same time" (vol. 1, p. 293).

For the Stoics, disasters make men aware of their plight, and teach them not to depend on fortune or cling to earthly possessions. Nor should humans place their hopes in the progress of their race. Civilization, in spite of its great accomplishments, brings about man's corruption. Seneca thought he had been witness to such a decline during his long life of some ninety years. Furthermore, in Seneca's pessimistic view, the golden age that follows destruction is always short-lived: "Every living creature will be created anew and the earth will be given men ignorant of sin, and born under better auspices. But their innocence too will not last, except as long as they are new. Vice quickly creeps in. Virtue is difficult to find; it needs a director and guide. Vices can be learned even without a teacher" (vol. 1, p. 297).

The theatrical works attributed to Seneca which became very popular in Europe during the sixteenth and seventeenth centuries mirror the violence of his age. They often juxtapose tragic horror with examples of purity and innocence. Descriptions of the golden age in these dramas enhance the contrast between the evils of the iron age which arise from man's passions and the peace of the earliest times when humans lived innocently and in harmony with nature. In the *Hippolytus*, the young man's chastity and love of nature contrast with his stepmother's unnatural passion for him, which she describes thus: "A malady feeds and grows within my heart, and it burns there hot as the steam that wells from Aetna's caverns" (vol. 1, p. 327).[37] The volcanic fire of her passion eventually destroys everything surrounding her and can be considered a metaphor for the *ekpyrosis* that comes at the end of the iron age. Hippolytus, who has lived a life free and pure in a bucolic environment akin to a golden age, must answer to temptation. He rails against city and court which embody disharmony in his eyes, and strives to portray his simple pleasures and rustic ways which are in accord with "man's ancient ways" (vol. 1, p. 357). In this he emulates Horace's *Epode* II as well as Virgil's *Georgics* II. The notion that man's present fallen state is due to sinfulness is found in Virgil as well as in Stoic teachings.

The contrast between the peace of the countryside and the turmoil of the court is but a prelude to Hippolytus's evocation of the golden age: "Twas in such wise, methinks, they lived whom the primal age produced, in friendly intercourse with gods" (vol. 1, p. 539). He describes the golden age through a series of negative statements.

There were no ships or swords at the time, nor did teams of oxen till the land since nature gave freely from self-productive fields to the men who upheld its laws. But Hippolytus lives in a different age, a period that has lost innocence, where passion ignites and lust destroys. The young man, in spite of his vision of the golden age and in spite of his innocence, becomes a victim of his times. Although he upholds the laws of nature, the disharmony of the present transforms him into a tragic hero. Theseus, Hippolytus's father, thinking him guilty of unnatural love for Phaedra, calls on Neptune to destroy his son. A monster arises from the sea and consumes the chaste and innocent youth. Two of the Greek elements, fire and water, have risen up against Hippolytus. The first is seen in Phaedra's passion, described as the fires of a volcano, while the second is presented as a result of his father's cruel judgment. The monster that arises from the sea represents both elements; it is a creature of Neptune but can also be symbolic of the passions—Phaedra's lust and Theseus's ire. At the play's conclusion, then, the fragile vision of a golden age has been destroyed by flood and *ekpyrosis,* as in the final catastrophe at the end of the *magnus annus.*

During the sixteenth and seventeenth centuries, Europeans were particularly fond of a play attributed to Seneca, the *Octavia,* in which again the notion of the golden age is evoked amidst events that exemplify the evils of an iron age. In the *Octavia,* Nero's wife learns that her husband wants to divorce her in order to marry another. He is even plotting to have her assassinated. Octavia recalls the many evil deeds of her "monster" husband, but in the end becomes a victim of her times, being helpless against his might. Her defeat by a "monster" recalls Hippolytus's death. Seneca is a character in his own play, trying to teach the emperor to control his passion through Stoic philosophy. His presence on a stage replete with victims of Nero's passions mirrors his own future fall. Indeed, it is Seneca himself who, in a soliloquy, recalls a younger world "when Saturn held the kingdoms of the sky. Then did that virgin, Justice, goddess of mighty sway, from heaven sent down with holy Faith to earth, rule with mild sway the race of men" (vol. 2, p. 439).

The gentle rule of Astraea evoked by Seneca stands in sharp contrast with the realities of the tyranny of Nero. The description of the golden age turns to negative statements describing the failure of future ages, such as Seneca's own time. New inventions are seen in the Stoic manner as partly responsible for the downfall. Astraea's escape during the third age is described in a manner reminiscent of Aratus and Ovid: "Away from earth that scorned her, from the wild ways of men and hands defiled with bloody slaughter, fled the maid, Astraea, chief glory of the firmament" (vol. 2, p. 441). With Astraea's exile, "all-potent lust" (vol. 2, p. 441) prevails among men. Octavia and Seneca can only sing of a past age, like the poet in the *Works and Days*. In the *Octavia*, the song of Hesiod's nightingale-poet, although compelling, is weak. The tyrants and hawks of the *Works and Days* also prove to be powerful destructive forces in this drama. The personal tragedies of Octavia and Seneca stand as symbols of the departure of justice from the land.

Seneca's tragedies present brief glimpses of an idyllic age so that the horror of the tragic and apocalyptic present will stand out in high relief. In this, the dramas resemble the vision presented in the *Naturales Quaestiones*, where descriptions of the destruction of the universe far outweigh mentions of the return of a brief golden age. This rather negative view of earthly existence taints even Seneca's portrayal of our goddess. In the *Thyestes*, the Chorus is afraid the heavens are crumbling and that gods and men are going to be overcome again by "formless chaos" (vol. 2, p. 159). The vision of falling constellations includes Astraea-Virgo. Thus, rather than depicting the return of Astraea, the *Thyestes* recalls her fall, along with that of Justice-Libra: "The Virgin shall fall to the earth she once abandoned, and the Scales of justice with their weights shall fall and with them shall drag the fierce Scorpion down" (vol. 2, p. 161).

Even more disturbing is the description of the chaste and just Astraea in *Hercules furens*. Here the Chorus, grieved at the hero's madness, calls on Sleep to provide Hercules with the only possible haven for his misery: "And do thou, O Sleep, vanquisher of woes, rest of the soul, the better part of human life, thou winged son of thy mother Astraea, sluggish brother of cruel Death, thou who dost mingle false with true, sure yet gloomy guide to what shall be; O thou, who art peace after wanderings, haven of life, day's respite and night's comrade . . . sweetly and gently soothe his weary spirit (vol. 1, p. 95). The goddess of the golden age has become the mother of Sleep and Death. Taken to an extreme, these lines in *Hercules furens* may seem to imply that Sleep and Death are the only "golden ages" of peace and harmony allowed to the man of the iron age. Yet Hercules, refreshed by Sleep, does not succumb to the temptation of suicide.

In a second play on the Hercules theme, *Hercules Oetaeus*, the mythic figure attains heroic stature through his struggles to bring justice to a chaotic land. His deeds, however, have imperiled the very heavens. Hercules laments, "Now have the gods no peace; the freed earth sees in the sky all creatures which she feared; for there hath Juno set them. The crab I slew goes round the torrid zone, is known as Libya's constellation, and matures her grain; the lion to Astraea gives the flying year" (vol. 2, p. 191). Not even in heaven does the goddess attain that harmony she once enjoyed during the reign of Saturn.

The rule of Nero, the historical equivalent to Seneca's fictional milieu, did not survive the death of the Stoic philosopher by many years. Eventually, a tyrannical empire was replaced by "just rule." Paganism gave way to Christianity as the official religion. Constantine's conversion signaled a new wave of hope. Astraea, as in Virgil's *Fourth Eclogue*, is seen as the virgin who returns to earth to implement a new golden age. It is ironic that the *Fourth Eclogue,* a poem so clearly rooted in a pagan and cyclic conception of history and Empire, should have become a quasi-religious text for Christians. The transformation of pagan vision into messianic prophecy began with the Emperor Constantine, who simply proclaimed that the virgin who returns is none other than Mary. The child is Jesus, the serpent that shall cease to be is the devil, and the balsam which will grow is the Christian race.[38]

But even during the late Christianized empire, the pagan myth preserved one of its functions, that of eulogizing the ruler by prophesying, or at least expressing the hope, that he would bring about a golden age. Claudian, for example, asserted that justice returns to earth as Theodosius ousts tyrants; and Themistius imagined that "the earth will offer her fruits and the sea her fish" in the new era.[39] Pagan myth and Christian reinterpretation could coexist since they assumed different roles. The pagan myth became a secular expression of the desire for just rule devoid of sacred and cyclic implications; the Christianized version was used to buttress a key mystery in the newly predominant religion. Poggioli summarizes the Christian metamorphosis: "Christians read the poem as a miraculous announcement of the Nativity, seeing in Astraea an allegory of the Virgin and interpreting the Golden Age to come not as a worldly order of the *pax romana*, but as the metaphysical order of the *pax Christiana*, to be reestablished through the new covenant between man and god. . . . While for the pagan poet the salvation of mankind meant conjuring away the curse of war, for his Christian readers it meant the redemption of the human race from original sin."[40]

The Middle Ages accepted the messianic interpretation elaborated by Lactantius and Augustine. But as the centuries passed, a political dimension was reintroduced into the association of religious conversion with the return of the age of gold. Constantine's ambiguous pronouncements on Astraea led to the merging of the religious and the imperial interpretations of the goddess of justice. In the year 800, the German Charlemagne was crowned *Augustus* and *Imperator* in the city of Rome by the pope. Christianity now had two leaders, a spiritual and a temporal one, with a geographical source of power in what was again the eternal city. According to the statements of Pope Sergius II two generations later, this coronation created a *concorporatio* that "united in one body the Empires of Romans and Franks."[41] The survival of the empire and its new double axis, Germany-Rome, was explained through the theory of translation: "As Constantine had translated the Empire to the East, so now in Charlemagne it was translated back to the West."[42] Fears of the empire's destruction and the consequent dissolution of the universe, prevalent in Roman times, were now Christianized and applied to the Holy Roman Empire centered in Germany. Apocalypse, the pursuit of the millennium, became part of the political vision of the epoch: the end of the world is at hand when the emperor becomes ruler of the world. World peace under one ruler is but a signal of the return of Astraea.

A famous early medieval play treats this subject. The *Ludus de Antichristo* (c. 1160) portrays the emperor of the Romans in the process of becoming ruler of the world.[43] The historical parallels with Frederick Barbarossa (1122-90) are striking. This German emperor was then expanding the territorial limits of the empire and battling with the pope. His excommunication further excited the apocalyptic furor, which did not even subside with his death. Many, awaiting the unification of the empire, considered that he still lived. Frederick Barbarossa would share this legend with the second of his name, Emperor Frederick II (1194-1250).[44] Ernst Kantorowicz has carefully demonstrated how Frederick II was intent on praising and emulating the ancient empire. For the medieval emperor, the age of Augustus represented the fullness of time which Christ had chosen for his birth, "the only *aurea aetas* of peace since Paradise." Frederick believed that his mission as ruler was to return that second epoch of peace. In other words, he envisioned his reign as the third golden age in which peace and justice would prevail on earth. Unfortunately, the pope came to believe that Frederick, as *Dominus Mundi*, posed a threat to his authority. The consequent enmity between the two great European powers led to rumors and prophecies concerning the end of the world. People debated whether Frederick should be considered the Antichrist or the Prince of Peace. When the death of the emperor was suddenly announced in the year 1250, few believed the news since no apocalyptic resolution had taken place. It was then rumored that the *Dominus Mundi* was not dead, but was concealed in Mount Aetna and would soon return.[45] A symbol of justice had once again retired from earthly conflict. Frederick and Astraea await a propitious time to return. While she remains in the heavens as the constellation Virgo, he hides in a volcano that has sheltered departed heroes such as King Arthur.[46]

Among those who aided the emperor in "foreseeing" his future was Michael Scot, the court astrologer. Indeed, the emperor had surrounded himself with a number of scholars and philosophers versed in this occult science. His reign foregrounded the revival of astrology, which had virtually disappeared with the fall of Rome: "Not until the twelfth century, with its discovery of Aristotle and the science of the Moors, did astrology regain a position of prominence in the intellectual life of Europe."[47] What Augustine had severely condemned, reacting to the fatalism of the Stoics, would soon receive a more positive commentary from Thomas Aquinas. Following Aristotle, Aquinas states that the stars can influence matter. Consequently, they have an impact on the corporeal organs of man, affecting the humors and spirits. On the other hand, Aquinas is careful to point out that man has free will and can reject inclinations stemming from the lower appetites. The human being also possesses an intellect that cannot be directly affected by astral influences. In spite of intellect and free will, however, astrological predictions dealing with human actions often come to pass. "The majority of men, in fact, are governed by their passions, which are dependent upon bodily appetites." There are some, the text explains, who are not subject to the stars: "Few indeed are the wise who are capable of resisting their animal instincts."[48] When astrologers state that a wise man rules the stars, they simply mean that he controls his passions.

In spite of astrology's new credibility during the later Middle Ages, it was still considered a dubious undertaking since it lent itself to magic through characters, herbs, stones, or amulets that captured or transformed the influences of a particular planet or constellation. The well-known astrologer from Bologna, Cecco d'Ascoli, was burnt at the stake in 1327, a clear example of the perils of practicing this occult science at the time. Frederick II's astrologer met a worse fate, albeit only in literature. Dante placed him in the eighth circle of hell, next to Guido Bonatti, another famous astrologer who frequented the court of Frederick II and who reputedly delved into astral magic in order to know "all things":

Quell' altro che ne' fianchi è così poco,
Michele Scotto fu, che veramente
de le magiche frode seppe 'l gioco.
Vidi Guido Bonatti . . .[49]

Interestingly, it is Virgil, the developer of Astraea as an astral imperial myth, who speaks thus in Dante's poem. The learned commentaries from late antiquity by Donatus, Servius, and Macrobius had enhanced Virgil's reputation during the Middle Ages. One reason why Dante chose Virgil as his guide was that this poet was one of the "canonized" authors of antiquity who were read for their didactic content. Superimposed on this learned tradition was popular belief. Dante's guide through the *Inferno* and the *Purgatorio* had acquired a reputation as a magician during the Middle Ages, for his description of Aeneas's *katabasis*, for the magic involved in Dido's funeral rites, and for his predictions of a child savior. In his guise as prophet, "he trod, indeed haunted, the boards of mystery plays, sometimes accompanied and sometimes replaced by the Cumean Sibyl."[50]

The clearest indication of the high regard Virgil and his prophecies enjoyed during the Middle Ages can be found in the twenty-second canto of the *Purgatorio*. Here Virgil meets Statius, who tells how he was converted to Christianity when he realized that in the *Fourth Eclogue* the pagan writer was announcing the coming of Christ forty years before the event. Dante goes so far as to translate verses 4-7 of the *Fourth Eclogue* and include them in this *Canto:*

". . . Secol si rinova;
torna giustizia e primo tempo umano,
e progenie scende da ciel nova."[51]

During the Renaissance, the myth of Astraea can be said to have become a commonplace supported by key classical and medieval texts. Her popularity was such that Marsilio Ficino's disregard for the godess in spite of his concern with Saturn seems puzzling. The founder of the Platonic Academy in Florence learned astrology as an aid to medicine from his father. From a very young age he became preoccupied with the influence of Saturn since his horoscope showed this malefic planet located in the sign Aquarius, the night or negative house of Saurn. Furthermore, Mars, the second most malefic planet, was conjunct with Saturn. Such was Ficino's fear of the seventh Ptolemaic planet that he delved into astral magic in order to mitigate its influence. Yet, as a Platonist, he was compelled to see Saturn as the embodiment of man's highest aspirations. Thus, he developed a fa-

cinating theoretical system that stressed Saturn's bipolarity. In his
writings, this planet emerges not only as a destructive force, but also
as a symbol of a new intellectual elite who suffer Saturn's melancholy
in order to receive its most precious gift, wisdom. This wisdom is the
basis for just rule and the establishment of a philosopher king. If
Saturn is the just king, then Astraea represents the blissful life that
can be lived in a world where justice prevails.[52]

Christoforo Landino, a member of the Platonic Academy and a
friend of Ficino, represents a different viewpoint. In his commentary
on the *Fourth Eclogue,* he equates Apollo with Octavius. He believes,
however, that Virgil must have had an unconscious knowledge of the
coming of Christ. Thus, the virgin's child in the poem refers to both
a political figure and a religious savior. This type of speculation, often
including the prophetic powers of the sibyl, abounded among hu-
manists. The many controversies surrounding the messianic interpretation of the Astraea myth during the Renaissance have been
studied by Don Cameron Allen.[53] Harry Levin, concerned with its
political and literary implications, asserts that "if we trusted the panegyrics of the courtly poets, we should have little doubt that the
golden age had been reborn in the Renaissance. There would be
some disagreement among them, however, as to whether that rebirth
had taken place under the Medici or the Valois or the Tudors or the
dynasty of Spain and Austria. Whoever happened to ascend the
throne at the moment, of course, was always the new Saturn or Astraea."[54]

The myth's popularity continued through the sixteenth and sev-
entheenth centuries. As Elizabeth Armstrong has shown, Pierre Ronsard utilized the return of Saturn to praise or exhort Henry II and his
successor Charles IX. Ronsard added an international dimension to
the laudatory use of the myth, since he used it to praise Queen Elizabeth I of England when he was asked to honor her as France's ally.[55]
Ronsard's poetry often elaborates on the contrast between the age of
gold and the age of iron. His verse oscillates between hopeful praise
that envisions future perfection and satire of corrupt contemporary
conditions. The poet often laments that in the present age man is
overly concerned with the metal gold, a preoccupation absent in the
happiest age where gold was the metaphorical perfection of the soul.
In spite of Ronsard's insistence on the theme of the golden age, the
name of Astraea is absent in these poems. The *Hymne a la justice,* an
early example of the use of the golden age myth, presents justice as a
blindfolded goddess holding the scales. Ronsard names her Themis,
not Astraea. It may be that the absence of our goddess's name in most

of the political and satirical poems by this French poet is related to the fact that he composed a series of sixteen pieces entitled *Sonets et madrigals pour Astrée* where the goddess of justice is metamorphosed into a contemporary lady. These love poems do not even mention the age of gold, but do contain allusions to the constellation Virgo.[56]

The best-known example of the presence of Astraea in French literature is Honoré d'Urfé's pastoral romance *L'Astrée*, composed at the beginning of the seventeenth century. For some critics, this pastoral subverts the very notion of the golden age since the happiest of epochs appears as a deliberate artifice, something that is irrelevant to the real world.[57] But even if we accept the notion that the text overturns many of the pastoral assumptions, it is still clear that the setting, the names, and the myth stand as a challenge in a conflictive period. The Arcadian setting that portrays the shepherds of Forez in the fifth century A.D. is reminiscent of the first age. The heroine's name is that of our goddess, chastity being one of her major attributes. The dedication includes political overtones, since Henry IV is addressed as "pasteur souverain." In a period of religious wars, the dream of Arcadia, of the happiest of epochs, surfaces again. Henry IV is dressed in shepherd's clothes so that he may realize that beyond conflict lies the hope of peace and prosperity in a period of religious tolerance.[58]

In England, poets such as Sidney and Spenser viewed Queen Elizabeth as a just virgin whose rule revealed the qualities of the virtuous inhabitants of the first age. References to Astraea may be discovered even in a play attributed to Shakespeare. *Titus Andronicus* has as its protagonist a general maddened by the wrongs of Saturnine, emperor of Rome. He laments the lack of justice at this sublunary level: "Terras Astraea reliquit" (4.3.4).[59] Titus then orders a search for the goddess: "And sith there's no justice in earth nor hell, / We will solicit heaven and move the gods / To send down Justice for to wreak our wrongs" (4.3.49-51).

Titus's companions shoot arrows at the heavens and are told that Saturn and not Saturnus abides in the seventh sphere. The god Saturn, ruler of the golden age and dispenser of justice, is sharply distinguished in this play from the malefic planet of the astrologers. The former is associated with Astraea and must be sought out, while the latter seems to be causing havoc, supporting tyranny, and inflicting melancholy. Of all the archers, it is Titus's son Lucius who strikes "Virgo's lap" (4.3.64). Not surprisingly, he becomes the next ruler and attempts to restore justice in a chaotic environment. By striking Astraea and becoming the next emperor, Lucius takes on the character-

istics of Virgil's child-savior in the political realm. The play's conclusion is a happy one, hinting at future harmony with a true Saturn as
emperor.

The demise of the Virgin Queen did not signal the disappearance
of Astraea in English letters. The seventeenth century would display
the imperial and the messianic interpretations of the myth in two
outstanding writers. While Dryden's *Astraea Redux* is a laudatory
poem on the restoration of Charles II, Milton's *On the Morning of
Christ's Nativity* is a Christian pastoral that, according to Poggioli,
owes much to Virgil's *Fourth Eclogue*.[60] Milton's interest in the Astraea
myth is also evinced by the fact that he read and annotated Aratus's
Phaenomena. That this English poet studied two classical texts dealing
with Astraea is clear proof of the power the myth still held over man's
imagination during the seventeenth century.

A lengthy voyage has been undertaken in just a few pages. In
Chaldea, Greece, pagan and Christian Rome, we have encountered
poets, astronomers, mythographers, philosophers, and theologians
who have expressed their views on the golden age of man. For some,
Astraea was simply the goddess of justice who lived in a remote past.
Through catasterism, she left earth to be perceived as the constellation Virgo. Yet, her new abode was not beyond the changing. In some
cyclical accounts of world history that echoed the conception of the
Indian *yuga*s, the universe was created, destroyed, and regenerated.
Even linear accounts placed paradise at the beginning and at the end
of time. Astraea can return. This longing for a golden age was at
times tempered by people's fear of the catastrophe which would precede it. Some asserted that such an *ekpyrosis*, or destruction by fire,
was not a necessary precondition for regeneration. Rome was not
doomed to destruction. During Augustus's rule, the city was considered an *urbs aeterna*, with Astraea serving as the imperial virgin.

When the goddess of chastity and justice assumed a Christian
garb, imperialist concerns lost their sway, and the possible demise of
the city was again discussed. The *pax romana* was metamorphosed
into a *pax Christiana*, while Astraea became an allegory for the Virgin
Mary, albeit concealing in some instances traces of the imperial goddess. Christians believed that the golden age had been ushered in by
Christ, the child of the *Fourth Eclogue*. Some argued that the reason
why all were not enjoying the fruits of this golden epoch was that it
had resurfaced as an inner state of joy, piety, and equity in the blissful
hearts of the chosen. Others looked forward to the arrival of the mil-
lenium. With the Renaissance, the myth of Astraea became a commonplace in the verses of courtly poets. But the allusiveness and

power of the goddess did not disappear. Sixteenth-and seventeenth-century writers as diverse as d'Urfée, Ronsard, Shakespeare, and Dryden found in the goddess a source of inspiration. The virgin with the *spica* or child appeared time and again to the poet, visionary, or seeker of truth and justice who searched for her in the world, in the heavens, or within the self.

CHAPTER TWO

Astraea in the
Spanish Golden Age

SPAIN, although mentioned only in passing by scholars who have delved into the Astraea myth, contributed as much or even more to its popularity than Italy, France, or England. The first major utilization of the myth occurs during the reign of the Catholic kings. In the *Bucólicas*, Juan del Encina renders into Spanish verse Virgil's ten *Eclogues*. Not all agree on the merits of Encina's work. Menéndez Pelayo believes that the freedom with which the poet of Salamanca deals with the Latin poems is a sign of irreverence and parody. Others take a more positive and balanced approach, stressing the historical importance of Encina's contribution. Henry M. Sullivan summarizes them aptly: "The *Bucolics* constitute the first attempt by any Spanish poet to render a Latin Verse classic in the native meters of Castile. While it is true that attempts were made previously in the fifteenth century to translate some major works of antiquity . . . these had not been in verse. Encina's attempt to render Virgil impresses us both by its vaulting ambition and its quaintly Spanish costume."[1]

Some of the eclogues, particularly I, II, IV, and V, are best viewed as imitations that endeavor to relate the poems to contemporary personages or ideas. The prophecy of the *Fourth Eclogue* is applied to the times in which Encina lived. Echoing other European writers, Encina provides the reader with a political interpretation. The dawn of a new golden age is represented by the reign of the Catholic monarchs, whose son, Prince John, is the child described by Virgil: "aplicada al nacimiento bienanventurado del nuestro muy esclarecido príncipe don Juan, su hijo, adonde manifiestamente parece Sibila profetizar dellos, y Virgilio aver sentido de aqueste tan alto nacimiento, pues que, despues del, en nuestros tiempos avemos gozado de tan crecidas vitorias y triunfos y vemos la justicia ser no menos poderosa en el mayor que en el menor" (p. 271).[2] The poem carefully reworks the Sibyl's prophecy:

los bienes comiençan, los males fenecen
segun que Sibila lo canta y lo reza,
gran orden comiença en su realeza,
los reynos saturnios en el rebivecen.
La mesma justicia con el ha venido,
del cielo nos vino tal generacion,
¡o Virgen Maria! tu da perfecion
al príncipe don Juan ya nacido.

[p. 272]

The reign of Saturn is returning with Prince John. He has brought with him justice from heaven. The unknown child of the prophecy is the future Spanish monarch who will complete the Catholic kings' task of bringing about a new Christian golden age of justice and harmony. By appealing to the Virgin Mary, Encina brings together the political and religious interpretation of Astraea. The virgin is both political justice and the mother of the Christian messiah. The new golden age is the fulfillment of Christian and secular desires.

In this adaptation of Virgil's *Eclogue*, Encina is echoing the imperial messianic aspiration of the times. All of Europe was acutely aware of the crucial role being played by the Catholic kings. As Marcel Bataillon puts it, "En Europa, o, por mejor decir, en la cristiandad de entonces, la España de los Reyes Católicos ocupa una posición singular. Al mismo tiempo que acaba de arrojar al Islam a Africa, abre un Nuevo Mundo a Cristo. Y esto ocurre en el momento en que la unión de Aragón y Castilla y los venturosos resultados de su política en Italia ponen a la doble monarquía en primer rango entre todas las potencias."[3] This Christian hope centered on the kings of Spain is reflected in their being associated with the return of Astraea. When *El Sofí*, king of the Persians, was converted to Christianity soon after the great triumph at Oran, Charles Bovelles wrote a very telling letter to Cardinal Jiménez de Cisneros on March 20, 1510. In the letter, Bovelles tells an anecdote concerning the cardinal himself that suspiciously resembles the legend of Rodrigo, *el último godo*, who lost his Christian kingdom to the Moors. He also introduces the Astraea myth: "Bovelles, durante los días que pasó en Toledo, oyó contar que Cisneros había descubierto, entre los escombros de una vieja iglesia, una vasija en que se veían imágenes de moros derribados por tierra, con una inscripcion que decia: 'Cuando esto aparezca ante los ojos de los hombres, será inminente la destrucción para aquellos cuyas imágenes se ven aquí contenidas.' ¿Sería cierta o falsa esta historia? Cisneros lo sabrá mejor que nadie. Sea lo que fuere, haga Dios que su voluntad se cumpla en la tierra como en los cielos. Haga venir los tiempos cantados por Virgilio: *Iam redit et virgo.* . . . Que la paz sea, y que aparezca en el mundo entero la concordia. Que una sola fe, que un solo Príncipe reine por fin en todas partes."[4] Virgil's prophecy has again been applied to the reign of Ferdinand and Isabela.

If the Catholic kings had a Spanish and French bard announcing the return of the golden age, we would expect nothing less of Charles V, whose title of emperor gave him the opportunity of reviving the concept of *dominus mundi*. However, a purely messianic interpretation is found in Juan Luis Vives's *Bucolicarum Virgilii expositio potissimum allegorica*. Published three years before his death, this work evinces Vives's "constant admiration for the author of the *Aeneid*."[5] As expected, the Spanish humanist explains that Virgo is both the justice of Christ and the Virgin Mary, while the child is Christ, who has come to cleanse man of original sin. He urges the literal-minded to be silent and recognize the messianic prophecy in Virgil's *Fourth Eclogue*.[6]

The best-known "foretelling" of just rule for Charles V is found outside of Spain, in canto 15 of Ariosto's *Orlando Furioso*. Here Astolfo is told that from the union of the houses of Austria and Aragon will be born a child who will bring about a new golden age (15.25). Charles V will restore Astraea-Justice along with the other virtues that were exiled with her as the world grew more corrupt. Once the sixth and seventh ages of man pass, a new emperor will arise, more just and prudent than the Roman Augustus (15.24). The use of prophecy, the notion of the return of a golden age, the mention of Astraea-Justice, and the parallel between the perfect future emperor and Augustus are clear reminiscences of Virgil's *Fourth Eclogue* and the *Aeneid*.

Within Spain the outstanding literary example of the imperialist concerns that surfaced during Charles V's rule is Hernando de Acuña's sonnet announcing the coming of a glorious age:

> Ya se acerca senor, o es ya llegada
> la edad gloriosa en que promete el cielo
> Vna grey, y vn pastor, solo en el suelo,
> Por suerte a vuestros tiempos reseruada.[7]

In the manner of Virgil's *Fourth Eclogue*, Acuña's sonnet assumes a prophetic tone. Charles V is bringing about a new Augustan age of universal empire, characterized not only by political unity but also by religious harmony. The latter is expressed through the use of the metaphorical *grey* and *pastor*. In one of the few critical essays that attest to the importance of the myth of Astraea in Spain, J.H.R. Polt convincingly argues that this Spanish poem has as its source the fifteenth canto of Ariosto's *Orlando furioso*. Studying Acuña's famous line "Vn Monarca, vn Imperio, y vna Espada," Polt notes the absence of the sword from Ariosto's canto, but adds, "Si nos acordamos de la representación típica de la justicia con balanza y espada no será difícil ver la conexión entre la metonimia de Acuña y la justicia personificada de Ariosto."[8] The sword thus stands for Astraea's justice.

Acuña's imperialist poem became a model for prophetic utterance in the Spanish epic, which is fitting since the sonnet is based on Ariosto's Italian epic. According to Polt, passages in three Spanish works were influenced by Acuña: Juan Rufo's *La Austríada*, Cristobal de Virués's *Historia de Monserrate*, and Bernardo de Valbuena's *El Bernardo*.[9] This vision of a universal monarch holding Astraea's sword parallels Titian's equestrian portrait of Charles V, where the ruler is depicted holding the *hasta, summa Imperii* of the Roman emperors.[10] Art and poetry view the emperor as a new Augustus.

And yet, this image of Charles V was not all-prevailing. Studying political thought in the Iberian peninsula through the writings of Francisco de Vitoria, Domingo de Soto, Francisco Suárez, and Luis de Molina, Bernice Hamilton proves that the medieval notion of a lord of the world was rejected by these writers. In their discussion of kingship, they contend that a community appoints a king, and in so doing transfers its authority to him. Once the power is shifted, the ruler is greater than the community. Since the community derives its power from God, the king, through the transfer, now rules by divine right. Thus the power of the king originates in divine and natural law. No such explanation is forthcoming for the emperor, who does not derive his power from these sources. Suárez and Soto suggest and discard several premises that would back the notion of imperial world rule: "that the empire is an inheritance from Rome (but the Romans were not lords of the world); that it was instituted by Christ (but no trace of such a donation has been found, and many separate kingdoms continue to flourish); that it was a papal donation (but the pope has no temporal power and so cannot bestow it)."[11]

Antonio de Guevara, the historiographer of the emperor, seems somewhat closer to the notion of imperial world rule. In *Una década de Césares* (1539), he "emphasizes or invents similarities between the good Roman emperors and Charles V."[12] His attitude is not as positive as it first may appear, however, as is clear from the *Libro aureo de Marco Aurelio*. Guevara begins with a prologue to Charles V, stating that the ruler should imitate the virtuous rulers of the past in order to obtain the fame he desires. The modern emperor is not equated with the Augustus who, according to Virgil, brought back the golden age, but is asked to learn a lesson from the "fictionalized biography"[13] of Marcus Aurelius. An expanded version of the *Libro* entitled *Relox de príncipes* contains several allusions to the age of gold. Studying these passages, Augustin Redondo concludes that Guevara sees the earliest of ages as a communistic community of virtuous men. He attributes the fall from this paradise to the desire for property and power that destroys virtue and brings about war and tyranny. Redondo notes that Guevara includes agriculture in the first age: "Guevara s'eloigne de l'évocation classique de l'Age d'Or sur un point important: les hommes, pour lui, avaient besoin de travailler pour vivre."[14] We have seen how the ancients were divided on this matter. Guevara is conforming to a tradition that he seems to have studied carefully. The third book of the *Relox de príncipes* deals with the particular virtues that these rulers must exemplify. Guevara begins his discussion with justice (chapters 1-2), and tells the appropriate poetic fiction concerning Astraea. Here he cites Nigidius Figulus rather than Virgil, but it is clear that he knows his subject well. In the discussion he fails to apply the prophecy of the return of the virgin to imperial *renovatio* during the rule of Charles V.[15]

Guevara uses many classical examples of just rule and paradisiacal conditions as contrasts to the present age. In the *Menosprecio de corte y alabanza de aldea* he even states that present corruption is such that man has gone beyond the iron age into the age of clay: "Gozaron nuestros passados del siglo férreo y quedó para nosotros míseros el siglo lúteo, al qual justamente llamamos lúteo, pues nos tiene a todos puestos del lodo."[16] Asunción Rallo asserts that Guevara uses the myth of the golden age as *contrapunto* for the realities of the times. The end of the golden age is the result of tyranny and greed. An excellent example of tension between imperial expansionism and the harmony of the first age is found in Guevara's anecdote concerning Alexander the Great's attempted conquest of the *garamantes* in India, as described in the *Relox de príncipes* (bk. 1, chs. 32-34). A second example is the famous episode of the *villano del Danubio* (bk. 3, chs. 3-5).[17] These chapters represent an indictment against the desire for conquest and expansion symbolized by the Roman Empire, which in turn can be associated with Charles V's expansionist desires. The expression "quiere (Dios) que un emperador sea monarcha del mundo" in the *Relox de príncipes* (bk. 1, ch. 18) does not mean that Guevara accepted imperialist policies. Influenced by a vision of the New World as the last refuge of Astraea,[18] and steeped in the classical

myth of the golden age, the bishop dreamed of paradise and condemned war. His ideal was a just and peaceful kingdom. Astraea, for
him, should not be clothed in a martial tunic or wear the *hasta* of
modern imperialism. She should be seen as a representative of *pax*.

With the ascent of Philip II to the throne, we come to the end of
Spanish leadership over the Holy Roman Empire. Immediately following the abdication of Charles V in favor of Philip, the University
of Alcalá set out to receive the new monarch and assure his continued
patronage. For this occasion, two dramatic representations were prepared. The second play, dedicated to Philip II, deals with the ages of
the world. From the *relación* of the festivities we learn that "el argu-
mento de la comedia era representar en los cinco actos las quatro
edades, que Ouidio y los otros poetas fingen auer auido en el
mundo."[19] In the first act the *Príncipe* marries virtue during the happiest of ages. In the second act, his son inherits the kingdom and
brings about the silver age, since virtue no longer prevails. As the
play continues, we witness the further deterioration of man and his
environment. Finally, the monarch is defeated in an iron age war.
Realizing his mistakes, he embraces virtue. Between the acts,
nymphs relate the dramatic action to the historical situation: "Entre
vn acto y otro de la comedia, ciertas Nymphas cantauan cosas, con
que aplicauan todo lo que se representaua a la fiesta Real." The author of the *relación* adds that the nymphs utilized *mucho ingenio* to
accomplish this and, indeed, Ronald Surtz wonders at the suitability
of the topic of the decline of the ages for such an occasion: "The songs
interpolated between the acts must have required all the ingenuity
the university poets could muster, for despite the 'happy ending' of
the play, there existed the rather unflattering parallel between the
behavior of the prince in the play and the possible royal career of
Philip II in the audience."[20] Correct interpretation would have been
difficult, since the audience must have been well aware that Charles
V had been considered by many as the emperor who would bring
back the golden age. It was also clear that his son's rule began with
the dashing of desires for Spain's universal imperial rule. Indeed, it
was rumored throughout his reign that Philip II sought the title of
Emperor of the Indies.

In spite of the absence of the imperial title, Spanish expansionist
policies continued under the new monarch. When in 1580 the crowns
of Spain and Portugal were united, adding to its American conquests
the Asian possessions of the Portuguese, Spain seemed to be on the
brink of universal rule again. This climactic moment in the history of

the peninsula was followed by sudden and unforeseen catastrophe and the beginnings of a pessimistic attitude towards empire. But during most of Philip's reign the imperial vision prevailed,[21] hand in hand with a longing for a past age of peace, truth, and harmony.

The recollection of a past and perfect age is at times presented in Christian form, as in Jerónimo de Campo's *Manual de oraciones* (1573), where the early church is evoked as "tiempo dorado y tiempo de amor."[22] More often shepherd's clothing reveals the old dream of Arcadia-Golden Age.[23] With the publication of Jorge de Montemayor's *La Diana* (1559), pastoral concerns permeate Spanish literature. Indeed, a late pastoral has the golden age in its title: *Siglo de oro en las selvas de Erífile* (1608). As Juan Bautista Avalle-Arce points out, however, the title may be misleading, since Bernardo de Balbuena actually expresses doubts about the myth in his work.[24] In this connection we should heed the warning of Anthony Cascardi: "In much pastoral literature, the artist conjures up the Earthly Paradise, but also leaves that Paradise behind, sometimes destroying it as he goes."[25]

The *novela pastoril* coexists with eclogues and other types of bucolic poetry, where similar concerns are expressed. The *beatus ille*, already encountered in Antonio de Guevara's treatise *Menosprecio de corte*, reaches its height in the poetry of Fray Luis de León. In a manner reminiscent of Garcilaso de la Vega's *Egloga segunda*, Fray Luis's *Vida retirada* elaborates on the Horatian contrast between city and country life.[26] This poem, together with several other compositions by Luis de León, contains reminiscences of Virgil's *Georgics* II and *Fourth Eclogue*, and—more importantly—of Seneca's *Hippolytus*.[27] In Seneca praise of the country and blame of the city immediately precede description of the golden age. As in the Roman tragedy, the countryside in *Vida retirada* recalls the moral purity of the inhabitants of the golden age, a quality that has been lost in the present urban age:

> A mi una pobrecilla
> mesa, de amable paz bien abastada,
> me baste; y la vajilla
> del fino oro labrada,
> sea de quien la mar no teme airada.[28]

The golden utensils can be taken as the corrupting "inventions" of developed civilizations condemned by the Stoics. Their gold is not the harmonious quality of the golden age, but the metal that brings about wars. Significantly, this image is followed by a reference to a man who does not fear the sea. Navigation came into existence after the happiest age and was often used as a sign of decline. As Gareth

Davies points out, gold and sea are mentioned after the description of a table "de amable paz," that is, a table that partakes of the qualities of that happiest of ages where nature provides spontaneously for man's needs and where there is tranquility as opposed to strife.

While Davies discusses numerous points of contact between classical works like the *Hippolytus* and *Vida retirada,* Poggioli demonstrates the Spanish poem's uniqueness. He sees its originality in the implicit praise of solitude which is "envisaged as an inscape into self-company as well as an escape from the company of others." For Poggioli, Fray Luis's poem presages Góngora's *Soledades,* where "solitude ceases to be a retreat from and becomes a triumph over the world."[29] This triumph of self over world, which transcends solitude, is not unique to these poems. It is found in works as varied as Lope's "A mis soledades voy" and Bartolomé de Argensola's *Rimas.* The triumph has as its basis the notion of Christian conversion which is the source of an inner paradise. The golden age has as one of its definitions the *pax Christiana* encountered in the soul that has attained knowledge of God through quiet prayer and meditation. This inner bliss is clearly exemplified in the writings of the Spanish mystics during this period. Their outlook is very similar to that of Fray Luis de León.

Fray Luis is also known for his translations of Virgil's *Eclogues,* a task that was attempted by numerous scholars of the epoch.[30] He renders into Spanish the key verses of the Messianic Eclogue thus:

> La postrimera edad de la Cumea
> y la doncella virgen ya es llegada,
> y torna el reino de Saturno y Rea.
> Los siglos tornan de la edad dorada;
> de nuevo largos años nos envía
> el cielo y nueva gente en sí engendrada.[31]

His translation lacks the political overtones of Encina's. Yet Fray Luis does modify the intent of the original work, as in this passage introducing the Christian notion of original sin:

> Lo que hay de la maldad nuestra primera
> deshecho, quedarán ya los humanos
> libres de miedo eterno, de ansia fiera.

The *Fourth Eclogue* had a particular significance for Fray Luis since he was most interested in apocalyptic matters. He believed, for example, that the Turkish Empire was to be considered the fifth and last, the beast of the *Apocalypse.*[32] According to his view, the world would last six thousand years, each day of creation being a millennium. He places the end of the world in the year 1656, citing among his authorities the sibyl. The seventh age belongs to Christ.[33]

The significance of the number seven, as the seventh day of the week, the sabbath or day of rest, reappears in a different context in *Noche serena*. Here, as he asks man to contemplate the heavens, Fray Luis directs his description upwards through the spheres of the seven Ptolemaic planets, recalling the Platonic ascent of the soul found in writers such as Ambrose and Dante. The seventh sphere is described as being ruled by "Saturno, padre de los siglos de oro,"[34] and thus linked with the second golden age, the return of Astraea, or the sabbath of the Christian soul. It may be that Fray Luis derived his inspiration in these matters from Bartolomé Barrientos's recent edition and commentary on Cicero's *Scipio's Dream*.[35] At any rate, what is striking here is that for Fray Luis inner peace is often projected outwards either to the countryside which reminds him of the happiest of ages or to the seventh sphere where Saturn, father of the gods and ruler of the golden age, grants rest to the traveling soul.

From the few examples presented here, we can see how the writings of Luis de León combine many aspects of the Astraea myth: the pursuit of the millennium; the role of Saturn as the highest planet and ruler of the golden age; and the *beatus ille* tradition contrasting the countryside of the golden age with the corrupt inventions of present-day civilization. His sources are varied, from Virgil to Seneca to Cicero. Throughout, the priest from Salamanca stresses the inner peace of the Christian soul for which the *beatus ille* is but a metaphor.

The theme of the earliest of ages is a constant preoccupation in Cervantes's works, according to Américo Castro.[36] Don Quijote's speech on the golden age is addressed to goatherds who seem as far removed from paradisiacal felicity as the tortured Marcela and Grisóstomo. In spite of their closeness to nature, they lack many of the qualities of the mythical golden race. Through satire and ambiguity, Cervantes attempts to liberate the myth from its exile to the Arcadian regions and from the enslavement of having become a *topos* utilized for religious and political purposes.

The golden age can also be detected in the description of the gypsies in *La gitanilla*; and it is found in several passages of Cervantes's last work, the *Persiles y Sigismunda*. Most interesting from our perspective is the episode of Soldino in the third book of the "Greek" romance. Soldino, an old man of over eighty years of age with a long white beard, leads several of the main characters to his cave, after accurately predicting a fire at the inn. As the pilgrims descend the steps into the dark cave, they are surprised to find bright daylight

and idyllic natural surroundings: "Se descubrió el cielo luciente y
claro y se vieron unos amenos y tendidos prados que entretenían la
vista y alegraban las almas" (p. 395).[37] This *locus amoenus* was created
by Soldino after retiring from what Fray Luis termed the *mundanal
ruido*: "Aquí no suena en mis oídos el desdén de los emperadores, el
enfado de sus ministros"(p. 395). The discordant notes of the court
give way to harmony; worldly wars are replaced by peace and tranquility. Indeed, this peace is communicated to the visitors as soon as
they enter this mysterious realm. We are told that their souls become
happier on perceiving the fertile valley. This subterranean abode also
rewards the visitor with nature's spontaneous gifts, a characteristic of
the golden age: "La hambre, que en ese mundo de allá arriba, si así
se puede decir, tenía, halló aquí la hartura" (p. 395). Yet, as the pilgrims prepare to depart, Soldino seemingly contradicts the previous
description of nature's gifts to man: "Y por agora no mas, sino vá-
monos arriba; daremos sustento a *los cuerpos* como aquí abajo le he-
mos dado a las almas"(p. 397). Studying this episode, John Weiger
rightly concludes that "we are meant to interpret the *locus amoenus*
figuratively (or spiritually), not literally."[38] Hunger and satiety are references to spiritual need and fulfillment. The descent into the cave
can be equated with a descent into the self. It represents the silence
or solitude necessary for self-knowledge. It is similar to the inner
paradise of the Christian soul that can be attained in communion
with God through prayer, meditation, or contemplation. Soldino sees
the cave or the self as the closest road to God: "Aquí tengo mi alma
en mi palma, y aquí por vía recta encamino mis pensamientos y mis
deseos al cielo" (p. 395).

In spite of the scene's debt to the Christian tradition of the paradise within,[39] Cervantes is careful to point out that this cave is not to
be interpreted solely in the traditional Christian manner. Soldino is
neither a pilgrim nor a priest, and he dresses as neither: "Venía ves-
tido ni como peregrino, ni como religioso" (p. 392). He is an astrologer whose science enables him to accurately foretell future events.[40]
Soldino's knowledge is a direct result of solitude: "Aqui estoy, donde
sin libros, con sola la esperiencia que he adquirido con el tiempo de
mi soledad" (p. 396). The intimate relationship between microcosm
and macrocosm is implied in this episode. By knowing himself, Soldino is able to be a true astrologer, comprehending intuitively the
movement of the planets and the stars: "He contemplado el curso de
las estrellas y el movimiento del sol y de la luna" (pp. 395-96). According to Leonard Barkan, astrology is actually microcosmic: "Man
is the crucial and central term in the astral cosmos, and since all the

bodies in the cosmos influence all the others, man must contain within him the distillation of the whole astral system."[41] It may be said, then, that Astraea abides within Soldino. His cave or inscape is permeated with virtues such as truth and justice. As a harmonious microcosm, it contains all the constellations.

The theme of solitude as related to self-knowledge is an important one in the *Persiles*, as John Weiger has noted. This critic has also demonstrated how each instance of isolation and self-knowledge in the romance contains a reference to Charles V. This evidence leads him to speculate that the emperor's withdrawal to the monastery at Yuste at the end of his life may have been the model for Cervantes's repeated depiction of oases of solitude.[42] Soldino, like the emperor, abandons the concerns of the world in order to attune himself with divine intelligence. The notion of the golden age and the return of Astraea in Cervantes is not so far removed from the question of empire. In these last years of his life, Cervantes may be expressing the belief that Astraea can return, not through imperial *renovatio*, but through man's abandonment of worldly concerns in imitation of the Holy Roman Emperor who himself relinquished the crown and imperialist wars in order to attain inner peace.

On the other hand, the younger Cervantes, the warrior of Lepanto, resembles the youthful Soldino who fought for his country during the reign of Charles V. In his earlier works, Cervantes comes closer to the belief in imperial *renovatio*. In *La Numancia*, the prophecy of future glory and empire expressed by the river Duero can be equated with Virgil's vision of Rome's rebirth in the *Fourth Eclogue*.[43] A description of the age of gold is found in another early play by Cervantes, *Los tratos de Argel*. Aurelio, a Christian captive in Argel, laments his plight in a soliloquy recalling the happiest of ages:

> ¡Oh santa edad, por nuestro mal pasada,
> a quien nuestros antiguos le pusieron
> el dulce nombre de la edad dorada!
> ¡Cuán seguros y libres discurrieron
> la redondez del suelo los que en ella
> la caduca mortal vida vivieron![44]

Sweet liberty, he adds, is one of the qualities of the first age that is now missing. In its stead, there is slavery and war, arising from the desire for the metal gold. Aurelio blames the corruption of man on the discovery of this metal: "Descubrieron los rubios minerales / del oro que en la tierra se escondía" (p. 148). Although the *comedia* exalts Christian heroism in a war against Islam, a quest that spurred Spanish imperialism, Aurelio's lament represents a longing for a golden age of peace, where sweet liberty will reign and bloody wars will vanish. Interestingly, Aurelio's evocation of the happiest age comes in a moment of solitude. Silence once more triggers in the self a vision of harmony. Inner peace again is contrasted with imperial *renovatio* in Cervantes's continuing concern with the myth of Astraea, a goddess who is not mentioned by name in these commentaries on the age of gold.

Lope de Vega seldom uses the name Astraea in his *comedias*, but he frequently contrasts the iron age and the age of gold. In two early dramas where the Emperor Nero is a character, Lope may be emulating the *Octavia* attributed to Seneca, where the differences between the just and peaceful rule of Augustus and the tyranny of Nero elicit the image of the first and fourth epochs. *Los embustes de Fabia* (1588-95)[45] depicts the lack of moral structure and the absence of justice in the political realm of Nero. As in many of Lope's *comedias* evoking another time or place, the ambience remains much closer to his own Spanish environment. *Los embustes de Fabia* is an exception to Bruce Wardropper's theory that *capa y espada* plays concern life before marriage, while honor plays concern life after.[46] This is not an honor drama, even though Fabia, the central character, is married. The tone and structure are similar to the *comedias de capa y espada*, with the implication that marriage is devoid of social or religious force in an age of moral, religious, and political decadence. The chaotic family and social structure in the play mirrors the actions of Nero, who divorced his wife and had her murdered to satisfy his lust for another woman.

Los embustes de Fabia revolves around the amorous tricks of Fabia, a woman of many loves, although married to the senator Fabricio. Revenge, the most common motivation in Seneca's tragedies, rivals lust as a main ingredient in this *comedia*. Fabricio, Lelio, and Vitelio, for example, waver between revenge and desire for Fabia's favors. The lady herself plots to have her husband murdered by one of her suitors so that she can enjoy Vitelio's love. When discovered, Fabia locks herself in a tower and threatens to kill her child, recalling Medea's actions in Seneca's drama. When Lelio accuses the senator to the emperor, Nero bemoans truth's departure from earth:

> Bien dicen que la edad pasó dorada
> y que, de verse la Verdad corrida,
> al Cielo se volvió, de donde vino.
> Mas no permitiré que mientras viva
> se diga que con ella juntamente

> la Justicia se fue, que pienso agora
> hacerla muy de veras . . .
>
> [p. 99][47]

The many deceptions perpetrated in the *comedia* are evidence that truth has indeed abandoned the realm. Nero's claim that Astraea's other virtue, justice, still prevails in his realm proves to be false. Lelio and Vitelio remain in the Emperor's presence and attempt to explain the many confusing events that have occurred. The poetic portrait of Fabia drawn by these two lovers moves the emperor, whose behavior demonstrates that his passion does not arise from the lady's spiritual qualities but from his desire to possess that which others consider unattainable.

If truth and justice are absent from the age of Nero, so is Astraea's third major quality, chastity, as is manifested in Fabia's entanglements and the emperor's increasing desire for her. As Nero seeks to satisfy his desires, Fabia's husband intervenes to protect his honor. The emperor recalls the lustful Spanish kings in Lope de Vega's dramas:

> No me pienses tu enseñar;
> ¿no sabes que soy tu Rey? . . .
> Pues quien hace la ley
> ése la puede quitar.
>
> [p. 107]

The senator tries to educate the emperor, to make him understand that rather than taking away the honor of others, the ruler should confer it and act in accordance with the laws. When Nero reveals that he will stop at nothing to obtain Fabia's favors, the senator swallows poison from his ring, and foretells the future of Nero's rule as being worse than an iron age:

> Tendrá perpetuo destierro
> de tus hijos la verdad,
> será muy peor edad
> que la de alambre y de hierro.
>
> [p. 108]

The senator's death comes close to imitating the tragic demise of the innocent victim in Seneca's tragedies. The emperor is unconcerned by his death and attempts to seize Fabia. Imitating her husband, she takes poison and dies, as the emperor leaves the scene in rage and frustration. The *comedia* does not end on this tragic note of Senecan horror, however. After all, the play is called *Los embustes de Fabia*. She has only pretended to swallow poison, and now that her old husband is dead, Fabia can leave with the dashing Vitelio. This "happy" ending betrays the immorality of Nero's times. Lope has presented an epoch where rulers are lustful tyrants and where a woman can turn her back on her dead husband in order to fulfill "all-conquering lust," in Seneca's words. Beneath a false happy note, akin to the ending of the *comedias de capa y espada*, lurks the horror of an age devoid of virtues, be they honor, justice, or chastity. Beneath the merriment lies the realization that these characters know nothing of the *devenir responsable* of which Wardropper speaks when analyzing the conclusion of the cape and sword plays. The weak prophetic voice of the inept senator is ignored. This is precisely the kind of era depicted in the *Octavia*. But the philosopher's voice in the Roman play is here replaced by the mutterings of a senator who is considered an old fool.

Nero reappears in *Roma abrasada* (1598-1600),[48] another early play by Lope de Vega portraying the corrupt life of imperial Rome. This *comedia*, whose structure Menéndez Pelayo calls "irregular y mon-struosa," is a dramatization of Nero's worst excesses. Menéndez Pelayo adds, "El poeta no nos perdona ningún acto de la vida de Nerón; ni siquiera la escena en que, después del parricidio, contempla con lascivos ojos el cadáver de su madre."[49] MacCurdy minimizes the influence of Seneca on *Roma abrasada*, in spite of the fact that the philosopher is a character in the *comedia*.[50] I believe that this link should be reconsidered. The inclusion of Seneca as a character in *Roma abrasada* is probably inspired by his presence in the *Octavia*, a work that Lope had already utilized for certain scenes in *Los embustes de Fabia*. Many of Nero's actions in the *Octavia* are repeated in *Roma abrasada*. At the beginning of the *Octavia* Seneca reminisces about his early years in the country, where he had been able to pursue his studies, including the motion of celestial bodies. Lope's Stoic philosopher is an astrologer, whose horoscope of Nero in the first act reveals that he will murder his own mother if he becomes emperor.

Agripina rejects Seneca's prediction, stating that "Esa ciencia es disparate" (p. 417).[51] Even if it were true, she would not desist in her efforts to make her son emperor: "Tenga un hijo emperador, / que yo huelgo que me mate" (p. 417). To fulfill this goal, she must conspire with her son to poison the present emperor, her husband Claudius. In a sonnet, Agripina justifies through example this murder as well as the possible future matricide:

> Semíramis no diera muerte a Nino
> Ni el hijo airado fuera matricida
> Ni le quitare Rómulo la vida
> Al fuerte hermano que pasó el camino,

> Si el imitar á Júpiter divino,
> Que del padre Saturno fue homicida,
> Ya no fuera disculpa conocida . . .
>
> [p. 417]

The key example in this sonnet is the father-son conflict that is the basis for the myth of Jupiter's parricide. In works not concerned with the decline of the ages, Saturn's death is positive, since the tyranny of his rule is replaced by Jupiter's benevolent reign. In this passage, Agripina hopes that her son will be another Jupiter, even if this means that he will kill her. The characteristics of the two supreme gods evoked by Nero's mother are mirrored in the aspects of the planets of the same name. According to medieval astrologers, Jupiter was the most auspicious of planets, while Saturn was considered a malefic influence. In *Roma abrasada*, the opposition between the planets is described in precisely these terms by Otón, as Seneca leaves to cast Nero's horoscope:

> Júpiter vaya contigo
> Y el se muestre tan amigo
> En la parte que es planeta,
> Que en cuanto influya y prometa
> Venza a Saturno enemigo.
>
> [p. 416]

The *comedia* presents the triumph of the Saturnine qualities in the emperor which lead Seneca to eventual suicide. In *Roma abrasada*, Saturn is never the planet of highest wisdom evoked by the Renaissance Platonists nor is he the just ruler of the golden age. Instead, Saturn is consistently described as both the malefic planet of medieval astrologers and the tyrannical figure who was murdered by Jupiter. While *Los embustes de Fabia* contrasts Saturn and the golden age to the iron age of the Romans, *Roma abrasada* stresses the opposite aspect of Saturn; and while *Los embustes de Fabia* manipulates the Senecan contrasts found in the *Octavia*, *Roma abrasada* takes Senecan horror to the extreme.

In later plays Nero is not forgotten, although the early Senecan experiments have evolved into more mature *comedias*. In *La Niña de plata* (1607-12),[52] Zulema casts a horoscope of the future King Peter the Cruel where this monarch is compared to Nero. After five years of just rule, Pedro, like Nero, will become a tyrant and will kill Enrique de Trastamara's mother:

> Que también Nerón romano
> Cinco años gobernó

Su república de suerte,
Que una sentencia de muerte
Con mil lágrimas firmó.
Séneca dél se admiraba;
Pero matóle después;
Y esta blancura que ves
En Pedro, ya el curso acaba.
A doña Leonor, tu madre,
Ha de matar . . . [53]

The mention of Nero, Seneca, and matricide by the astrologer recalls Agripina's sonnet in *Roma abrasada* where the Saturn-Jupiter rivalry is presented. *La niña de plata* includes many allusions to the ages of the world. The juxtaposition of the words *hierro* and *yerro* form a pun in the *comedia*, where the mistakes of an epoch akin to the iron age are presented. Jupiter rules over the ideal epoch, the silver age, while Saturn is related to the metal gold and to tyranny. In the first age, ironically transformed into the iron age, the prince's passion threatens to make of Dorotea the innocent victim often depicted by Seneca. Tragedy is averted in the end and Dorotea is able to marry the man she loves, don Juan. As in many of Lope de Vega's comic plays, the malefic Saturn of the medieval astrologers complicates the action and causes delays and disasters; but in the end, Venus rules over the happy denouement.[54]

Even though Astraea is never a character in Lope's plays, her presence can be gleaned from emblematic descriptions in certain *comedias*. Alan Soons, for example, perceives her in a scene from *El despertar a quien duerme* (1613).[55] Allusions to the goddess of justice can also be found in Lope's *Isidro* plays, which will be discussed in the following chapter as precursors of Calderón's *La gran Cenobia*. In general, however, Astraea's prominent role in Calderón's dramas contrasts with her conspicuous absence from Lope's *comedias*.

Although the myth of Astraea must be sought in Lope's *comedias* through references to the ages of the world, astrology, the Saturn-Jupiter rivalry, and emblematic representation, her name is often found in his poetry and even appears in some prose works. The traditional association of the astrological sign Virgo with the myth of Astraea, however, is ignored by Lope in favor of a lesser-known link. In this, Lope may be exhibiting his knowledge of astrology.[56] For example, the fifth book of the pastoral romance *La Arcadia* (1598) contains a description of the sign Virgo. Rather than relating Astraea's story, Lope recalls the myth of Erigone's catasterism described by Manilius and Hyginus. Icarius, Erigone's father, was killed by some *villanos* who became intoxicated when he shared with them Bacchus's drink. Erigone goes in search of her father: "Guiada Erígone por un perro donde su padre estaba, murióse de dolor, por cuya piedad Júpiter la puso entre los signos."[57] Lope has selected Erigone's pity over Astraea's justice and chastity as the genesis of the zodiacal sign Virgo. Six years later, Astraea appears in *El peregrino en su patria:* "Diez veces había el sol por otros tantos paralelos cercado el cielo casi en la sazón que Astrea igualaba las balanzas al equinocio."[58] Here Astraea is related to the scales and to the equinox. The scales, although at times utilized by Virgo as Justice, are most often related to the sign Libra. The equinox occurs at the beginning of Libra, as Lope reminds us in *La Arcadia:* "Libra, signo celeste, en quien entrando el sol hace el equinoctio autumnal."[59] We can assume that in *El peregrino en su patria* our poet is associating Astraea with the sign Libra.

Libra and the equinox reappear in association with Astraea in the epic poem *Jerusalén conquistada* (1609). In the sixth book we encounter the following verse: "Passo la Libra ygual el Sol ardiente" (vol. 1, p. 243).[60] In a note, Lope explains his use of *ygual:* "Libra ygual porque subiendo el sol por ella en Octubre haze el Equinoctio Autumnal" (vol. 1, p. 484). In the seventh book a more extensive reference is found, this time including the name of Astraea: "Tocaua el Sol el peso, con que Astrea / Dias y noches, premio y pena yguala" (vol. 1, p. 274). Again Lope chooses to explain his statement in a note, where a more complete exposition of his views on Astraea can be found: "Assi llamaron a la justicia los Poetas en la edad dorada. Ouid. prim. Meth. y de alli tomó la Astrologia llamar Astrea á la Libra, por que entrando en este sino el Sol por Otubre se causa el Equinocio autumnal"(vol. 1, p. 490). Following Ovid, Lope associates Astraea with the goddess of justice who inhabited the earth during the golden age. Lope adds that in astrological terms, Astraea is the sign Libra, although we know that our goddess is most often associated with Virgo.

The relationship of Astraea (Justice) with Libra is based on the scales, an icon of both goddess and zodiacal sign. This relationship was a commonplace in Lope's time. In Piero Valeriano Bolzani's *Hieroglyphica*, a work "which brought together the hidden meanings of almost all things beneath the sun,"[61] we encounter a hieroglyph or emblem of Astraea, suspended in the heavens between the scales and the lion. Valeriano, in his prose explanation, repeats the story of Astraea's flight to the heavens and adds "qu'elle se meit entre le Lion & la Balance, laquelle mesme luy est atribuee, pour y peser ce qui est deu á un chascun." Valeriano adds that the reason Astraea-Virgo is placed between the scales and the lion is so that the lion will give her courage and generosity while the scales will allow her to weigh "les crimes & les merites d'vn chascun."[62] Thus, Astraea assumes a most important role in the heavens while the two adjacent zodiacal signs are seen as her helpers. Valeriano's hieroglyph reminds us of the figure of Justice in the Tarot cards. Here, she is not between two heavenly constellations, but is seen holding two instruments in her hands which aid her in her duties. Noting that this Tarot figure holds a sword in one hand and the scales in the other, J.E. Cirlot echoes Lope's statement in the *Jerusalén conquistada*: "The enigma is related to Libra, the sign of the Zodiac. . . . Astronomically speaking, Justice is Astraea."[63] The link established by Lope between Libra and Astraea probably led him to use another myth—that of Erigone—to explain Virgo's catasterism.

The use of Libra-Astraea to denote the equinox did not require much erudition. Yet Lope insists on relating it to classical literature. If we are to trust his show of ancient learning in both *La Arcadia* and *Jerusalén conquistada*, we should search Virgil's *Georgics* I for the passage he had in mind. The following may be Lope's source (I am using Luis de León's translation):

> Cuando la Libra iguales horas diere
> al sueño y a la vela, y justamente
> la redondez por medio dividiere
> entre la noche y la luz . . .[64]

It may be that Lope's stress on the word *igual* in his description of the zodiacal sign is derived from the *Georgics*. The term *igual* refers not only to the equal length of day and night, the equinox that takes place while the sun is in Libra, but may also imply the equality of all men under the law, since Astraea is justice. At any rate, Astraea-Libra as an equalizer of light and darkness is a commonplace in Lope's works. Another example occurs in a sonnet dedicated to Mira de Amescua, found in the *Rimas*:

> Viendo que iguala en su balanza Astrea
> los rayos y las sombras desiguales,
> Dauro no ha reparado en las señales
> de la extranjera vega que pasea.
> [p. 121][65]

This allusion to Lope de Vega's visit to Granada (note the use of the word *vega* to refer to the poet), begins with a description of the equinox as Astraea's scales equalizing light and shadow.

The "Descripción de la tapada" included in *La Filomena* (1621) is a poem dedicated to Teodosio II, seventh Duke of Braganza. One of the laudatory techniques utilized by Lope in the work is to compare the duke to the twelve signs of the zodiac, showing how this human microcosm mirrors perfectly the celestial macrocosm. Virgo and Libra are described thus:

> ¿Dónde mejor que en vos la bella Astrea,
> Teodosio excelentísimo, se mira;
> la Libra, la igualdad que os hermosea,
> peso que el mundo en vuestra gloria admira.
>
> [p. 714]

The passage is different from examples cited above in that Astraea is here equated with Virgo,[66] but her just qualities are also shared by Libra. In these verses Lope merges the meaning of the two zodiacal signs: Teodosio reflects Astraea-Virgo's justice and is admired for his Libra-like qualities of *igualdad*, that is, evenhandedness or justice.[67] *Igualdad* carries the two meanings common in Lope. First, Libra is the equalizer of days and nights as in Virgil's *Georgics* and Manilius's *Astronomica*, which describe the equinox in this manner. And second, the balance delineated by the stars in the constellation also reflects the equality of justice among men. The stanza concludes with a discussion of the next sign of the zodiac, Scorpio.

The "Descripción de la tapada" may serve as a bridge in our discussion of Astraea in Lope de Vega, leading us from astrological descriptions where equality and justice are emphasized to verses where truth is hailed in the guise of our goddess. In the second part of *La Filomena*, the central poem in the collection that includes the "Descripción de la tapada," the idea of Astraea as truth is expressed by the nightingale (representing Lope) who has just heard the song of the thrush (standing for his enemy, Torres Rámila). The nightingale speaks:

> "Senado ilustre y claro
> —dijo el ave amorosa,
> templando el pico en la primera rosa—;
> si con largo y retórico proemio
> solicitar adulación quisiera,
> en este siglo avaro
> de la divina Astrea,
> que con doradas alas
> se fue a juzgar a las etéreas salas,
> huyendo la mentira atroz y fea,
> temiera el justo premio . . .
>
> [p. 641]

Lope (the *ruiseñor*) assures his audience that he will not subject them to a "largo y retórico proemio." Even though Justice-Astraea has fled to the heavens, he is afraid he would receive his just reward—censure—if he so dared. By saying this, Lope criticizes the *tordo*, Torres Rámila, for just such a speech. In the next stanza, Lope adds that his enemy's words have revealed his *arrogante ingenio* and his *envidia*.[68] He labels him a *mísero gramático* (p. 641). The nightingale will avoid such vices and excesses. Entrambasaguas explains that the beautiful bird's efforts will be directed at demonstrating "que procurará ser menos violento y más justo."[69] The reference to Astraea-Justice is more complex than it appears at first glance. The goddess with the scales denotes evenhandedness, a characteristic of justice; thus, Lope will not indulge in excessive rhetoric and will attempt to be fair with his enemy. The fact that Astraea left earth attempting to escape *mentira atroz y fea* is significant because for Lope, Torres Rámila is the embodiment of such a lie. His negative vision based on envy and pride is typical of the worst of ages. In contrast, Lope de Vega as the nightingale sings an evenhanded and beautiful song. Through these qualities shines Astraea's truth, and the *ruiseñor's* song is an evocation of the happiest of ages.

It may be that in choosing the nightingale, Lope recalled Hesiod's poem on the happiest of epochs where the bird represented the poet. The envy, lies, and excesses found in Torres Rámila's inflated rhetoric typify the worst of times. Astraea as truth is often counterbalanced in Renaissance iconography by envy or calumny.[70] Lope could be characterizing his poetry as Astraea's truth while Torres Rámila's attacks are calumny based on envy. The lies of the powerful, he claims, although compelling, should not be accepted. Lope argues that men should listen to his nightingale's truthful voice. In the autobiographical song of bucolic beauty reminiscent of the golden age, the beautiful bird alludes to many works written by our poet. Thus, the nightingale's song is not only the poem at hand, but all of Lope's poetic production. Art based on nature and grounded in philosophy (p. 643) is the truth of the bird's song. Even though elsewhere Lope indulges in bitter satire during his literary war, *La Filomena* captures that longing for the golden age through the idealized self-portrayal of a poet who prefers to speak the sweet truth and evoke the beauty of the golden age.

In a sonnet from the *Rimas* entitled "A la Verdad," Lope again recalls the exile of Astraea at the advent of the iron age:

> Hija del Tiempo, que en el Siglo de Oro
> viviste hermosa y cándida en la tierra,
> de donde la mentira te destierra
> en esta fiera edad de hierro y lloro.
>
> [p. 117]

The use of the present tense to mark Astraea's exile makes the iron age an immediate concern. Every lie one hears uttered is one more justification for the goddess's departure. Her beauty and virtuous nature gone, the present age is characterized by fierceness and weeping. As with the Biblical tale of the fall, Astraea's departure signals the beginning of man's suffering. The sonnet contains many typical oppositions between the present age and the happiest of epochs, such as peace versus war and chastity versus covetousness, yet it is more concerned with transcending these opposites. In the last two verses, the poet reveals Astraea's true nature after admitting he can never write enough in her praise; "¿qué puedo decir en tu alabanza, / si eres el mismo Dios, Verdad divina?" (p. 117). In an age of iron where wars and uncertainties reign, divine truth is man's greatest treasure (*Mayor tesoro*). It is a window through which God's light shines (*del sol de Dios ventana cristalina*).

Lope's image of truth as God's light parallels Marsilio Ficino's own perception of this virtue: "Absolute truth is in itself the light of God." Ficino hopes that man will discard the shadow of earthly pleasures and blissfully experience "the supreme treasury of truth." The Italian philosopher also speaks of the divine light with reference to a second attribute of Astraea, justice. He ends a letter with an invocation to the goddess: "Justice that is blissful life! Justice that is heavenly life! Mother and Queen of the golden age, sublime Astraea seated among the starry thrones! Goddess, we beg you, do not abandon your earthly abode, lest we miserably sink into the iron age. Heavenly goddess, we beseech you, ever live in human minds, that is, in citizens who belong to the heavenly country."[71] As in Lope, Astraea's departure has a certain immediacy here. Without her, men will live in an iron age of suffering, but as in Lope, she can be recaptured in human minds.

Lope, I believe, is also evoking the inscape of happiness, the blissfulness of the inner paradise in the soul of man where peace can be attained in spite of the world's turmoils. The golden age is the treasure within, the divine truth. This perception helps us to understand the first words of the sonnet, where Astraea is not presented as the daughter of Themis and Zeus, but as the offspring of time (Chronos). In this, Lope is following a tradition based on the classical line "veritas filia temporis." This phrase became well known in the Middle Ages through Lactantius's allusion to it, and was popular in Lope's epoch as envinced in La Perriere's emblem that begins "Le temps chercheoit sa fille Verité."[72] Lope merges Astraea, the last of the immortals to leave earth, who represents justice, chastity and truth, with a tradition that considers personified Truth as the daughter of Father Time. In a pseudomorphis described by Erwin Panofsky, Time (Chronos) becomes infused with characteristics of Saturn (Kronos). The god who devours his own children is during the Renaissance an allegory of time, the ever-changing relative that devours whatever has been created.[73] Lope's sonnet speaks of Astraea as Time's daughter. Lope's distrust of Saturn is evident once more in this sonnet: instead of focusing on the planet that stands for wisdom according to Ficino, he transfers this quality to his new daughter, Astraea-Truth. Like Jupiter, she somehow survives Saturn's bloody banquet. When the golden age, defined within space-time limitations, is over, and Saturn is deposed, the goddess remains accessible to men. Yet her supreme value lies in the eternal realm which is accessible to man through his perceptions of her virtues which shine with divine light. Ficino describes his experience thus: "[God] has shed light into the mind beyond any limit of time, by which it rises from the currents of time to the stillness of eternity."[74] Astraea's supreme value is the eternal moment, the transcending experience when historical time disintegrates through a vision of the eternal.[75]

Lope de Vega's continuing concern with Astraea as a perception of divine truth is evinced in a sonnet in Los pastores de Belén. In the prose passage following the sonnet, Lope elaborates on his concept of Astraea-Truth. One of the characters laments for the many that have suffered to uphold truth on earth: "O quantos, dixo Aminadab entonces, han padecido en el mundo, por decirla muertes y afrentas" (p. 69).[76] Tebandra replies that writers continue to tell the truth in spite of the threats of tyrants: "Pues a su pesar de los tyranos principes se saben sus vicios, desde el principio del mundo hasta la edad presente, y se sabran los que huviere por el discurso de los años hasta su fin" (p. 69). Tying this theme to the nativity, the subject of Los pastores de Belén, Tebandra adds that Herod's crimes are well known. Yet the thrust of the passage is Lope's view of the writer. He sees the writer as the individual charged with revealing the truth of the world.[77] In this sense, Astraea, the embodiment of truth, is the writer's ideal. The optimistic notion that truth will be known throughout historical time is maintained. Yet Astraea is more than earthly truth. She is the eternal and divine *verdad*:

> Sol que nuestras tinieblas hermosea
> y thesoro, que hallado regocija,
> pues quando mas obscuridad te aflija
> no haran los años que lo que es no sea.
> [p. 68]

As in the previous sonnet, Astraea is linked with the light of the sun, God's light. No matter how much darkness envelops man he can find solace in her unchanging nature. The goddess is again a *tesoro*, meaning a heavenly gift, that momentarily dispels the darkness of the present. Here Astraea is also called "de los tiempos hija," following the classical dictum "veritas filia temporis." Although manifested in time as man's ideal, she exists beyond it: "santa Verdad eternamente fixa / de tu Hacedor en la suprema idea" (p. 68).

The theme of Astraea-Truth is eminently suited to *Los pastores de Belén*. The story of Christ's birth would be incomplete without a reference to the virgin-goddess whom Constantine equated with Mary, mother of Christ. Her son brings to man that divine revelation, that *verdad divina* that can transform human existence into a paradise or golden age in the hearts of the faithful. For Lope, Christ is the truth within and beyond history that brings peace now as the eternal moment, and in the eternity that will follow historical time. Without the vision of the transcendent, present time is conflict and suffering, as in Fabio's tale in *El peregrino en su patria:*

> guerras el mundo afligían
> por la mar y por la tierra;
> que faltaba en aquel siglo
> la paz y la bella Astrea.[78]

Platonic aspirations and religious fervor have led to the conception of Astraea as an inner paradise. The outer world, devoid of her divine light, is filled with shadows and conflict. The tension created by these opposite states is further reinforced by the poet's own outward pursuits of love, fame, and pleasure. As his life comes to a close, the earlier enthusiasm for the ideal, although leaving its mark, tends to fade as Lope learns to cope with unfulfilled desires in the presence of time's destructive force. Alan Trueblood perceptively describes Lope's *desengaño:* "Out of his attachment to what is impermanent, his growing sense of impermanence within himself, arises the wistful disenchantment peculiar to the mood of *La Dorotea*, one of *desengaño en el goce vital* . . . a mood bittersweet, not bitter, melancholy but acquiescent."[79] The poet who had previously denied the wise Saturn in favor of the dazzling Astraea is now influenced by the planet that rules old age. *La Dorotea*, although still celebrating Venus in the guise of Dorotea, turns inward and projects the *soledad* and melancholy typical of those ruled by Saturn. When Astraea appears in the *acción en prosa*, she is no longer dressed in divine light, but is surrounded by the shadow of *desengaño*. The passage in question is found in the poem "A mis soledades voy."[80] Astraea has simply departed from earth, and man is alone, discoursing with the self and with the temporal world:[81]

> Dixeron que antiguamente
> Se fue la verdad al cielo;
> Tal la pusieron los hombres,
> Que desde entonces no a buelto.
>
> [p. 89][82]

As Trueblood notes, the fragility of all imaginable worlds resounds in the poem through the image of splintering glass:

> No puede durar el mundo,
> Porque dizen, y lo creo,
> Que suena a vidrio quebrado
> Y que ha de romperse presto.
>
> [p. 89]

This is a further departure from Ficinian enthusiasm. The verses come closer to the Stoic emphasis on endings. As the poet contemplates the evils of the present age, he feels that dissolution is at hand and expresses this in a Christian context: "Señales son del juizio" (p. 89). Envy, the ugly goddess banished from Astraea's radiant presence in previous poems by Lope, is now found at his side. With a final effort, the poet dismisses her, remaining alone, in silence: "A mis soledades voy, / De mis soledades vengo" (p. 91). Perhaps in this quiet inner state revealed at the end of "A mis soledades voy," without Astraea or Envy, Lope is able to reconcile within the self the opposites of existence—the transitory nature of the universe and the longing for an eternal golden age.

Carlos Vossler records an important act at the end of Lope's life: "Mencionaremos tan solo el hecho, casi simbólico, de que veinticuatro horas antes de su muerte el mismo Lope de Vega compuso una silva moral cantando en versos amables y transparentes aquella lejana edad dorada."[83] This silva is Lope's most complete statement on Astraea and the myth of the golden age. The first and longest section describes the happiest age, utilizing most of the traditional details such as peace and eternal spring. Elements that are absent from the epoch are also discussed, for example, navigation, martial pursuits, and the oxen used for agriculture.

In the happy times when men wandered on the face of the earth without jealousy or interés, with God as their ever-present companion, a beautiful virgin appeared. Lope's detailed and delightful description of Astraea and men's admiring reaction to her occupies more than fifty verses. When asked who she is, the virgin responds, "Yo soy . . . la Verdad" (p. 381).[84] The poem concludes with the corruption of men and the goddess's departure from earth. Her *felicidad* gives way to man's *soberbia*. Although examples of *tristeza melancólica* may be gleaned from the *silva*,[85] what is significant here is that Lope revels in the description of the ideal age, which is much longer than the condemnation of the present age. He also delights in the description of Astraea. She is once again equated with divine light and truth. If *verdad divina* had faded in the worldly Dorotea, she returns now to guide the poet in his last moments of earthly existence as a symbolic presence. The poet's final admonition to his fellow men deals precisely with the notion of the evanescence of earthly existence:

> Viendo, pues, la divina Verdad santa
> la tierra en tal estado...
> la muerte no temida,
> y para el sueño de tan breve vida
> el hombre edificando,
> ignorando la ley de la partida,
> con presuroso vuelo
> subiose en hombros de sí misma al cielo.

In 1635, Lope de Vega left this world, having sung of Astraea and the notion of life as a dream. At approximately the same time, Calderón composed *La vida es sueño*.

LOPE DE VEGA'S extensive use of Astraea in his poetry is not an isolated phenomenon. The largest number of references to Astraea in the seventeenth-century in Spain occur in poetic compositions. Astraea's presence among the poets may be linked to her preeminence in laudatory verse since the Renaissance, and to her importance in classical poetry from Aratus to Ovid and Virgil. Perhaps Lope de Vega was aware of this double tradition when he chose to include the goddess in his verse compositions and exclude her from most of his *comedias*. Yet he was certainly aware of Seneca's treatment of Astraea and the golden age in the tragedies. Whatever Lope's motivation may have been, others seem to have followed him. Poets as diverse as Lope de Vega, Góngora, Quevedo, and Villamediana were interested in our goddess, while few playwrights included her in their works, the major exception being Calderón de la Barca.

Lope de Vega often portrayed Astraea holding the scales of justice, linking her to the sign Libra rather than Virgo. The scales are very popular among the poets of the epoch, who often place this instrument in the hands of Astraea. The scales also appear quite independently from our goddess in many metaphysical poems, as evinced by Daniel Heiple's carefully documented study on mechanical imagery in Golden Age poetry.[86] Justice holding the scales is also a common figure in pictorial arts. Justice with the balance and sword is a card in the Tarot, and she is also seen with the scales in the emblematic tradition. The *Emblemas morales* (1610) by Sebastián de Covarrubias Horozco picture a lady holding a sword in one hand and a pair of scales in the other. The author does not give a detailed explanation, stating simply that "La figura del emblema, es la comun pintura de la justicia."[87] A second Spanish emblem book, Francisco de Villava's *Empresas espirituales y morales* (1613), includes an *emblema* of a hand supporting the scales. The pans contain a sword and a feather. Since the balance functions by lowering and raising its pans, it conveys the idea of Astraea's movement. She is first seen leaving earth and taking with her her heavenly gifts: "Por ventura por esto fingieron los antiguos fabulistas que la virgen Astrea se volvio al cielo, por quien significava la justicia, la qual, segun su razon universal, significa y abarca todo genero de bien."[88] The movement upwards of Astraea-Justice leaves man without divine guidance in an iron epoch. But Villava will also discuss the downward movement of one of the pans. Here Astraea is portrayed as returning through Christ's sacrifice. Heiple explains that "the image of the balance expresses with precision the relationship between Christ and man—the humiliation of God for the exaltation of man."[89] Villava points to the Cumaean Sibyl's prophecy of Christ as found by Christian writers in Virgil's *Fourth Eclogue*. Virgil's verses and the pictorial tradition of justice holding the scales have produced a Christianization of the myth. She represents divine gifts that are taken away from earth or brought to man. The balance's two pans serve to show her at the two key moments of departure from earth and return. These are explained through Christian doctrine as the expulsion of man from paradise and Christ's redemption. The sword, the second instrument associated with Astraea in pictorial representations, is also included in Villava's emblem. It is not the golden sword that points to heaven as portrayed in the Tarot, but the sword of vengeance that keeps man from attaining paradise. The sword was replaced with Christ's mercy.

Although rich in innovations dealing with the Astraea myth, the emblematic tradition was no match for the variety of anecdotes and allusions found through the erudition of the mythographers. Perhaps the most complete overview of the Astraea myth during the

Spanish Golden Age appears in the fifth book of Baltasar de Vitoria's *Teatro de los dioses de la gentilidad* (1620). The author tells how, from Aurora and the Titan Astero were born two children, Astraea and the Winds (p. 732).[90] Vitoria then attempts to provide a rational and historical explanation for this goddess. He states that Astraea is related to justice because her father had been "vn Principe muy recto y justo" (p. 733). The story of her ascent to heaven becomes logical, according to Vitoria, if we consider it conceptually: "y por ser la justicia cosa tan soberana, dixeron, que se auia subido al cielo" (p. 733). Examples of her catasterism are provided from classical authorities. A rather lengthy astrological discussion of the sign Astraea-Virgo follows. Most of his material was common knowledge for the period, but Victoria adds the curious datum that Virgo is found in the house of Mercury, a god of prudence and wisdom, "porque para librarse vna virgen de los hombres, y guardar su honestidad, es menester mucha prudencia, y mucho auiso" (p. 734).

The poets of the epoch had a rich tradition from which to draw when dealing with Astraea. Some use the Astraea myth as a laudatory vehicle. This is the case with Francisco López de Zárate. He alludes to Astraea in a poem composed to commemorate Philip IV's birthday,[91] but it is in a second poem, written to celebrate the "Natalicio al Principe Nuestro Señor Baltasar Carlos Felipe," that he develops the myth more fully. López de Zárate refers to Philip IV's son with the words, "Varon a los del Cielo semejante, / Con menos parte de Austria que de Astrea."[92] The similarity between *Austria* and *Astrea* leads the poet in this pun to proclaim that Baltasar Carlos, although a Hapsburg from the "house of Austria," truly belongs to the "house of Astraea." The return of Astraea means a return of the golden age. In typical fashion, López de Zárate speaks of the coming peace and harmony.

Not all poems of the period hail the return of Astraea. In fact, the lament for her absence is a more prevalent theme. In a manuscript that contains poems by authors from Antequera, collected between 1606 and 1627, appears a sonnet by Luis Martín de la Plaza in praise of Francisco de Alfaro. The poem begins by noting Astraea's flight from earth after the disintegration of the golden epoch. The cause of corruption, according to this poet, is covetousness:

> Después del siglo del metal mas puro
> de ti, codicia vil, huyendo Astrea,
> desterrada en el cielo se pasea,
> interponiendo a tu poder su muro.[93]

In the second stanza, Astraea vigilantly watches earth from one end to the other of the stellar constellations, but sees few who are not affected by this vice. The third stanza poses a question: "Mas, ¿quién, hollando la cudicia, raro / milagro ostenta, y con igual balanza / reluce Astrea, de la tierra austente?" The answer given in the final stanza is Francisco de Alfaro, the subject of the poem: he is not touched by the *monstruo*, greed. Instead, he is the true representative of Astraea on earth, dispensing justice without any thought of gain. Since he carries the scales of justice (*balanza*), he is deserving of the highest praise (*alabanza*). The poem, although emphasizing the virtues of a particular man, presents a negative view of the times, which are described in terms of the iron age.

The chaos and confusion of the present iron age lead another poet in the collection to write about Astraea's offspring. Agustín de Tejada makes no reference to the savior-child of Virgil's *Fourth Eclogue*. For this poet, Astraea's child is Sleep:

> Sueño, domador fuerte del cuidado
> hijo ligero de la madre Astrea,
> dulce alivio que al ánimo recrea
> reposo alegre al pecho fatigado . . .[94]

This genealogy can be traced back to Seneca's *Hercules furens*, where Sleep is the "winged son of thy mother Astraea, sluggish brother of cruel death"(vol. 1, p. 95). In Tejada's poem, however, sleep is not depicted as Death's brother but "de la helada muerte idea." This would seem to make Death and Astraea the parents of Sleep. Although I have not been able to determine the exact source of this concept, it might be that it is related to the image of Father Time. In some versions Astraea-Truth is presented as the daughter of Time, who in turn can be portrayed as an old man with a sickle, a figure akin to Death.[95] Thus, while Seneca describes Death as one of Astraea's sons, the Father Time tradition suggests that death is Astraea's father. From these confusing genealogies and correspondences, Tejada may have derived his own version where Death is Astraea's mate and the father of Sleep.

At any rate, both Sleep and Death in the poem have power over all, be they kings or servants. Applying an image commonly used with Death, Sleep is described in the poem as providing a harbor (*puerto*) for the weary pilgrim of life:

> tú al alto rey, al mísero criado
> vistes de una color y una librea,

y, siendo de la helada muerte idea,
del trabajo eres puerto deseado.

The inequities of the iron age are replaced by a kind of "balance" provided by the son of the maiden with the scales. Sleep like Death is a powerful equalizer, providing momentary peace and the illusion of a "golden age" in times of trouble. Rather than a symbol for Christian *renovatio*, this poem seems to take a Senecan image to its extreme and express the pleasures of oblivion through the figure of our goddess.

Francisco de Quevedo's treatment of Astraea is also unconventional and negative. In a sonnet, he portrays the goddess with the two instruments she holds in the Tarot, but he orders her to throw away the scales and keep only the sword:

Arroja las balanzas, sacra Astrea,
pues que tienen tu mano embarazada;
y si se mueven, tiemblan de tu espada:
que el peso y la igualdad no las menea.[96]

Justice, for Quevedo, has become a farce. The scales do not represent justice, the sword does. He speaks neither of the golden sword pointed to heaven as found in the Tarot, nor of the instrument of celestial vengeance as in Villava's emblem. Instead, the sword is a symbol of power, and the only law, since legal tomes are written with men's blood: "Ya militan las leyes y el derecho, / y te sirven de textos las heridas / que escribe nuestra sangre en nuestro pecho."

While Agustín de Tejada links Astraea with Sleep and Death, Quevedo compares her to the Fates in the last stanza of the sonnet: "La Parca eres, fatal para las vidas." She actually becomes the third of the Fates, death. Thus, in these two poems the goddess of the golden age has become the handmaiden of death and destruction. Her scales are now "homicidal," and her sword serves to inflict injury. Although this may appear to be a surprising turn of events, it does not actually do violence to the myth. The destruction of the present civilization (iron age) is often seen as a prerequisite for the return of the happiest of ages. By juxtaposing Astraea, a goddess linked to beginnings, with the Fates or the figure of Sleep, who refer to endings, the poems recall the cyclic nature of the myth where opposites are seen side by side. In her destructive garb during the iron age, Astraea may be presaging the drastic destruction and chaos that precede the age of greatest harmony and order.

Alonso de Ezquerra in a reply to Bartolomée Leonardo de Argensola does not rail against Astraea, but against the present times. He explains that her name has acquired such negative connotations because men invoke her when they wish to commit a crime:

> Dice que los delitos mas atroces
> son los que se cometen a su sombra:
> ¡ay cuán bien sé que esta verdad conoces!
> ¡Ay cuántas veces la doncella nombra,
> levantándola falso testimonio
> quien la debiera honrar! ¡El mundo asombra![97]

In this topsy-turvy world those that ought to be the representatives of justice are the first ones to commit perjury. The worst crimes are commited under Astraea's umbrage. As the goddess of truth,[98] she knows this well, but is far removed from earth during the iron age. The lament on present conditions is followed by a kind of *beatus ille* that stresses the happiness of those who flee the cares of the world. Predictably, solitude is the means to acquire individual peace: "¡Dichosa soledad, seguro nido / de las águilas reales, que contemplan / el claro sol con ojo no torcido!"

The image of the eagle, which will be discussed in detail in our analysis of Segismundo's dream in *La vida es sueño*, connotes the contemplative man who is able to meditate upon the divine sun of God's illumination. This solitude is very different from that of Lope's "A mis soledades voy." It pertains to the Christian who wishes to come in close contact with the deity. If *soledad* befriends him, he will surely abandon all worldly riches in order to enjoy this blissful state: "Amada soledad, hazme tu amigo, / y al punto dejaré, si poseyera, / todo lo que perdió el godo Rodrigo."

The reference to Rodrigo, whom we have already encountered in the apocryphal tale about Cardinal Cisneros, recalls the wars of Islam and the question of Spanish imperialism. The previously mentioned eagle could also serve as a symbol for empire. The poem ironically emphasizes the precarious nature of worldly possessions through Rodrigo's loss. Christian expressions of solitude and mystical flight inform these verses. Although the poem begins with a pessimistic view of the present iron age where war and injustice prevail, it concludes in an optimistic tone. The reader realizes that although Astraea as imperial goddess has brought about wars, and although as the justice of the iron age she is invoked by criminals, her true nature can only be perceived in the silence of the Christian soul. Soaring in the inner spaces, communing with the divine sun, the solitary man is given a treasure greater than all earthly riches, the *pax Christiana* or interior paradise that illumines the soul.

The importance of solitude, the contrast between the golden age and the present epoch, and the utilization of Astraea as a laudatory vehicle are elements that are also present in the poetry of Luis de Góngora. In a sonnet in praise of Juan de Acuña, this magistrate's equitable actions are equated with the justice of Astraea:

> éste, ya de justicia, ya de estado,
> oráculo en España verdadero,
> a quien por tan legal, por tan entero
> sus balanzas Astrea le ha fiado . . .[99]

The scales of justice, the goddess's icons, are given to Juan de Acuña, a model of Astraea's justice who fights the "monsters" of the present age.

Although Góngora does not stress the contrast between the present iron age and the idyllic golden age in this sonnet, the dichotomy surfaces in the *Soledades*. Already in the seventeenth century we encounter the belief that Góngora was here attempting to depict the ages of the world and man. Pellicer, for example, states that "su principal intención fue en quatro *Soledades* describir las quatro edades del hombre. En la primera, la Juventud, con amores, prados, juegos, bodas y alegrías. En la segunda, la Adolescencia, con pescas, cetrería, navegaciones. En la tercera, la Virilidad, con monterías, caías, prudencia y oeconómica. En la quarta, la Senectud, y alli Política y Govierno. Sacó a luz las dos primeras solamente."[100] This division is common in the literature of the period. Baltasar Gracián divides the *Criticón* into three parts that encompass the four seasons and the four ages of man. The participant in this constant cycle of life, death, and rebirth comes to see his path as a *peregrinatio vitae*, ending in paradise. Gracián like Góngora equates protagonist with pilgrim. In the *Criticón* the pilgrim travels through an environment lacking the qualities of the golden age. Gracián utilizes the myth of Astraea to describe present conditions in a discussion of wisdom's departure from earth: "Muchos años ha que se huyó al cielo con las demás virtudes en aquella fuga general de Astraea. No han quedado en el mundo sino unos borrones de ella en estos escritos que aqui se eternizan."[101]

The fourfold division is also encountered in Cervantes's *Persiles y Segismunda*. Periandro and Auristela are again described as "pilgrims," and an example of the inner paradise is seen in Soldino's cave. The pilgrims' destination is Rome, the center of Christianity and presumably the location of the gates to paradise. After a brief sojourn in Rome, the pilgrims sail to the "Isla de la Inmortalidad." Although the final stopping place does not conform to the traditional

Christian paradise, it does represent a higher plane: "It is the immortality of preservation in men's memories, the secular but nonetheless everlasting glory of the hero that awaits them."[102] The pilgrim of Góngora's *Soledades* may also aspire to this kind of immortality. As Juergen Hahn reminds us, the term *peregrino* indicates something out of the ordinary, a surprising or unexpected occurence. Therefore the reader of a *peregrina aventura* expects wonderment from the events described. Life through the poet's gaze becomes replete with the marvelous, which is reflected in the language of the poem. In this sense, Góngora and his *peregrino* are analogous figures: "As the *peregrino*-lover gropes his way through the unknown land, so the *peregrino*-poet, whose steps are the verses, explores the no-man's land of a new concept of poetry."[103]

Góngora has modified a Christian *peregrinatio vitae* into a poet's journey. His interpretation of the four ages, according to John Beverly, is original, not necessitating an outward fourfold division. The poem is complete as it stands, not requiring two more *Soledades* to complete the cycle: "Ovid's myth of the Ages of Metals acts as an *informing shape* for Gongora's sequence of presentation." The gold and silver ages are the models for the *Soledad primera*, where the *serranos* and the *labradores* stand for each of these two periods. The *Soledad segunda* moves through the landscapes of the bronze and iron epochs, culminating in the castle. Beverly adds that "the end of the cycle in the *Soledad segunda* is not yet the landscape of the Court and empire: that will be the pilgrim's tragic homeland of the next day." Ovid's description of the ages of man culminates in a flood which destroys civilization so that happier days can return. "The Flood, which comes to abolish the disorder of the present and prepare the return of the Golden Age, is the poem itself: something which 'confuses' the normal terms of experience, throws us back to our beginnings, atomizes and reforms."[104]

Instead of guiding the reader to Christian paradise, the *Soledad segunda* leads to personal introspection. The open-ended fate of the pilgrim who has not attained "paradise" in the traditional sense, but who has lived through the cycles of human history, calls for a questioning of personal and political destinies. As an "anti-imperialistic pastoral,"[105] in the words of R.O. Jones, the poem rejects the prevalent belief in expansionist wars at a time when the decline of Spain was becoming evident. The inner Christian paradise is as conspicuously absent from the poem as the notion of imperial *renovatio*. Devoid of its traditional connotations, the myth of the golden age and the notion of the cyclic nature of time await new meaning. The poem-flood has served to "purify" the reader's and the author's vision, the silence of solitude providing the necessary conditions for introspection.

In 1617, Góngora abandoned his self-imposed exile and returned to the court. The *Panegírico al duque de Lerma*, written that year, contains a curious reference to our goddess. Atropos, the third of the Fates, is related to Astraea:

> En el mayor de su fortuna halago,
> la que en la rectitud de su guadaña
> Astrea es de las vidas, en Buitrago
> rompió cruel, rompió el valor de España . . .[106]

The basis for the conceit is that the third of the Fates does not show favoritism as she cuts the thread of life. As in Quevedo and Tejada, Góngora's *Panegírico* links Astraea and Death through their equitable actions and their role as equalizers. All men are the same in the eyes of justice and death, so the scales, the sword, and the sickle become icons of inevitability. The previous stanza is also related to Astraea in its emphasis on justice and destruction, extolling Spain's role in bringing back divine justice by destroying the pirates from Argel. The goddess of the golden age has a destructive aspect. She must invoke the aid of Atropos in order to eliminate negative forces before harmony can be restored and she can again reign on earth.

As a panegyric, the poem represents a positive portrayal of the Lerma family and an optimistic view of history. Recent reverses caused by Atropos or Fortuna are part of a larger picture involving the return of Astraea. This optimistic view is most evident in the prophecy uttered by the river nymph Napea, with its reminiscences of Virgil's *Fourth Eclogue*.[107] In the *Panegírico*, the river nymph foretells the great future of a child, the duke being praised in the poem. Rather than mentioning Atropos, the nymph refers to Clotho, the Fate who spins the thread of life. Napea sees a bright future for both the future duke and his king. The duke, through his counsel, will lead Philip III along the steps of Emperor Augustus. Yet Góngora is not content with these two glorious futures. He also narrates the baptism of another child, the future Philip IV. The proliferation of savior-children serves to underscore the notion of *renovatio*, each new birth embodying the hope for the return of a golden age. The image of the *phoenix* used to describe the plaza after the fireworks in honor of the future king is fitting. Representing the square's new existence after the consuming fire, the phoenix also stands for Spain's renewal through its children. Atropos is thus powerless, for with every death there arises new life through which Astraea can pursue her goal.

In spite of the association of Astraea with Atropos, the message of the panegyric is clear: a golden age is possible if Philip III follows the advice of the Duke of Lerma and creates a new era resembling Augustus's *pax romana*. The poet's hopes for peace and harmony are soon dashed by the realities of court intrigue. The fall of Lerma in 1618 is the first step in Góngora's second fall from grace. The hope of personal triumph and the vision of a future golden age have been as fleeting as time itself. Góngora, towards the end of his own *peregrinatio vitae*, views his past adventures through the lense of *desengaño*: "¡Cuánta esperanza miente a un desdichado! / ¿A qué más desengaños me reserva, / a qué escarmientos me vincula el hado?"[108]

A poet of the school of Góngora, Juan de Tassis y Peralta, second Count of Villamediana, was particularly fond of Astraea. The references are often laudatory and are frequently triggered by the birth of a child to the royal family. The verses citing Astraea or foreseeing a future golden age often have as their subject the *infante* Carlos or the future Philip IV,[109] thus recalling the laudatory poems by López de Zárate. Direct references to the goddess are avoided in works where the prophetic tone makes obvious the notion of imperial *renovatio*. According to Juan Manuel Rozas, "Igualmente hay un eco lejano en todos estos versos de Virgilio, de su misteriosa *Egloga IV*, tenida en tiempos como seudoprofética."[110] His specific example is a sonnet concerning the future Philip IV, where the would-be monarch is equated with the sun, since he will be the fourth of his name and the Ptolemaic luminary occupies the fourth sphere (*Ro.*, 53, p. 133). The speed and brilliance of this monarch who imitates the sun will be that of lightning and of a comet; his actions will create a sense of wonderment like that caused by these two celestial phenomena. But he will not have the negative influence associated with these heavenly portents, but the effect of a benevolent planet, bringing about the liberation of Asia. The sonnet's imperial designs are most clearly expressed in the last two verses of the second quatrain: "uno el ovil, una la ley perfeta, / habrá un solo pastor y un solo imperio" (*Ro.*, 53, p. 133). The one law will be Astraea's Christian justice, implemented by one shepherd, the future king. The term *pastor*, usually reserved for Christ or a minister of his church, is applied to the secular ruler whose empire will encompass the whole world.[111] Villamediana's sonnet proposes a future golden age attained through expansionist pursuits with the Spanish king as the central figure in the Christian world.

Villamediana's notion of imperial *renovatio* and of a Spanish universal ruler must be tempered by the negative vision expressed in his satirical poetry; it must be questioned in view of his association with

Góngora, who became in his mature years an anti-imperialist poet; and it must be balanced against his admiration for the French monarch, Henry IV. Villamediana wrote four sonnets in Henry's praise. Luis Rosales concludes that the proliferation of sonnets on Henry IV by Spanish poets during the reigns of Philip III and Philip IV is a sign of *desengaño:* "Si el enemigo se ofrece a los ojos como ejemplo y dechado, el propio espíritu desarmará nuestro brazo en el combate. Tal actitud, en lugar de servirnos de emulación, acortó nuestro ánimo. Era la acción del desengaño." Praise of Henry IV is motivated by satire: "Si en ellos la intención expresa es admirativa, la intención tácita es satírica. El tono de alabanza envuelve una censura. Sugieren más que dicen y, en fin de cuentas, si se refieren a Enrique IV, se dirigen a Felipe III."[112] Yet it is not only Henry's integrity and his moral qualities that are contrasted with Philip's behavior. I believe that Villamediana is contrasting the French monarch's tolerance and Spain's warlike, imperialist stance. Frances Yates has noted how Henry's tolerance in religious matters and his independence of the papacy earned him an important place among those who hoped for religious liberalization and an end to Christian division. Henry IV was seen as a king whose peaceful designs could bring back the harmony of the golden age. Yates asserts that "the return of Astraea was the most constantly used symbol of the reign of Henry IV."[113] It is in this context that we should examine Villamediana's sonnet concerning the French monarch.

The first quatrain expresses Henry's greatness in terms of a series of oppositions:

> Haze el mayor Enrique quando lidia
> En el marcial honor de la estacada,
> Corona el Yelmo, y Cetro de la Espada,
> Paz de la guerra, y Fe de la perfidia.
>
> [*Ob.*,p. 70]

Crown and scepter, peace and faith triumph over negative and warlike objects and qualities. The power of harmony exerted by a just king dispels all negative influences. The second quatrain restates these notions, portraying the French monarch as forgiving those he fights:

> Cesar renace, y Alejandro enbidia
> Piadoso perdonar con mano armada,
> Y en los peligros la virtud osada
> Despreciando el morir, vence la enbidia.
>
> [*Ob.*,pp. 70-71]

As in the first stanza, the portrayal of a bellicose ruler fades here in the presence of a peaceful king. His courage and daring dispel the mutterings of the envious. The theme of imperial *renovatio* is introduced when we are told that Caesar is reborn in Henry IV. The French monarch is also compared to the model of world rule, Alexander the Great. The Greek conqueror's legendary generosity is also found in the French monarch, whose qualities of forgiveness shine even in war.

The first tercet reiterates Henry's mercy. Here, the king "castiga rebelados, perdonando" (*Ob.*, p. 71). Paradoxically, he punishes rebels by forgiving them. The tercet ends echoing the imperial concerns introduced in the second stanza. Utilizing the Virgilian prophetic technique, Villamediana foresees the creation of a "nuevo Imperio sin segundo" (*Ob.*, p. 71). The poem ends with a closing within the sonnet: the temple of justice can shut its doors since it is no longer needed in a harmonious age, when Astraea can again descend to earth.

> El templo de la paz cierra, y baxando
> Del cielo Astrea, su valor mantiene
> Con freno a Francia, y con la fama al mundo.
>   [*Ob.*, p. 71]

Astraea, the goddess of *pax* to whom Augustus built a temple, has returned to earth to stand next to the peaceful ruler, Henry IV. The peace is based on valor; the fame of Henry and his country is assured.

This sonnet is perhaps Villamediana's most complete statement on Astraea, revealing his pacifist, tolerant, and anti-imperialist concerns. The warlike Caesar and the magnanimous Alexander pale before this almost godlike image of courage and compassion that indeed keeps company with a goddess. It is interesting, however, to note that the formula "Caesar plus Alexander" is also used by Villamediana in an already cited poem where Philip IV is called "Alejandro español, Cesar cristiano" (*Ro.*, 114, p. 194). Virgilian prophecy is utilized to describe Philip's future imperial wars and not the triumph of peace. It may be that after Henry's demise, the count shifted his hopes to the future Spanish monarch. But his praises of Philip IV sound hollow, while the sonnet in praise of Henry IV appears more daring and truthful.

In addition to being utilized for laudatory, prophetic, political, and astrological (*Ro.*, p. 220) purposes, Astraea is also included by Villamediana in a sonnet dealing with the Day of Judgment. The poet portrays the goddess as singing God's praises with the angels: "Y con Angeles mil la bella Astrea / Himnos en su alabanza repetia" (*Ob.*, p. 56). As *justicia*, she must be present on that final day when all men are forever divided between the righteous and the damned.[114] She is not portrayed as a punishing deity, but as part of celestial harmony.

Astraea, having survived medieval and Renaissance transformations, has become a multifaceted figure utilized by numerous writers during the Spanish Golden Age. For those ignorant of her many metamorphoses, treatises such as Baltasar de Vitoria's *Teatro de las dioses de la gentilidad* or emblems created by Francisco de Villava and Sebastián de Covarrubias provided the needed examples. In her imperial and religious garb, Astraea is utilized during this period as a laudatory vehicle by authors who wish to portray the Catholic kings, Charles V, Philip II, and even Philip IV as a *dominus mundi* who will bring about world order and peace. Others such as Fray Luis de León and Miguel de Cervantes move away from the imperial goddess and prefer to view the golden age over which she presides as being actualized in the hearts of individual believers. It is among the poets that Astraea fares best, mirroring her importance in classical poetry from Aratus to Virgil. Figures as diverse as Lope de Vega, Quevedo, Góngora, and Villamediana pursue her astral implications and at times subvert her imperialist traits by composing works that favor religious tolerance or reject world conquest. The literature of the Spanish Golden Age thus provides numerous examples of Astraea's presence.

CHAPTER THREE

The Priestess of Justice and Fortune

A SENSE OF WONDERMENT could be felt throughout Madrid and Aranjuez as a succession of astonishing and unpredictable events filled the year following Philip IV's accession to the throne. The Spanish court in 1622 did not have to turn to Cervantes's *Persiles y Sigismunda* or to Góngora's *Soledades* to experience a *peregrina aventura*. The accidents of fortune and the balancing of the scales of justice set the stage for happenings stranger than those encountered in fiction. While exiles and enemies of the previous king returned triumphantly to the court, scores of noblemen left Madrid in disgrace. Some were imprisoned; others were executed. These events triggered opposing reactions, ranging from the hope of a new golden age to a lament for the lack of justice. Courtiers vied for the young king's good will, as Olivares slowly rose to supreme power.

Art flourished in these chaotic months under a French queen who delighted in Spanish theater. Queen Isabel prepared a celebration at Aranjuez for her husband's birthday where two literary styles were represented in plays by Lope de Vega and Villamediana. The celebration, postponed until May 15, ended with a tragic fire and rumors of royal infidelity. A month and a half later, attention shifted from scandal to canonization as the city celebrated the naming of four new Spanish saints by the pope. Lope de Vega presided over the festivities for Isidro, patron of Madrid, and presented two plays on the saint's life. On August 21, Villamediana was murdered. By October, the mysterious assassination was forgotten as rumors filled the court concerning the sudden death of the Count of Lemos. Poison was suspected. La Barrera aptly summarizes the events of 1622: "El reinado de Felipe IV, el poeta, se inauguraba entre el cadalso, el puñal, el veneno y la canonización de cuatro santos."[1]

The prophetic and enigmatic Astraea made her appearance on the stage at the two most publicized dramatic events: the festival concerning the canonization of Isidro and the palace performance for the king's birthday. The virtually unknown Pedro Calderón de la Barca earned third prize for a *canción* at the festival commemorating San Isidro. He was also successful with his entries on San Francisco Xavier. His interest in Astraea as a dramatic figure may derive from these celebrations. Calderón probably watched with interest Lope de Vega's *La niñez de San Isidro*, where the figure of Astraea is introduced with laudatory intent. He may also have seen Villamediana's *La gloria de Niquea*, where Astraea is hailed by a figure mounted on an eagle. As we have seen, both Lope de Vega and Villamediana had consistently utilized the myth of the goddess of the golden age in their poetry. In 1622, they both included Astraea in theatrical representations.

Philip IV's seventeenth birthday was celebrated on May 15, a month late. The *fiesta* took place at Aranjuez and included the performance of two spectacle plays, Lope de Vega's *El vellocino de oro* and Villamediana's *La gloria de Niquea*. The count's festival play is composed of three sections—an introduction and two *escenas*.[2] The introduction, which contains the passage on Astraea, can be subdivided into four moments represented by four ladies who praise Philip IV. The first figure represents the Tagus river, appropriate since the performance takes place on an island in Aranjuez, which comes to represent the ship of state. The Tagus assures the monarch that his will be an exemplary life.

A second triumphal car enters representing a sign of the zodiac: "Tirava un Toro su florida máquina, como signo que visita el Sol en la estación de sus días" (*Ob.* p. 7). The lady riding on the car is dressed as a mythological figure: "Donzella Europa, amante robo del transformado Jupiter" (*Ob.* p. 7). Europa speaks to the king in verses that include a direct citation from Góngora:[3]

> El que ves toro, no en la selva nace
> A mis floridos yugos obediente
> En campos de Zafiro estrellas pace,
> Signo tuyo feliz siempre luziente.
>
> [*Ob.* p. 9]

This bull that grazes in the heavens is of course the sign Taurus, referring to the fact that the play is taking place while the sun is in the sign of the bull. The scene is laudatory in tone since the bull is Jupiter, a symbol of kingship. Europa was played by Francisca de Tavora, a lady reputedly favored by the Spanish monarch.[4] The myth of Jupiter's rape of Europa may function as an allusion to Philip's amorous pursuit of Francisca. As such, it might have been taken either as a compliment to the monarch or as a dangerous indiscretion on the part of the writer.

As Europa sings the praises of Jupiter, an eagle descends from the heavens. The eagle is another of the notorious transformations of Jupiter, and its appearance serves to reinforce the linkage between god and monarch. Indeed, the bird's relation to empire had been brought out by Villamediana earlier in the narrative of the *fiesta:* "Nunca se ha visto el Tajo con tan honrosa ocasión de disculpada vanagloria, ni quando la ponposa Roma ilustró sus márgenes con las Aguilas de su Imperio" (*Ob.,* p. 5). In the play, the eagle descends carrying a lady so beautiful that she "parecía Imagen de aquellos dorados siglos que han aguardado tantos" (*Ob.,* p. 11). Her laudatory speech combines the elements of empire and the lost golden age:

> Siempre feliz, y tan capaz de aumento
> Soberano señor, tu Inperio sea,
> Pues dexó de pisar el firmamento,
> Por asistir a tu govierno Astraea.
> [*Ob.,* p. 11]

By hailing the return of Astraea, the figure mounted on the eagle implies that Phillip IV is the child king prophesied by Virgil who will bring back the golden age. The eagle is the symbol of the Roman empire to which Philip is "heir."

The fourth lady embodies the *loa,* and thus provides us with the subject of the play. She emerges from a tree, since she represents the mythological figure of Daphne, beloved of Apollo, thus praising the king as yet one more deity. Apollo is the sun god who, in astrological terms, rules the fourth sphere. Philip shares this numerical value with the luminary, being the fourth of his name. Soon after the presentation of *La gloria de Niquea,* Lope de Vega would include the equation monarch-sun in the *loa* of one of the two plays he wrote to celebrate Isidro's canonization in 1622. In *La juventud de San Isidro* we read, "Cuarto sois de los Felipes / el sol en su cuarta esfera / de su luz."[5]

The number four in *La gloria de Niquea* has other values. It represents the four corners of the world, ruled by Philip, and the four elements that constitute the sublunary realm.[6] The two triumphal cars that appear at the beginning represent the two heavy elements that tend to fall towards the center of the cosmos—water and earth. The Tagus river is obviously water, while the myth of Europa and the bull represents earth. Each figure, in addition, combines these two heavy elements. The Tagus (water) speaks of an island-ship, Philip's kingdom on earth, while the bull (earth) also represents a ship carrying Europa through the ocean's waters, their destination an island where love can be enjoyed. The descent of the eagle signals a shift to the light elements air and fire: "En un Aguila bañada en *ascuas* de oro, que batiendo las alas parecia que le servia de alfombra la region del *aire*" (*Ob.*, p. 10). The eagle, fiery in appearance, descends through air, his own element. His fiery appearance recalls Apollo's element since he represents the sun.

The introduction to *La gloria de Niquea* is thus organized around four figures that praise the monarch and represent the four elements, signaling his control over the constituents of this sublunary realm. These elements, have battled with each other since the fall of man. Their harmony expresses the coming world harmony or the return of the golden age. The descending figure on the eagle, calling on Astraea, symbolizes the descent of our goddess from her heavenly exile. The bird itself is charged with significance. It represents the lighter elements, including fire, as it blazes through the air like the sun-Apollo-Phillip. The eagle is also one of Jupiter's transformations. Finally, it is the bird of empire and thus signals imperial *renovatio* under the fourth of the Philips.

The performances that evening ended in a catastrophic fire. The story spread that Villamediana had deliberately set fire to the stage during his own play in order to rescue the queen in his arms. This supposed love affair was said to be the cause of his assassination some months later. Whatever the historical truth may be, the blaze of fire recalls the *ekpyrosis* feared by Virgil's contemporaries as a prelude to the golden age.

The next major celebration was also highlighted by two plays, both by Lope de Vega. On June 28, 1622, Madrid celebrated the canonization of its patron, Isidro. The two *comedias* prepared for the festivities were viewed by King Philip and Queen Isabel, as Lope himself points out in the *relación de las fiestas*. He glorifies the new king and the four new saints by using the figure of Astraea, perhaps following Villamediana's lead. His praise is both political and religious.

The *loa* that precedes the first play, *La niñez de San Isidro*, proclaims the return of Astraea now that Philip IV is king. The church also profits from this new age, exhibiting her new treasures, the four Spanish saints:

> En el tiempo feliz que reina Astrea
> Por Felipe divino, con decoro
> Debido á su valor, para que vea

Tantos siglos perdido el siglo de oro,
La iglesia de su reino se hermosea
Del sacrosanto espléndido tesoro
De cuatro hijos suyos, à honor suyo,
En que su dicha y gloria constituyo.

[p. 505][7]

The new monarch, like the four saints, will enrich the world, bringing forth *abundancia*. This term recalls nature's gifts to man during the
golden age.

Philip's marriage to Isabel de Borbón is presented in the *loa* as the
fruition of the peace overtures between France and Spain begun
under Philip II and Henry IV of France, perhaps a reference to the
peace of Vervins (1598). The importance of the young monarch's father is downplayed in the *loa*, mirroring the tension that existed between father and son. The grandfather, Philip II, is not only praised
for his foresight but is compared to Solomon: the Escorial is a build-
ing akin to the Biblical temple.[8] Henry IV is also praised, recalling
Villamediana's admiration for the ecumenical French monarch. Lope
calls him a son of Mars. The *fénix* praises Henry IV as the father of
Isabel de Borbón, Philip IV's wife. Reference to the French king and
to peace between Spain and France should not, however, lead us to
think that Lope prefers anti-imperialist policies. Quite the contrary,
Lope emphasizes Spain's imperial destiny.[9] Freed from wars with its
neighbor, Spain can turn on the infidel and defeat him by the Jordan
and Nile rivers. Then the world will render homage to the Spanish
king with the emblem of the Holy Roman Empire, obtained from a
third river: "Águilas te dará sagrado el Tibre / y tres veces laureles
Alemania" (p. 506). In *La gloria de Niquea*, Astraea had been evoked
by a figure descending on an eagle. In Lope's *loa* the goddess is again
related to the Roman bird. The subsequent mention of Germany links
the Roman Empire to its present seat, doubly emphasizing the imperialist aims of Philip IV.

The *comedia* stands in sharp contrast with the *loa*; contemporary
political and imperialist concerns give way to a portrayal of bucolic
tranquility and virtue in a remote past. Yet there are many points of
contact between *comedia* and *loa*. First, there is a sense of continuity
provided by images of the sun and the dawn in both *loa* and the first
speech in the play. These images are no longer applied to an earthly
monarch and his wife. They describe God, the "Rey eterno y soberano" (p. 506), and the Virgin Mary. In this first speech, Inés prays to
the Virgin for a saintly son. Since she is a poor woman, all she can
offer the Virgin is her husband's labors. The wheat he gathers in the

field is their treasure. Inés hopes "que cada grano de espiga / precioso diamante fuera" (p. 506). The image of *spica* is the key to Inés's prayer, and we know that it is more than earthly wheat. It is the wheat held by Virgo in the zodiacal belt. The hope that the *espiga* will be a precious diamond likens it to the star which shines clearly like the precious stone. The Virgin with the *spica* is often equated with the Virgin with child, the wheat being a symbol of fertility.[10] In *La niñez de San Isidro,* the offer of wheat to the Virgin results in the birth of a saintly child whose canonization hundreds of years later will signal the advent of a golden age. Play and *loa* thus deal with the return of Astraea in spite of their different tones. In the political realm of the *loa,* the child of Virgil's *Eclogue* is King Philip, heir to empire. In the religious sphere of the *comedia,* Isidro is the child. He is related to Virgo through Inés's prayer to the Virgin and the offering of wheat.

La juventud de San Isidro is also prefaced by a *loa* praising Philip and the newly created saints. These saints are considered the new treasures of the church, each equated with a precious stone.[11] Ignacio is a ruby, Xavier is an emerald, Teresa is a sapphire, and Isidro is a diamond, recalling Ines's prayer comparing the *spica* to this stone. The stress on numerology is greater in this *loa.* The king in typical fashion is described in terms of solar imagery, since being the fourth of his name he can be equated with the fourth Ptolemaic planet. The saints are also four, an essential number in creation:

> Cuarto sois de los Felipes;
> El sol en su cuarta esfera
> Da su luz; cuatro los santos
> Que hoy nuestra España celebra.
> Número cuatro componen
> Tres personas y una esencia,
> Las potencias con el alma,
> Y las partes de la tierra.
>
> [p. 532]

The *loa* concludes with the hope that the victories of the fourth Philip and the glories of the church adorned with four new saints will be enough to impart fear in four evil figures:

> Cuyo trono excelso tema
> El moro, el Hereje, el Turco
> Y la envidia, que contempla
> Los triunfos de vuestras armas
> Y la gloria de la iglesia.
>
> [p. 532]

Envy is the link between the *loa* and the *comedia*. Just as she watches Philip and the church in order to bring them down, *Envidia* provides the conflict in the *comedia* by attempting to soil Isidro's saintly reputation. She emerges from a dark cave anxious to spill her poison. She is a fitting image to combat Isidro since, as we have noted, Lope considers her the antithesis of divine Truth-Astraea. This is emphasized by the fact that *Envidia* calls *Mentira* to her aid. There are echoes here of *La Filomnea*, published the previous year. Recall that in that poem dealing with a literary war, the nightingale's simple yet truthful song triumphed over the *tordo's* rhetorical and learned style infused with envy. In the *comedia*, *Envidia* is allied with the *sabios*, while truth is equated with the simplicity of the peasant saint. *Envidia* justifies herself thus:

> Que no llegue a tanta gloria
> Un labrador destra villa,
> Sin letras y sin valor;
> Que es lo que Agustín decía,
> Que a veces los ignorantes
> El cielo a los sabios quitan.
>
> [p. 537]

With the aid of God and as a representative of divine truth, Isidro is able to avoid envy's snares. His triumph and glory can be equated with that of Spain during Philip IV's reign. To stress this correspondence, Lope includes towards the end of the *comedia* a lengthy prophecy concerning Spain. The *siglo de oro* will return when four Spaniards are canonized and a seventeen-year-old prince is admired by the world (p. 551).

THE YEAR FOLLOWING the appearance of Astraea on the Spanish stage, Pedro Calderón de la Barca composed his first *comedia*.[12] *Amor, honor y poder*, as the title suggests, deals with three forces that will be ever-present in Calderón's theater. *Poder* is represented by the king, whose willful and lustful nature is subdued through the virtuous lessons on honor and love provided by his subjects. In this earliest play, we already encounter the conflict between a figure of authority whose acts appear arbitrary and a young protagonist whose freedom and happiness seem threatened by the actions of one in power. The authority of family, church, or state often triggers the action in Calderón's *comedias*. Robert ter Horst takes this notion to its extreme: "Power is the first impulse in the genesis of the play, but rebellion against the absolute is the second, equally vital, equally important movement. The idea of might in Calderón is orthodox—God, King, Religion, Monarch—but the artistic construct by means of which we perceive might is hostile, negative, heterodox."[13]

Although some critics reject the use of biographical material in the study of the *comedia*,[14] others argue that the conflict with authority in Calderón's dramas has its basis in his relationship with his father. In some early *comedias*, as Alexander Parker points out, the father-son conflict and the opposition between authority and liberty or personal desire are common themes expressing the poet's own inner struggle, which will eventually lead him to the priesthood. The father-son conflict, according to Parker, is poetically resolved in *La vida es sueño* (c. 1635), where Rosaura-Astraea inspires in Segismundo a desire for reconciliation.[15] Robert ter Horst finds a "contrapuntal melody of struggle" in the reactions towards authority portrayed in Calderón's theater.[16] Rebellion leads to renewal. Parker, on the other hand, stresses the mercy and forgiveness that emerge from Calderón's internal conflict as expressed in his literary works. Whatever the answer to this dichotomy may be, we can affirm that opposites are central to Calderón's dramaturgy. His first *comedia* brings into play the basic concepts that will battle for supremacy onstage.

Amor, honor y poder bears a close resemblance to *La estrella de Sevilla*, a play that may reflect political events of 1622. The king's murder of a loyal subject in *La estrella de Sevilla* and *Amor, honor y poder* could be linked to Villamediana's death on August 21, 1622. The count was mysteriously murdered at a time when he had befriended the king's beloved, Francisca de Tavora. It was rumored that his death was caused by *un impulso soberano*. Plays with political allusions attempting to educate the prince were common at this time, according to Ruth Lee Kennedy.[17] The lustful young monarch of *Amor, honor y poder* could indeed reflect Philip IV. The repeated use of *Sol* to refer to the monarch in this play, although a common occurrence in the *comedia*, could very well point to the *Rey Planeta*. We have seen how Lope and Villamediana chose the title *Sol* as a central motif in their laudatory verses addressed to Philip in 1622. Now, the Sun-King is taught a lesson on stage.

Curiously, the budding playwright turns silent after this production. Perhaps his disappearance was due to political motives, for once more the young Calderón had defied authority. As Manuel Durń notes, "from 1623 to 1625 he does not seem to live in Spain at all."[18] Just as unpredictably, Calderón returns to the Spanish capital in 1625 where he now resolutely pursues a career as a playwright, intimately linked to the court.

1625 was an *annus mirabilis* for the Spanish monarchy and for Olivares's expansionist aims. That summer both the surrender of Bredá and the capture of Bahía gave the regime spectacular strategic triumphs to bolster morale and revive the bellicose spirit of the nation. Both victories soon appeared in pictorial and dramatic art. Bahía was immortalized in Lope de Vega's *El Brasil restituído* and Maino's *Recapture of Bahía;* Bredá was preserved in art by Calderón's *El sitio de Bredá* and Velázquez's *Las lanzas.*[19] The paintings became part of twelve canvases commemorating Spanish victories in the Hall of Realms at the Retiro, a project directed by Olivares. The plays were also intended for viewing at court.

Calderón's *El sitio de Bredá* was presented at court under the auspices of Olivares soon after June 15, 1625, when the news of the triumph reached Madrid.[20] The climactic surrender is depicted in chivalrous fashion. Spínola's words to the defeated Justin of Nassau express "the triumph of the spirit as well as the triumph of arms."[21] This *comedia* is a far cry from *Amor, honor y poder.* Instead of a struggle against authority, the play is a masterful depiction of Spanish heroism, affirming the Spanish spirit. The *loa* by Antonio Hurtado de Mendoza describes how the news of the victory arrived at court and how both the royal family and Olivares's relatives received it. King and *privado,* as Shirley Whitaker notes, are given equal prominence.[22] As is to be expected, the monarch is portrayed as an heir to the Roman Empire.[23] Praise of Philip is expressed in solar imagery: "Filipo poderoso, / quarto planeta de la luz del día."[24] With this statement, the Calderón who opposes the frailties of a very human monarch seems to vanish in favor of a poet intimately linked with the aspirations of those in authority.

As time passes and victories give way to defeat, the courtly spectacles fashioned by Calderón and others lose their basis in political and social reality. Brown and Elliott comment that "not even the magical artistry of a Calderón could ensure a suspension of disbelief. The count-duke was perpetually demanding an unquestioning loyalty to himself and his works, and the poets and hacks who undertook to supply it inevitably sounded false outside the circle of the faithful."[25] Durán goes further in his assessment of Calderón's production after 1636: "Calderón is very much a part of a subtle conspiracy of Olivares against Philip IV. . . . It was a deliberate and successful attempt to mesmerize the King—to distract his attention by turning his mind away from the matters of State so that he, Olivares, could become, for all practical purposes, the real ruler, the true King of Spain."[26] Durán's presentation does not do justice to the inner tension portrayed in Calderón's dramatic art. As noted above, Calderón's theater often dramatizes the playwright's own struggle between rebellion and submission to authority.

On June 23, 1625, only days after the announcement of the surrender of Bredá, *La gran Cenobia* was staged by the company of Andrés Vargas.[27] The play, like Calderon's first *comedia*, deals with love, honor, and power. Set in imperial Rome, it scrutinizes authority taken to extremes through treason and tyrannicide. This *comedia* marks the first appearance of Astraea in Calderón's theater. The goddess, from the first, is associated with imperial concerns, and with the pitfalls of power.

While not a single play by Lope de Vega, Tirso de Molina, or Ruiz de Alarcón lists Astraea as a character, Calderón includes her in thirteen instances.[28] A character named Astraea, sharing many characteristics of the goddess, plays a crucial role in three *comedias—La gran Cenobia, Las armas de la hermosura,* and *El privilegio de las mujeres—* which have Rome as a backdrop and deal with questions of authority, justice, and empire. In three other plays—*La vida es sueño, El monstruo de los jardines,* and *Los tres afectos de amor*—a character assumes the name of Astraea and shares traits with the mythological figure. In six other plays, a character named Astraea has a minor role: *El golfo de las sirenas* (loa and comedia), *La hija del aire, El mayor encanto, amor, Ni amor se libra de amor, La puente de Mantible,* and *Los tres mayores prodigios.* Astraea also appears in two *autos sacramentales: El árbol de mejor fruto* and *La lepra de Constantino.* Clearly, the goddess interested our playwright throughout his career. Her role is intimately tied to key notions and basic conflicts dramatized in these works.

La gran Cenobia, the earliest Astraea play, contrasts with the optimistic *El sitio de Bredá.* In the first act Astraea, priestess of Apollo, guides the Roman soldiers to Aureliano and crowns him emperor. Aureliano's initial soliloquy, and his future actions, reveal his fierce and tyrannical nature. As the play opens, we see him dressed in skins, like Segismundo in the tower. Living alone in a *selva,* his pride and ambition lead him to consider himself "rey de las fieras," since he has no humans over whom he can exert his power: "Lleva pieles que simbolizan la fiereza de su espíritu y sus pasiones sin control, incompatibles con las condiciones del buen soberano."[29] Astraea's act of granting rulership over the empire to such a proud and ambitious man does not appear to be just. As ruler, Aureliano will not hold justice in high regard, being guided by personal desires and wishing to stand above all, including Fortune. This initial sequence of events may lead us to question whether Calderón truly had in mind the goddess of justice when naming the priestess in this *comedia*. Only in her imperial and prophetic garb is Astraea recognizable in the first scenes.

According to critical opinion prevalent until recently, "*La gran Cenobia* es un espectáculo brillantemente construido sin idea palpable, del tipo de aquellas que consideramos como dramas de fantasía."[30] Yet, as recent critics such as Angel Valbuena Briones, Jesús Gutiérrez, and Juan Manuel Gómez have argued, the work achieves thematic unity through the concept of fortune.[31] Gutiérrez goes as far as stating that "*La gran Cenobia* podía haberse titulado 'El reino de la fortuna,' ya que la diosa campea soberana y muda 'a su antojo'—pero en paralelismos muy precisos—las situaciones y los personajes."[32] The turn of Fortune's wheel, the rise and fall from power, is an image often used in *comedias* to portray the pitfalls of exalted position. The higher one reaches, the greater can be the fall, as exemplified by the execution of Rodrigo Calderón ordered by Philip IV in 1621, an event that triggered the composition of a number of plays dealing with the tragic fall, according to Raymond MacCurdy.[33] The theme of fortune becomes allied with the thorny question of tyrannicide, the fall of favorites, and contemporary political allusions. In *La gran Cenobia* Aureliano is a study in the dangers of absolute power, Cenobia exemplifies the effects of bad counsel, while the actions of Decio and Libio work out the limits of authority and the justifications for tyrannicide. All these characters are linked by their responses to power and fortune.

The priestess Astraea at the inception of the drama grants Aureliano both power and good fortune. She appears at key moments holding together the different characters and actions. The priestess may thus be equated with a second pagan deity, Fortuna. She reverses Aureliano's *mala fortuna* and by her power makes him emperor. This act has tremendous repercussions. It changes the course of history, since the warlike Aureliano confronts Cenobia, who has acquired great power in the East. Her *buena fortuna* will be reversed by Aureliano's rise. The continuous spinning of the wheel in this *comedia* has led Guitiérrez to classify it as a salient example of the *fortuna bifrons*.[34] Decio, Aureliano, and Cenobia, along with several minor characters, are subject to sudden reverses in fortune which demonstrate the temper of their souls in both positive and adverse situations. The action of the play is but the unfolding of Astraea's initial turn of the wheel, raising Aureliano to power. As the plot develops, we see how every turn is mysteriously linked to the priestess.

Once this central equation, Astraea-Fortuna, is accepted, the priestess's behavior throughout the drama acquires meaning. On the other hand, the traditional attributes of the goddess Astraea—such as imperial power, justice, chastity, and prophecy—are significant only at certain points in the play and only in relation to her role as fortune. This confluence of Astraea and Fortuna in the character and actions of the priestess of *La gran Cenobia* is not an entirely original conception on the part of Calderón. It comes from an ancient (though not very well-known) source, Eratosthenes' *Catasterisms*, and is found in other classical authors who deal with Astraea such as Avienius, Germanicus, and Hyginus, as noted in chapter one. Bouché-Leclerq comments, "Ceux qui assimilaient la Vierge à la Fortune ne se contenaient pas de lui mettre un bandeau sur les yeux; ils lui enlevaient la tête." The difficulty in observing the Virgin's head in the heavens has produced one more association. Virgo-Astraea must be blindfolded Fortune, or better still, Fortune without a head (*sine capite eam pingunt*).[35] The figure of Fortuna who spins her wheel while blindfolded, expressing the capriciousness of her gifts, is equated with the figure of a Virgin without a head, floating in the ever-turning zodiacal wheel.

Frances Yates has attempted to unearth this classical equation in Renaissance Europe. She points to Valeriano Bolzani's *Hieroglyphica* as the key example for its diffusion. But even though the hieroglyph in question speaks of the headless Astraea-Virgo, she is related not to Fortuna, but to Justice.[36] The headless Astraea as both divine and earthly justice does not show favoritism, but acts in mysterious, secret, and egalitarian ways symbolized by the fact that she hides her head in the clouds or among the stars.

The equation Astraea-Fortuna is equally difficult to discover in Golden Age Spain. Pérez de Moya's *Philisophía secreta* was one of the most widely used handbooks of mythology by the authors of the epoch. He explains the concept of *fortuna bifrons*[37] and describes her iconography, such as the *rueda*. Pérez de Moya ends his description by giving the appropriate Christian evaluation of fortune as a minister or instrument of divine providence, and he warns: "Pierda, pues, el pueblo Christiano la mala costumbre que tiene de quexarse ni alabar a la fortuna, pues no hay fortuna ni hado, y pida a Dios fauor, pues dél se ha de esperar remedio y socorro en los trabajos y remuneracion de sus obras" (pp. 88-91). Although Pérez de Moya portrays fortune as blind ("Pintauanla ciega, como cosa que da sus riquezas sin examinación de meritos"), he never describes her as headless, and thus the connection Astraea-Fortuna cannot emerge. The link between the two goddesses based on the fact that Virgo's head is hardly visible is not a common one.

Although Calderón may have been unaware of the tradition that merged the two goddesses, he certainly knew of the enmity between Astraea and Fortuna. Angel Valbuena Briones, studying Fortuna as the unifying concept in *La gran Cenobia*, notes the similarities between Seneca's conception of the fickle goddess and Calderón's: "La caída de Cenobia y la victoria de Aureliano prueban el girar vertiginoso de la rueda de la fortuna, esa figura que, como dice Séneca en *Fedra*, 'no guarda a nadie fidelidad.'"[38] While Cenobia exemplifies the heroic qualities that emerge during adverse fortune according to Seneca's *On Providence*, Aureliano's good fortune leads him to disregard the warning that the higher one climbs, the easier and more catastrophic the fall can be, as expressed in Seneca's *On the Shortness of Life*. Although Valbuena Briones points to many parallels between Calderón and Seneca on the question of fortune, he fails to mention the opposition between Astraea and Fortuna. In the *Octavia*, the *Hippolytus*, and *Hercules furens*, the three Senecan tragedies that allude to Astraea and the golden age, we also encounter warnings against the mutability of fortune. In *Octavia* Seneca speaks of Fortuna in the same soliloquy where he invoked the virgin of the golden age. The philosopher's high station as advisor to the Emperor Nero makes him the more subject to Fortuna. To the uncertainties of his lofty yet dangerous post, Seneca prefers the pleasures of his previous simple life in the Corsican countryside. He links his earlier life with the first or golden age, while the present existence at court is equated to the iron epoch. The two goddesses are in opposition, one representing the earliest of ages and the other the chaotic period before the "last day . . . which shall crush sinful man beneath heaven's ruin" (vol. 2, p. 439). While the reign of Astraea represents new beginnings, Fortune's rule presages *ekpyrosis*. Seneca, like Decio in *La gran Cenobia*, warns the tyrant against his folly and reminds him of the mutability of fortune (vol. 2, p. 445). But Nero, like Aureliano, refuses to consider the possibility that fortune will turn against him. The tyrants do not realize that their actions strengthen the power of the illusory, fickle, and destructive goddess. Stoic belief in virtue and reliance on the self is discarded for the fleeting pleasures of Fortuna. Justice-Astraea has no place in the tyrants' universe. Calderón, well aware of the conflictive nature of Astraea-Fortuna, formulates the dramatic action of *La gran Cenobia* on a new conceit. By merging the two goddesses in the character of the priestess, the *comedia* expands the *con-*

cepto so that the whole action of the play reflects the Renaissance mystery of *discordia concors*.[39]

This opposition between Astraea and Fortuna is found in a Spanish text published two years after *La gran Cenobia*, Gabriel de Bocángel y Unzueta's *Declamación segunda, contra la fortuna*. The work begins with an invocation to Astraea: "Despues, ó bellisima Astraea, que huyendo de los engaños del mundo, assida à los filos, y balanzas que de tus atinados pulsos con infalible señorìo penden, nos dexaste embueltos entre las sombras de un segundo chaos, postrada la desvalida virtud à las violencias del hado, y armandose el ocio, y el vicio de tus robados despojos: desde entonces comenzò la Fortuna a introducir su Imperio." (p. 51)[40] Inspired by Juvenal, who includes both Astraea and Fortuna in his *Satires*,[41] but probably borrowing from Seneca, Bocángel sees Fortuna as having taken the place Astraea left vacant when she fled the earth. In spite of her nonexistence in the celestial pantheon, the very fickleness of fortune gives her a certain power over men since all want *buena fortuna*, not knowing that it destroys virtue more easily than *adversa fortuna*: "La otra lucha es mas violenta, y dificil de superar, y vencer, que es la que intima la Fortuna prospera" (p. 54). By elevating the wicked and creating hardships for the just man, Fortuna is able to make men forget about divine providence. Having exposed fortune's apparent injustice, Bocángel calls for the return of "Astrea santa" to extirpate this "monstruo" from the world. As in Seneca, Astraea and Fortuna rule over opposite ages. When man's wickedness obscures the workings of providence, then fortune, a nonexistent goddess, can expect the worship of those who wish prosperity rather than the opportunity to purify their souls in the flames of misfortune. In Bocángel, the opposition and enmity between Astraea and Fortuna is only apparent, for Fortuna is nonexistent. Behind her chaotic and illusory gift-giving and punishment, the person with steady intellect can detect the workings of providence, that is, divine justice symbolized by Astraea. The mystery of discord is resolved when we realize that the two goddesses are one in reality, thus establishing a *mysterium coniuctionis*. In *La gran Cenobia* the mystery of Astraea-Fortuna encompasses the whole action of the play as a representation of the workings of *discordia concors*.

The *comedia* begins with a soliloquy by Aureliano, who lives in a *monte* and considers himself to be king of the beasts. His salient trait is *fiereza*, which, although it enhances his bellicose nature and will eventually lead Rome to more glorious conquests, is associated with the lower realm of animals. His fiery temperament and his frustrated ambitions, nurtured in the wilderness, have caused an imbalance in his humoral constitution (*discrasia*), leading to a "mortal melancolía" (p. 4).[42] One of the effects of unnatural melancholy, as William Mc-Crary reminds us, is the propensity for prophetic dream visions.[43] Aureliano has a vision in which he sees Quintilio, with bloodied countenance, foretelling that he will be emperor, and giving him the symbols of rulership. Guided by his self-esteem and ambition, Aureliano, emerging from his trance, puts on the crown and exclaims, "Pequeño mundo soy y en esto fundo / que en ser señor de mí lo soy del mundo" (p. 5). Here Aureliano is applying the Renaissance theory of man as a microcosm. Since he rules himself, he claims, he can also rule the world, which is part of the macrocosm. This correspondence between man and the universe certainly applies to the play, but not in the way Aureliano perceives it. Francisco Rico explains that "cuando el hombre no es microcosmos cabal, dueño de sí, el macrocosmos se le rebela."[44] Aureliano claims to be master of himself, yet we know from his soliloquy that he is closer to the passionate beast than to a rational being. Rather than searching for a more human and universal quality, Aureliano becomes enamoured of his baser nature. Since he does not know himself and can not rule his passions, he certainly can not be an exemplary world ruler.

At this point the priestess, in the imperial aspect of Astraea and in the guise of Fortuna, enters with Roman soldiers, making true Aureliano's dream vision. Astraea leads the soldiers to this place, inspired by Apollo's oracle just as the Cumaean Sibyl was given prophetic powers by Apollo. Since this sibyl's key prophecy was the return of Astraea, the two figures were at times confused.[45] Calderón's prophetic priestess of Apollo who shapes imperial destiny is a figure akin to the goddess Astraea who returns to renew the decadent empire, as she had done during the time of Augustus. The priestess relates to Aureliano how Quintilio's fortune "subió mucho y duró poco" (p. 6). Now that he is dead, killed by his own soldiers, it is Aureliano's turn to be emperor according to "el cielo propio" (p. 7). The earthly Astraea delivers a warning based on the inconstancy of her nature as fortune, exemplified by Quintilio's rapid rise and fall. Behind fortune's disguise lies the hand of providence: the heavens have decreed that Aureliano be emperor and he is to obey the "secretos misteriosos" (p. 7) conveyed to him by the priestess. Any attempt to ascribe the lack of justice to the "unfortunate" choice of Aureliano to be emperor must be tempered by the recognition that behind fickle fortune stand the immutable and eternal laws of providence. This is part of the mysterious secret embodied in Astraea.

Aureliano briefly ponders the mysteries of existence, not knowing whether he should trust his senses. His intellectual and rational probings of reality are immediately obscured by his passions and his desire to rule. He concludes: "Sea César, aunque luego / despierte; que al cabo todos / los Imperios son soñados" (p. 8). Although Aureliano admits the evanescence of worldly pursuits, utilizing the dream metaphor that informs *La vida es sueño*, he fails to draw a lesson from it. Aureliano wants to enjoy the ephemeral relative and ignore the timeless absolute, relying on the evidence of his senses and not using his higher faculties to unravel truth. Throughout the play he is guided by his fierce instincts, his cruel nature, and his ambitious will. Disregarding the absolute, he also ignores providence and the obligations it imposes on him. He must perforce accept the rule of Fortune in the guise of Astraea: "Si me ofrece la fortuna / el bien, ¿por qué no le gozo?" (p. 8). Blinded by good fortune and the enjoyment it brings, he forgets her other side, acting as if Fortuna were not a fickle goddess. Trusting her, he swears that he will enter Rome in bloody and amazing triumph, in a golden chariot.

Decio's arrival, like Astraea's speech, includes a lesson on mutability. The great general has been defeated by Cenobia's force as well as by her beauty. On hearing of the loss, Aureliano becomes choleric and throws the general at his feet. Decio's dishonor and fall contrast with Aureliano's rise:

> ¿Puedo ser vencido yo?
> ¿Puedo yo mudança alguna
> padecer en tanto honor?
> Dí, ¿tiene el tiempo valor,
> tiene poder la fortuna?
>   [p. 14]

Aureliano has been totally blinded by good fortune, forgetting that her domain includes both rise and fall. Unable to conceive of his exalted state being taken away from him, his response to others' misfortunes is one of cruelty and indifference.

Although most treatises on Fortuna describe remedies for *adversa fortuna*, Bocángel, following Petrarch, claims that good fortune is even more insidious. "La otra lucha es mas violenta, y dificil de superar, y vencer, que es la que intima Fortuna prospera. . . . La leccion moral de las Historias en la observada verdad de los passados exemplos, comprobarà ser raros los que ayan sabido manejar sin despeño el desfrenado cavallo de la dicha" (pp. 54-55). The *caballo desbocado*, a common image used by Calderón to refer to the lack of control over the passions,[46] is here used by the Bocángel to refer to the usual outcome of good fortune. In *La gran Cenobia*, Aureliano can be equated with the reckless beast whose passion and good fortune lead to destruction. Decio, as an ideal subject, acts as a mirror to his ruler, pointing out the new emperor's lack of vision. In the manner of the "Mirrors of Princes," Decio attempts to educate Aureliano through the concept of fortune:

> Sí, que ay en el tiempo engaños,
> ay en la suerte venganças,
> en la fortuna mudanças,
> y en mi vida desengaños.
>
> [p. 14]

The new emperor refuses to listen to the mirror of *desengaño*. Choosing to live in his dream of empire, he is not concerned with Stoic remedies for fortune. Now that he possesses *buena fortuna*, he discards the goddess: "Ni la temo, ni respeto. / Témela tu, que en efecto / es la fortuna muger" (p. 15). *Fortuna* and *mujer* are linked because they are supposedly adept at *mudanza*.[47] Aureliano also ignores this fickleness, adducing that woman, like fortune, is weak. He is too powerful to be controlled by her. Aureliano extends the equation weakness-woman-fortune to include Cenobia. He will ride against her, bringing her back to Rome as a triumph over woman and fortune. Decio curses the emperor, who has dishonored him and now prepares to conquer his beloved.

Calderón has carefully prepared for Cenobia's initial appearance. The audience, without having seen her, is moved by her loveliness and astonished by her valor. Aureliano's war against her thus becomes more immediate. The two ruling figures are also carefully contrasted. We have seen how Aureliano considers himself a microcosm, although his passions obscure his relationship to the harmonious universe. Decio describes Cenobia in a similar manner:

> que en ella los estremos se igualaron;
> Luna, Saturno y la mayor estrella
> le rindieron metales que engendraron;
> Mercurio ingenio, Iúpiter ventura,
> Marte valor y Venus hermosura.
>
> [p. 11]

All the benefic influence of the seven planets are reflected in Cenobia. She is truly a microcosm, a perfected being who is a mirror of the universe. She encompasses within herself that mystery of the universe of which Calderón and other writers of the epoch so often speak, the conjunction of opposites. The most obvious representation of *discordia concors* is the harmony derived from the opposite planets and gods, Mars and Venus. The offspring of their unlawful union was Harmonia. Cenobia harmonizes martial valor with the beauty and softness of Venus, whereas Aureliano's martial qualities represent an extreme not tempered by the influence of benefic planets. The mystery of *coincidentia oppositorum* eludes him as he rides the crest of fame and fortune to catastrophe. Aureliano, the *caballo desbocado* led by passion and good fortune, contrasts with Cenobia as she emerges to do battle with Decio:

> tan firme en un cavallo, que creyera
> que a los dos en espiritu regía
> porque mostrava, aunque de furia lleno,
> que se pudiera governar sin freno.
>
> [p. 13]

These first few scenes, which are not modeled after Calderón's historical source, the *Historia Augusta*, may have been inspired in some degree by Petrarch. They provide the conceptual basis for the unfolding of the action. Astraea has appeared in her imperial garb, acting like fortune, but alluding to the "secretos misteriosos" (p. 7) of providence. She has triggered Aureliano's rise and the play's action. The new emperor becomes a Petrarchan example of the perils of good fortune. Yet the goddess is *bifrons*. As Aureliano rises, Decio falls: "Los dos estremos seremos / de la fortuna y la suerte" (p. 14). Mighty opposites are portrayed in a *comedia* where contrast is the key to the action.

Having presented Aureliano's character and goals, the action of the play shifts to Palmyra and focuses on Cenobia. This queen's positive portrayal was a commonplace. The Spanish translation of Boccaccio's *De las ilustres mujeres* (1494) begins by stating, "Cenobia: fue reyna de los palmerinos y fue mujer de tan excellente virtud y tan grande: dando testigo desto los libros antiguos: que en nobleza de fama: es de anteponer a todas las otras gentiles."[48] Juan de Pineda comments, "mas en la reina Cenobia, viuda, mucha estima mereció atreverse contra el imperio romano, y romper en batallas con él, y no se espantar de las amenazas del emperador Aureliano, aunque ella carecía de marido, que la pudiera favorecer y esforzar."[49] Her dramatic portrayal by Calderón, however, has elicited different critical opinions. Melveena McKendrick feels that "Calderón's attitude to Cenobia is one of unequivocal admiration. In her he has created a model of all he thinks the perfect leader should be." Pursuing this line of reasoning, McKendrick finds that as drama, *La gran Cenobia* is defective: "The issues are too clear cut, the contrasts too extreme, the protagonist too blandly perfect." Dian Fox views Cenobia in a negative light: "She is herself a vain, ambitious woman, and not the rightful heir to her deceased husband's rule."[50] I believe the answer lies somewhere between, but much closer to McKendrick's description of the queen as the perfect ruler.

As the scene shifts to Palmyra, we see Libio plotting with Irene to murder Cenobia's husband, Abdenato. Libio is afraid that if he does not succeed to the throne immediately, the people will eventually disregard the law that a male must inherit the kingdom and offer the crown to the more qualified Cenobia (p. 18). Libio's devious, violent, and ambitious nature justifies the people's desire to withhold the crown from him. On the other hand, Cenobia's qualities make of her an almost ideal ruler. As the queen enters, she is conducting the affairs of state with prudence, always deferring to her now very old husband, with the result that her subjects are eager to obey her every wish. Libio expresses the only discordant note: "¡Y qué envidia! ¡Estoy rabiando!" (p. 20). In Lope de Vega's poetry *envidia* was often pitted against the truth and justice of Astraea. Here, Cenobia's integrity confronts the schemes of the envious Libio. Her just rule can be equated with Astraea's. But this parallel is somewhat disorienting, since the priestess named Astraea seems to favor the Roman emperor who is bent on triumphing over the present queen of Palmyra.

The names of those conspiring against Cenobia can be linked to the Astraea myth. Libio recalls the astrological sign Libra, the scales of justice, while Irene is the name of Astraea's sister, the goddess of peace in Roman times. These two characters ironically represent the negation of their mythical namesakes. Libio disregards equity and justice in his pursuit of personal gain through treason. Irene is indifferent to peace and revels in conflict. Cenobia will not be able to rule successfully and defeat the Roman army mainly because she is surrounded by people whose names reflect positive values, but who are actually utilizing negative traits to destroy her. This name confusion recalls the apparent opposition encountered earlier in the play between the two pagan goddesses Astraea and Fortuna. In the first scenes, Aureliano was not able to comprehend Fortuna's true nature since he looked only at surface values without attempting to reconcile opposites at a deeper level. Cenobia is also deceived by appearances, not understanding that a name does not necessarily reflect the character of the bearer.

Cenobia is not the perfect ruler, although she approaches this description. Her downfall is the result of a very specific flaw in her nature, her inability to judge character. Daniel Heiple explains that "the buffoon whom she trusts to protect her is a cowardly imposter, and Libio and Irene, her confidants, are murderers and traitors."[51] In defense of Cenobia it must be pointed out that she is aware of Libio's plots and warns him of the consequences on a number of occasions. In this case, her error is not so much her lack of judgment but her excessive tolerance.

By implicating her close associates in Cenobia's downfall, the play touches on an important political consideration. At a time when *privados* such as Lerma and Olivares seem to tower over the two Philips, the quality of a monarch's counselor does become a question of utmost significance. This subject is considered in treatises such as Quevedo's *La política de Dios*. *La gran Cenobia* is less direct in its presentation of the problem. Rather than portraying a *privado* who gives improper advice to the king, Calderón diffuses the issue by introducing a fool posing as a brave soldier and a diffident confidante who listens to her mistress and plots against her. Calderón turns away from commonplace and direct political allusion to more intriguing portraits and situations.

As the first act comes to an end, truth emerges in the guise of Decio. He comes to Palmyra to warn the queen of Rome's imminent attack on her country. Cenobia offers Decio the *bastón* of her army, but he declines, torn between honor and love, not knowing how to salvage either. His decision contrasts with the actions of Libio, whose treachery will bring victory to the Roman camp. Decio's loyalty to Rome in spite of its ruler will also help to bring about the imperial victory he dreads and that would make his love for Cenobia impossible. As if he realized the consequences of his decision, Decio's speech to Cenobia is replete with images of disillusionment where both life and good fortune are seen as transitory:

> y esta vida breve flor
> que se consume a sí misma
> gusano de su botón;
> un almendro de hojas lleno,
> que ufano con ambición,
> a los suspiros del austro
> pompa y vanidad perdió.
>
> [p. 29]

The description of a budding almond tree subjected to a winter storm arouses a multitude of associations. The fierce wind can be equated with the Roman army led by the fierce Aureliano, coming to destroy the beautiful queen and her kingdom. The storm can also be related to *mala fortuna*, the winds of fortune that bring down a virtuous and valiant leader. In the context of the speech, the storm may even refer to death itself. The almond tree as tragic foreshadowing is a common image in Golden Age drama.[52] This image prepares the spectator for the reverses of fortune in the following act.

The second act begins with a recapitulation of the major motifs. Libio appears as a personification of murderous ambition and envy. Although he has poisoned Abdenato, the people have chosen Cenobia to rule instead of him. Aureliano's power and ambition are also evinced as he repeatedly attacks Palmyra. Against the onslaughts of men and fortune, Cenobia stands firm, further gaining the audience's favor and admiration. Libo speaks of Cenobia's *varonil valentía* which shines next to her *mugeril belleza* (p. 33), reintroducing the notion of *discordia concors*, as the queen combines the beauty of Venus with the valor of Mars.

Irene adds that her mistress spends the evening writing a book entitled *Historia oriental*. Cenobia is again showing that opposites can be incorporated within the self, mirroring the completeness of the eternal diurnal and nocturnal circle. Lengthy polemics on which was the most worthy, *armas* or *letras*, were common. Don Quijote's speech on this subject is perhaps the bests-known example of the debate, although other important Renaissance writers, such as Castiglioni and Erasmus, treat this topic.[53] Cenobia combines the two "roads" in her activities, creating a particularly amazing example of *coincidentia oppositorum* since these two roads are to be followed by the male. Cenobia's sex adds one more opposition that is reconciled within herself. As if to pictorially convey to the audience the wonder of this union, Cenobia appears on stage "con armas negras, vestida de luto, leyendo en un libro" (p. 34). Book and sword are emblematic representations of *sapientia* and *fortitudo*, the two key virtues of the epic hero as portrayed in Ulysses and Achilles.[54] It may be that Cenobia's entrance can be linked to Raphael's painting *The Dream of Scipio*, in which three gifts are offered—book, sword, and flower. Raphael's painting, derived from Macrobius's treatise, expresses the Platonic scheme of the tripartite life: the contemplative, the active, and the pleasurable. Cenobia exhibits all three gifts. She holds sword and book, emblems of *fortitudo* and *sapientia*. In addition, her beauty is like that of a flower, her outer appearance reflecting the harmonious nature of her inner self where opposites are mysteriously reconciled.

But this flower may be the early-blossoming almond tree. The tragic consequences of perfection in an imperfect world have been predicted by the arboreal image. Cenobia at this point resembles the

Senecan tragic hero who is destroyed by the injustice of the iron age. As the scene shifts to the opposite camp, the empire's might becomes evident, and Cenobia's plight appears the more desperate. Aureliano is surrounded by his imperial army as his pride and ambition direct him against Palmyra. The courageous Decio is present, his face hidden with Cenobia's *banda*, but ready to fight against her. Aureliano is accompanied by the priestess Astraea, who announces that according to Apollo's prophecy this is the time for victory. Cenobia has no such array of forces. Instead of Decio and Astraea, she is accompanied by Libio and Irene, and the only prophecy she hears is that of the almond tree. Although her army behaves bravely, she trusts the foolish soldier Andronio. As the battle begins, the audience realizes that Rome has the advantage, and is backed by prophecy and foreshadowing images.

But surprise once again overtakes the spectator of this drama where fortune's fickleness is constantly made evident. Rather than seeing the prophecy fulfilled, the audience witnesses the defeat of Aureliano. Astraea attempts to save her credibility and influence, claiming that she interpreted Apollo's oracle erroneously. The irate Aureliano focuses on her mendacity:

> Sacerdotiza engañosa
> baticinante mentida,
> sirena falsa y fingida,
> profetisa mentirosa . . .
> [p. 39]

By referring to her deceitful nature, Aureliano contrasts the priestess's character and the image of the goddess Astraea as truth. Again appearance and reality, name and essence, seem to be at odds. Aureliano's choleric temperament clouds his reason and he tries to kill Astraea by throwing her off a cliff into a cavern.

As Aureliano departs, Cenobia enters the scene looking for a solitary place in which to tend a wound incurred in battle. She hears a strange, faraway voice which we know to be Astraea's. The priestess's lament fills the queen with horror. She takes it as an omen of what is to come. Astraea speaks of an "infelice muger" who is "herida y sangrienta" (pp. 40–41). This is precisely Cenobia's plight. The voice then proclaims that a traitor and an emperor will triumph over her. Although Astraea is speaking of herself, her lament becomes a true prophecy of Cenobia's doom. Thus, in her darkest moment the priestess assumes her true role. As a figure akin to the Cumaean Sibyl, given oracular powers by Apollo, she predicts the future from a cave. When the saddened queen departs, Libio enters. He too hears the uncanny voice, which urges him to be fierce, proud, and tyrannical. The words impel him to accomplish his treacherous intent. Again, the content can be interpreted in two ways. First of all, it represents the priestess's lament. Second, it represents Astraea in her role of fortune, influencing the outcome of the war. Decio is also caught by the spell of the apparently disembodied voice. The priestess labels him emperor of Rome. Unlike Cenobia and Libio, Decio discovers the source of the voice. As he rescues the priestess, he realizes who she is, calling her "Divina Astrea" (p. 43). She, in turn, expresses her hope tht Decio will deliver Rome from a tyrant and become emperor. She is no longer either the prophetic sibyl or the personification of fortune. Decio has recognized her as divine, and she grants him a gift based on her role as imperial goddess. All three characters have heard a voice, then, that may be taken as their own inner voice, their intuition. From this voice, Cenobia discovers the sadness of the immediate future; Libio finds the vitality to perform his evil deeds; and Decio finds hope and solace in his confused state. Astraea, the inner voice, has assumed the roles of sibyl, fortune, and imperial goddess.

Characters who listen to mysterious voices and take them as prophetic are common in the theater of the Spanish Golden Age. Usually the voice is that of a character who does not know that the lament is synchronically describing an unknown listener's doom. In most cases the foretelling is accurate.[55] One such tragic foreshadowing is the image of the almond tree in Lope de Vega's La inocente sangre, published in 1622. Here, a gardner's apostrophe to the tree is heard by others and taken as prophecy.[56] Perhaps Calderón was inspired by Lope's play in his use of the almond tree in fashioning the prophetic scene. At any rate, the priestess's triple role as the earthly representative of the goddess of fortune, truth, and empire seems to crystallize in this scene. At the same time, a new twist in the wheel of fortune is perceived. Aureliano verbally dismissed the pagan goddess as weak in the first act. Now he has tried to murder the embodiment of Fortuna. The "fickle" goddess will now shift her allegiance. Astraea, although committed to the destruction of Palmyra and the triumph of Aureliano, envisions a less immediate future when Decio will be proclaimed emperor.

The fleeing Aureliano offers Decio his bastón and an equal place in the empire if he is able to stop Cenobia. Decio positions himself in front of a bridge, challenging the whole army of Palmyra. In this, Decio imitates the actions of countless heroes of chivalric romances.

Amadís de Gaula guarded bridges, and historical heroes emulated these chivalric practices. Suero de Quiñones, a historical personage, defended a bridge over the river Obrego in 1434 as a tribute to his lady. The situation is reversed in *La gran Cenobia*. Rather than using the bridge to bring honor to his lady, Decio must use it to defeat her in battle and bring honor to the Roman camp, thus recovering his own honor. Cenobia approaches the mysterious guardian of the bridge and recognizes him as Decio. Cenobia understands that Decio must defend the bridge, and that his love for her can attain fulfillment once his honor has been restored. A chivalric commonplace has been transformed by Calderón into another example of mighty opposites, from which both queen and lover emerge tragically resolute. The chivalric bridge has become a bridge between extremes that must remain undisturbed, awaiting the appropriate time for reconciliation, or crossing.

Since Decio and Cenobia have achieved a certain stasis through their understanding of opposite forces, Fortuna must find another agent. Libio goes to the Roman camp and offers to kidnap Cenobia. Aureliano promises Libio a crown and a position equal to his own in the empire, an offer he has earlier made to Decio. The obvious falseness of the offer makes us aware that Aureliano never meant to fulfill his promises to Decio. His reign is far removed from the influence of the goddess Astraea: neither truth nor justice are his guides. Libio, not perceiving the emperor's mendacity, congratulates himself on having listened to the voice of Fortuna. Like Aureliano, he does not understand the fickleness of the pagan goddess. He concentrates on *próspera fortuna*, disregarding her other face. When Cenobia is brought to Aureliano's camp and Libio asks for his reward, he is given the crown, but *próspera fortuna* immediately shows her other side. Aureliano orders that Libio be thrown off a cliff. In this, Aureliano is following an ancient tradition that urges the ruler to use treason and pay for it, but at the same time punish the traitor.[57]

The third act commences with Decio informing Astraea that Cenobia is to be brought in triumph through the streets of Rome:

> A Roma llegas a tiempo
> de ver la mayor tragedia
> que en el teatro del mundo
> la fortuna representa.
>
> [p. 61]

The common Baroque metaphor of the world as stage is here utilized to reintroduce the topic of fortune. According to Decio, it is this pagan goddess who has "staged" the great tragic "triumph" that is about to be witnessed by all. To the common notion that God is the *autor* (producer) or director of the play of life, Decio is grafting the concept that Fortuna is the cause. Thus, he is hinting at an important link in the *comedia*, that between fortune and providence.

Decio's description adds that the emperor is seated in the triumphal chariot, "a imitación / hermosa de algun Planeta" (p. 61). Aureliano's choleric temperament and bellicose disposition link him to the planet Mars. Guy Marchant, in the *Kalendar and Compost of the Shepherds*, describes this planet as follows: "The planet Mars is called the god of battle and of all war. . . . This planet Mars is the worst of all others, for he is hot and dry, and stirreth a man to be very willful and hasty at once, and to unhappiness."[58] Aureliano fits the description perfectly; he is willful, warlike, choleric, and hasty, qualities which will bring him unhappiness. Aureliano's martial qualities are particularly fitting to a Roman emperor, since Romulus was the son of Mars and Ilia. What is lacking in Aureliano is some benevolent influence to temper the excessive heat and fury of Mars.

If Aureliano is Mars, then Cenobia is Venus in her beauty. As Aureliano enters Rome in his martial planetary chariot, he holds in golden chains Cenobia or Venus. In this, he is reversing the Platonic iconography of *discordia concors*. To explain the mystery of harmony, Renaissance Platonists portrayed benevolent Venus subjugating bellicose Mars.[59] *La gran Cenobia* dramatizes a triumph where Aureliano is not tempered, but exhibits his most extreme and tyrannical nature. He points to the humbled queen and considers her defeat as his triumph over Fortuna:

> Esta que veis a mis pies
> muger humillada, esta
> que, a ser mortal la fortuna,
> la misma fortuna fuera,
> assombro ha sido del Assia . . .
> miralda agora ¡que humilde!
> [pp. 63–64]

In the first act, Aureliano linked women to fortune, thinking them both weak and manageable. Now that he has triumphed over Cenobia, he forgets how close he came to *adversa fortuna*. At the height of his power, he believes himself to be in control of the macrocosm, although we know from the initial scenes that Aureliano does not even have control over his own self, the microcosm.

Cenobia reminds him of *mudanza*, an attribute of both *fortuna* and *muger*. She utilizes several images—such as fortune's wheel and the daily circumference of the sun's path—to remind Aureliano of his precarious position. Rather than considering any of the Stoic remedies for fortune, Aureliano blindly reasserts his superiority and minimizes Decio's curse pronounced in the first act:

¿Cómo este tiempo no llega?
O no osa ya la fortuna
o me teme o me respeta.
Ni la estimo ni la aprecio;
Bueno fuera que temiera
a una muger y an un cobarde.
[pp. 65–66]

Aureliano will not look at fortune's other face. He considers her a weak woman or a cowardly deity. These are the qualities he also confers on Cenobia and Decio. Yet we know that Cenobia is powerful, not weak, and that Decio is valiant, not cowardly. Aureliano's *anagnorisis* has not yet come. He lives a life of deception. Hearing his name, Decio makes himself known as the brave soldier who defended the emperor. Aureliano's response comes as no surprise. He calls Decio a coward, adding, "Esta / es la justicia, que manda / hazer la fortuna fiera" (p. 67). Aureliano claims as his own the power of justice and fortune, two attributes of the goddess Astraea. We know that he possesses neither. His self-deception also negates Astraea's third major quality, truth.

Decio decides to assassinate Aureliano. His motives are various.[60] As a person, he has been deprived of his honor, while his beloved is unjustly humiliated. The emperor's tyrannical, choleric, and vengeful nature has not been altered or softened; he feels that he is above fortune and even all the other gods. Since Aureliano is a tyrant, he can be deposed.[61] We know that Decio will succeed in this enterprise when the priestess Astraea, the earthly image of Fortuna, vows to help him. Irene and Libio are also in Rome. They also wish to murder the emperor. Yet this pair is treacherous, willful, and ambitious. They wish to advance themselves rather than thinking of what is best for the empire. By directing both pairs to the emperor's palace, the play follows its constant contrastive structure.

Aureliano, seated on the throne, is a parody of the just ruler. Not the least interested in his subjects' welfare, he exclaims, "¡Qué cansados pretendientes!" (p. 77). Finding the situation tedious, he becomes sleepy, as Libio and Irene enter dressed as *pretendientes*. As Libio prepares to stab the emperor, Astraea and Decio enter through the other door. The priestess remarks that Aureliano's dream has been sent by heaven ("Efeto del cielo fue / el sueño," p. 79). Not only will this sleep enable them to approach the emperor and end his life, it also takes us back to the first scenes of the play when Aureliano, seeing a vision, was not sure whether he was awake or asleep. Rather than learning the initial lesson of the evanescent quality of all earthly gifts, the emperor has deluded himself into believing in the permanence of terrestrial good fortune. It is thus fitting that he die at the hands of real people whom he thinks are phantoms. He has created his own illusions and will die with his self-deceit, blaspheming against a heaven he cannot control and does not wish to accept. As Astraea and Libio rush towards him, Aureliano awakes in astonishment. Two people he has supposedly killed are standing by him with threatening daggers:

> Fantasmas ¿qué me queréis?
> Libio, yo te di la muerte,
> Astrea, yo te maté,
> por traidor, por engañosa;
> no traición, justicia fue;
> no tiranía, piedad . . .
>
> [p. 80]

The emperor attempts to justify himself by speaking of *justicia* and *piedad*, two qualities he does not possess. At this point, Decio enters and actually kills Aureliano, who dies at his feet, as the curse predicted. The emperor dies raging against the gods. In contrast with Aureliano's meaningless blasphemy, Decio's action takes place while he is flanked by Astraea and Libio, figures whose names recall two adjacent heavenly constellations, Virgo and Libra, the signs of justice. Aureliano's fall from fortune is dramatically depicted by his fall at Decio's feet. Fortuna "bifrons" now shows her prosperous countenance to Decio who is cheered by the imperial soldiers for having rid Rome of a tyrant. He is also proclaimed emperor, as Astraea-Fortuna predicted. This ending provides the spectator with a glimpse at the true workings of the supposedly fickle goddess. Aureliano's rule served to test the temper of Decio's soul. Decio has acted bravely against the onslaughts of fortune. Now he can utilize his experience to rule wisely. His demonstrated heroism is soon translated into just action. Following ancient custom, he orders the traitors Libio and Irene killed. Any fear that his martial qualities might lead him to Aureliano's extremes is soon dispelled. He announces that he will marry Cenobia, who has also proven herself during adverse fortune. Her Venus-like benevolence will temper any martial excesses. Indeed, she immediately pleads for the life of Libio and Irene.

The harmony that arises out of contrariety, the peace that

emerges from brutal wars and treacherous actions, and the marriage of enemy rulers form the mystery of *discordia concors* pondered by the Platonists. Mighty opposites also reveal Astraea's nature. In this *comedia* she is a human figure with failures as well as virtues. Yet her actions correspond to the will of the celestial goddess whose name she bears. This deity appears as Fortuna to the man who views events uncritically. Man in his ignorance cannot understand the mysterious workings of God's laws and creates a fickle and blind goddess.[62] Yet there are moments when heavenly purpose emerges through the "accidents" of fortune. Beneath fickle Fortuna the observant person may detect its opposite, the perfect ordering intelligence that rules the universe. Calderón explains this link in *No hay más fortuna que Dios:*

> fingir una
> deidad que el nombre equivoque
> de la siempre sabia, augusta
> distributiva Justicia,
> haciéndolos que presuman
> que de la Fortuna nace
> lo que halaga o lo que angustia.[63]

In this *auto sacramental*, the devil wishes to frustrate *Justicia* or the celestial Astraea. To accomplish this, he interposes the feigned Fortuna between man and God. As Robert Fiore puts it, "The plan is to confuse man so that he will not understand the distributive justice of God and thus will be discontented with his status on earth."[64] Aureliano dies despising the feigned goddess. He only understands the surface values of life, attempting to win, in his ignorance, a contest against a nonexistent deity. The wiser man knows that the reverses of Fortuna-Astraea have their source in the absolute, since "no hay mas Fortuna que Dios." On the world's stage as presented in *La gran Cenobia*, the wheel of fortune spins creating opposing effects that mysteriously achieve a lasting peace and a just rule akin to Astraea's golden age. The just Decio and the benevolent Cenobia form a balance of opposites that can lead to imperial *renovatio* after catastrophic events. Chaos gives way to order in the concluding scenes of a drama that transforms a historical narrative into a meaningful poetic fiction where Cenobia marries the new emperor, an event that has no basis in history. This transformation of history into timeless art revives the hope that the imperial goddess can return to earth, bringing back the happiest of times, the mythical first age. The complex actions of this play mirror the fickle and whimsical Fortuna, yet the careful craftsmanship and the artful conclusion reveal an ordered cosmos. They are the work of a poet whose theocentric craft imitates and thus worships the creative intelligence that structures relative existence. The earthly Astraea has become a celestial goddess. Fortune's wheel has been metamorphosed into the eternal circle of the zodiac where universal laws are inscribed in mysterious and contrary signs.

CHAPTER FOUR

The Fallen Virgin

APPROXIMATELY TEN YEARS after the portrayal of Astraea as the priestess of fortune and justice in *La gran Cenobia*, Calderón returned to the goddess in his masterpiece, *La vida es sueño*. Her importance in this *comedia* has been ignored by most critics, since the dramatist himself seems to downplay her role.[1] Mention of this deity occurs in the second act when Rosaura pretends to be Clotaldo's niece, adopting the name Astraea. This scene belongs to the secondary action of the play, which has been labeled as "frivolous" by some critics.

The subordinate plot centers around Rosaura. Her plight, according to Melveena McKendrick, is a particularly common one in golden age drama. "The plays with a maiden errant in search of a recalcitrant lover are too numerous to mention. The intention is to make the gallant consent to marry her. . . . The grievance is normally slight because the affair has rarely progressed beyond the *reja*." *La vida es sueño* is an exception since the grievance is more real: "Rosaura's grievance against Astolfo becomes identified with the play's themes of free will and moral reality."[2] The secondary plot of *La vida es sueño* has attracted interest mainly as it relates to the main action. Ever since Menéndez Pelayo referred to the Rosaura episode as "una intriga completamente pegadiza y exótica,"[3] critics have felt compelled to justify the prominence of the subplot. A.E. Sloman explains how the main and secondary actions are linked. Other critics, such as E.M. Wilson, William M. Whitby, Michele Federico Sciacca, Jackson I. Cope, and Harlan Sturm, consider Rosaura to be central to the *comedia*, since she parallels the protagonist's actions and also serves as Segismundo's guide, leading him to "conversion."[4]

Even though modern criticism has accepted this interpretation, a number of critics of *La vida es sueño* evince a certain hesitancy over the frivolous aspects of the subplot. A. Valbuena Prat complains that "la galantería se enreda en el discreteo frívolo, muy lejos de la inten-

THE FALLEN VIRGIN 89

sidad de los problemas de la existencia," while Sloman reluctantly admits that the tone of the two plots "is often quite different." Some recent appraisals echo Menéndez Pelayo's attitude, in particular V. Bodini's structural analysis where the terms superficial and extraneous are applied to the subplot.[5]

Rosaura is not just the simple stock character of the jilted woman. Further evidence of her crucial role emerges from the name substitution in the midst of the supposedly frivolous action during the second act. Even if Calderón's audience did not remember the importance of this goddess in *La gran Cenobia*, Astraea was such an important myth for the Renaissance and Golden Age that they may have been aware of her role as an astral-imperial deity associated with the happiest of ages. The myth of the golden age is fully developed in *La vida es sueño*, as are the astral-imperial concerns. The mention of Astraea serves to trigger our associations. While she is not the central figure, her presence, on one level, is the actualization of myth in history.

Eleanor Jean Martin insists that in imagery and in the questions of prophecy, treason, and deception, Calderón relied on *La gran Cenobia* as a key source.[6] Her case would have been greatly strengthened if she had considered the myth of Astraea in the elaboration of both *comedias*. The themes of justice and empire coalesce at the end of *La gran Cenobia* when the tyrant Aureliano is murdered in the temple of justice, while Decio is crowned emperor in the presence of Astraea, the priestess who helped to bring about the new order. Tyranny and justice are also central to *La vida es sueño*. At the end of the play, Segismundo's "humiliation" of Basilio is reminiscent of the Decio-Aureliano situation in *La gran Cenobia*. There is of course one central difference: Segismundo forgives and is forgiven, while Decio must kill or remain dishonored. Both Segismundo and Decio are able to triumph with the aid of what one may term their spiritual guides, two women, Astraea in *La gran Cenobia* and Rosaura-Astraea in *La vida es sueño*. In addition, both of these female figures are present at the denouement in order to underline that justice and harmony have been restored in a new golden age.

But the many similarities in plot and characterization as well as certain thematic links between the *comedias* should not obscure the divergent natures of these two works, written ten years apart. *La gran Cenobia* keeps a character named Astraea constantly on stage. Yet this early play seems to turn its back on the celestial goddess as it focuses on the abuses of power. Roman history is presented as a mirror to contemporary deeds and habits. Astraea as Fortuna overshadows the message of the constellation Virgo, and the final resolution depicts a golden age in strictly imperial terms. Myth is here in the service of history. In *La vida es sueño*, Astraea is most conspicuous for her absence. The few allusions to her have the opposite effect to that in *La gran Cenobia*. Rather than acting in history to preserve the Roman Empire, Rosaura-Astraea becomes a conceptual trigger to "obrar bien." In *La vida es sueño*, the "displacement" of myth[7] is so contrived as to preserve a mythical ambience in a fallen world. A.A. Parker notes that Segismundo's tower becomes a Calderonian myth. While Astraea becomes for Segismundo the timeless and eternal, the tower, in Parker's words, is "a symbol of mankind's subjection to death: we are, each of us, imprisoned in a Tower." This critic also refers to it as the tower of human guilt, since, as the Fates promised, "men would bring dissension, violence and strife into the world."[8] Tower and Astraea are thus the opposite poles in the play: they represent death and immortality, guilt and redemption, violence and harmony. It is the tension between these two aspects of man, the relative and the absolute, that triggers the action. Segismundo's quest leads him from the tower through the worldly palace to the eternal values of existence. Emphasis on the fall at the beginning of the *comedia* elicits a desire for its opposite—a golden age. History becomes subservient to myth, and empire becomes subordinate to inner transformation. *La gran Cenobia* consists of action and history; the focus is on the tyrant Aureliano, his violent deeds, and the strife that leads to his annihilation. *La vida es sueño* focuses on man's innermost desires and views secular history through the lens of timeless myth. The ironic presentation of a chaotic landscape, a fallen virgin, and a bestial man lead to the dawn of an age which is the source and goal of historical time. This shift in emphasis is accompanied by an astounding density of images, motifs, and meanings, enriched by Calderón's readings in the ten years between the early historical play and his materpiece. A brief overview of antecedents will place certain themes in perspective.

A.E. Sloman has argued that "the debt of *La vida es sueño* to *Yerros de naturaleza y aciertos de la fortuna*, is unmistakable," as has J.A. Van Praag.[9] There are indeed numerous points of contact between the two *comedias*. Even character names such as Segismundo and Rosaura appear in both works. Written by Antonio Coello y Ochoa in collaboration with Calderón, probably the year before the composition of *La vida es sueño*, *Yerros* is based, in turn, on a Byzantine romance by Enrique Suárez de Mendoza y Figueroa entitled *Eustorgio y Clorilene, historia moscóvica* (1629). The education of the prince in *La vida es sueño* has been carefully analyzed by Everett W. Hesse.[10] Segismundo's development is reminiscent of Eustorgio's in Suárez de Mendoza's romance. After many trials and tribulations, Eustorgio emerges as a magnanimous ruler who forgives his tyrannical aunt Juana. Possibly recalling this romance, Calderón shifts his attention from the proud and egotistical ruler to his future replacement, delving into their relationship. The unrelated rulers of *La gran Cenobia* are transformed into brother and sister, Polidoro and Matilde, in *Yerros de naturaleza;* and finally into father and son in *La vida es sueño.* This shift is related to Calderón's particular concern with the father as a figure of authority.

In *Yerros,* the conflict centers around the twins Polidoro and Matilde. Matilde usurps the Polish throne and orders her brother killed. Instead, he is imprisoned in a tower, and eventually recovers the throne. The tower immediately calls to mind Segismundo's imprisonment in *La vida es sueño;* both Polidoro and Segismundo pass from incarceration to rulership. However, the point that interests us here is the conflict between twins. For René Girard, one of the main triggers for violence is precisely the birth of twins. The lack of difference between them, the inability to place one above the other in a social or political structure, destroys the society's hierarchical pattern. Noting that in primitive societies twins inspire a particular terror and are often put to death, Girard views them as a potential source of violence.[11] This attitude towards twins often extends to brothers. Calderón appears to avoid enemy brothers in *La vida es sueño,* after having utilized the theme the year before in his collaboration with Coello. The powerful figure of Basilio draws our attention away from this danger and focuses it on the father-son conflict.

The twins of *Yerros* are metamorphosed into cousins in *La vida es sueño,* so that another threat, that of incest, fades, or at least appears to do so at first glance. Parker notes the importance of the incest motif in brother-sister pairs in *La devoción de la cruz, Las tres justicias en una,* and *Los cabellos de Absalón.* But he fails to analyze the Segismundo-Rosaura relationship in this context. Their plight, as many critics have noted, is very similar; their road from oblivion to success traverses the same landscapes. Both have secrets in their families: Rosaura does not know her father, while Segismundo is imrisoned in a tower and is ignorant of his parentage. Rosaura, we know, was born from an illicit relationship. We will see in the next chapter how Segismundo could also be regarded as an illegitimate child. In romance, lack of knowledge of one's parents by two children of opposite sexes often results in the discovery that they are siblings. Calderón used this motif in several plays, but changed it from the happy anagnorisis of romance to a tragic view: Lope and Violante from *La tres justicias en una* and Eusebio and Julia from *La devoción de la cruz* are typical examples of couples who love each other not knowing their fraternal relationship. Although it would be almost impossible for this to be the case in the Segismundo-Rosaura relationship, the many similarities with other couples certainly suggest this theme. Indeed, Edwin Honig views the pair as the mythical twins.[12]

A kind of continuity emerges between *Yerros de naturaleza* and *La vida es sueño* when we study human conflicts in the two plays. But while Coello's conception of the twins belongs to the mythical enemy-brothers tradition, Calderón alters this when writing individually, making use of his own life experience and of a universal myth. Segismundo and Rosaura have a conflictive relationship from the start and demonstrate a violence that reminds us of Girard's notions of lack of difference in twins: she is threatened by him with death and rape. In spite of this potential violence, their actions and reactions serve to bring about a harmonious resolution. This is not tragedy, which Girard defines as "the balancing of the scale, not of justice but of violence."[13] The violent mimesis of which this critic speaks gives way to a mysterious reconciliation, not the destructive opposition of Greek tragedy, since Rosaura-Astraea triumphs in the end. She is elevated to her proper place with the aid of Segismundo, and he gains in wisdom through a conceptualization of her beauty and goodness.

The mythical "twins" of *La vida es sueño* may be viewed as two aspects of the self attempting to achieve wholeness. Their final reconciliation, as well as Segismundo's atonement with the father, can be understood in terms of the hero's quest and the integration of the personality, themes which will be discussed in the next two chapters. In the end, Rosaura regains her honor by marrying Astolfo, while Segismundo marries Estrella. The double wedding is the final barrier against incestuous tendencies, and a sacred bond that restores order and balance to an environment that had suffered from selfish attitudes and narrow viewpoints. The wholeness achieved within Segismundo's double nature assures that Rosaura will regain her honor. By conceptualizing her attributes into eternal truths, the prince learns the full value of the object of perception and is not caught any longer in the fragmented world of selfish desire. The golden age hinted at by Rosaura when taking the name Astraea is one that begins in the individual, proceeds through human relationships, and extends to the whole country.

The violence that was unleashed soon after the mythical "twins" first met has now been banished from the land. Male-female twins are the preferred symbol for the *mysterium coniunctionis* in alchemical treatises. Reconciliation of opposites through the creation of the philosopher's stone may be a more appropriate approach to Calderón's play than Girard's view of twin phobia. The "order restored" at the end of the play is that mystery pondered by Platonists and alchemists alike, the merging together of opposite and fragmented values into a cohesive whole, the individual's transformation from corruptible metal into gold. The play exemplifies this heroic quest for integration, and the dramatic structure is in itself a triumph of wholeness over a conflictive world. At the denouement, Astraea's just balance resides in Segismundo's heart but her truth is the poet's song, the frail nightingale that must oppose the tyrants of the land.

In the ten years that elapsed between *La gran Cenobia* and Calderón's masterpiece, Astraea appears only once in his plays, and then only as a minor character. She is one of Floripes's ladies in the chivalric drama entitled *La puente de Mantible* (1630). From the above discussion, it should not come as a surprise to discover that this play begins with an incestuous brother-sister relation. The beautiful Floripes is the sister of the fierce Fierabrás. Although born of the same parents, they are as different as winter and spring. This relationship provides the playwright with the opportunity to expound on the theme of like-opposites. Floripes states:

> no es mucho que de una causa
> (calle la modestia aquí)
> naciésemos, para ser
> él ocaso, yo cenit,
> él adelfa, yo clavel,
> él la sombra, yo el matiz,
> él la concha, yo la perla,
> él enero, y yo el abril.
> [p. 1854][14]

She is beauty, spring, and light. He is winter, the setting sun, shadows. They have one characteristic in common which bridges these oppositions—their martial nature:

> Sólo lo que nos ha hecho
> hermanos, fué el varonil
> espíritu, el corazón
> de que adornada me vi.
> [pp. 1854-55]

This keeps them side by side in the wars against the twelve *pares* of France. However, Fierabrás wants more from his sister: "Tu hermano y tu amante soy" (p. 1861). She rejects his advances: "Como a mi hermano te sigo, / pero no como a mi amante" (p. 1861). Floripes is in love with one of Charlemagne's knights, Guido de Borgoña, and he reciprocates. After much chivalric courtesy, challenges, and confusion, the first act ends when the French army is defeated by the Turks and Fierabrás takes Guido prisoner. Unbeknownst to Fierabrás, his sister's martial spirit has been tempered by Venus. She did not participate in the conflict since her beloved, Guido, was a member of the opposition. As the battle rages, all she can do is to call on her ladies, Irene and Astraea, and wonder at the loss of her warlike instincts (p. 1862). These are appropriate maids for Floripes. Irene, it should be recalled from discussion of *La gran Cenobia*, is Astraea's sister and represents peace. The love of a Christian has now dispelled the remaining link between Floripes and her brother.

Guido, along with three other French heroes, Oliveros, Ricarte, and Guarinos, is imprisoned in Mantible, a tower described in much the same manner as Segismundo's prison in *La vida es sueño*. It is a *sepulcro*, a *tumba* (pp. 1863-64), and a cave (p. 1864). Whatever its appearance, the tower-cave was built by a magician and is impregnable (p. 1864). The confusion between cave and tower and the introduction of a magician recall the many legends of the tower and/or cave of Hercules in Spain. These legends were later adapted to the caves of Salamanca and Toledo, which became places of forbidden knowledge, presided over by the devil. Calderón is infusing the landscape with reminiscences from old, popular legends so as to increase the feeling of wonder and terror in the spectator and to underline the desperate plight of the Christian heroes. If the demonic aspects of the cave-tower are a cause of terror, the vague recollection that such structures had their origin in Hercules must be seen as a source of optimism and strength. The prisoners' difficult situation changes when Floripes comes to rescue her beloved Guido. Guido is seriously wounded, but Floripes has brought magical unguents to effect his cure (p. 1865).

The demonic and destructive magic of Fierabrás, symbolized by the frightful tower-cave built by a magician, is now opposed by Floripes's healing arts. Again, brother and sister take on opposing qualities. Her rescue of the captive heroes, however, is not entirely successful, since Fierabrás arrives. The four followers of Charlemagne lock themselves in the tower, together with Floripes and her maids. Irene's peaceful nature is translated into Guido's pleas to Fierabrás:

"de paz en la torre trataremos" (p. 1867). This request is rejected by Fierabrás, who rages with anger and jealousy. He cannot conquer the tower since it is magical and is defended by four great heroes. In a raid to obtain food, Guido is captured by Fierabrás.

As the third act opens, another battle ensues and this time Floripes and her three maids, Irene, Astraea, and Arminda, rescue Guido, but misfortune is still upon them. Trapped in the dark tower of demonic magic and surrounded by Turkish and Moorish enemies, they choose Guido to serve as messenger to Charlemagne. Since the bridge is carefully guarded, Guido crosses the green water of the infernal river Lethe. The use of the mythical river reinforces the demonic qualities of Fierabrás's domain. Guido is reminiscent of mythological figures like Orpheus and Hercules who were able to journey to the underworld and come back to earth. Indeed, the use of the magical cave-tower makes clear the parallel since, as stated, Hercules built such a structure in Spain.

In the end, the Christian forces predictably defeat the pagan, even though the enemy has enlisted two giants (p. 1884). The wounded Fierabrás calls on the emperor to administer to him the last blow. Charlemagne replies, "Llevadle donde le curen / como a mi persona propia" (p. 1885). The contrast that was established between Floripes and Fierabrás now distinguishes Charlemagne from the pagan king. One is intent on destruction, while the other believes in healing wounds. The conclusion of the *comedia*, although abrupt, is appropriate. The peace (Irene) that has been established in the political realm is translated into individual happiness in the marriage between Floripes and Guido. This marriage establishes a bridge between pagan and Christian cultures. Charlemagne orders tower and bridge destroyed. The emperor thus makes war on the demonic forces at the same time that he expands the boundaries of his empire. The result he has in mind is the creation of world peace and harmony, reminiscent of that happy age when Astraea lived on earth. His was the first attempt at world rule by the Christianized Roman Empire. Indeed, he storms the enemy bearing "las aguilas de Roma" (p. 1882). The return of the golden age through imperial rule and the consequent era of peace and happiness had been foreshadowed by Floripes's initial contrastive speech. At the end of La puente de Mantible, the ravages of winter have given way to an amorous and happy spring; demonic darkness has been dispelled by the emperor's Christian light; and the setting sun of Fierabrás's kingdom gives way to the dawn or rising sun of a new age.

Although preserving imperial connotations, *La puente de Mantible* moves away from the historical ambience of *La gran Cenobia* towards the world of romance. References to demonic rivers, magical towers, and ancient heroes bring the work closer to myth, to the wish-fullfilment dream. As in *Yerros de naturaleza*, the protagonist must descend to the depths and darkness of tower and cave before becoming a true hero. Floripes, aided by her maids Arminda, Astraea, and Irene, heals the wounded Guido in the tower of human suffering. In *La vida es sueño*, Segismundo will also pass through this perilous tower. But Rosaura will be able to guide her "brother" in suffering, Segismundo, to a vision of truth, whereas Floripes simply serves as a contrast to her destructive, lustful, and incestuous brother, Fierabrás. In *Yerros* too, the twin brother and sister exhibit opposing tendencies. Only in *La vida es sueño* will the pair surmount lustful and even incestuous desires to attain a harmony based on higher values.

In his plays, Calderón often develops parallels between the protagonist and Hercules. We have seen an example of this in *La puente de Mantible*, but the connection becomes even more apparent in *La vida es sueño*. Clark Colahan and Alfred Rodríguez have pointed out similarities between Segismundo's double nature and the dual characterization of Hercules as it appears in the two plays on the subject by Seneca: "El trágico romano presenta, en su *Hercules Furens,* al protagonista en su fase violenta y animalizada, y subraya, en su *Hercules Oetaeus,* su evolucionada personalidad estoica y controlada."[15] Among the many parallels cited, the authors note the importance of *sueño* in both Spanish and Roman dramas. Sleep is addressed directly and is labeled both truthful and mendacious. More important, in both *La vida es sueño* and *Hercules Furens* the transformation of the hero from violence to control occurs precisely after a long sleep. These two critics have overlooked a key point of contact between the plays. Seneca's Chorus describes Hercules' sleep after his violent and murderous behavior with a reference to Astraea: "And do thou, O Sleep, vanquisher of woes, rest of the soul, the better part of human life, thou winged son of thy mother Astraea, sluggish brother of cruel Death, thou who dost mingle false with true. . . . O thou who are peace after wonderings . . . sweetly and gently soothe his weary spirit" (vol. 1, p. 95).

It may be that this reference to Astraea was instrumental in structuring the manner of Segismundo's transformation in *La vida es sueño*. The prince, after creating havoc at the palace, is given the narcotic potion by Clotaldo and returned to the tower, where he awakens and is told that the palace episode has been a dream. Clotaldo then advises him that "aun en sueños / no se pierde el obrar bien" (vv. 2146-

47).[16] Alone, Segismundo ponders on the nature of life and tries to decipher his role in it, in the famous soliloquy at the end of the second act. The situation is akin to that of Hercules in *Hercules Furens*. After perpetrating acts of violence, both protagonists sleep. Their awakening signals the beginning of an inner change. While Hercules is still asleep, the Chorus calls on Astraea, the mother of Sleep and Death. This pessimistic statement that points to life as a struggle and to peace as the state of sleep or death could be interpreted in a more positive manner. In sleep, the protagonist comes in touch with deeper truths and a feeling of well-being that lead him to question the nature of reality and search for eternal values within the self. Astraea can be considered the mother of sleep since in this state of consciousness man can come closer to his "true" nature. Thus, sleep and death can guide man away from the relative towards the absolute. This may have been Calderón's interpretation of Seneca's scene. He thus portrays Segismundo's awakening as a realization of higher values after a dreamlike struggle with the passions and with violence that culminates in a peaceful sleep. The two children of Astraea, sleep and death, lead him to the mother, the unconscious in man. As he delves deeper within the self, he discovers some of the wisdom of which Clotaldo speaks. While Seneca ends *Hercules Furens* at the point of awakening, Calderón continues his drama by showing Segismundo's reaction to Rosaura-Astraea when he meets her for the third time. Although the prince is once again involved in political struggles, he now has the experience from the palace and the wisdom acquired in the peaceful times that followed the violent sojourn. He acts with a broader vision based on an inner peace. The golden age thus begins as a dream of man, who wants to escape the prison of violence, desire, and suffering.

The impact of Seneca on *La vida es sueño* and the notion of the golden age does not stop here. But with every reminiscence, Calderón adds a touch of optimism to the Roman dramatist and philosopher who viewed *ekpyrosis* as a necessity, and the happiest of ages as a recurring but fleeting moment in the history of man's iniquities and failures. Two more references to Astraea in Seneca should be recalled. In *Hercules Oetaeus*, the hero, in a moment of despair, fails to find tranquility even in the heavens. In fact, he feels responsible for heavenly turmoil: "But what avails it to have freed the race of men from fear? Now have the gods no peace; the freed earth sees in the sky all creatures which she feared; for there hath Juno set them. The crab I slew goes round the torrid zone, is known as Libya's constellation, and matures her grain; the lion to Astraea gives the flying year; but he, his burning mane upon his neck back tossing, dries up the dripping south-wind and devours the clouds" (vol. 2, p. 191). The peaceful Astraea, who retired to the heavens fleeing man's vicious nature in the worst of ages, is now surrounded by violent and monstrous creatures in the sky. This is the firmamental violence that Basilio perceives in casting his son's horoscope. He focuses on the threatening creatures, as Hercules had done, forgetting that the music of the spheres reveals an eternal harmony, and that providence as written in the stars is the most perfect order. Basilio does not focus on the celestial Astraea, but on what to him appears to be a threatening sky. By incarcerating Segismundo he brings about his own downfall. The son will eventually look at Rosaura-Astraea and learn from her. He will restore a harmony on earth that mirrors the perpetual celestial tranquility based on the mystery of the reconciliation of opposites.

Astraea also appears in Seneca's *Thyestis*. Here the Chorus comments on an unnatural darkness over the world, and expresses fear of an apocalyptic destruction when the constellations will drop from the sky: "The Virgin shall fall to the earth she once abandoned, and the Scales of justice with their weights shall fall and with them shall drag the fierce Scorpion down" (vol. 2, p. 161). This portrayal of the fall of Astraea from the sky may have inspired Calderón to make Rosaura a fallen woman. What more perfect emblem for the depths of the iron age than a celestial Virgo who has fallen from the heavens and has lost her virginity, literally falling into the darkness of Poland at the very doors of the tower which symbolizes man's guilt, suffering, and imprisonment?

An apparently wise man who sees violence in the stars, but not the harmony of the spheres; a celestial sign that drops from the sky, losing its nature as Virgo; and a man's sleep that leads to the transformation of the self—these are some of the Senecan images and themes that may have contributed to Calderón's masterpiece.

WHEN *La vida es sueño* is approached from the perspective of the Astraea myth, an underlying cohesiveness becomes apparent. If the figure Rosaura-Astraea is taken as the embodiment of returning justice and truth, then the main action can be directly related to the subplot, since the father-son conflict can be translated into the Saturn-Jupiter rivalry that put an end to the first age. Astraea as truth is depicted as the daughter of Saturn or time in emblems that follow the motto *veritas filia temporis*. Thus, Saturn's "children" are Jupiter and Astraea, in other words, Segismundo and Rosaura-Astraea. In this sense, they are truly brother and sister. All these references must have been easily accessible to an age where the survival of the pagan gods in the guises of veiled Christian symbols was a reality. When, in the midst of the so-called frivolous action of the second act, Estrella turns to Rosaura and addresses her as Astraea, the audience may have reviewed the previous action in light of the new role assumed by the heroine.

La vida es sueño begins with Rosaura's arrival in Poland, dressed as a man, exclaiming that she could not control the horse-hippogriff she was riding. Critics such as Valbuena Briones, Bandera, and Maurin have noted the symbolism of Rosaura's fall from the horselike creature.[17] The inability to control a horse has been related, since classical times, to the inability to control one's passions. Rosaura's fall is thus a moral one: she has been dishonored by Astolfo. The hippogriff, a monster described in terms of the confusion of the four elements, represents the chaos created by lack of control over the sexual appetite, as Cilveti points out.[18] It also serves to set the tone for the first scene of the *comedia*, where chaos reigns. Indeed, *hipogrifo* is the first word uttered in *La vida es sueño*, and its crucial placement may be indicative of further implications. In the *Orlando furioso*, the hippogriff plays an important role since it is utilized by Astolfo in travels and battles. He listens to Andronica's prophecy of a new golden age that will dawn during the reign of Charles V. Calderón's first mention of Astraea coincides with Rosaura's attempt to recover her portrait held by Astolfo. The duke's name and title, in the minds of a seventeenth-century audience, were probably linked with Ariosto's character and therefore with the myth of the golden age and with the mythical hippogriff. The Astolfo-Rosaura-Astraea connection in the second act propels us back to the first scene of the *comedia*. We then realize that Rosaura's fall from the hippogriff, Astolfo's beast, is a most appropriate image.

The Rosaura-Astolfo connection reveals the bestial side of the human being and represents a moral fall that can be equated with the Biblical fall of man or with the descent of the ages in classical mythology. The chaos that reigns in the first scene and the lack of harmony among the elements[19] are typical of the landscape that prevails after the expulsion from the terrestrial paradise or after the loss of the golden age. A nature that provides man with bounteous gifts has been replaced by a "confuso laberinto / de esas desnudas peñas" (vv. 6-7) that proves harmful to Rosaura. Visually, Rosaura's fall from the hippogriff is not as dramatic as her descent from the *monte eminente* (v. 15) to the dark depths where a prison dominates the landscape.

This is reminiscent of the fall of the constellations to earth as depicted in Seneca's *Thyestes*. Yet there is a kind of ambiguity here. The celestial sign may have fallen to earth, signaling the destruction of the universe, or Astraea's fall may be taken to mean that she has returned to earth at a time of deepest darkness to herald the return of a golden age. The chaos and confusion of the sublunary realm during the depths of the iron age are to be transformed into peace and harmony.

This type of visualization of Virgo's fall and/or return is not unique to Calderón. It may be found in Vélez de Guevara's *Vitrudes Vencen Señales*[20] and in Shakespeare's *Titus Andronicus*, where Titus and his friends shoot arrows at the constellations, attempting to make the gods aware of man's plight under the tyrannical rule of the wicked Saturnine. Lucius hits the zodiacal sign Virgo, bringing this goddess to earth. Significantly, Lucius is the one who restores justice in the empire at the play's conclusion. Rosaura's initial arrival in *La vida es sueño* can be considered auspicious, but is also replete with images of descent. She falls from a horse and she falls into Poland; she is a fallen woman and maybe even a fallen constellation. Rosaura's relationship to Astraea-Virgo leads us to ponder if her fall signals the destruction of the world or heralds a new age.

It may seem ironic that Virgo-Astraea should have returned as a dishonored woman. Yet this is a most appropriate "disguise" for Kali Yuga, the Indian equivalent of the iron age, a time when lust and violence are said to prevail. We soon discover that Rosaura seeks to restore her honor. Taking her place as an oppressed and suffering human in a dark age, the "goddess" may be able to lift others to the highest level of fulfillment as she lifts herself. Cesáreo Bandera has argued that Rosaura brings violence into Poland: "Es decir, lo que ve Basilio en los signos del horóscopo es lo mismo que introduce Rosaura en el reino . . . una violencia catastrófica."[21] I would take the opposite stance: she is the hope for future harmony, and the violence that takes place is simply the ordering of the land. The violence visualized by Basilio is but a small part of the whole. He never looked beyond to the silence after a great upheaval. Rosaura may be seen as the cause of violence, but her true nature is found in the myth of the return of Astraea.

Rosaura and Segismundo, critics remind us, should be studied as parallel lives. We have seen that this is also the case when approaching the work from a mythical perspective. They are both children of Saturn. The bipolarity of this god and planet is clearly revealed in the work. As children of Saturn, both Rosaura and Segismundo should be capable of descending to the most unfathomable depths or of attaining the highest wisdom. Bestiality is one of the malefic qualities of the planet. Rosaura succumbed to the bestial side when she was thrown by the "hippogriff." Segismundo also acknowledges his bestial nature: "Soy un hombre de las fieras / y una fiera de los hombres" (vv. 210-11). In his first soliloquy, he complains that the beast has more freedom than he does. Segismundo must come to realize that the tower of guilt and suffering can be overcome.

Rosaura is the divine aid who will lead him beyond his present limitations. Her appearance at the tower and his unexpected response, as William Whitby has pointed out, are the first hint of his future transformation. When Segismundo realizes that he has been overheard, his wrath descends upon Rosaura. His pride and vanity are countered by her humility and compassion. When she first heard Segismundo cry out, she was filled with "piedad" (v. 173). Now that he is about to murder her, she does not hesitate to kneel, to humble herself before him and appeal to his compassion: "Si has nacido / humano, baste el postrarme / a tus pies para librarme" (vv. 187-89). From the very beginning of the *comedia*, Rosaura's influence on Segismundo is a positive one. She tempers his fiery nature ("un volcán, un Etna hecho," v. 164) with her softness. This recalls the Mars-Venus imagery in *La gran Cenobia*, where Decio's martial nature is balanced by Cenobia. Yet there is much more here than a harmonizing of the emotions. When Rosaura kneels before the imprisoned prince she neutralizes the malefic celestial portents observed by Basilio, teaching Segismundo humility and eliciting from him tenderness and compassion. In the third act, the defeated Basilio will prostrate himself at the feet of his son in fulfillment of the omens. Segismundo's forgiveness of his father has its roots in the earlier scene.

From the very beginning Rosaura, in her role as Astraea, is preparing the way for future harmony. Her plight arouses compassion, but her beauty creates admiration, being a reflection of the eternal values contained within the self. Segismundo claims that he has studied all of nature, but only the presence of this stranger has aroused such wonderment in him:

> tú sólo, tú, has suspendido
> la pasión a mis enojos,
> la suspensión a mis ojos,
> la admiración al oído.
> [vv. 219-22]

This can be the reaction of man in the face of the eternal. But the physical Rosaura, even though she is dressed as a man, also affects the prince, foreshadowing his passionate response to her at the court. In the confusion of this world they do not recognize themselves and each other as children of Saturn. They are, however, brothers in suffering, rejection, and incarceration. In spite of the labyrinth of earthly confusion, Rosaura has not lost her way. She has fulfilled her purpose at this time: "Hoy el cielo me ha guiado" (v. 249).

Rosaura's role as Astraea is further clarified in her conversation with Clotaldo. He orders Rosaura and Clarín arrested, and she again has resort to kneeling:

> Ya que vi que la soberbia
> te ofendió tanto, ignorante
> fuera en no pedirte humilde
> vida que a tus plantas yace.
> Muévate en mi la piedad.
> [vv. 339-43]

But Clotaldo seems at this point as blind to Rosaura-Astraea as Basilio was when he prophesied the future without envisioning her truth. The fathers of Segismundo and Rosaura seem caught in a labyrinth that offers no hope. It is the younger generation that must bring about the fulfillment of a myth. Rosaura, being told that she must die, wants to hand Clotaldo her sword so that he will remember the virtue of compassion: "Y si he de morir, dejarte / quiero, en fe desta piedad, / prenda que pudo estimarse" (vv. 366-68). Clotaldo does begin to feel pity and compassion on receiving the sword since it is the one he gave Violante, Rosaura's mother, when he departed from Muscovy, leaving her pregnant. Rosaura states in handing Clotaldo the sword:

> Que la guardes
> te encargo, porque aunque yo
> no sé que secreto alcance,
> sé que esta dorada espada
> encierra misterios grandes;
> [vv. 370-74]

On the surface, the mystery of the sword is that it belongs to Clotaldo and identifies Rosaura as his son (daughter). Yet, as Everett Hesse has noted, Rosaura's sword is also significant as a symbol of justice.[22] We also note that it is a golden sword, and thus related to the harmony of the earliest age. This is the real mystery of the weapon. Indeed, the word *misterio*, as Edgar Wind reminds us, had a particular meaning for the Renaissance, since the Florentine Platonists related it to the unveiling of truths behind certain myths.[23] Calderón often uses it to alert the audience to deeper meanings in his *autos*. The mystery of the sword is more than Violante's and Rosaura's dishonor; its highest meaning is the paradoxical descent of Astraea-Virgo in the guise or "veil" of a dishonored woman.

As Rosaura points to the *misterio* of the golden sword in the tower, Basilio reveals a related mystery to Astolfo and Estrella at the palace. It is fitting that Astolfo be in attendance since, like his counterpart in Ariosto, he will witness the foretelling of an astral-imperial occurrence. Basilio, as T.E. May notes, is a kind of Renaissance magus.[24] His knowledge of astrology allows him to read the celestial signs, while his study of other occult sciences leads him to an interpretation of dreams and omens. Having described to the courtiers the political turmoil that he foresees if Segismundo is allowed to rule, Basilio recounts the amazing astral phenomena that he noted at the prince's birth and that led him to imprison him:

> éste fue, porque, anegado,
> el orbe entre incendios vivos,
> presumió que padecía
> el último parasimo.
>
> [vv. 692-95]

In these words, the king is evoking that apocalyptic fear of destruction present in myths from many cultures. It recalls the *pralaya* or dissolution at the end of Kali Yuga[25] more accurately, it describes the Roman fear of *ekpyrosis*, since Basilio describes the possible end of the cosmos through fire. A child's destructive destiny, as evinced by the fact that even at birth he would kill his own mother like a "víbora humana" (v. 675), had to be stopped, claimed Basilio. It was this fear that led him to incarcerate his own son at birth.

Basilio's actions parallel those of Saturn, who chose to devour his own children when he was told that one of his offspring would dethrone him. Calderón could have derived the idea of a king who imprisons his own son due to an astrological forecast from Lope de Vega's *Lo que ha de ser*, a play where the Saturn myth is central to the action.[26] In addition, Lope de Vega's *El gran duque de moscovia*, a literary antecedent of *La vida es sueño*,[27] includes a ruler also named Basilio who kills his son. Immediately preceding the killing, the son compares himself to Jupiter and his father to Saturn. Calderón's interest in the myth, derived from his personal concern with the father-son relationship, may have become associated with the horoscope motif from these two plays. In utilizing this myth he includes one more element of the Astraea story and thus adds cohesiveness to the work,

since Saturn was the ruler of the golden age. Any discussion of Basilio's role in *La vida es sueño* must take into account the ambivalence
of this astral god, who could act as the benign ruler of an idealized
world or become the tyrant who must be dethroned by Jupiter.

Indeed, the proud and determined Basilio has second thoughts
and becomes somewhat magnanimous as he continues to discuss Segismundo's plight, finally explaining his resolve to free his son:

> porque el hado más esquivo,
> la inclinación más violenta,
> el planeta más impío,
> solo el albedrío inclinan,
> no fuerzan el albedrío.
>
> [vv. 787-91]

In these words, Basilio is espousing the medieval Catholic attitude
towards astrology as expressed in the writings of Thomas Aquinas.
Predictions usually come true since human beings follow their passions and instincts which arise from material stimuli. Only the wise
man can invalidate the astrologer's horoscope by using his reason
and free will to overcome the passions. Basilio stresses that Segismundo will be able to overcome the stars if he acts with *valor* and
prudencia (v. 1109). The prince certainly evinces valor during his stay
at the palace. Yet, as Robert Pring-Mill points out, Segismundo cannot show *prudencia* since, according to Thomas Aquinas, it is not an
innate virtue, but one that is acquired through experience, something
the prince lacks due to his imprisonment.[28] The father has prepared
a test that his son must fail. Saturn was recognized by Renaissance
astrologers as the *planeta mas impío* (v. 789). Basilio can be viewed as
that malefic influence that is leading Segismundo to disaster.

Paralleling Segismundo's failure at court, Rosaura is unable to restore her honor. All she can do is to recapture her portrait from As-
tolfo, before it falls into Estrella's hands. Segismundo's meeting with
Rosaura-Astraea at the court also appears as unfortunate on the surface, but acquires positive significance when carefully analyzed.
Since she is now dressed as a lady, she arouses the prince's passions.
On the surface, their meeting is tense, filled with lust and violence.
Yet Segismundo's courtly language is at odds with his avowed purpose. He again brings up certain images he had used in praise of
Estrella, but now he takes them to extremes, ascribing to Rosaura the
highest values in visible creation:

> Pues ¿cómo, si entre flores, entre estrellas
> piedras, signos, planetas, las más bellas

prefieren, tú has servido
la de menos beldad, habiendo sido
por más bella y hermosa,
sol, lucero, diamante, estrella y rosa?

[vv. 1612-17]

This apparently conventional praise reveals a dichotomy in Segismundo's self. On the one hand, he wants to possess, to do violence to Rosaura. On the other hand, he places her far above others, including Estrella. Segismundo establishes five categories: flowers, stars, signs, stones, and planets. He then presents Rosaura as the best example of each. She is the most beautiful flower, the rose; the ruling Ptolemaic planet, the sun; the most shining of stones, the diamond; and the leading star, *lucero* or Venus. The fifth correspondence, however, seems somewhat confused. Segismundo has mentioned that she is the most prominent *signo*, but in the summary, the only term left to match is *estrella*. This appears as a mistake at first glance: "star" is not a zodiacal sign. But we should not pass over this apparent mistake lightly. Rosaura's name (which he is not supposed to know at the time since she has assumed another identity) includes the most beautiful flower, *rosa*. She is also the sun since her name is an anagram for *auroras* (dawn). Her beauty is like that of Venus, while her firmness of purpose is like the diamond. Rosaura's name at court is Astraea, which means star-maiden. By saying that her sign is *estrella*, the prince is referring to the fact that Rosaura is Astraea-Virgo. In spite of passionate violence, there is a beginning realization in Segismundo.

In spite of glimmers of order and truth at the palace, it all ends in potential disaster since Segismundo is returned to the tower and Rosaura-Astraea begins to worry again about an alliance between Estrella and Astolfo which would dash her hopes of marrying the duke and restoring her honor. The dazzling world of the court may have proven unconquerable for the siblings in suffering, Segismundo and Rosaura. Yet she has been using her *ingenio* and he has begun to recognize and follow his true "star." Segismundo's return to the tower is not ill-advised at this point. The tower is no longer a mere jail, since the freedom to indulge in serious conversation and quiet meditation without the lure of the palace brings Segismundo closer to enlightenment. The process of Segismundo's transformation, to be discussed in chapter six, now accelerates as Clotaldo explains to the prince that the palace "dream" was the result of his going to sleep while listening to a story about an eagle.

The soaring eagle described by Clotaldo previously in his effort to ready Segismundo for the palace experience is tied to the notion of *imperio*. It recalls the Hapsburg eagles but, more important, it is reminiscent of the twelve eagles seen by Romulus on the founding of Rome. They are related to the mythical substructure of our play since they represent the twelve months of the Great Year, a cycle that would end in the destruction of imperial Rome.

After quiet moments of reflection at the end of act two, the third and final *jornada* is given to fast-paced action. It begins with a violence that seems to enact the fulfillment of the horoscope. The cosmic battle between the two luminaries, the sun and the moon, is mirrored in the civil war between father and son, king and prince. The darkest of ages seems to be ending in an *ekpyrosis*. Yet there are hints that this epoch "sin orden ni ley" (v. 3037) may lead to a new golden age. Segismundo's behavior shows a certain control in spite of the all-pervasive violence. This is first seen when the rebel soldiers come to rescue him from the tower. He acts in a guarded manner, dispassionately, recalling an example from nature: the impetuous almond tree that blossoms early in winter, but soon loses its *pompas* to the cold north wind (vv. 2307-37). Since the uncertain glories of life are like an insubstantial dream ("sé bien que la vida es sueño," v. 2344), it is best to act with the guidance of prudence and absolute principles.

Rosaura appears on a horse, recalling her first arrival in Poland. Now she does not fall, but controls the animal, the passions. She is also carrying the sword, symbol of Astraea's justice. She represents the infusion of the celestial into this relative realm of existence. Her role is of necessity subtle, but is not necessarily passive. The woman-goddess actively brings about a transformation within the prince. On seeing her, Segismundo exclaims, "El cielo a mi presencia la restaura" (v. 2689). Indeed, heaven is about to restore justice and harmonious rule through the figure of Astraea-Rosaura by completing Segismundo's transformation. He is now aware that Rosaura is both the suffering being who came to his tower and the beautiful vision he saw at the palace. He brings these two together, but settles for the highest vision, the celestial sign that has shown him how to be humble and have compassion. Opposites come together. The "twins" merge. The different aspects of the self are reconciled, but the higher values are preferred. Rather than take advantage of the *pompas* (v. 2954), Segismundo utters his famous line, "acudamos a lo eterno" (v. 2983). Relative existence acquires value and permanence only when it is infused with the absolute.

The meeting with authority, his father and his king, can now be productive. Although he triumphs over the father, fulfilling the horoscope, he also triumphs over his baser instincts, forgiving him and thus healing the wounded land. Segismundo's response of compassion triggered by Rosaura reminds us of Plato's alternate reading of the four ages in the *Republic*. In an "audacious fiction" Socrates tells the citizens that their youth was but a dream. Actually, they were formed and raised in the womb of the earth. Those that have the power to command are made of gold. Segismundo's youth, like that of the citizens of the Republic, could be called a dream. His transformation has made him one of the *gens aurea* that can lead the state.[29] Rosaura, an anagram for *auroras*, has subtly changed Segismundo, since the dawn of the new age must be conceived in the heart.

The horoscope has been fulfilled. The king has been humbled. The malefic planet Saturn no longer reigns supreme. Basilio's limitations allowed him to read but part of the celestial map, concentrating on the purgation that precedes enlightenment. The change of rulership from Saturn to Jupiter does not signal the end of the earliest age, but the actualization of a new golden age which has been brought about by the benefic influence of Astraea. Segismundo can be related to the child-savior of Virgil's *Fourth Eclogue*.[30] The new ruler will restore the empire according to the mandates of heaven he can now perceive in the "papeles azules / que adornan letras doradas" (vv. 3162-63). The return of the virgin has brought about the desired effects. According to Manilius, "She will produce a man to direct the laws of the state and the sacred code, one who will tend with reverence the hallowed temples of the gods."[31]

CHAPTER FIVE

The Serpent Star

ASTRAEA-VIRGO is but one of many features in the celestial map of *La vida es sueño*. Yet all references to the firmament can be linked to Astraea in that they either instill fear of apocalyptic destruction or build up hope for the coming of a new golden age. These celestial occurrences are always focused on Segismundo, since he is the person that serves to trigger future events in Poland. The prince, following the portents, has the potential of becoming the universal ruler who will reestablish the happiest of ages. Thus, while Rosaura-Astraea points to the possibilities and guides Segismundo, it is through him that we perceive how the astral-imperial elements of the myth become part of the historical process. In addition, Segismundo stands as the microcosmic pivot of the play. The links between stars and dreams, between myth and history, are to be found within his self.

Laurens Van der Post asserts that "at all times for all men, the dream was some sort of admiralty chart by which their lives were navigated and spread out, like Mercator's epic projection, on a map specially designed for their searching selves."[1] In the next two chapters, dreams will be taken as a point of departure. In *La vida es sueño*, this inner map is closely paralleled by the "papeles azules / que adornan letras doradas" (vv. 3166-67), the heavens where golden letters or stars form a book that can be deciphered through astrology. Inscape and cosmos, microcosm and macrocosm, are inextricably interrelated in the Spanish masterpiece where chart and book reveal mysteries that affect Basilio's actions and Segismundo's quest.[2] The journey towards Astraea, the constellation that presages a new golden age, takes place within the prince's own self.

The significance of the dream metaphor in *La vida es sueño* has been the subject of a number of studies. Some have dealt with the sources of this image; others have been concerned with Segismundo's moral response to this metaphor; while a third group has stressed the Platonic implications of the notion. Closer to our approach are essays by Everett W. Hesse and Julian Palley. Hesse adopts a Jungian approach to *La vida es sueño*. "Según la psicología de Jung, el subconsciente parece tener el poder de investigar los hechos y sacar conclusiones de ellos, como lo hace el consciente. . . . El subconsciente llega a sus decisiones instintivamente."[3] Palley espouses a more clearly Freudian interpretation of the *comedia* with its concomitant Oedipal complex. Yet Palley's views echo Hesse's: "Our waking life is interrelated with our dreams, the work of our subconscious, and we progress from one stage to another with the aid of our dreams."[4] Our approach will partake of this general view. But Palley and Hesse concentrate on the *notion* of dreams or on the *false* dream at the palace. In these two chapters we will deal with the *substance* of the two key dreams in *La vida es sueño* and their relationship to astral occurrences that mirror the action of the *comedia*.[5] In this chapter, the dream of the serpent will be analyzed, while chapter six will deal with the eagle.

At the conclusion of the first act, Basilio assembles his courtiers, including Estrella and Astolfo, the possible heirs to the crown of Poland, to reveal that he has a son and heir to the throne who, having been imprisoned shortly after birth, is now to be tested in order to determine his suitability as future king. Significant for our purposes are the reasons given by the king for his past behavior. His deep understanding of the *ciencias*, Basilio believes, challenges time itself since through this knowledge he can glimpse the future and thus strip coming events of surprise and wonder:

> pues cuando en mis tablas miro
> presentes las novedades
> de los venideros siglos;
> le gano al tiempo las gracias
> de contar lo que yo he dicho.
> [vv. 619-23]

At first glance this *ciencia*, which he calls at one point *matemáticas sutiles* (v. 614), may be equated with astrology.[6] The sky becomes a book that reveals the geography of future time (vv. 633-39). However, a careful look at the *prodigios* (v. 663) consulted by Basilio at the birth of his child reveals that they are not limited to astral occurrences. They can be divided into three types: astral, psychic, and sublunary, relating to the heavens, to man's inner world, and to the outer world. The eclipse is of the first type, the dream of the second, and the earthquake of the third. A *magus* such as Basilio would concentrate on those planes where the writings of providence would be most clearly expressed. God's purposes could be most easily deciphered from heavenly portents and dreams. Since man was considered to be a microcosm, heavenly writings could be mirrored in that inner chart that surfaces as a *sueño*. Indeed, Clorilene's dream as explained by Basilio is as ominous on the personal or microcosmic level as the eclipse is on the universal or macrocosmic plane. The dream foreshadows Clorilene's own death and Basilio's political and personal tragedy:

> su madre infinitas veces,
> entre ideas y delirios
> del sueño, vió que rompía
> sus entrañas atrevido
> un monstruo en forma de hombre,
> y entre su sangre teñido,
> le daba muerte, naciendo
> víbora humana del siglo.
>
> [vv. 668-75]

The dream has as its subject the birth of a *monstruo*. In the serpent conceit, Segismundo is described as human in form but viper in disposition.[7] Following Pliny's account, the violent birth of the snake had become a commonplace. A bestiary begins its description of the *víbora* with the statement that "the viper (*vipera*) is called this because it brings forth in violence (*vi*). The reason is that when its belly is yearning for delivery, the young snakes, not waiting for the timely discharge of birth, gnaw through the mother's side and burst out to her destruction."[8] During the Spanish Golden Age some doubts were expressed as to the veracity of this anecdote, but authors such as Juan de Pineda and Sebastián de Covarrubias repeat it: "los vivoreznos, los quales siendo en número muchos, los postreros que han tomado más cuerpo y fuerça, malsufridos y cansados de esperar, rompen el pecho de la madre."[9] The viper was also a popular emblematic subject. In the *Empresas espirituales y morales*, for example, Juan Francisco de Villava admonishes the offspring of this serpent in the following manner:

> Buen pago à vuestra madre le aveys dado
> Biboreznos traydores,
> Con una impiedad tan conocida,
> Pues rompiendole el lado,
> Con terribles dolores,
> Le days la muerte, porque os dio la vida.[10]

Golden Age poets were also fond of the image. In a passage by Lope de Vega, Belisa laments the departure of her lover and wonders if she ought to take revenge on the child that will be born from the affair. She fears, however, that the child will be like the viper off-spring, "que será vívora fiera, / que rompiendo mis entrañas, / saldrá dejándome muerta."[11] This classical anecdote was also found in Hor-apollo's *Hieroglyphica*, a book of symbols supposedly written by an Egyptian priest. According to Don Cameron Allen, the manuscript was found in 1419, printed in Greek in 1505, and reprinted at least thirty times in different languages during the sixteenth century. Its popularity during the period was immense, establishing the vogue of the emblem book. Renaissance writers believed that the Egyptians possessed a most ancient and thus a very pure kind of wisdom. In-deed, Marsilio Ficino was convinced that Horapollo's work supported the conjecture "that hieroglyphs were pictures of the Platonic Ideas."[12] This ancient book of symbols clearly states that "the viper is not born, but devours the belly of its mother as it emerges."[13] The *sabio* Basilio could not ignore such a statement.

Confirmation of the dream's validity through the death of Clori-lene and verification of the universal significance of the symbol of the viper would lead a *magus* such as Basilio to delve deeper into the hidden significance of this powerful image. The obvious implications of the dream are described by Covarrubias: "La ingratitud de los hijos pintavan los egypcios en el parto de la bívora." The lesson to be learned from this "hieroglyph" or emblem is described by Juan Fran-cisco de Villava: "La reverencia y piedad que se deve a los padres es una de las cosas que se encarecen en ambas leyes, escritas y de Gracia por si viniere alguno tan pervertido que, no le ·despierte el impulso natural." Yet the image refers to more than *ingratitud* versus *piedad*. We are told that the birth of vipers "symbolized children plotting against their parents."[14] The king's prediction that his son "había de poner en mí / las plantas" (vv. 720-21) is thus partially justified by the dream and the ensuing occurrences.

A seventeenth-century audience would also be acquainted with a second symbolic meaning of the birth of a viper. St. Ambrose con-siders the viper the most vile kind of beast due to its cunning in mat-ters of lust. The male viper was often depicted in unnatural copula-tion with a sea eel (Murena), while the female viper was a favorite image of misogynists. Beryl Rowland adds that in the sixteenth cen-tury, the *víbora* signified "a common woman or harlot lying in the way, to sting men with the contagion of her wantonness and lust."[15] Such behavior was often associated with adultery. Thus, while Basilio addresses himself to the negative aspects of his offspring, he is silent about the other possible connotations of Clorilene's dream, which would cast doubt on his honor and on Segismundo's legitimacy.

In Clorilene's dream, the son was described as a *monstruo*, a term applied to Segismundo throughout the play. It is derived from *monstrum* or divine portent of misfortune and was used to name a creature that was often composed of different species of animals, or of animals and man. Segismundo in *La vida es sueño* accepts the term to describe his own double nature. Speaking of monsters to Rosaura, he refers to the chimera (v. 210), which is part lion, part goat, and part serpent. In this manner, the notion of carnal love is introduced, since this fabled creature was associated with lust in medieval times.[16] Segismundo then refers to himself as a *monstruo humano* (v. 209), a composite of man and beast. His initial behavior towards Rosaura reinforces belief in his monstrous character: "Sólo porque me has oído / entre mis membrudos brazos / te tengo de hacer pedazos" (vv. 183-85). The description of the *membrudos brazos* is reinforced visually, since the spectator observes that Segismundo is chained and is dressed in skins.

According to Augustine, it was possible for humans to have monstrous offspring who would still have souls.[17] In certain traditions, *monstruos* were thought to be the result of illicit sexual relations. John O'Connor, studying the French version of the *Amadís de Gaula* and its influence in Elizabethan England, notes that in these chivalric romances "incest is frequently another source of monstrosities." He mentions in this connection the offspring of Gregaste and her son— a Cavalyon, which is part horse, part man, and part lion. O'Connor also refers the reader to the description of the dreaded Endriago, who was born of the incestuous union of the giant Bandaguida and her father. O'Connor adds that "the sin and terror surrounding monstrous births contrast sharply with the circumstances under which heroes enter the world."[18] Basilio's son seems to belong to the tradition of monstrosities rather than to the heroic mold.

The imagery associated with Segismundo tends to support the contention that he is a monster resulting from an illicit sexual relationship. Margaret S. Maurin has studied the image of the *monstruo* and *La vida es sueño*. "The monster image thus signifying the domination of reason by violent passions, its identification with Segismundo ends from the moment he assumes his basic humanity, and accepts the restraining power of his reason."[19] At the conclusion of the play, the viper's *ingratitud* is transformed into its opposite, *piedad*, in the figure of Segismundo who pardons Basilio. Calderón thus incorporates in his *comedia* both the warning contained in the viper emblem and the lesson that should be derived from a study of this image. Among the several monsters linked to Segismundo, Maurin mentions the Minotaur, since the image of the labyrinth is a salient one in the *comedia*. "Both are considered prodigies and kept from public view, hidden in a labyrinth, real or figurative, but nourished and cared for."[20] But the significance of the Minotaur in the *comedia* is not fully understood by Maurin. Basilio refers to his son as a *monstruo* immediately after describing heavenly *prodigios*. Latin-Greek lexica of the Middle Ages connected both words with the Greek *teras*. Both terms deal with amazing natural phenomena that are signs of divine power and will. The Romans were particularly apt at divination from these occurrences. In the *De Diferentiis Vocabulorum*, Marcus Cornilius Fronto notes the similar meanings of these words, but insists that the student should be careful to distinguish between them: "*Monstrum* is something against nature, as for example the Minotaur. *Prodigium* is something from which detriment is expected."[21] The terms *prodigio*, *monstruo*, and *Minotauro* are thus closely linked. They refer to amazing examples of God's power and wisdom, usually with negative connotations. Maurin also fails to mention that this *monstruo*, part human and part bull, is the result of an illicit relationship. In Knossos, the capital of the Cretan Empire, Queen Pasiphae was seduced by a magnificent bull. From this union the Minotaur was born. King Minos had the labyrinth built to hide his offspring just as in Poland Basilio incarcerates his son in a tower.

Calderón, aware that both the tradition of the monster offspring and the image of the birth of the viper could be related to lust and illicit sexual relations, carefully blends them in another play, *La devoción de la cruz*. In the second act, Curcio narrates his wife's pregnancy and childbirth in the same manner as Basilio explains the birth of Segismundo in *La vida es sueño*. Curcio mistakenly believes that the children are the product of an adulterous relationship, and warns his wife, Rosmira:

> En tus entrañas
> como la víbora, traes
> a quien te ha de dar la muerte.
> Indicio ha sido bastante
> el parto infame que esperas.
> [p. 405][22]

Thus in both *La devoción de la cruz* and *La vida es sueño* a wife is called a viper in a lengthy *relación* told by a husband who is attempting to justify his cruel behavior. Explaining Curcio's actions in *La devoción de la cruz*, Edwin Honig notes, "It is evident that by accusing his wife of infidelity and seeking to kill her on admittedly groundless evidence, Curcio touches off a series of actions which end in the death of his three children and his wife."[23] Basilio's behavior and its results are very similar. His actions bring Poland to the brink of civil war. His veiled references to Clorilene's lustful intentions and possible infidelity are probably as unfounded as Curcio's suspicions. Yet his interpretation of his wife's dream will affect events as significantly as Curcio's imaginings: in both *comedias* a son will come to believe that he is in fact a monstrous offspring.

Indeed, Eusebio, the child left in the *monte* in *La devoción de la cruz*, is described as a kind of *fiera* or *monstruo*. He attempts to kill his nurse in a manner reminiscent of the offspring that kills the maternal viper. Eusebio's "diabólica fuerza" (p. 393) is the same kind of energy that impels the Endriago in the *Amadís*. But while the monsters in the chivalric romance have few redeeming qualities, both Segismundo and Eusebio clearly evince that soul of which Augustine speaks. In both *comedias* then, the conflict is not so much an exterior confrontation as it is an interior one. The protagonists are not concerned with the destruction of a dragon or Minotaur, since the archetypical battle takes place within their own psyche: they must vanquish their own bestial nature. If there is a significant outer conflict, it is between father and son. The close relationship between *La devoción de la cruz* and *La vida es sueño* posited by Alexander Parker ought to make the images of the viper and the monster as significant a link between the plays as the presence of an authoritarian father figure.

Joseph Campbell, taking King Minos as an example of the authoritarian father, refers to him as "tyrant Holdfast—out for himself."[24] The tyrant, he claims, is an aspect of the dragon that the hero must deal with. In *La vida es sueño*, the images of the viper, the monster, the Minotaur, and the figure of the tyrannical father as King Minos possess an archetypical significance. By conquering his own viper-nature, the selfish passions, Segismundo becomes the epitome of the hero who can overcome Basilio's prediction. Conquest of the self, Campbell explains, is equal to atonement with the father, since both are seen as rejections of the notion of egocentric self-aggrandizement. In order to arrive at this state, "the hero may derive hope and assurance from the helpful female figure. . . . For if it is impossible to trust the terrifying father-face, then one's faith must be centered elsewhere."[25] In *La vida es sueño*, Rosaura is such a figure. We have seen in the previous chapter how Rosaura-Astraea leads Segismundo to inner transformation and outer wisdom. She is a figure that both parallels the hero and guides him. From the textual evidence presented thus far, we may argue that the suspicion of an illicit parental relationship looms not only in Rosaura's but also in Segismundo's past, thus adding one more element to that "fearful symmetry" carefully constructed by the playwright.

We have seen how Clorilene's dream has become a reality that mirrors certain archetypes and myths. This should come as no surprise since, in Campbell's view, "dream is the personalized myth, myth the depersonalized dream; both myth and dream are symbolic in the same general way of the dynamics of the psyche. But in the dream the forms are quirked by the peculiar troubles of the dreamer, whereas in myth the problem and solutions shown are directly valid for all mankind."[26] Clorilene's dream of past sin and future disaster is the "personalized myth" of act one. Let us cast a glance at the heavens and see if the *prodigios* there reveal similar mysteries and provide clearer indications of the cosmic implications present in the individual *sueño*. Basilio notes that Segismundo's birth is marked by an eclipse:

> Nació en horóscopo tal
> que el sol, en su sangre tinto,
> entraba sañudamente
> con la luna en desafío . . .
> El mayor, el más horrendo
> eclipse que ha padecido
> el sol, después que con sangres
> lloró la muerte de Cristo,
> éste fué . . .
>
> [vv. 680-92]

The eclipse is described by the king in terms of the battle between the two Ptolemaic luminaries, the sun and the moon, the latter overcoming the source of light, although briefly. Campbell, delving into the motif of the slain Minotaur, which plays such a significant role in *La vida es sueño*, considers it as a recurring image and refers to a plaque from ancient Sumer (*circa* 2500 B.C.). The picture is an ancient echo of Theseus slaying the monster since it "shows the ever-dying, ever-living *lunar* bull, consumed through all time by the lion-headed *solar* eagle."[27] The opposition moon-sun, then, is related to the images of the Minotaur and the eagle. In other words, this is the same kind of opposition that exists within Segismundo's psyche and that is reflected dynamically in the play by the presentation of the labyrinth motif in act one and the eagle dream in act two, where Clotaldo

explains the palace episode in terms of this imperial bird: "Como habíamos hablado, / de áquella aguila, dormido, / tus sueños imperios
han sido" (vv. 2140-42).

When Basilio observes the eclipse of the sun, he associates it with
the death of a solar hero, Christ. Noting that a portent of death occurs
at the birth of his son, he concludes that the child will be linked to
forces associated with destruction and chaos. He does not realize that
Segismundo, as a microcosm, will embody the universal conflict of
mighty opposites as inscribed in the heavens. He also fails to note
that the eclipse was a brief occurrence—after death there may be resurrection. Basilio's negative interpretation of inscape and horoscope,
equating Segismundo with the viper that kills the mother and the
moon that dims the light of the solar hero, externalizes a conflict and
places the son in opposition to the father. Yet by incarcerating Segismundo in the tower, Basilio is actually embarking the child upon the
hero-quest.

Bruce Wardropper has analyzed the beginning of La vida es sueño
as an exposition of the pains of childbirth. Following his lead, Everett
W. Hesse considers the tower as a symbol of the womb. Referring to
the quest of the solar hero, Erich Neumann ties the images of womb
and labyrinth into one: "The labyrinthine way is always the first part
of the night sea voyage, the descent of the male following the sun
into the devouring underworld, into the deathly womb of the Terrible
Mother."[28] He adds that this group of archetypal symbols is com-
pleted by the moon, identical to the womb in this context, and by the
serpent, noting the crescent moons depicted on the snakes held by
the hero in designs by the Chimu Indians of Peru. Thus moon, snake,
Minotaur, and a tower that stands for labyrinth or womb are the images that attend Segismundo from birth to the advent of his helper,
Rosaura. With her aid and the guidance of the inner chart of dreams,
he will be able to soar, to defeat the bestial side of his nature and
become the eagle, symbol of the solar hero. The eclipse, the "night
sea voyage," will give way to "resurrection," the return of the hero
or, utilizing the language of La vida es sueño, rebirth.[29] After all, the
serpent image could be a positive symbol. Commenting on a passage
in the Gospels (Matthew 7:13), Augustine asserts, "He who sheds his
skin, like the snake in flight, readies himself to enter the strait gate
of Heaven."[30] Segismundo will become the newly born serpent or the
eagle that soars to heaven.

The Segismundo of the first act, with whom we are concerned in
this chapter, is far from achieving the heroic qualities that would
identify him with the perfect prince.[31] Instead, the atmosphere of loss

and confusion, the animal and monster imagery together with the nightmarish ambience, situate the action in a demonic realm as defined by Northrop Frye in his study of the structure of romance. The importance of the highest plane, the heavens, in the first act as reflected in Basilio's casting of a horoscope, should not obscure this identification. Frye argues that any level can be ambivalent. Indeed, the malefic stellar and planetary influences encountered here are typical of themes of descent.[32]

Although the eclipse is the only explicit information concerning the heavens that is provided in the first act of *La vida es sueño*, past audiences may have speculated on the actual astrological chart prepared by Basilio. Such an investigation, particularly in the case of a "monstrous" birth, would have been encouraged by the heated discussion on this matter that took place in scholarly circles at the time. A. Bouché Leclerq comments: "Les ouvrages des astrologues de la Renaissance abondent en examples des naissances monstreuses." According to the astrological treatises of the epoch, the placement of the luminaries would be of particular significance in determining monster births. In our case, the eclipse would certainly bode ill for the child. Bouché Leclerq adds, "Si, de plus, des 'luminaires' se trouvent en des signes 'quadrupèdes' ou 'animaux,' le monstre n'aura pas forme humaine. Ce sera un animal sauvage."[33] The zodiacal sign or constellation in which one of the luminaries was present at Segismundo's birth should be in the shape of the animal he resembles at birth. Yet the signs of the zodiac do not seem to yield a figure that would "cause" the formation of a viper. Interestingly, one astronomer writes that "out of the twenty-five days, from the 21st of November to the 16th of December, which the sun spends in passing from Libra to Sagittarius, only nine days are spent in the Scorpion, the other sixteen being occupied in passing through Ophiuchus."[34] He thus considers that Ophiuchus is more of a zodiacal sign than Scorpio. In the heavenly map, this constellation is drawn as a man holding a serpent, which some associate with the figure of St. Paul with the Maltese viper. The negative connotations of the viper are counterbalanced by the identification of Ophiuchus with Asclepius, the king of medicine who lent his name to the best-known hermetic treatise and who associated serpents with wisdom and prudence.[35]

Seventeenth-century audiences may have linked Segismundo's viper birth with the presence of a luminary, at the time of an eclipse, in Ophiuchus. Clorilene's dream would thus mirror figures in the heavenly chart. Segismundo's negative side would be associated with the viper, while his subsequent conversion could reflect the positive interpretation of the constellation as Asclepius. Indeed, the fact that prudence is the serpent's central attribute has a direct bearing on Segismundo's conversion since this is the virtue Segismundo most lacks during the palace adventure.[36]

An examination of the geographical and chronological setting of *La vida es sueño* may aid us in further establishing that Segismundo was born under the sign of Ophiuchus. Ervin Brody claims that "Calderón succeeded in recreating the historical Poland of Sigismund III in the midst of the turbulent Russian Time of Troubles."[37] These years (1604-13) are characterized by civil wars related to Polish candidates for the throne of Moscow; the reluctance of the Polish nobility to accept Muscovites as rulers, as in the case of Boris Godunov; and Polish support for Demetrius as reflected in Lope de Vega's play *El gran duque de Moscovia*.[38] Brody adds that Basilio is a composite figure, not only reflecting the political turmoil of the epoch, but also the astrological debates that reached their climax with Galileo's trial: "Calderón united the philosophy of the two unorthodox astronomers—the Pole Copernicus and the Italian Galileo—and resurrected it in the pseudo-scientific experiment of King Basilio of Poland."[39] Although Galileo's trial may have inspired Calderón to create the figure of Basilio, however, resemblances between Corpernicus, Galileo, and Basilio are negligible.

In a recent article, Hana Jechová convincingly argues that the setting is a blend of Polish and Czech motifs. Basilio comes closer to reflecting the interests of Emperor Rudolph II than those of King Sigismund III.[40] The contention that Rudolph II delved into the occult sciences is supported by R.J.W. Evans's study of the Hapsburg monarchy. He notes that Central European humanism flourished late, during the second half of the sixteenth century. Humanistic studies reached their peak at the court of Rudolph II in Prague (1576-1612),[41] and were focused on astral magic and the problem of the reconciliation of opposites. Both of these concerns are central to *La vida es sueño*. Basilio's interest in the occult parallels Rudolph's, while the images of eagle and serpent central to the two major dreams in the *comedia* are traditionally associated with the contrariety inherent in nature.

Another point, which Jechová fails to mention in her important article, is that Rudolph did not just delve into the occult sciences, but was fond of surrounding himself with the best European minds interested in alchemy, astrology, and even magic. At the start of his reign, Johann Kepler had already acquired great fame in Europe, not so much for his discovery of the elliptical orbit of planets, but for having predicted in his first almanac "a major cold spell and a Turkish invasion, both of which duly occurred."[42] At the death of Tycho Brahe, Kepler was made imperial astrologer, and charged with keeping track of the heavenly map in order to interpret astral portents and predict furture events.

When a new star, or *nova*, appeared in the heavens in 1604, Kepler was pressed by the emperor to come forth with an accurate astrological forecast. This was the second new star to appear in the sky. The first *nova* had intruded on the heavens in the year 1572. According to Lynn Thorndike, this event was more of a shock to Europe than Copernicus's theories.[43] After all, there was supposed to be neither generation nor corruption in the sphere of the fixed stars and yet this shining apparition of 1572 slowly faded and finally disappeared in 1574. Astrologers, philosophers, and theologians argued about its nature. They called it a new star, a new divine creation, a comet, and a meteor in the ethereal regions. Tycho Brahe, Kepler's predecessor at court, had been much preoccupied with this matter. This greatest miracle of nature in the eyes of many announced great political and religious events. It was followed by several comets which kept up astrological speculation in 1577, 1580, and 1585. It was no wonder that when the 1604 *nova* appeared Kepler was pressed to explain its nature and meaning. To add to the excitement over heavenly portents, the 1604 *nova* became visible just one year after a most important conjunction between Jupiter and Saturn had taken place in Sagittarius, one of the signs of the fiery trigon. Such a meeting occurred at approximately eight-hundred-year intervals, and the two previous ones had signaled the birth of Christ and the end of the Dark Ages with the advent of Charlemagne as Holy Roman Emperor.[44] Tommaso Campanella, believing that Spain was destined to expand its rule into a universal empire shortly before the end of the world, wrote a treatise on how and why Spain was to accomplish this. He points to this Jupiter-Saturn conjunction as one of the signs that reveal such a destiny since the Great Conjunction takes place in Sagittarius, which is the constellation of Spain. He adds that this event "will discover many secrets," upon which he will discourse at a later time.[45]

Campanella's was one of many interpretations. All of Europe became obsessed with deciphering this double portent. Max Caspar explains that "there were many interpretations. There was talk of a universal conflagration, of the Day of Judgment, of the overthrow of the Turkish kingdom, of a general revolution in Europe, of the appearance of a great new monarch: *Nova stella, novus rex.*"[46] The imperial astrologer dedicated an entire book to this matter. This monograph, which appeared in 1606 and was the source of much controversy, was entitled *De stella nova in pede Serpentarii*. The fact that the star appeared in the constellation of the serpent and meant for some the end of the world, while for others it signified the arrival of a universal empire, may have led Calderón to fashion the figure of Basilio as a composite of Rudolph II and his wise astrologer Kepler, although keeping in mind that the celestial events could well apply to a future Spanish emperor as Campanella had predicted. Segismundo's birth would clearly be signaled by that new star in the Ophiuchus constellation, where the eclipse that rivaled the one at Christ's death had also taken place. These portents were the macrocosmic reflections of the dream of the snake birth experienced by Clorilene. Opposing predictions based on these events could very well fit Segismundo, since he is an ambivalent figure at the beginning of the *comedia*.

Basilio's son does have a historical counterpart in the annals of Rudolph II's reign, according to Jechová: "Un fils illegitime fou, dont jusqu'à nos jours les guides rancontent des histoires effrayantes à Cesky Krumlov où il a été enfermé."[47] Calderón was bound to know this story of Rudolph's mad child, don Giulio, and his audience could have easily understood the connection between Segismundo and the historical figure. After all, the Spanish court kept close contact with the imperial Hapsburgs, in spite of the continuing antagonism between the two branches of the family. Rudolph was a well-known figure in Spain, where he spent the eight years from 1563 to 1571, together with his brother Ernst, "on the insistance of their uncle Philip II."[48] Furthermore, Rudolph's youngest natural daughter, Ana Dorotea, was taken to Madrid in 1624 when she was only twelve years old. There she entered the convent of the *Descalzas Reales*. A guide to the monastery notes: "Período de singular florecimiento para las Bellas Artes en el Monasterio, fue el de los años en que en él vivió sor Ana Dorotea, Marquesa de Austria, hija del Emperador Rodolfo II."[49] Dispatches from the Tuscan Embassy in Madrid, preserved today in the *Archivio di Stato* in Florence and dated 1633 and 1634, the years in which Calderón was in the process of composing *La vida es sueño*, demonstrate Ana Dorotea's visibility at court and her closeness to King Philip IV.[50] It is thus plausible that Calderón is alluding to historical events well known in Madrid.

These parallels with don Giulio add new dimensions to Calderón's masterpiece. The historical prince is said to have exhibited many of the questionable traits of the Hapsburgs. Robert J.V. Evans states that "the family history of the Habsburgs affords numerous examples

both of extreme awareness of rank and instability of temperament."
Segismundo evinces this excessive awareness of rank in his behavior
at court during the second act. The instability of temperament in don
Giulio's case includes excesses "both homicidal and sexual."[51] Segismundo is seen as murdering a servant and attempting to satisfy his
lust even by force during the second act.

But Rudolph's child is not a totally negative figure. Evans adds
that "don Giulio reveals in an advanced form certain of his father's
tendencies: the Caesarist illusion, the life of fantasy."[52] By introducing Rosaura in the guise of Astraea, the goddess of imperial *renovatio*
evoked by Virgil in his Messianic Eclogue, Calderón reveals to the
audience that Segismundo ought to be viewed as a possible candidate
for universal empire. He shares the Caesarist illusion of many Hapsburgs. There is thus a certain timeliness in Calderón's portrayal of a
"monstruo humano" who may be heir to the throne. Peace through
universal empire or devastating conflict and oppression triggered by
a mad and cruel ruler are equally possible outcomes given the ambiguity of characterization at the beginning of the *comedia*. The blend of
historical allusion and astrological speculation infuses the play with
the tensions, fears, and aspirations of the European population during the first part of the seventeenth century.

References to an actual mad Hapsburg and to celestial portents
also lend a certain verisimilitude to a play that comes closer to the
mythical mode.[53] Robert ter Horst asserts that "*La vida es sueño* is both
in and against time, historical and anti-historical, specific and ab-
stract."[54] The allusive historical texture must have added a certain
vibrancy and immediacy to the almost predictive tone of the work.
Campanella's reference to Spain as the last universal empire would
not have escaped a learned audience. Premonitions of glory and disaster weaved together with lessons to astrologers, cruel kings, and
proud princes must have certainly triggered political speculation. It
may be that the prominent place accorded by Calderón himself to *La
vida es sueño* as the first *comedia* in the *primera parte* of his published
plays was the result not only of its mythical timelessness, but of its
timeliness.

Jechová hesitates to make a definitive statement on the parallel
between Rudolph's child and Basilio's offspring since the mad and
fierce historical personage died in prison at the age of twenty in the
year 1609, and was the illegitimate son of the emperor. The notion of
illegitimacy, as we have seen, should not stand in the way of such an
attribution. Calderón was not trying to create an exact historical parallel, but to produce an allusive texture that would provide a mythical

plot with a certain immediacy. The images of the monster and the viper in Clorilene's dream reinforce the parallel between Segismundo and don Giulio, Rudolph's illegitimate child. The snake in the *sueño* may also point to the heavenly portent that occupied the minds of astrologers during the first half of the seventeenth century. Kepler watched the serpent star, the comets, and the Grand Conjunction, attempting to explain these heavenly mysteries as signals for earth-shaking events; Basilio observed similar celestial occurrences, noting the great impact his son was to have. Kepler's theories are in accord with Basilio's examination of the "monster" birth. The imperial as-trologer thought that such births were even more significant omens than great celestial portents.[55] Yet Basilio's excessive trust in the lan-guage of the stars was probably derived from Rudolph, who not only delved into every occult science, but was also most superstitious, fearing certain ominous predictions and forgetting that man has free will and can overcome his fate.[56]

In the calendar for the year 1604, the year of the new serpent star, Kepler writes, "I may say with truth that whenever I consider in my thoughts the beautiful order, how one thing issues out of and is de-rived from another, then it is as though I had read a divine text, writ-ten into the world itself, not with letters but rather with essential objects, saying: man, stretch thy reason hither, so that thou mayest comprehend these things."[57] In *La vida es sueño*, the essential objects encountered in the inscape of dreams and the heavenly space of stars and luminaries contain within their multiple meanings the basis for the drama. Basilio's reading of Minotaur and viper, serpent star and eclipse, provides the conflict, the labyrinth of earthly confinement. Segismundo's dealings with his own viper nature and the final atone-ment with the father provide a resolution that is in keeping with in-ner and heavenly portents. The monster-son, guided by Rosaura-Astraea, has the potential of becoming a solar hero who will bring peace and happiness to mankind. Chaos and harmony, serpent and eagle, moon and sun, as Kepler hints, issues one from the other in that wonderful book written by the divine hand. Calderón mirrors this eternal truth, revealing aspects of the heavenly text inscribed in stars and souls in a work that aims at transcending conflict through a vision of wonderment at the ways in which God's creation unfolds.

CHAPTER SIX

The Imperial and Mystical Eagle

AT THE BEGINNING of the second act of *La vida es sueño* Clotaldo, Segismundo's teacher and jailor, recounts to Basilio how he has been able to transfer the prince from prison to palace. He has utilized knowledge of the hidden properties of certain plants in order to induce a deep sleep in Segismundo. As the prince is about to drink the potion, Clotaldo speaks to him of an eagle's flight in order to "levantarle más / el espíritu a la empresa" (vv. 1034-35). The avowed purpose of the anecdote is to aid Segismundo in assuming his proper role at the court. Clotaldo can thus be viewed as the wise teacher whose knowledge of nature enables him to perform amazing deeds and help others to improve themselves. Indeed, E.M. Wilson, although not focusing on the eagle's flight, views Clotaldo as an admirable figure, linking him to Rosaura. These two figures serve as guides to the prince.[1] Other critics tend to emphasize Clotaldo's less positive traits. Eugenio Súarez Galban discusses Clotaldo's vascillation, while Angel L. Cilveti notes "el servilismo y debilidad del padre (de Rosaura)," explaining that his eventual success is due to "la acción de la Providencia."[2] Perhaps the most comprehensive study of Clotaldo has been undertaken by C.A. Merrick, who associates him with Basilio: "As Basilio's agent in the main plot and close analogue in the subplot, Clotaldo illustrates the way in which a father and a teacher—the guardians of truth and order in the lives of those they rule—may pervert their proper roles, deny their commitments and divorce their charges from personal and social fulfillment. In both plots the petty egotism of the old constrains and endangers the young until the young break free."[3]

There are flaws in the characters of Basilio and Clotaldo, yet there is much knowledge and some wisdom as well. Both men are quite proficient at occult sciences. While Clotaldo is learned in terrestrial phenomena such as herbs and fauna, Basilio prefers to deal with celestial portents. Both men are concerned with man's inscape, with the dream. This chapter will discuss how Clotaldo's description of the eagle's flight affects the prince's behavior in the "false" dream at the palace. It will also help us to comprehend the mechanics of the prince's transformation. Furthermore, it supports and clarifies a key theme in the *comedia* and the subject of this study: the astral-imperial concerns emerging from Rosaura's role as the goddess Astraea. The eagle is the bird most often associated with our deity's imperial concerns. From Virgil through Dante to Calderón, the eagle is the emblem of a would-be universal ruler.

While the viper dream is associated with the element earth and is recounted by Segismundo's father, Basilio, in order to justify his cruel actions, the second dream is triggered by Clotaldo, Segismundo's surrogate father. The subject of the dream, the eagle, is a mystical and imperial bird associated with the lighter and higher elements, air and fire. Clotaldo mentions these two elements in his description of the flight:

> que, despreciando la esfera
> del viento, pasaba a ser,
> en las regiones supremas
> del fuego, rayo de pluma.
> [vv. 1039-42]

The eagle's upward voyage from the earth, through air, into the highest element covering the sublunary region, typifies images of ascent described by Northrop Frye.[4] It signals the eventual regaining of identity, position, and honor by both Segismundo and Rosaura, and thus mirrors the movement of the action in acts two and three. While the earthly viper represented displacement,[5] the eagle will aid in the convergence of fallen man with mythical identity.

Yet the few critics who have studied the image of the eagle in *La vida es sueño* have stressed its negative aspects. Vittorio Bodini shows how the anecdote of the imperial bird takes "il superbo titanismo di Sigismundo sino al parossismo." He sees the bird as an ambiguous symbol at best, "il quale da una parte è segno di generosa grandezza e nel contempo di superbia e di rivolta: segni contrari impliciti nella struttura del monarca potenziale."[6] Merrick points to Segismundo's immediate reaction to the eagle as proof that it was an ineffective lesson on Clotaldo's part.[7] This chapter will contend the opposite—that the eagle does teach Segismundo how to behave properly.

A study of the eagle motif must take into account Calderón's conception of the natural world. His presentation is usually hierarchical and orderly. The playwright's description of the four elements often includes the creatures and objects that typify each one. They, in turn, have their own ruler. At times, descriptions of elements are combined with other classifications; in other instances, trans-elemental imagery reflects the confusion created by man.[8] In *La humildad coronada de las plantas*, an *auto sacramental* produced in 1644, the *plantas* have gathered to select a monarch, since God expects this hierarchical organization:

> así entre las plantas hoy
> quiere que haya Rey, que siendo
> superior, presida; bien
> como el águila, en los vientos;
> como el delfín, en los mares,
> y el león en los desiertos.[9]

While the two heavier elements, earth and water, are presided over by the lion and the dolphin respectively, the eagle is the ruler of a lighter and higher element, air, according to Calderón's scheme. As such, it is used as the typical creature of this element in many *comedias*.[10] Since the *águila* rules over air, it must also preside over all birds. This is precisely what Clotaldo emphasizes to Segismundo in an attempt to bring out his royal nature in preparation for the palace ordeal:

> Encarecí el vuelo altivo,
> diciendo: "Al fin eres reina
> de las aves, y así a todas
> es justo que prefieras"
> [vv. 1044-47]

The eagle's exalted position in Calderón's *comedias*[11] is not an unusual feature. Since ancient times, this bird was the companion of ruling gods. In Indian mythology it was called Garuda and was the sun bird of Vishnu, enemy of serpents. In the classical period the eagle was Jupiter's bird. In Medieval times, the eagle becomes a symbol of empire. Emperor Frederick II, for example, conceived of his reign as a new golden age in the manner of Augustus Caesar's. He imitated the ancient ruler's coins, preserving the imperial eagle on the reverse side but portraying himself rather than Augustus on the front. The eagle's application was much broader even than this, since it denoted any sovereign rule. Covarrubias traces its significance from Alexander the Great to seventeenth-century Spain: "El águila con las dos cabezas significa el uno y otro Imperio, Oriental y Occidental; y éstos le pronosticaron a Alexandro Magno las dos águilas que aparecieron el día de su nacimiento, y han quedado incorporadas en las armas imperiales y en las de los Reyes de España, cuya potencia se ha estendido del Oriente al Poniente." The *Tesoro de la lengua* also mentions a Sigismundo, King of Poland, who "tuvo la empresa del águila que sube por el aire."[12]

Clotaldo's choice of the eagle as an anecdote to be recounted to one who is passing from a lowly state to that of prince is a most appropriate one, fitting both a Polish and a Spanish prince. In the first act, Basilio had rejected his own newly born son partially because of his wife's dream of a viper. Now Clotaldo is taking an image which stands in opposition to the first one and inducing a dream in Segismundo that will counterbalance his negative image of himself. Instead of a chthonic creature associated with treachery and the devil, Clotaldo will have Segismundo focus on a being from a higher element who is undertaking a flight to even loftier regions, a creature that has been associated with the solar hero, lofty enterprises, rulership, and empire.

The juxtaposition of serpent and eagle in the two dreams of *La vida es sueño* reveals that the conflict of opposites taking place within Segismundo is of mythical dimensions. Rudolp Wittkower explains: "Fights between eagles and snakes have actually been observed. . . . The greatness of the combat gave the event an almost cosmic significance. Ever since, when man has tried to express a struggle or a victory of cosmic grandeur, the early memory of this event has been evoked." This archetypical battle fits well within the Christian mold. In the Pseudo-Ambrose's *Sermones*, for example, we find the standard interpretation: "The devouring of the snake by the eagle is interpreted as a simile for Christ overcoming Satan." Just as in ancient times the victory of the eagle represented immortality and material triumph and was associated with magician and ruler, in the Christian era it stands for eternal salvation and also for secular triumphs. When the Spanish King Philip IV, patron of Calderón, died in 1665, "the Jesuits erected an eagle tearing a serpent with its claws, because by his victory over his enemies Philip had achieved for his peoples what Christ had won for humanity by the victory over Satan."[13] Although victory and salvation can be the end result of this ever-recurring cosmic battle, the powerful image itself deals with the prevalence of mighty opposites in the sublunary realm of generation and corruption. In *La vida es sueño* Segismundo is just such a composite of opposites. He is both *hombre* and *fiera* (vv. 209-12), viper and eagle. By speaking of the serpent's opposite, Clotaldo triggers in Segismundo a process that will effect his transformation into a solar hero who defeats the serpent but is able to incorporate the chthonic elements into an integrated vision.

The anecdote of the eagle brings out an appropriate response in Segismundo. His royal lineage has provided him with a temperament suited to rule over men: "la sangre / le incita, mueve y alienta / a cosas grandes" (vv. 1052-54). The notion of *la fuerza de la sangre* was a commonplace in the epoch, and a theme that provided material for numerous Golden Age plays, where *natura* triumphs over *nutritura*.[14] On hearing of the eagle, Segismundo's royal nature emerges. Segismundo asserts that, although imprisoned since birth, he can identify with the soaring and majestic bird. If he were free, none could defeat him:

> "¡Que en la república inquieta
> de las aves también haya
> quien les jure la obediencia!
> En llegando a este discurso
> mis desdichas me consuelan;
> pues, por lo menos, si estoy
> sujeto, lo estoy por fuerza
> porque voluntariamente
> a otro hombre no me rindiera."
> [vv. 1055-63]

This is certainly not a "perverse moral," as Merrick would have us believe, but a conclusion consonant with Segismundo's inherited place in the social structure as conceived in the epoch. Segismundo's kinship with the eagle is based on the doctrine of correspondence between macrocosm and microcosm. The pattern of universal and hierarchical order which is present in the natural world corresponds to man's social structures. Each man has a distinct part to play just as different animals and stones have different instincts and properties. Sir Walter Raleigh clearly summarizes this Renaissance and Baroque concept: "For that infinite wisdom of GOD, which hath distinguished his Angells by degrees which hath given greater and lesse light and beautie to Heavenly bodies, which hath made differences between beasts and birds, created the Eagle and the flie, the Cedar and the Shrub, and among stones given the fairest tincture to the Rubie, and the quickest light to the Diamond, hath also ordained Kings, Dukes and Leaders of the People, Magistrates, Iudges and other degrees among men."[15] Segismundo's degree is that of king, which corresponds to the eagle in the sphere of air. Each should be allowed to rule over his own element.[16] Clotaldo does not reject Segismundo as a viper or a monster, but attempts to transform his apparently inhuman nature through the influence of a creature whose qualities should resonate in the soul of a would-be king.

There is further wisdom in Clotaldo's selection of the eagle. Bestiaries, emblems, and patristic writings tell the story of how the eagle casts out its unworthy young: "It is claimed that the eagle presents his young to the sunbeams, and holds the children up to them in middle air with his talon. And if one of them, when stricken with the sun's light, uses a fearless gaze in his eyes, with an uninjured power of staring at it, that one is made much of, because it has proved the truth of its nature. But the one which turns away its eyes from the sunbeam is thrown out as being degenerate and not deserving such reward. Nor is it considered worth educating such a molly-coddle, as if it were not worth bothering about it."[17] This bestiary tale was well known in Golden Age Spain. The anecdote appears in Covarrubias' *Emblemas morales:*

> Muchos autores graves han escrito,
> El Aguila provar a sus polluelos,
> Si miran cara el sol, de hito en hito,
> Y sino, los derrueca por los suelos.[18]

Andres Ferrer de Valdecebro repeats the tale following his picture of the eagle in the *Govierno general, moral y político:* "Prueba ser sus polluelos legítimos, ofreciéndolos en lo más alto de un risco a los rayos del Sol, los que acobardan cerrando los ojos los desecha, los que resisten, y vencen los cría y sustenta."[19]

Since Segismundo has studied from the "book of nature" aided by his teacher, Clotaldo, he must be well aware of this test. Clotaldo is thus imprinting on the prince's mind, immediately before the drugged sleep, the image of a creature that must be tested before it can assume its lofty role. Basilio, many years before, had rejected his own son, equating him with the offspring of the viper, an animal that, according to zoological lore, would show its cruel and treacherous nature by killing the mother at birth. Clorilene's "monstrous" birth and her subsequent death would have been taken by many to be the result of an illicit relationship. Segismundo would thus be considered illegitimate. Now Clotaldo, the surrogate father, looks again at nature, but this time the result promises to be more positive. The teacher superimposes the image of the eaglet on that of the viper offspring, inspiring in Segismundo a desire to pass the required test and thus become the legitimate and worthy heir to the crown of Poland.

In his drugged state, Segismundo is transported to the palace, where he awakens. Basilio represents the eagle or ruler who has taken his child or eaglet to a high place to be tested. The king states:

> Esto quiero examinar,
> trayéndole donde sepa
> que es mi hijo, y donde haga
> de su talento la prueba.
>
> [vv. 1112-15]

The eaglet, by staring directly into the sun, reveals its true nature. Segismundo, by his actions at the palace, will also reveal himself to the court and particularly to the two teachers on nature, Basilio and Clotaldo. Analogical thinking was considered a high form of wisdom during the Renaissance and Baroque eras. It was the dominant pattern in the occult sciences, and we know that Basilio delved into astrology.[20] Clotaldo must believe that Segismundo understands the link between himself and the eaglet. He hopes that the prince will act on this knowledge. When Segismundo awakens, Clotaldo points out to Segismundo that his palace sojourn is to be a test of his temperament. He tells him that he can triumph over his horoscope, being *magnánimo* (v. 1287). This is one of the chief qualities associated with the eagle: "Leonardo da Vinci in his bestiary considered that the eagle stood for magnanimity, because of a legend that it always left some of its prey for lesser birds unable to forage for themselves."[21] Both Covarrubias and Ferrer de Valdecebro concur in referring to the eagle as "generosa," a term that appears in Clotaldo's description of the bird's flights in one of the texts of *La vida es sueño*.[22] Although this term can mean "noble" from the Latin *gens*, it can also have the present meaning of "generous." This virtue, stressed by Clotaldo, does not appear to concern Segismundo during his stay at the palace. When he discovers that he is the rightful heir, he rages against Basilio and Clotaldo, who have been unjust to him. The prince behaves like the majestic bird who subdues all.[23] He answers Clotaldo's admonitions, exhibiting his *soberbia* and *poder* (v. 1299). His proud and bellicose nature is not held in check since he now has power. He is like the tyrant Aureliano in *La Gran Cenobia*, a formidable adversary whose choleric and martial inclinations are not tempered by benefic influences. When courtiers play music to entertain Segismundo, he objects that "las músicas militares / sólo he gustado de oir" (vv. 1258-59).

It is fitting for a ruler to exhibit the qualities of the god and planet Mars. Ever since the founding of Rome by Romulus, emperors were expected to resemble this god. But Segismundo's pride, belligerence, and majesty must be tempered. Opposing qualities like those of Venus must be cultured so as to create a *coincidentia oppositorum*, a harmony out of contrariety. Segismundo is capable of this since in the first act his fiery nature gave way to tenderness on hearing Rosaura speak: "Tu voz pudo enternecerme" (v. 190). *Fiereza* and *ternura* can coexist in the heart.[24] But in the palace, the generosity and magnanimity of the eagle are not in evidence. Segismundo has understood only part of the lesson taught by the divine book of nature. The eagle, for Segismundo, is indeed the imperial bird of his teacher. But the flight upwards to the higher realms is motivated by selfish and proud motives. Rather than being concerned with the kingdom, the prince is preoccupied with the fulfillment of his passions—violence, revenge, and desire. His choleric disposition, which resembles that of Aureliano in *La gran Cenobia*, has as its primary quality, heat. His initial soliloquy in act one reveals this. Describing and desiring the freedom of *pez*, *bruto*, and *ave*, inhabitants of the elements of water, earth, and air, Segismundo laments his own incarceration, using the element of fire to characterize his response:

> En llegando a esta pasión,
> un volcán, un Etna hecho
> quisiera sacar del pecho
> pedazos del corazón.
> [vv. 163-66]

Studying the *sistema icónico* of several *autos* and *comedias* by Calderón, Javier Herrero emphasizes the playwright's use of the volcano as an image of "caos cósmico." He also notes the mountain's demonic connotations: "El demonio es el señor del ardiente centro de la tierra."[25] Volcanic fire belongs to the devil, is associated with chaos, and is truly the opposite of the celestial element to which the eagle's flight aspires. Segismundo's lust and rage at the court are thus foreshadowed by his description of his inner self as a Mt. Aetna. When Bodini speaks of the prince's *titanismo*, he must have in mind this image.[26] Titans and giants are often confused in myth. Both were defeated by the gods and were buried beneath the earth, "usually in volcanic regions."[27] The giant Encelades, for example, is supposed to struggle under Mt. Aetna, creating tremors and eruptions. Other writers claim that it is Typhon, the most vicious of the giants, who is buried there.[28] At any rate, the monstrous, savage, and proud nature of Segismundo is described with reference to this Sicilian mountain. The giants' as well as Lucifer's attack on heaven resemble Segismundo's actions at the court. He plunges the palace into chaos, threatening to dispose of his teacher and his father. The prince's ascent to the palace is a demonic rather than a celestial journey. His fiery nature has little in common with the highest element to which the eagle aspires; his choleric temperament is akin to the destructive and demonic fire under the earth.

Most symbols during the Medieval, Renaissance, and Baroque periods could be interpreted *in bono* or *in malo*. The eagle, for Segismundo, is indeed the imperial bird of his teacher. Yet the flight upward does not lead him to perceive higher truths, since his journey is not motivated by a desire for enlightenment, but by selfish, lustful, and proud motives. The eagle *in malo* is the symbol of the tyrant. Diego Saavedra Fajardo describes the cruelty and haughtiness of the bird in *empresa* 92: "Aun las plumas de las aves peligran arrimadas a las del águila, porque éstas las roen y destruyen, conservada en ellas aquella antipatía natural entre el águila y las aves. Así la protección suele convertirse en tiranía."[29] Segismundo is like the proud eagle in Saavedra Fajardo that destroys other birds that need protection, since it considers them inferior and has a natural *antipatía* for them.

Segismundo's palace sojourn recalls the voyage of Icarus who, neglecting Daedalus's advice, flew too close to the sun and fell to his death when the wax in his wings melted. Icarus is often portrayed as a negative example of conduct since he does not follow the "middle road." Segismundo's downfall is also due to excess. Pérez de Moya speaks of Icarus's *soberbia*.[30] Segismundo is also guilty of this vice. When the prince is returned to prison, Clarín alludes to the Icarus myth when speaking of Segismundo's actions at court: "¿Arrojé del balcón yo / al Icaro de poquito?" (vv. 2038-41). The courtier whom Segismundo threw from the balcony into the sea is described by Clarín as a lesser Icarus. Indeed, his flight did not last long. Clarín's joke serves a dramatic purpose. It points to a more apt comparison, between the mythical flyer and the prince. Both fall as a result of their pride and their propensity towards excess. In addition, the *gracioso's* pun serves to pinpoint the moment when Segismundo's own descent begins. As he tosses the courtier from the balcony, he is structuring his own downfall.

Basilio, on hearing of this senseless murder, refuses to embrace his cruel son. The killing confirms the king's suspicions concerning the violent and tyrannical nature of Segismundo (vv. 1468-75). Basilio's renewed fear of Segismundo has its foundation not only in the prince's cruel behavior but also in mythical images such as the giants' storming of heaven, Icarus's disobedience and pride, and the tyrannical eagle viewed *in malo* as the destroyer of other birds. Clotaldo's potion is used again, and the prince is returned to the tower. To lessen the prince's pain, Clotaldo explains to him that his palace adventure was a dream triggered by the eagle anecdote: "Como habíamos hablado / de aquella águila, dormido, / tu sueño imperios han sido" (vv. 2140-42). Thoughts of the majestic bird before sleep cause a dream concerning *imperios*. We also learn from Clotaldo at this point that the eagle was not a mere anecdote he recounted in order to teach Segismundo a lesson; it was something he actually did see in the sky before giving the prince the potion:

> ¿Todo el día te has de estar
> durmiendo? ¿Desde que yo
> el águila que voló
> con tarda vista seguí,
> y te quedaste tu aquí,
> nunca has despertado?
> [vv. 2092-97]

The eagle's flight must have seemed to Clotaldo as important an omen as Clorilene's viper dream which led to Segismundo's imprisonment at birth. By recounting the flight to his pupil, Clotaldo was attempting to impart to Segismundo the *in bono* image of ascension and empire, since he must have been certain that the celestial apparition portended great things. Furthermore, when Clotaldo first describes the flight to the prince, he compares it to a "desasido cometa" (v. 1043). By linking the eagle to the comet, the teacher is inflating the prophetic implications of the flight. The *Cometomantia* of 1684, a tract dedicated to answering "Whether the Apparition of Comets be the Sign of Approaching Evil," asserts that their visitation often presages "the sudden death of many Great Ones."[31] To this continuing interest in comets as omens was added a heightened degree of speculation, beginning in 1572 and extending throughout the seventeenth century. A *nova* was sighted that year in the constellation Cassiopea. This was considered one of the greatest "miracles" of nature, since no new creations could take place in the immutable realms above the sphere of the moon. Many tracts were written attempting to explain the apparent generation and corruption that was visible among the stars. A second *nova* appeared in 1604 in the constellation Serpentarius, fueling further speculation. Comets were included in these discussions since new discoveries pointed to the possibility that these bodies also existed above the sphere of the moon, a notion contrary to Aristotle's arguments.

Calderón may be reflecting these heated astronomical and astrological arguments in *La vida es sueño*. We have noted in the previous chapter how Clorilene's dream of the viper may have been mirrored in the heavens by the *nova* appearing in the constellation of the serpent. Clotaldo's comparison of eagle and comet may in fact refer to a specific heavenly portent such as the appearance of a comet in the constellation Aquila, the eagle. Like the serpent, the eagle is an emblem from the divine book of nature. It is as much a part of the inscape of dreams as of the outer space of stars and constellations. In all their forms, the opposing animals can be construed as omens. Basilio had interpreted the inner, outer, and heavenly signs of the serpent in a totally negative manner, and imprisoned Segismundo in an attempt to change what he believed would be an apocalyptic future. Clotaldo does not ignore the fact that man has free will and control over his actions, something Basilio tends to ignore. Clotaldo tries to teach the prince a lesson from the book of nature. The apparent failure of his pupil at court does not deter him. He reiterates the importance of the eagle and adds a new image to his teaching, that of the dream. If the eagle stands for the pomp of empire, then the dream can represent the vanity of human wishes in this mortal existence.

Segismundo is left alone to ponder the new correspondence. The second soliloquy signals the beginning of this transformation. The eagle provides the path followed by the prince. In Theobaldi's *Physiologus*, a "compendious form of that bestiary lore which was a vital part of European culture for over a thousand years," we find a description of how the eagle renews itself.[32] A typical bestiary describes this journey: "And it is a true fact that when the eagle grows old and his wings become heavy and his eyes become darkened with a mist, then he goes in search of a fountain, and, over against it, he flies up to the height of heaven, even unto the circle of the sun; and there he singes his wings and at the same time evaporates the fog of his eyes, in a ray of the sun. Then, at length, taking a header down into the fountain, he dips himself three times in it, and instantly he is renewed with a great vigour of plumage and splendour of vision."[33]

Segismundo, like the eagle, has ascended to the heights of the palace. There he has beheld the sun of kingship and empire. This has led to an explosion of his choleric and lustful temperament, previously held in check in a heart compared to Mt. Aetna. The eagle's heat is legendary. In classical times, Pliny ascribed the bird's swiftness to this quality. The eagle is also described as being a hot and dry creature.[34] These are the two qualities that make up the choleric temperament. Once Segismundo is burnt by his fiery passions arising from the predominance of choler in his system, and once he is also burnt by the closeness to power and beauty, often symbolized by the sun, he dips down like the bestiary's description of the eagle. He awakens in a prison. This descent is signaled by the fall of a courtier into the waters, and is related to Icarus's drowning in the ocean. Segismundo's descent, on the other hand, does not represent extinction. The eagle plunges into the "foundation of the Lord" which heals and renews, according to the bestiary.[35] The fountain is the source of creation, the strength Segismundo must find within the self.

The second soliloquy indicates that the process of regeneration has begun. The mist of the passions that clouded the eagle's eyes has been removed. With the power of his will, Segismundo exclaims, "pues reprimamos / esta fiera condición" (vv. 2148-49). Segismundo has been purified through an experience of opposites, the destructive power of passionate fire and the restoring force of the peaceful waters. This inner transformation is what the bestiary recommends, and what Clotaldo probably had in mind when he kept insisting on the eagle: "Do the same thing, O Man, you who are clothed in the old garment and have the eyes of your heart growing foggy."[36] We have passed from the realm of the imperial eagle to that of the mystical flight.[37]

Segismundo's vision of himself and his surroundings is now based on Clotaldo's second image, that of life as a dream. His descent to the prison is a descent into himself. Aided by Clotaldo, he now views the glories of the world with suspicion, "y el mayor bien es pequeño" (v. 2185), since its dream or illusion will fade in death: "¡que hay quien intente reinar, / viendo que ha de despertar / en el sueño de la muerte!" (vv. 2165-67). Paradoxically, the realization of the dream of life implies the awakening of the soul or inner self. Act three will portray a second ascent. This time it will trace a flight towards the higher reaches of awareness.

A Gnostic myth, *The Hymn of the Pearl*, ties the eagle and the dream motifs and may be of aid in our understanding of the link and its importance in Segismundo's transformation.[38] A prince, having left his parents' home, is imprisoned in Egypt. He soon forgets his identity and lies "in deep sleep." Hearing of this tragic situation, the father sends him a letter "in the likeness of an eagle," to rouse and bring back the son. On receiving it, the sleeper awakens, remembers his heritage, and returns home. For the Gnostics, "the desire to experience the body" leads the soul to forget itself and become identified with the material aspects of existence. Mircea Eliade explains that "waking implies *anamnesis*, recognition of the soul's true identity."[39] Segismundo begins the process of awakening and remembering his divine and earthly heritage through the messenger, the eagle anecdote as recounted by Clotaldo. He first hears the secular and political message of the imperial eagle—the fact that he is heir to an earthly kingdom. The first ascent to the palace is violent, unsettling, and purificatory since Segismundo does not understand the full message. On returning to the tower and pondering on the notion of life as dream, he begins to awaken to the eternal values. The "desire to experience the body" through the senses and the passions is now restrained: "pues reprimamos esta fiera condicion" (vv. 2148-49). The second ascent is characterized by the mystical eagle whose motto could well be "acudamos a lo eterno" (v. 2982).

The pomp of empire no longer distracts Segismundo from his duty, from the performance of virtuous acts since, according to Clotaldo's admonition, "aun en sueños / no se pierde el hacer bien" (vv. 2146-47). When the soldiers free him from the tower in order to "restaurar / tu imperial corona y cetro" (vv. 2298-99), Segismundo responds with prudence. Before, he would have needed Clotaldo to advise him and present to him anecdotes and analogies from the divine book of nature. Now his wisdom begins to emerge and he is able to produce such emblematic images from his own self. Faced with the desire for power and glory, he compares the pomp of empire to the flowering almond tree that loses its beautiful buds during a winter storm (vv. 2326-37).[40] The almond not only represents the tragic consequences of hasty and unthinking acts; it also reveals the contrast between the impermanence of outer phenomena, *majestades fingidas*, and the eternity of the soul. Rather than contemplate the precarious blossoms of the almond tree, a hero must ascend like the eagle to the higher reaches of awareness. A link between tree and bird may have been suggested to Calderón by a passage in Pliny's *Natural History:* "At the rising of Aquila, the almond blossoms first of all in the month of January."[41] The constellation of the eagle in the realm of the fixed stars watches over the mutability of the sublunary realm, where fortune appears to rule and where the almond tree exhibits tender blossoms that can be easily destroyed by a winter storm.

The will to *obrar bien* is not enough. Segismundo's transformation is gradual, as critics have pointed out. He must contend with his own desires—the chthonic viper feared by Basilio—and vanquish them in a manner reminiscent of the mythological contest between serpent and eagle. After the rebel soldiers release him from prison, Segismundo meets Clotaldo. At this point, it is clear that the prince makes an effort to restrain his fiery and fierce nature (vv. 2410-13). He also shows Clotaldo how he has made several of his teacher's warnings his own, including the notion of life as dream and the consequent need to *obrar bien* (v. 2400) The prince's struggle for control over himself is most evident in his third meeting with Rosaura. As A.E. Sloman has pointed out, this is a key scene in Segismundo's transformation: "Rosaura, and Rosaura only, can convince Segismundo that his visit to the palace was real. And only in the knowledge of this can his conversion be complete—the knowledge, that is, that life itself is as fleeting and unreal as a dream. Rosaura is the means of Segismundo's conversion."[42] This is indeed true, although this chapter shows that the eagle is also of significance in Segismundo's transformation. William Whitby, who has carefully analyzed Rosaura's role in the *comedia*, adds that during his third meeting with Rosaura, the prince "realizes in this moment that both natures exist in him together, on one plane of existence."[43] In terms of our study, these two natures are represented by the serpent and the eagle. Although the celestial creature triumphs in the contest, the viper is still a part of Segismundo's nature. This coexistence of opposites within his awareness reflects the mystery of *discordia concors* pondered by the Renaissance Platonists and often expressed iconographically in the triumph of Venus over Mars. With the aid of Rosaura, a figure akin to the Celestial Venus of the Platonists, Segismundo has been able to temper his choleric and martial fire.

This personal triumph corresponds to a political victory in Poland. Before this can take place, Segismundo will have to come to terms with that desire for power and empire (*pompas* and *majestad*) expressed in the almond tree anecdote. When the prince marches out with his newly acquired army, his martial qualities lead him to fantasize extreme actions:

> Si este día me viera
> Roma en los triunfos de su edad primera,
> ¡Oh, cuanto se alegrara,
> viendo lograr una ocasión tan rara
> de tener una fiera
> que sus grandes ejércitos rigiera,
> a cuyo altivo aliento
> fuera poca conquista el firmamento!
>
> [vv. 2656-66]

Segismundo conceives of himself as a fierce Roman warrior, guided by the martial eagle, establishing a vast empire. He even aspires to conquer heaven, like the giants and Titans of mythology. Their fiery nature, presumptuousness, and pride led to interment under Mt. Aetna. Yet this mighty volcano is not only a prison for those who attempt to undo the celestial order (or the political establishment in Segismundo's case); it is also the abode of great monarchs such as King Arthur and Frederick II, who await the appropriate moment to return to relative existence and become world rulers in a last great age.[44] Perhaps it was this thought that changed Segismundo's *in malo* flight of fancy: "Pues el vuelo abatamos,/ espíritu" (vv. 2664-65).

This newly acquired control over passions such as lust and pride reaches its climax in his magnanimous attitude towards his vanquished father at the end of the play. Basilio recognizes Segismundo's transformation and considers that he has been reborn (vv. 3248-50). His rebirth is like that of the eagle. Destroyed by his fiery actions during the first imperial flight, Segismundo has been renewed by a realization of the transcendental aspects of life. He can now exhibit the magnanimous qualities of the imperial bird. The eaglet that was cast out by the stern father returns in glory, able to glance at the sun of power without passion. The eaglet anecdote transcends the Basilio-Segismundo relationship. The son has transformed himself, the relationship, and consequently the anecdote. The casting out of the eaglet may now mean the dismissal of unworthy thoughts. This is a process that began in the tower, a place that can be compared to the monastic cell described by Rafael de Osuna in the *Abecendario espiritual:* "Onde muy bien se pueden comparar los varones recogidos en sus celdas á las águilas en sus altos nidos; las cuales, según se dice, desde allí examinan sus hijos, volviéndolos hacia el sol, é parando mientes si lo miran derechamente sin pestañear, é si no lánzalos de su compañía; cuasi de esta forma hacen los justos, cuando se entran en sus nidos, que son sus celdas, donde examinan todos sus propósitos y deseos, que son como hijos suyos; é si conocen que se enderezan cumplidamente al sol del glorioso mundo, que es Dios, afírmanse en ellos é críanlos hasta los poner en perfección; empero si los ven pestañar, no siendo tales como deven, lánzanlos de sí é afírmanse en los buenos."[45]

Segismundo emerges from the tower, nest, or cell armed with this newly found wisdom akin to that of the mystical eagle. He is indeed the Great One announced by the comet and other celestial portents; but he comes as a just ruler and not as a tyrant. The prince has tamed his lower nature as the eagle defeats the serpent. Yet these mighty opposites coexist within himself in a *mysterium coniunctionis.* Other mysteries are now solved. Rosaura, his guide, represents and is an anagram for dawn. Her other name is Astraea, the last of the immortals to leave earth as corruption set in. She has been watching over men as the zodiacal sign Virgo, and now returns to the planet with the sword of justice at the dawn of a new golden age. Segismundo must then be the new universal ruler announced by portents as varied and significant as a comet, an eclipse, and the dreams of serpent and eagle. He rises from Mt. Aetna, from the fire of passion, in a flight toward a purer fire. He harmoniously combines within the self powerful opposites such as magnanimity and strength, eternal values and political wisdom, eagle and serpent. Clotaldo was correct in inculcating in Segismundo admiration for the eagle. In both its imperial and mystical aspects the emblematic creature exhibits the qualities Segismundo emulates in his flight from the chaotic world of displacement to the sphere of myth where Rosaura rises to the role of celestial virgin who hails him as universal ruler. The emblematic creature from the natural world is also an omen. In the sky, it resembles a comet, a celestial phenomenon that portends great changes. It is also the constellation Aquila. Manilius notes that this celestial image "rises on the left of the youth who pours, whom once it carried off from earth."[46] The astrological poet is here describing the proximity and kinship between Aquila and Aquarius. The youth who pours is Ganymede, who should be next to Aquila since he was taken to heaven by Jupiter, metamorphosed as an eagle. This flight is often described as a mystical one.[47] The water-bearer also signals the approach of the Aquarian age or new golden epoch. Celestial portents in La vida es sueño do more than indicate the coming universal harmony. They point to the prince's transformation. Manilius's Astronomica describes one born at the rising of Aquila: "He that is born on earth in the hour of its rising will grow up bent on spoil and plunder won even with bloodshed; he will draw no line between citizen and foe, and when he is short of men to kill, he will engage in butchery of beast. He is the law unto himself, and rushes violently wherever his fancy takes him; in his eyes to show contempt for everything merits praise. Yet, should perchance his aggressiveness be enlisted in a righteous cause, depravity will turn to virtue, and he will succeed in bringing wars to conclusion and enriching his country with glorious triumphs."[48] The imperial, mystical, and celestial eagle is an emblem and an omen for Segismundo's rise to power.

CHAPTER SEVEN

The Maids of Autumn

SOON AFTER *La vida es sueño*, Calderón wrote *El mayor encanto, amor* for presentation at the Buen Retiro. In his first mythological spectacle play, Calderón continues to reflect an intense interest in astrology. In this *comedia*, Astraea, who had played such a significant role in *La vida es sueño* and in *La gran Cenobia*, becomes a minor character who, together with Libia, attends the witch Circe. The following year (1636) Calderón again prepares a play for the Buen Retiro during the night of Saint John. In the first act of *Los tres mayores prodigios* Jason meets Medea, another witch versed in the occult sciences, particularly astrology. Her attendants are again named Astraea and Libia. There is yet another play that follows this pattern, the second part of a work that has been called by Francisco Ruiz Ramón an "espléndido drama."[1] In *La hija del aire* II we encounter Semíramis, a cruel queen who controls political events and also worries about a horoscope and celestial portents. Once again, the maids of a powerful and sinister woman interested in astrology are called Astraea and Libia. Many of the events in this third *comedia* parallel the other two plays. But since some have questioned Calderón's authorship of *La hija del aire* II,[2] this chapter will concentrate on the first two plays, *El mayor encanto, amor* and *Los tres mayores prodigios*.

El mayor encanto, amor was scheduled for the night of Saint John, 1635. The presentation of plays before the king to celebrate this festival was common at the time. In 1631 Lope de Vega, commissioned by the Conde-Duque de Olivares, wrote the delightful *La noche de San Juan*, which has attracted critical attention for its *costumbrista* description of folk beliefs.[3] Calderón's *El mayor encanto, amor* was intended not only to celebrate Saint John's night but also to commemorate the completion of the Hall of Realms, the most significant addition to the Buen Retiro, which was to serve as a throne room from which the king could witness ceremonies and entertainments. The palace and gardens of the Buen Retiro, with the extravagant festivities held therein, were a cornerstone for the Conde Duque de Olivares's policies. In fact, the Buen Retiro was often called his palace, and became one of the most despised symbols of his power. In spite of criticism over extravagant spending, Olivares held on to the idea that the king must be properly entertained at his new palace. This conviction carried with it several assumptions concerning the function of celebrations. Their most important purposes were: 1) to amuse; 2) to exhibit the power and glory of the Spanish Empire; 3) to bolster the regime's policies and commonly held assumptions and beliefs; and 4) to praise monarch, ministers, and courtiers, thus maintaining and exalting the ruling class. Artists became indispensable members of the court and agents for propaganda: "The count duke was perpetually demanding an unquestioning loyalty to himself and his works, and the poets and hacks who undertook to supply it inevitably sounded false outside the circle of the faithful."[4]

While certain poets composed incidental poetry to delight king and minister, others preferred to uphold their artistic integrity. With the commission to prepare this entertainment, Calderón had to deal with political and artistic pressures. His *comedia* had to include a celebration of the regime as well as amazing *tramoyas* with which to astound the royal audience. From the first, he stressed his artistic independence by rejecting a *memoria* from Cosme Lotti.[5] The Italian scene designer had sketched a plot to include all the *tramoyas* he wished to build for the occasion. Calderón wrote in a letter, "Yo he visto una memoria que Cosme Loti hizo del teatro y apariencias que ofrece hacer a su Magd. en la fiesta de la noche de San Juan; y aunque está trazada con mucho ingenio, la traza de ella no es representable, por mirar más a la invención de las tramoyas que al gusto de la representación. Y aviendo yo, señor, de escribir esta comedia, no es posible guardar el orden que en ella se me da."[6]

The quarrel between poet and architect was raging throughout Europe at this time. In England it was seen in the battle between Ben Jonson and Inigo Jones.[7] The issue of whether the verbal or the visual takes precedence was of great importance to Lope de Vega who, in 1621, "laments the new popularity of plays of spectacle in which the machinery and elaborate stage trappings were emphasized at the expense of delicate metaphor and lovely poetry."[8] Thus, when Calderón wrote his letter concerning Cosme Lotti's *tramoyas*, he had behind him a tradition of poets who wished to uphold the primacy of verbal art. Rather than accept Lotti's dictates, Calderón composed his play independently of the *memoria*, although incorporating many of the central ideas and a few details. He also took into account the kinds of *tramoyas* Lotti wished to construct. He used as his immediate source the *Polifemo y Circe*, a play which he had written in collaboration with Mira de Amescua and Pérez de Montalbán.[9] The new product is a much simplified story that focuses on Ullyses' adventure in Circe's island and palace. We follow the Greek hero's initial defeat of her magic; his eventual fall at the greatest of all enchantments, *amor*; and his final escape from Circe's embraces, having recovered his *virtus*. Such a plot not only contains magical feats that can be performed with elaborate *tramoyas*, but it also traces the symbolic journey of a hero. A.E. Sloman concludes that "for Calderón as for his compatriot Gracián, the voyages of Ulysses symbolized the journey of life, and his encounter with Circe, the human conflict between duty and passion, between reason and lust."[10] Such a universal moral would certainly be considered appropriate for a play to be presented at the palace. Ullyses' triumph could be interpreted as a mirror of the king's *virtud*, or to the more critical eye, the trials of the hero could serve as education for the prince.

Circe is an appropriate choice to represent the danger or temptation encountered by the Greek hero. Both Cosme Lotti and Calderón agreed on her presentation as a figure opposed to *virtud*.[11] This particular confrontation between hero and witch reflects the rituals of the night of St. John, perhaps the most "magical" night of the year. Egla Morales Blouin has discussed the many folk customs associated with this night and their presence in the Spanish ballad.[12] But this feast was not limited to Spain. As James Frazer has observed, it is one of the most ancient festivals of mankind: "A faint tinge of Christianity has been given to them by naming Midsummer Day after St. John the Baptist, but we cannot doubt that the celebration dates from a time long before the beginning of our era. The summer solstice, or Midsummer Day, is the great turning point in the sun's career, when, after climbing higher and higher day by day in the sky, the luminary stops and thenceforth retraces his steps down the heavenly road. Such a moment could not but be regarded with anxiety by primitive man so soon as he began to observe and ponder the courses of the great lights across the celestial vault."[13] Frazer states that bonfires are built on this night to protect against dragons, trolls, witches, and evil spirits. Calderón's play can be seen to partake of this ritual. Ullyses is the solar hero who is lured and brought down by the witch or the forces of darkness. Like the sun, he will eventually regain his strength and rise out of the isle of darkness. The bonfires of Saint John have their counterpart in the purificatory fire at the conclusion of the *comedia*. Ullyses' journey in *El mayor encanto, amor* is precisely one of initial triumph, descent to darkness, and final reversal towards *virtud*.

As the play begins, the Greek hero's ship is blown by a storm towards the coast of Trinacria. As the travelers land, they are amazed at the inhospitable character of the terrain. The animals emit "quejas . . . lastimosas y severas" (p. 1511); the trees appear as "funestos ramos" (p. 1511); and the birds are "nocturnas sí, agoreras aves" (p. 1511).[14] This is then the realm of night, ruled by Circe who in her dark kingdom wishes to see Ulises' fall. She offers his men a magic potion that metamorphoses them into animals. One of Ulises' followers does not partake of the magic cup and is able to escape and tell the Greek hero of Circe's enchantments.

The description of Circe's palace and its riches recalls the newly built palace of the Buen Retiro where this performance took place. In the previous year, 1634, Calderón had included the palace as a central motif in his *auto sacramental* entitled *El nuevo palacio del Retiro*. But Calderón's praise in the *auto* could not stop the mounting tide of criticism over extravagant expenditure on buildings, decorations, and celebrations. In their study of the many controversies over the palace, Brown and Elliott conclude that 1635 was a particularly difficult year. Furnishing the Hall of Realms had been a most expensive operation at a time when the country could ill afford it, especially with the new French war: "It was not the ideal moment for the King to be enjoying himself, and a satirical piece making the rounds early in June spoke mordantly of the King of France being on campaign, and the King of Spain in retreat (*en el Retiro*). In response to the public mood the usual St John's day festivities were suspended, but Calderón's new play for the occasion, *El mayor encanto, amor,* was put on a few weeks later, at the end of July."[15] The popular mood is reflected in Calderón's play, although his criticism is of necessity somewhat veiled. The beautiful palace is metamorphosed into the abode of a witch, while the creatures who in the *auto* had lived happily in the Retiro are now lamenting their fate.

If we compare Cosme Lotti's *memoria* with Calderón's *comedia*, we find a most significant omission. In the *memoria*, when Virtud convinces the hero to leave Circe towards the end of the play, an old giant appears, dressed as a hermit (the Retiro arose on the grounds of the monastery of San Gerónimo), and tells Ulises that he is "el Buen Retiro, y que lo que le conviene para colocarse en el templo de la eternidad y hacerse famoso, ilustrando su nombre con grandes glorias, es seguir el Buen Retiro; porque menos que siguiéndole, no podrá

apartarse de los vicios y amar la virtud, que sólo se puede hallar re-
tirándose de todo lo que le puede divertir de ella. Con que Ulises
determinado de seguir el Buen Retiro, se abrazará de la virtud."[16]
Through this figure, Lotti made sure that Circe's palace would not be
confused with the Buen Retiro. No such hermit appears in Calderón's
play.

In Calderón's play, Circe's palace is not the "casa del sol," the
panegyrists' term for Philip's abode. Instead, it is the palace of the
moon—"alcazar de la luna" (p. 1539). The moon reflects the rays of
the sun and may thus be taken to represent the king's favorite. As
noted, many believed that the Retiro was actually the Conde Duque's
own palace. There is further evidence that links Circe's abode in Calderón's *comedia* with Olivares's Buen Retiro. When the witch appears
before Ulises, she relates to him the many occult sciences she practices. Reading the celestial symbols is too easy a task for her. Circe
need not turn to the sky to see the future in the stars, since she can
read it in birds and flowers. She is also an expert in *quiromancia, geo-
mancia,* and *piromancia.* Her powers are such that she can change the
weather, transform men into beasts, trees, or inanimate objects, and
control the movement of celestial luminaries and all other heavenly
bodies and constellations, thus changing the course of history:

> Esta soy, y con mirar
> el sol a mi voz rendido,
> la luna a mi acción atenta,
> obediente a mi suspiro
> toda la caterva hermosa
> de los astros y los signos.
> [p. 1517]

Like that of Basilio in *La vida es sueño,* Circe's vision is limited to the
hero's fall, and does not take into account the cyclic return of the sun.
Her blindness will bring about her destruction. Basilio and Circe are
followed in the next years by Medea and Semíramis as characters in
Calderón who wish to control human events yet fail. I believe that
this literary pattern reflects a historical situation.

In the middle and late 1630s Calderón may have taken a dim view
of the Conde Duque's reputation as a conjurer of evil spirits to gain
and maintain power. Olivares's inordinate thirst for power is well
known. As Gregorio Marañon comments, "Pero Olivares sentía,
desde lo mas hondo de su organismo, como uno de sus impulsos más
eficaces, el afán de mando por el mando mismo, y a ésto sacrificaba
todo lo demás, incluso su fortuna y su vida." This urge to control
found an outlet in the occult sciences: "Creía en los mayores dispar-

ates con la misma buena fe que sus contemporáneos; y creía, además, en algunos que su situación y cultura le debían impedir aceptar."[17] Among the occult sciences that interested the Conde Duque, alchemy plays a significant role. As the economic situation worsened, alchemy seemed to provide an easy manner of obtaining gold. He went so far as to build a laboratory for one of his practitioners in the Buen Retiro.

For Olivares, obtaining funds was a minor concern compared to his need of the king's support for his policies. His standing depended directly on the king. As early as 1622 we find an instance of his use of the occult to influence the monarch. The president of the Royal Council investigated in that year the claims of a Leonorilla that certain philters she was selling were "los mismos que el conde de Olivares daba al rey para conservar su privanza."[18] According to some, Olivares had no need for philters. His magic powers were derived from a spirit in the *muletilla* he always carried with him because of his gout. The *Cueva de Meliso*, a work released after his fall and containing all manner of rumors and accusations against the former *privado*, is an excellent indicator of popular belief. Olivares is described as going to the magic cave of the wizard Meliso, who forecasts his future and hails him as "gran maestro, de toda ciencia mágica el más diestro que vieran las edades, oráculo mayor de las verdades."[19] Ruth Lee Kennedy has demonstrated how Olivares's magic is satirized in Tirso de Molina's *La fingida Arcadia*.[20] Calderón's *El mayor encanto, amor* seems to serve a similar purpose. The use of the witch Circe to attack Olivares and his policies is not a device limited to Calderón's play. In the vignette *La isla de Monopantos* included in Quevedo's *La hora de todos*, we read, "La moneda es la Circe, que todo lo que se le llega o de ella se enamora, lo muda en varias formas."[21] In an essay that describes how Quevedo's work satirizes the programs for political, social, and economic reform put forth by Philip IV's *privado*, Conrad Kent explains that the leader of the Monopantos, Pragas Chincollos, is an anagram of Gaspar Conchillos, or Olivares.[22] Circe and Olivares attempt to control and change nature, with disastrous results.

Calderón's play was performed for the king and his favorite. Any intent to express opposition to Olivares had to be thoroughly disguised. The allegory of Ulises as Philip IV may have helped to veil satirical intentions. The many *tramoyas* may have served to divert the intellect away from political matters. Even with these precautions, the possibility of discovery was there. The praise of Philip as Ulises, a solar hero portrayed at the time of the sun's greatest exaltation during the summer solstice, may not have been sufficient to disguise criticism of a vain palace built by a witch who tries to control the hero.

When Circe offers to Ulises a beverage that the audience knows can change him into an animal she can control, some may have thought of Leonorilla's magic philter reputedly used by the Conde Duque to control the king.

When Circe's admiration for the hero turns to love she describes the many occult sciences she has mastered. Circe claims that if Ulises stays on the island with her, she will transform her disposition and the landscape:

> Verás trocado mi extremo
> de riguroso en benigno,
> con el gusto que te hospedo,
> con la atención que te sirvo,
> siendo el Flegra desde hoy,
> no ya fiero, no ya esquivo
> hospedaje de Saturno,
> siempre en roja sangre tinto,
> selva sí de Amor y Venus
> deleitoso paraíso . . .
>
> [p. 1518]

Circe states that her disposition will be changed from *riguroso* to *benigno*. Students of astrology will recall that Saturn was considered the most *riguroso*, the most *maligno*, of the seven Ptolemaic planets. Baltasar de Vitoria, after calling it *maligno*, asserts that it rules over certain night creatures such as owls and bats.[23] At the beginning of the play, the sailors had seen "nocturnas . . . agoreras aves" (p. 1511) on the island. Vitoria adds that Saturn rules over *agoreros* and *hechiceros*, of which Circe is one. Both the landscape and the lady who presides over it are thus ruled by the most malignant of planets. According to some astrologers, Saturn has a special power over the sign Cancer.[24] This is probably due to the fact that Saturn rules Capricorn, the sign of the winter solstice, standing in opposition to Midsummer Day. Both Circe's lunar and Saturnine nature are in conflict with the sun, since the moon rules the night and Saturn presides over winter. This clearly sets up the conflict between Circe and Ulises, who is the solar hero in the play. Furthermore, the rulership of Saturn in a horoscope has adverse effects. Vitoria asserts that Saturn "significa cárceles, caminos largos, trabajos, tardanzas," precisely the adverse situations encountered by Ulises and his men on the island of Circe.

Circe, through her magic, has promised to transform a dark, somber, and Saturnine landscape into an earthly paradise ruled by Venus. The notion of paradise is presented in the speech concerning the seventh planet. Most writers of the epoch were aware of Saturn's essential bipolarity.[25] Medieval and Arabic treatises of astrology viewed it as the most malignant of heavenly bodies, while Renaissance Platonists added that it could also represent the highest wisdom. As god, Saturn could be regarded as a tyrannical figure or as the benign ruler of the golden age. By associating paradise with Saturn, Circe hopes to evoke images of a new golden age. Yet we know that her paradise is but a vain appearance that disguises the malignant nature of her intentions.

At the time of Philip IV's coronation in 1621, a gazeteer announcing that the new monarch would bring back the fabled "siglo de oro" created a laudatory commonplace for Philip's reign.[26] Villamediana, when he wished to praise the king in his play *La gloria de Niquea*, called Aranjuez a Spanish paradise and recalled the "dorados siglos" (*Ob.* p. 2). Villamediana's praise of Aranjuez contrasts with Calderón's portrayal of the Buen Retiro. The new palace in *El mayor encanto, amor* is a vain and proud edifice constructed by a witch who wishes to control the solar hero. It houses a malignant Saturn and not the benefic ruler of the golden age. *La gloria de Niquea* contains further praise of Philip IV. An eagle descends from the sky, carrying a beautiful lady who "parecía imagen de aquellos dorados siglos que han aguardado tantos" (*Ob.* p. 11). Addressing the monarch, she hails the return of Astraea. In *El mayor encanto, amor*, Circe's two trusted maids are called Astraea and Libia or Licia.[27] A character who played a central role in *La gran Cenobia* and *La vida es sueño* by helping to bring about harmony has been relegated to the minor role of Circe's servant.

Following our astral-political interpretation, it may be argued that Astraea is merely a term used by Circe (Olivares) to evoke a paradise that has turned out to be false. The wars do not seem to lead to universal empire but to financial distress. The Buen Retiro is a costly and false mirror of the ideal epoch. The debasement of Astraea in the play is further indicated by the fact that she is paired with Clarín, the lowliest of the two *graciosos*, whom Circe eventually transforms into a *mona*. The fact that Astraea serves Circe, a woman versed in astrology, may be of significance. Circe claims control over the heavens, and Astraea's subservience to her is an instance of her malignant control over the stars. Not only is a zodiacal sign in her control, but she also has it act in a manner which is opposite to its basic qualities. Astraea, as the sign of justice, serves a tyrannical ruler. As a sign of chastity she is paired with a servant whose transformation represents his own bestial nature.

Astraea representing the sign Virgo is closely connected with the second maid, Libia.[28] This is a pattern that Calderón will follow in the other two plays as well. The presentation of Astraea and Libia as servants to three powerful women versed in astrology and desiring control over human events may imply that Circe, Medea, and Semíramis command both the heavens and the earthly realm. In the 1602 edition of his *Rimas*, Lope de Vega defends the use of commonplaces. He begins by arguing, "Usar lugares comunes, como engaños de Ulises, salamandra, Circe y otros, ¿por qué ha de ser prohibido, pues ya son como adagios y términos comunes, y el canto llano sobre que se fundan varios concetos?"[29] Lope then defends his own use of *arenas* and *estrellas* as images of near-infinity, citing many classical works where the sands of Libia and the stars refer to a countless number. If Calderón was going to create "varios concetos" from Ulysses and Circe as Lope recommends, why not add the *arenas* and *estrellas* as characters? Circe thus controls the countless stars through Astraea, which means star maiden. The witch also rules over the world, the countless grains of sand in the desert of Libia. Even if Calderón were not aware of Lope's discussion, these matters were well known.

There is a second and more interesting possibility. Virgo, the sign of the grain and the harvest, is followed in the zodiacal belt by Libra, the sign of the autumnal equinox. As noted previously, writers of the period associate Astraea with both Virgo and Libra, the reason being that the latter's scales represent justice, one of the attributes of the star maiden. Naming the two maids Astraea and Libia could serve to recall the two constellations found at the end of summer and beginning of autumn respectively. In *La gran Cenobia*, Decio kills the tyrannical Aureliano and restores justice and peace to the Roman Empire at a time when he is flanked by Astraea and Libio. In *El mayor encanto amor*, the two maids will evoke the notion of a golden age of justice and harmony in contrast to Circe's tyrannical rule.

The connection between the two maids and the two contiguous signs Virgo and Libra explains one more astrological allusion. Circe would change the Saturnine landscape into a paradise of Venus. The sign of the autumnal equinox, Libra, is ruled by Venus.[30] On the opposite side of the horoscope, we encounter the sign Aries, the vernal equinox, ruled by Mars. Philip IV's birthdate is April 8, 1605, making him an Aries, a sign ruled by Mars. Appropriately, Ulises in *El mayor encanto, amor* is also ruled by Mars. Ulises is afraid of the wrath of Venus: "Venus, del griego ofendida / mis venturas descompone" (p. 1515). There is thus a Mars-Venus opposition in the play represented by Ulises and Circe, which reflects the rulership of the opposing equinoxes in the horoscope. The fact that Circe has Libia (Libra) under her control means that she rules the house of Venus, which, as noted, stands in opposition to Ulises or Mars. Circe brings the Greek hero to her palace and to her astrological house. Ulises' martial spirits are tamed by the sensuous nature of Venus. Overcome by passion, Ulises rejects the arms of Achilles for the arms of Circe:

> El grabado arnés ilustre
> de Aquiles a mis pies yace,
> torpe, olvidado e inútil.
> Bien está a mis pies, porque
> rendido a mi amor se juzgue,
> y segunda vez en mí
> amor de Marte se burle.
>
> [p. 1541]

Mars overcome by Venus is a common image in Renaissance iconography, and one that frequently appears in Golden Age drama.[31] In astrology, Mars in the house of Venus is a negative position.[32] As his martial spirit is restored, Ulises calls on Juno, the goddess of marriage. Perhaps in this scene we can detect a veiled appeal to Philip IV. The *comedia* exorts the king to rise from the blandishments of the Buen Retiro and concern himself with the wars that rage in Europe.[33] The call to Juno should also be heeded by the monarch. His wife, Isabel de Borbón, was neglected by the king for other amorous pursuits. The ambassador from Venice writes in 1632: "la reina, poco contenta de ver al Rey tan dado a los placeres y de tenerla a ella casi abandonada, vive mísera vida."[34] Philip should pay more attention to the royal family and less to the courtly entertainments which can be interpreted as the magic enchantments of Circe. Such a message contains an implied criticism of the spectacle play, where the visual overcomes the "soul" or meaning of the words.[35]

The frustrated and angry Circe, seeing Ulises escape, sets fire to the palace and kills herself after freeing the imprisoned spirits. When Libia and Astraea ask how they may escape the fire and destruction brought about by the angry witch, they hear the words of Circe:

> Cuantos espíritus tuve
> presos, sujetos y humildes,
> inficionando los aires
> huyan a su centro horrible.
>
> [p. 1544]

No longer will justice and chastity be virtues degraded by the desire for power. Astraea will once again be free to guide mortals in a historical progression towards a golden age.

For Circe, this has been a "noche triste" (p. 1544). Ulises as Mars has rejected the influence of Venus. Her lunar magic has little effect on his solar and martial vitality. Ulises' strength reflects the time of the year. The sun is at its most exalted position during the summer solstice. The forces of darkness have no power on St. John's night. This is a time when bonfires are built to increase the fertility of the soil, to keep away witches and evil spirits, and to cement promises of marriage. Circe's despair at the hero's rejection of her leads her to collaborate unwittingly with the solar forces. She transforms her palace into an erupting volcano at the end of the *comedia*. Its flames are the play's ritual bonfire for St. John's night. The solar hero has triumphed. For him, and for his followers, this is a "noche felice" (p. 1545). Ulises has followed the path of the greatest luminary from exaltation to its lowest point in the winter or slumber in Circe's arms, and has climbed back to a new position of prominence. Having escaped the danger of Venus-Circe, he returns home to his beloved and patient wife, guided by Juno, goddess of marriage. *El mayor encanto, amor* represents the triumph of the sun and Mars over the dark lunar and Saturnine forces.

A SIMILAR *fiesta* was scheduled for the following summer and Calderón was again commissioned to write a play for the occasion. The summer of 1636 turned out to be a most successful one for Spanish arms, and celebration was in order.[36] Like *El mayor encanto, amor, Los tres mayores prodigios* is linked to the festival, and this is but one of the many resemblances between the two plays. Each portrays a woman who describes herself as "sabia," an enchantress whose exploits are taken from classical mythology. In *Los tres mayores prodigios* she is Medea. Like Circe, she abides in a remote corner of the world, an island where she practices her magical arts. Both *comedias* begin with the arrival by water of strangers to the sorceress's domain. A foreign hero is in danger of falling under the magician's spell, but we soon realize that the greatest enchantment is not one she controls—it is love. It is this force that seems to direct the action, although it is challenged by the power of Mars. The Mars-Venus opposition is thus fundamental to both plays. Finally, Medea, like Circe, is accompanied by two maids named Astraea and Libia.

All these resemblances, however, arise from a comparison between the first act of *Los tres mayores prodigios* and the whole of *El mayor encanto, amor*. The other two acts of the 1636 play have little to do with the enchantress. To accommodate the three stories contained within this one spectacle play, three separate stages were prepared at the Buen Retiro.[37] In *Los tres mayores prodigios*, act two deals with Teseo's adventure in the Cretan labyrinth; the third act focuses on Hércules' pursuit of Neso, the centaur that has stolen his wife. The tragic ending, the death of Hércules, does not seem attuned to the atmosphere of rejoicing prescribed for an evening that is supposed to commemorate the sun's exaltation. Furthermore, errors of judgment by Jasón and Teseo in the first two acts cast a shadow on the already somber ending. The mood becomes progressively darker as the action unfolds. An analysis of the first act, exclusive of the rest of the play, would not give us a clear picture of Astraea's role in *Los tres mayores prodigios*.

This *comedia* has suffered from neglect precisely because of its apparently disparate nature. W.G. Chapman dismisses the play in a few lines as "una obra desafortunada, quizás la menos satisfactoria de estas comedias."[38] Yet a more recent study by A.I. Watson shows that the play is carefully constructed. Watson argues that the *comedia* is a kind of tryptich, the central panel being the third act, which was presented in the center stage, while the first two acts are auxiliary panels to the right and left of the main action: "The central position enjoyed by Act III immediately suggests the possibility that Hercules could be the central character of the entire play."[39] Teseo and Jasón are portrayed as friends of Hércules who help him to search for his wife, stolen by the centaur Neso. Jasón cannot find her in Asia, and becomes involved in the acquisition of the Golden Fleece in the first act, presented on the stage at the right. Teseo does not find her in Europe, and is sacrificed to the Minotaur in the second act, presented on the stage at the left. The third act takes place on the central stage. Hércules is able to locate Deyanira in Africa, where the three heroes finally meet at the end of the stipulated one year of searching. Watson contends that throughout the play the search for Hércules' wife is the central motive, while other adventures are subordinate. He then carefully analyzes the third act from the point of view of honor. Even though Hércules recovers his wife and has evidence that she resisted the advances of the centaur, he feels ashamed: "Calderón was concerned in *Los tres mayores prodigios*, as in his wife-murder plays, with the tragic consequences of moral cowardice and it was a stroke of pure genius to choose the strongest man in the Classical world to play the part of the Slave of Public Opinion."[40]

Watson's significant contribution to the honor theme in Calderón may have obscured the importance of the first two acts in the spectacle play. We will attempt to extend the kind of interpretation provided for *El mayor encanto, amor* to this puzzling work. The action commences with a song celebrating a pilgrim in the process of dedicating the Golden Fleece to the temple of Mars on the island of Colchis (p. 1548).[41] Medea and her three maids, Astraea, Libia, and Sirene, hear the song. The "witch" is irate since she considers herself the only deity worthy of worship in the area. Like Circe, she has remained in a secluded area of the world, accompanied by her maids, studying the hidden forces that control the universe. Medea has delved into the highest form of occult learning, astral magic. Her text is the heavens themselves: "son de tus estudios locos / libros esas once esferas / encuadernados a globos" (p. 1549). From the very beginning of the work, the playwright underlines the astral implications of the action. Medea, like Circe, believes she can control the heavens and has at her command Astraea and Libia, the maids of autumn, the constellations Virgo and Libra. The mention of Mars and the Golden Fleece at the beginning of the *comedia* introduces other celestial bodies in this astral drama. The god of war is also the fifth planet, and the Golden Fleece represents the ram or first zodiacal sign, Aries. As noted in the discussion of *El mayor encanto, amor*, planet and constellation are closely related since Mars rules the sign Aries.

Not only are the astral connotations manifested from the start, but so are the political implications of the action. Philip IV was born under the sign of Aries. By centering the action of the first act of the *comedia* around the Golden Fleece, Calderón seems to be paying homage to the king. The purpose of the summer celebration was to praise the king as a solar hero on the night of the luminary's exaltation, the summer solstice. Indeed, the *loa* that precedes the spectacle play speaks of the king as "Quarto Planeta de España,"[42] equating him with the sun.

As in *El mayor encanto, amor*, this praise of Philip must be tempered by other considerations. The many parallels between Circe and Medea recall the criticism hidden in the apparently laudatory spectacle play of 1635. The magicians in both *comedias* may well bring to mind the figure of Olivares, who was most interested in the occult arts. Circe's and Medea's attempts to control nature and man may refer to the Conde Duque's desire for control over Spanish policy and his well-known influence over the king.

El mayor encanto, amor commenced with the arrival of Ulises at Circe's island. *Los tres mayores prodigios* includes two arrivals by sea to Medea's island of Colchis. The first hero to appear is Friso, who wishes to consecrate the Golden Fleece to Mars. Questioned by the irate Medea, the pilgrim explains that he has been expelled, together with his sister Heles, from his father's kingdom. He is blameless, but was falsely accused by his stepmother, Nerida, who had used "un hechizo . . . amoroso" (p. 1549) to gain control of the king's affections and of the kingdom. Then, in order to rid herself of Atamas's children, she had bribed the priests to declare that the lack of fertility in the land could be remedied by the sacrifice of Friso and Heles (p. 1549). This lack of fertility began with Atamas's marriage to Nerida. The inhabitants do not realize that the new wasteland is a direct result of the breaking of nature's laws by their rulers. As Jessie L. Weston has posited, the relationship ruler-land is an essential one in traditional societies: "This close relation between the ruler and his land, which resulted in the ill of one becoming the calamity of all, is no mere literary invention, proceeding from the fertile imagination of a twelfth century court poet, but a deeply rooted popular belief, of practically immemorial antiquity and inexhaustible vitality."[43] The wasteland described by Friso is the result of the ill introduced by Nerida. A fertile land that produced wheat now abounds in thistles. The *espigas* (p. 1549) that are now absent recall *spica*, the most important star in the constellation Virgo, representing the wheat of fertility and abundance provided by Astraea to the inhabitants of the first ages. But Friso's homeland has been ravaged by the actions of a witch, who has wounded the king's heart with a passionate illness. Her attempts to manipulate nature and the king have resulted in catastrophe. Nerida's actions recall Circe's attempts to control nature in *El mayor encanto, amor,* as well as Medea's magical powers in *Los tres mayores prodigios.* In both *comedias,* Astraea, the celestial sign Virgo, is under the control of a witch. Her promises of fertility and abundance are subverted.

Friso's description of his homeland is essential to understanding the first act of *Los tres mayores prodigios.* It foreshadows a similar fate for any hero that falls under Medea's control. The passage is also essential for our political interpretation of the action. Nerida's behavior recalls that of Olivares, who was accused of purchasing a magical potion to control the king's will. Such control would only end in disaster. Fertility would give way to a wasteland. The inhabitants of the peninsula, fatigued and impoverished by wars, might be willing to listen to this warning. It is significant that a play performed on St. John's night, a magical night intended to bring fertility to the land, begins with the image of a wasteland. Calderón's imagery evokes a land that has been laid waste through the actions of a magician. Friso is the hero who can heal the land and the "father" or king.

Denial of birthright and expulsion from the land are typical beginnings of the hero monomyth.[44] To underline the heroic qualities of Friso, Calderón emphasizes that his miraculous escape from death is based on divine intervention. When Friso and Heles are abandoned and left to die, their mother Neifile appears to them in a cloud, lighted by Apollo, the sun. She gives them a gift from Jupiter, a golden ram to guide them to a place of safety:

Un ariete, cuya lana
de oro era. Humanos ojos
¿cuándo vieron que se diese
en traje de esquilmo el oro
brillante? Pues parecía
que en casa de tan hermoso
signo siempre estaba el sol,
sin acordarse de esotros . . .

[p. 1550]

On the surface, this represents another laudatory passage where Philip IV is praised through astral imagery. The golden ram is so brilliant that it appears as if the sun were always in its (astrological) "house," Aries, Philip's birth sign. The king's solar nature is emphasized, and his zodiacal sign is exalted above all others. Yet the magical ram has been given to Friso, who opposes Medea. Philip cannot be said to oppose Olivares. The link between mythical character and king is broken, bringing into question the previous laudatory comparison.

Friso's heroic quest continues as he traverses the ocean, riding the ram. As a test of his inner strength, he is asked not to look back to the land he has left behind. He is successful in this trial, but his sister fails. She falls to the ocean in an area that bears her name, the Hellespont. The young hero is able to land on the island of Colchis, where he is rescued by the king, Medea's father. Friso, aided by this ruler, and in spite of Medea's complaints, goes to the temple of Mars to offer the Golden Fleece to the helpful deity. Friso has survived an attempted murder, expulsion from his homeland, a long sea voyage, and a test of his inner strength. He has also withstood Medea's temptation and has offered the Golden Fleece to Mars as was his duty. The gift of the ram had expressed the benefic qualities of Sol and Jupiter, together with the power of the zodiacal sign Aries. To these he now adds the martial spirit of the fifth planetary deity, which is reinforced by the fact that Aries is the "house" of Mars. Friso is a hero supported by the gods and aided by the stars.

Medea rages against the hero. She does not want him to sacrifice to the gods, but would prefer that he render homage to her. The sorceress tells her maids that she could have granted Friso the boons he was given by the gods, if he had only prayed to her. Medea's maids attempt to counsel her, but she will not listen. The maids' advice may be interpreted as the benefic influence of the constellations Astraea-Virgo and Libia-Libra, who wish to lead her away from the chaotic course of forced control of the heavens and of nature, and towards an acceptance of the will of the gods. First Libia and then Astraea explain to Medea why Friso has taken the Golden Fleece to Mars, and warn her that the god may seek revenge. But it is the third lady, Sirene, who makes the most comprehensive statement of Medea's plight: "Que en Marte ofendes advierte, / a Marte, Venus y Amor" (p. 1551).

The presence of this third lady is rather puzzling. Her name refers to the *sirena* or mermaid, a creature that seems far removed from the sky. Astraea and Libia are names of goddesses who inspire humanity towards chastity, truth, and justice. Sirens, on the other hand, delude men and turn them away from their quest. There could be no more extreme contrast than that between Astraea, goddess of chastity and symbol of virginity, and the sirens who, according to Covarrubias, "significan las rameras que destruyen a los hombres, de su vista y blandos halagos engañados." Indeed, Marsilio Ficino compares the sirens to "bad demons," since by their traps and lures "souls are detained in bodily delights and do not turn back, therefore, to the port of their celestial home."[45] While Astraea and Libia may represent the "good demons" or astral forces described by Ficino as benefic to man, Sirene stands for the opposite, the obstacles in the soul's journey to the eternal realm.

In the hero monomyth as described by Joseph Campbell, the quester is faced with woman as goddess and as temptress. Medea has at her service both types. She is in control of both positive and negative forces—she is at the same time the goddess who leads man to his goal and the temptress who obstructs and destroys the would-be hero. Campbell adds that "woman, in the picture language of mythology, represents the totality of what can be known."[46] Medea attempts to control the knowledge of positive and negative forces in the universe. It should be recalled that sirens told Ulysses they were in possession of a complete knowledge of nature.[47] But their completeness and universality are false. Medea wishes to set herself above the gods and divert man from his duty. She represents a false and incomplete form of knowledge. She is as deceitful as the sirens, lacking the truth of Astraea.

Sirene's presence may serve more than a mere contrastive purpose. Baltasar de Vitoria, in his account of the creation of these creatures, relates them to the rape of Proserpine by Pluto, a mythological
event often associated with the summer solstice.[48] Proserpine's descent to Hades is equated with the sun's turning south, thus causing
the eventual onslaught of winter. Sirene can thus be associated with
the zodiacal sign Cancer, the beginning of the sun's decline. As such,
she is a figure akin to Astraea and Libia, who are also zodiacal signs.
Furthermore, Virgo and Libra stand for the autumnal equinox, a time
of equal days and nights. They point to a moment as important as
that signaled by the entrance of the sun in Cancer. This information
enables us to better understand why these maids are in Medea's service. Medea has in her control the two key moments in the heavenly
map that lead to the sun's downfall. As the sun passes Astraea-Virgo
and enters Libia-Libra, days become shorter than nights, the solar
power visibly declines. Sirene, as Cancer, the sign that immediately
follows the sun's highest position in the heavens, expresses the com-
mencement of decline. Calderón's *comedia* should celebrate the *rey-
planeta*'s power. Instead the first act of *Los tres mayores prodigios* presents a witch who controls the two principal moments of the sun's
descent. Just as the sorceress controls half of the sun's path, the
Conde Duque has a hold over much of the kingdom. His hold over the
rey-planeta, it is rumored, is based on his practice of the occult arts.
This new Circe or Medea is intent on domination. The night of St.
John, a time propitious for the destruction of witches and evil spirits,
witnesses their triumph at the beginning of Calderón's *Los tres mayores prodigios*. The "bad demons" divert the king and the country from
their proper quest.

Medea's desire to acquire the Golden Fleece and not have it sur-
rendered to Mars is also clarified through this astral-political interpretation. The sorceress now controls that half of the year when the
sun is in decline. Medea wants to possess the key sign of the sun's
ascent, the vernal equinox which occurs at the beginning of Aries.
Acquisition of the ram could be equated with complete control of the
heavens. According to classical astrology, although Aries is ruled by
Mars, it is also the sign of the sun's exaltation.

Jasón now appears, explaining that the wise Argos built for him
a ship in which he has come to Asia, searching for Hércules' wife (p.
1553). Medea praises the mariner for his valor, but deplores the invention of navigation, claiming that no place will now be safe from
man's ambition and pride (p. 1554). Argos and Jasón as the first
builders of boats[49] can be viewed either positively or negatively, de-

pending on the context. For some, navigation is essential to culture and progress. In the *Idea de un príncipe político cristiano*, Diego Saavedra Fajardo uses the Jasón voyage to praise navigation: "Es la navegación lo que sustenta la tierra con el comercio."[50] The notion of commerce as symbolized by Jasón's voyage may have political implications. As Conrad Kent has explained, Olivares encouraged Spaniards to become merchants so as to bring life to the country's sagging economy. Quevedo and many others rejected such policies: "If a nation engages in trade, he suggests, it ceases to be a rightful state and becomes a land of thieves."[51] It is ironic that Medea, the symbol for Olivares in *Los tres mayores prodigios*, worries about the impact of ships in the world, explaining that "no habrá mina tan secreta" (p. 1554) that sailors could not find. Spain had been relying for a number of years on such mines discovered in the New World, and the worsening economic situation and the constant wars demanded a more aggressive policy, according to the *privado*. Being aware of Olivares's mercantilist concerns, an audience may have wondered why Medea-Olivares would make such a statement on navigation.

A careful look at Medea's statements reveals that her attack is rather ambivalent. It combines worry with admiration. Secondly, subsequent actions will demonstrate her negative vision of shipping as untrue. Like the song of a siren, it is intended to lull the audience into a false sense of security. It is precisely the invention of navigation that will provide Medea with the opportunity to recover the Golden Fleece. Indeed, the sorceress's statement that gold mines would no longer be safe, no matter how remote, ironically refers to her future adventures. Now that she has available Jason's ship, Medea and the Greek hero will become the thieves described by Quevedo and steal the invaluable Golden Fleece. Thus, the siren Medea speaks falsely when she worries about navigation. As she lulls others with her pleasant chant, she plots how to use commerce for her own advantage. Like Olivares, she is exposed as a thief.

Medea's purpose is not to reward a hero, but to bewitch him, as Nerida had done to Atamas. Her weapons include her occult arts and her beauty. While Medea seeks direct control of the heavens, the gods act through mortals to bring about the punishment of the sorceress. *Amor*, using the impressions created by Mars through Jasón, lends fire to the conflict. Although Jasón appears to come in peace, and although Medea will use him for her purposes, he will turn out to be the gods' messenger of misfortune to a woman who has defied their power. And Jasón, in this astral-political interpretation, represents Philip IV. From this point of view, *Los tres mayores prodigios* is similar to *El mayor encanto, amor.* Ulises and Jasón, it could be argued, triumph over the magical powers of an enchantress, just as the king of Spain ought to overcome the influence of his *privado.*

The characterization of Jasón is more complex and ambiguous than the depiction of Ulises in *El mayor encanto, amor.* It is possible to question the laudatory intent based on the parallel Jasón-Philip IV in *Los tres mayores prodigios.* At first glance, the praise of the monarch appears too obvious to be denied. In 1622, Lope de Vega had adapted the Jasón myth in order to praise Philip IV. His play *El vellocino de oro* had been presented at court together with Villamediana's *La gloria de Niquea.* This second play had used Astraea and the golden age among its laudatory images. Now, Calderón combines Astraea and Jasón in one work, *Los tres mayores prodigios.* Instead of a prophecy concerning the golden age, we witness an imprisoned astral force, symbolizing Olivares's occult control. Jasón, however, is a hero who freely and valorously gains the Golden Fleece. This trophy, as Lope de Vega and Calderón were well aware, is found in the sky as the sign Aries, the constellation that presided over Philip IV's birth. Furthermore, the Golden Fleece is a chivalric order founded by Philippe le Bon, duke of Burgundy, and closely associated with the Hapsburgs.[52] The order had been created to unite Christendom against its greatest enemy, the Turks. Now the Spanish Empire had taken upon itself this mission. The Argonautica represents the Christian, chivalric spirit of the age. The order would welcome that universal ruler who could defeat all the enemies of Christianity and bring back an era of peace and harmony, a new golden age. The Jasón myth is thus embued with clear laudatory intent, when applied to a Spanish king.

It is true that Calderón regales his courtly audience with an abundance of laudatory commonplaces: the *rey planeta* is exalted at the time of the summer solstice; his reign includes Astraea, the goddess of the golden age; and he is Jasón, the chivalric hero whose quest can be interpreted as the establishment of a universal empire. If we go no further than the obvious meaning of these images, we will never understand the dramatist's artful deception. Indeed, if he is to criticize, he must do it carefully and deceptively. He must ironically be like a Circe or a Medea who lulls the audience while striking at their very heart. This is the genius of these spectacle plays: the presentation of positive signs and their veiled and clever subversion.

Medea receives two foreign visitors at Colchis: Friso and Jasón. Their contrastive nature and actions reveal much. Friso, the first to arrive, dedicates the fleece to Mars, avoiding the temptation of Medea. Having escaped one sorceress (Nerida), he is better able to deal with another. Jasón, the second to arrive, comes on a ship, a portent that signifies the decline of the ages. He is immediately taken by Medea's beauty. The sorceress decides to hold an *academia de amor* in the perpetual spring of her land. The fact that "es siempre primavera" (p. 1558) recalls the weather of the perfect first age. Yet at Colchis the perfect weather is not the result of nature's gifts to man, but is caused by Medea's control over the goddess who presided over the golden age. She invites to this academy the two strangers, Friso and Jasón. She cleverly excites the men to jealousy and passion, and then proposes they obtain the Golden Fleece. Jasón immediately accepts the challenge, but Friso is able to exert control over himself.

Jasón has aligned himself with Medea and against the gods. He will be her tool to obtain her desires. Ironically, he will also be a tool for the gods' revenge. Friso, on the other hand, shows reverence for Mars. He thus appears as a true hero. To further stain Jasón's character, the play depicts the witch calling on the dark forces to aid Jasón (p. 1559). His triumph against Mars is accomplished with the aid of infernal or demonic magic. Medea threatens the heavens and makes apocalyptic threats. She will destroy the sun in her attempt to steal the Golden Fleece from Mars. Philip IV is a solar and martial ruler according to his panegyrists. Here, Jasón and Medea use demonic magic to go against the luminary and the planet. Instead of evoking a golden age, the sorceress's language depicts apocalypse and destruction.

The act ends with a successful theft of the Golden Fleece. The pair escape in the ship, emblem of the fall. Since Jasón has taken the fleece at Medea's request, the theft lacks the justification found in the original legend. We may assume that Medea has taken along the maids, including Sirene. According to the myth of the Argonautica, on the return trip Jasón and his crew faced the danger of the sirens, but were able to pass unscathed. In Calderón's version of the myth, Sirene is within the ship. She is an aspect of Medea. The hero is lost.

The Chorus of Seneca's *Medea* evokes the first or golden age: "Unsullied the ages our fathers saw, with crime banished afar. Then every man inactive kept to his own shores and lived to old age on ancestral fields, rich with but little, knowing no wealth save what his home soil had yielded" (vol 1, p. 257). The Chorus contrasts that glorious past with the present age when the Argos sails. This is the world that Calderón portrays in the first act of *Los tres mayores prodigios*. The magical transport of the gods, the Golden Fleece, has become an object of greed. Proud man defies the deities and terrorizes other shores. In such a time, when the laws of nature are twisted for personal gratification, Jasón will betray and abandon Medea. But she will retaliate with the murder of their children. These events are not depicted in the Spanish play, but are foreshadowed by Medea's fear of the gods' revenge. In classical tragedy, Medea uses a "strategy of concealment" in order to "appear to herself and to us innocent and worthy of pity." This strategy includes the manipulation of the concepts of justice and of truth in her rhetoric, which also allows her to move from victim to master of the situation.[53] The notion that justice and truth (the two key attributes of Astraea) are manipulated by Medea is thus already found in Calderón's classical models.

One reason for the inclusion of the figures of Astraea and Libia in Calderón's first act may well have been to emphasize the manner in which the sorceress appropriated these qualities for personal gain. Sirene, on the other hand, may represent that "strategy of concealment" used by Medea. The siren is the sweet voice that subverts the values of the happiest of ages. Indeed, Calderón's first act is replete with images that negate the golden age and predict a wasteland. The ship as emblem of the fall, the eternal spring as demonic paradise, the lure of an enchantress and her siren, the imprisonment of astral signs, and the attempted control of the heavens are some of the dark images and actions that announce fall and apocalypse. Demonic powers and inventions, coupled with titanic pride and rebelliousness, link Jasón and Medea, who may be equated with the Spanish monarch and his *privado*, and are depicted as thieves and conjurers who disregard the will of the gods and are intent on personal gratification. Laudatory commonplaces have become images of censure and of impending doom. A brief review of the remaining two acts will show a similar subversion of heroic adventures.

At the beginning of the second act, Teseo arrives on his horse at the court of King Minos on the island of Crete. When soldiers lose two of the victims they are to sacrifice to the Minotaur, they naturally turn to the two strangers (Teseo and his servant) for substitutes. In the slaying of this monster, Teseo will be aided by a woman, just as Jasón was helped by Medea in his adventure. There are, however, significant differences between Ariadne and the sorceress of act one. Ariadne, like Medea, is the daughter of the king of the island, but she is not portrayed negatively. Rather than a manipulator of dark and occult forces, she appears helpless. Teseo, at the beginning of the act, saves her and her sister Fedra from a savage bear. The two sisters fall in love with the stranger, but it is Ariadne who saves his life when he is taken prisoner. She persuades Dédalo, the architect of the labyrinth, to provide Teseo with the means to kill the monster and find his way out of the maze. Indeed, Dédalo gives Teseo an "ovillo de hilo" (p. 1569) that he can follow to the exit, as well as "polvos" (p. 1569) with which to put the Minotaur to sleep.

When all is accomplished and Teseo has slain the monster, he readies to flee on his horse. The two daughters of King Minos plead with the hero to take them, but his horse can only accommodate one maiden. Ariadne reminds him that she has saved his life, but Teseo is enamoured of Fedra. Having to decide between *pasiones* and *honor* (p. 1573), he chooses the former, abandoning his savior, Ariadne. This episode establishes a link between Jasón and Teseo: both are ungrateful to the ladies who provided assistance to them in the performance of heroic deeds. The tragic fate of both heroes lies outside the scope of Calderón's play, although he points to the foibles that bring about the disastrous consequences. Seneca dedicates a drama to each of these two heroes. We have seen how in *Medea*, the sorceress murders Jasón's and her children. In the *Hippolytus*, Seneca shows how Theseus, after abandoning Ariadne, marries Phaedra, and how this brings about disaster. Phaedra is truly responsible for the death of Theseus's son, Hippolytus. This youth, at the beginning of Seneca's work, contrasts the life of the labyrinthine palace to that of the countryside, where the primal age can be relived without "monstrous love" (vol. 1, p. 331). Seneca declares that man does not live in a golden age, but in an iron epoch of selfishness, lust, and deceit.

Calderón's second act concludes in a manner reminiscent of the first act: an apparently happy pair of lovers leaves an island. The second act, like the first, includes a foreshadowing of tragedy that darkens the festive mood of the occasion. While in the first act Medea had envisioned the gods' revenge, here Ariadne curses Teseo. She hopes that he and Fedra will never be happy: "Si la quieres, te aborrezca" (p. 1574). Worse still, Ariadne wishes that Teseo will experience jealousy (p. 1574). This "fateful curse" will be partially fulfilled as Fedra will fall in love with her step-son, bringing destruction to both of them. The result of Ariadne's curse is not mentioned in Calderón's play, but his audience must have been familiar with the story and have understood the implications of the curse. In addition, it was believed that such curses were almost always fulfilled.[54]

Teseo, in the second act of *Los tres mayores prodigios*, is able to defeat the Minotaur and to ride his horse away from Crete. In spite of this, we see him make the wrong choice, being swayed by passion. Two actions emblematic of heroism have been rendered meaningless, and the myth has been subverted. If Teseo is meant as another image of Philip IV, then the king has much to learn. To commission a play about heroism does not alter the reality of the historical situation. Outward forms of power, virtue, and empire, when empty of content, subvert their obvious meaning. The first two acts of *Los tres mayores prodigios* exhibit the same tension between laudatory images and critical appraisals. Both Jasón and Teseo appear as admirable. They accomplish deeds worthy of great heroes. They seem fitting images of the Spanish monarchy. Yet, on a deeper level, it is obvious that these monuments of imperialism are tragically flawed. Heroes and king court disaster.

The third act portrays a third hero, Hércules. Robert Tate comments that "the political ascendency of Spain is heralded by a profusion of mythological history, created to serve a definite ideological purpose."[55] He considers Hercules to be the most important of these myths, since this hero is said to have saved Spain from the tyranny of Geryon and is thus taken as the founder of Spanish monarchy. It is well known that Charles V picked as an emblem of his empire the columns of Hercules. The mythological hero was said to have placed a warning on these columns made up of Mt. Atlas and Gibraltar: *Non Plus Ultra*. These elevations marked the end of the world man must not go beyond. Charles V's emblem contains the opposite statement: *Plus Ultra*. Frances A. Yates explains that "as well as its obvious meaning that his was an empire which extended further than the Romans, which had been bounded by the columns of Hercules, the device carried with it also this prophetic implication that the discovery of the new worlds was providentially timed to coincide with the coming of one who should be the *Dominus mundi* in a wider sense than was known to the Romans."[56] Thus, Hercules and his columnar device were obvious symbols for Spanish imperialism. The concept of a *Dominus mundi* and the hope for a return of the golden age are part of the myth as interpreted by the epoch. The use of this myth to praise Philip IV gained particular prominence when Zurbarán was commissioned to paint ten pictures representing the Labors of Hercules. They were to be exhibited in the Hall of Realms at the Buen Retiro. Zurbarán's commission was first documented in June, 1634, and Calderón's play was performed two years later, in June, 1636.

Calderón's third act, like the previous two, takes up a potent image of kingship and subverts it. *Los tres mayores prodigios* is not unique in its negative treatment of Hercules. In *La estrella de Sevilla*, King Sancho is equated with Hercules *in malo*.[57] In *Fieras afemina amor*, a late spectacle play by Calderón, we again encounter a negative image of Hercules. Thomas O'Connor writes: "A lo largo de los tres actos, Hércules es sometido a una inspección tan minuciosa y a una crítica tan severa que es posible y legítimo afirmar que Calderón se propone deliberadamente desmitificar al más grande héroe de Grecia y del mundo masculino."[58] This demythologizing is also characteristic of our third act. Here, Hércules is able to find Deyanira and her abductor, the centaur Neso. Like Jasón and Teseo, Hércules performs a valorous act. He slays the centaur. As half man and half beast, this creature has the same symbolic equivalence as the Minotaur. Once the action emblematic of heroism has been performed, the act proceeds to reveal the hero's weak inner self. Hércules has witnessed Deyanira's desperate fight against the centaur and knows that she is an innocent victim. At the same time, as A.I. Watson has demonstrated, this great hero succumbs to a false sense of shame, fearing "las malicias ajenas" (p. 1583). He tells his beloved wife that he will proclaim her death, and that she must remain in the wilderness, disguised as a *labradora*.

When Hércules decides to abandon his beloved, he is following a pattern already established in this *comedia*. Jasón, we know, will eventually abandon Medea. This action, although basic for the interpretation of this myth *in malo*, is justified by the fact that she is a sorceress. The second abandonment has much less justification. Teseo does not save his savior, Ariadne, since he prefers the passion of Fedra. Hércules' abandonment is the most negative. He recovers his true love, but rejects her for fear of gossip. Rather than functioning according to intrinsic honor, Hércules, like many Spaniards of the epoch, seems to be concerned with mere appearances. This false honor is made unbearable by the arrival of his friends. It is symbolized, according to Watson, by the tunic of shame that he wears. In the end, Hércules prefers death to the fear that is poisoning his existence, and hurls himself on the sacrificial pyre (p. 1589).

This immolation on a funeral pyre is often considered a "symbol of apotheosis."[59] But the context in which it takes place negates such an interpretation. Watson's comments are most perceptive: "The poison which burns into his flesh is merely the physical counterpart of the shame which is burning into and poisoning his soul. When, driven to distraction, he throws himself on the sacrificial pyre, the audience are witnessing the culmination of a spiritual crisis conveyed in emblematic terms."[60] On a superficial level the pyre is a symbol of apotheosis. The perceptive spectator may view it, on the other hand, as symbolic of the self-destructiveness of contemporary attitudes. Hércules' poison may be the poison that is destroying the Spanish Empire.

El mayor encanto, amor ended with the destruction of Circe in the flames of a volcano. The fire in that play has been related to fires of St. John's night. In *Los tres mayores prodigios*, the sacrificial pyre is also part of this folk ritual. In the 1635 play, it served its purpose: the witch died, the atmosphere was purified and the land made fertile again, proclaiming in veiled terms that the fall of the sorceress (Olivares) would restore harmony to the realm. *Los tres mayores prodigios* reflects a more somber attitude towards the future. One of the purposes of the St. John's fires is to destroy witches and evil spirits. In this play, Medea watches the death of Hércules in the sacrificial pyre. We know that she is an expert in *piromancia*, and this fire may be obeying her. A second objective of this most magical of evenings is to cement promises of marriage. Calderón's *comedia* reiterates the motif of abandonment. Even Hércules, the greatest hero, leaves his wife for fear of gossip. Future fertility and prosperity are a third purpose of the festival fires. From the beginning of the play, such hopes are dashed. Atamas married the witch Nerida and his country became a wasteland. Jasón falls for Medea, not knowing that the eternal spring she has created is in reality a demonic paradise, and that her song is that of a siren. This witch has in her control Libia and Astraea, the maids of autumn, symbolic of justice and the harmony of the golden age. In Colchis, nature is not providing her gifts freely to man, but struggles to be free of the sorceress's power. Even the gods are temporarily defeated as Medea threatens the universe with apocalyptic furor. The one hope for guidance in the *comedia* is Hércules, symbol of the Spanish monarchy. He immolates himself in a manner that recalls his Senecan counterpart. Yet the Spanish version of this mythical figure turns away from apotheosis to describe a man who abandons his wife and succumbs to poisonous gossip. In the crowd of onlookers one may detect Medea. In our astral-political interpretation, she stands for Olivares. The *privado* watches over the monarch's demise.

CHAPTER EIGHT

Empire Without End

THE STORY OF CORIOLANUS, a Roman patrician whose dislike of democracy led to his exile from the immortal city and whose stained honor demanded nothing less than the burning of Rome, is the medium through which Calderón reintroduces a character named Astraea into his theater. *El privilegio de las mujeres*, a play composed by Calderón de la Barca in collaboration with Antonio Coello and Juan Pérez de Montalbán, is considered the source for Calderón's recasting of the Coriolanus theme in *Las armas de la hermosura*. Both plays have been the subject of adverse criticism for their departures from historical fact and their glaring anachronisms. Menéndez Pelayo, for example, has argued that "la historia está falseada arbitraria y caprichosamente, no sólo en el espíritu íntimo que distingue unas épocas de otras, sino hasta en los lances y en los hechos más triviales y familiares."[1] Such negative evaluations of the two *comedias* have been countered by three critics. Perhaps the most far-reaching of these studies is by Alexander Parker. He justifies Calderón's alteration of the tragic ending as found in Roman historians such as Livy and Plutarch through the principle of poetic justice: "The death of a protagonist on the stage could only be punishment for a moral crime, but Coriolanus never at any stage actually commits one." In spite of the fact that he must change historical events significantly, Calderón chooses the Coriolanus theme, according to Parker, because it illustrates one of the playwright's major preoccupations, the "vengeance-forgiveness motif."[2] The overwhelming importance of this motif leads Calderón to a second major departure from history. In neither *El privilegio* nor *Las armas* is Coriolanus exiled from Rome for his patrician attitudes, as in the historical accounts by Livy and Plutarch. Instead, the Spanish plays make him a champion of women's rights. To underline the plight of women in Rome, Calderón identifies them as the abducted Sabines, even though the infamous rape had taken place three centuries earlier, at the time of Romulus. Rejecting Menéndez Pelayo's criticisms, Parker notes that this "telescoping of the action" has classical authority, since it is suggested by some lines in Plutarch.[3] Furthermore, these alterations of history not only serve to focus on the vengeance-forgiveness motif and on feminist concerns, but more importantly, they unify these two questions under the concept of honor. Coriolanus's victory and the consequent affirmation of women's rights in the city show, according to Parker, that "only if women rule in the domain of honour will there be the possibility of love, reasonableness and forgiveness ruling in the relations of human beings to each other."[4] These two *comedias* are then central to our understanding of the concept of honor in Calderón.

Albert Sloman's analysis supports many of Parker's contentions and adds that "Veturia's plea for mercy is superior to revenge." In order to show the "greater cohesion and unity" of *Las armas*, Sloman compares it to the source play, *El privilegio*.[5] Sloman's estimate that *Las armas* is a play of "first importance" is achieved by downplaying the significance of *El privilegio*, an earlier work that could very easily lack cohesiveness because it was written by three playwrights.

David G. Lanoue also focuses on *Las armas*, transforming one of Menéndez Pelayo's negative statements on this *comedia* into an argument for its artistic merit. Menéndez Pelayo had objected to the presentation of Coriolanus, "convirtiendo asi a aquel rudo guerrero romano de los primeros tiempos de la república, en un galante caballero de la corte de los Felipes."[6] For Lanoue, the Spanish flavor of Calderón's Coriolanus is essential to our understanding of the piece since the playwright wishes to emphasize the parallels between Rome and imperial Spain: "Calderón's courtly audience, whose taste for glittering escapist spectacles increased in proportion to the empire's decline, could well have recognized themselves in the feasting Romans at the beginning of the play. The history of Rome in the drama can be interpreted as a political metaphor for a ruling class in the process of losing its imperial dream."[7]

Much of importance has emerged from the renewed study of Calderón's Coriolanus plays. Yet all three approaches omit or negate a point of significance for the Astraea theme in Calderón. Parker, although pointing to three major alterations of history, fails to discuss the curious addition of a character named Astraea to the Coriolanus story. Sloman, in his attempt to show Calderón's craftsmanship in the composition of *Las armas*, relegates *El privilegio* to unjust oblivion. Finally, Lanoue, although interested in the parallels between Rome and imperial Spain, does not explore important ramifications of Calderón's utilization of the imperial model. This chapter will concentrate on the earlier play, El privilegio, and show how it—and consequently Las armas—is not concerned so much with the facts of history as with the myth of Rome as urbs aeterna. It is no coincidence that in both El privilegio and Las armas the purportedly eternal city is threatened by a queen named Astraea.

As El privilegio opens, the king of the Sabines readies to attack Rome. In a lengthy narration he recounts the history of the founding of Rome and the events that have led him to attack the city. The twins Romulus and Remus, descendants of Mars, were raised in the woods by a she-wolf (p. 1374).[8] The fierceness of the founders of Rome was derived from both their "father" and their adoptive mother. They and their followers are described as bandits, a common occupation for those ruled by the god of war.[9] The influence of Mars is also apparent in the way these men assure their succession, as described by Fritz Saxl: "The children of Mars are not satisfied with burning, murdering and stealing cattle; true to classical precedent they have added the abduction of women to their duties."[10] In the comedia, the king relates how the Romans invited the Sabines to a feast. Then they murdered many of them, stealing their women. King Sabino wishes to avenge the rape of the Sabines: "Solo venganza queremos" (p. 398). He is confident that he will succeed, since the rule of Romulus has given way to a senado.

The early days of Rome are described by this city's enemies in a manner that underlines the inhabitants' cruelty and fierceness. It is as if they were nurtured to exhibit the martial spirit of their god. Abductions, treacheries, and wars are far removed from the vision of tranquility and ancient peace portrayed by Virgil in the Georgics II: "Such a life the old Sabines once lived, such Remus and his brother . . . such was the life golden Saturn lived on earth, while yet none had heard the clarion blare, none the sword-blades ring, as they were laid on the stubborn anvil" (p. 153). King Sabino's presentation of the warlike Romans is very different, but the golden age is evoked in the first scene, through the arrival of a princess named Astraea. King Sabino is ready to destroy Rome with her aid. The end of the city could represent the end of the cosmos, since the two were tied together in myth. Mircea Eliade documents how "several times in the course of their history, the Romans underwent the terror of an imminent end to their city, whose duration—as they believed—had been determined at the very moment of its foundation by Romulus."[11] The twelve eagles or vultures seen by Romulus at the founding of Rome became a "mystic number" that revealed the duration of the city. As the number of months in a year, this cycle was linked to the Great Year, at the end of which the universe would be destroyed and regenerated. Describing the destruction of Rome, King Sabino states:

> Rojo diluvio de sangre
> sus anchas campañas cubra,
> ardiente incendio de fuego
> sus altas torres consuma.
>
> [p. 1375]

King Sabino's destruction will take the form of *diluvio* and *incendio*. Pythagoreans, Platonists, and Stoics drew their theories of universal conflagration from the Chaldean Berossus. The notion spread through classical antiquity that the end could take two forms, destruction by water or destruction by fire (*ekpyrosis*). The Sabine king combines both into an amazing conflagration where deluges of blood (his massacre of the Romans) would combine with fire. An audience versed in the myth of Rome would have thought it no coincidence that Sabino speaks of *diluvio* and *incendio* while accompanied by a figure named Astraea. Surely these are all presages of the end. Astraea's presence serves to confirm the *apokatastasis*, the notion that destruction of city, empire, or cosmos is followed by renewal.[12] Purification by fire and water would result in a new golden age for mankind.

Such an end takes place when men have been corrupted to such an extent that they live in the fourth or iron age. The third scene of *El privilegio* confirms the decadence of the people and the need for renewal. Even though the Sabine soldiers prepare to attack, most Romans refuse to fight, preferring the enjoyment of selfish pleasures within the city (p. 1376). Lack of patriotism, idleness, and lust are typical of the fourth or iron age. Such behavior is particularly abhorrent since it is contrary to the very nature of the Romans, who are the children of Mars. Indeed, Plutarch argues that valor is honored in Rome above all other virtues.[13] Calderón underlines the subversion of Roman *virtus* through the well-known opposition between Venus and Mars. The Romans are caught in the snares of the goddess who stands against the martial nature of the Roman deity: "Que estraga sus iras Marte / a los halagos de Venus" (p. 1377).

Rome has, however, a hero. With five hundred soldiers, Coriolano valiantly defeats the large Sabine contingent. While he is battling the enemy, the Roman senate debates the perilous situation. The result of the meeting is a *premática* where they afix blame for the decline of manly virtues on the women of the city. The decree forbids women to wear certain items of clothing and jewelry. It even prohibits them from riding in *coches:*

> Una premática han hecho,
> por bajar de las mujeres
> el exterior lucimiento . . .
> censurándoles su adorno,
> su estimación desluciendo,
> prohibiéndoles los coches,
> que es lo que ellas más sintieron.
>
> [p. 1378]

The *premática*, issued while Coriolano delivers Rome from the enemy, sidesteps male cowardice and instead takes away many of women's rights and privileges. The detailed description of the decree points clearly to the fact that Calderón was establishing a parallel between the action of the *comedia* and the contemporary situation in Spain. The *premática* described in *El privilegio* is so specific that it has enabled Cotarelo y Mori to date this *comedia:* "Fué escrita en este mismo año (1636), pues en ella (I, v) se alude a la pragmática publicada el 12 de octubre prohibiendo el uso de guardainfante y otros adornos." Although Sloman argues that "this seems to leave too narrow a margin for publication in that year," he accepts Ruth Lee Kennedy's assessment that *El privilegio* "was written in the 30's, probably not much before 1636."[14]

Threats from abroad, a declining empire, the scarcity of heroes, the decline in morals and customs, and the fact that women are blamed for man's lack of valor—these are situations and attitudes that can very well describe the Spanish Empire in 1635-36. Philip IV, as has been noted, was hailed by panegyrists as the monarch who would bring back the golden age, and he was often associated with Astraea. But Spain, like the Rome in the *comedia*, must wonder if a new age will be preceded by destruction, if Madrid's danger presages an *apokatastasis.*[15]

Returning in triumph to the city, Coriolano expects to be immersed in victory celebrations, but he soon discovers deep internal dissension over the *premática*. Veturia, his beloved, questions Roman men's *virtus* and thus their *valor:*

> Si sois valientes, decid,
> decid, ¿cómo habéis sufrido
> derogar de las mujeres
> los privilegios antiguos?
>
> [p. 1380]

Veturia is well aware that Roman soldiers have succumbed to vice and idleness, but she also knows that to afix the blame on the women is unjust (p. 1380). Roman women are the mothers of those that are now turning against them. Veturia's complaint reaches its climax in her description of the treachery of the males against their own mothers. To convey the odious nature of such behavior, she uses the image of the viper: "¡Oh víbora, que en el mismo / vientre que a beber le saca, / estrena el primer delito!" (p. 1381)

As we have seen in chapter five, the anecdote of the viper that is killed by its offspring at the time of birth is a well-known topic during the epoch, and one often utilized by Calderón. Indeed, the presence of the viper motif in El privilegio must be considered as one more element that confirms the fact that this comedia was composed in the mid-1630s. Calderón makes use of the viper image in at least two plays during this time, La vida es sueño (1635) and La devoción de la cruz (1637). A third play, La hija del aire II, although a work of uncertain date and of questionable authorship, could also be included in this group since many elements, including the viper motif and the presence of the "maids of autumn," are typical of this period.

In both La vida es sueño and La devoción de la cruz, a child is born as the mother dies. The events cast suspicion on both the mother and the child. Since she has given birth to a monstruo, albeit a metaphorical one, she is suspected of infidelity. The child is related to the viborezno and thus becomes an emblem and an omen of future treachery. In El privilegio the viper image continues the development of the mother motif in the comedia.[16] At the beginning of the play we encountered the she-wolf as the substitute mother of Romulus and Remus, the founders of Rome. The fierceness of the mother, along with the martial nature of the ancestor god, lends the Romans the necessary valor to begin to create an "eternal" city and a future empire. When this fierceness is forgotten, Veturia brings up again the image of the mother. The women of the city—and by extension, Rome itself—are being destroyed by the treachery of their own children, who prefer to raise their cowardly hand against them rather than acknowledge their own idlensss and vice. This image of Rome as the mother and of the males in the city as her treacherous viper offspring contrasts particularly strongly with accepted attitudes toward Rome. If this image is extended to imperial Spain, the play becomes a severe indictment of the customs and mores of Calderón's countrymen.

Weighing in balance the decree of the senate and the accusations of his beloved, Coriolano judges in favor of the women, thus fomenting civil unrest in the city. This new threat of violence brings to an end the first act of the *comedia*. The second *jornada*, written by Juan Pérez de Montalbán, centers around another judgment. Coriolano is tried for breaking "del senado los decretos" (p. 1382). The term *balanza* is repeated as the judges attempt to reach an equitable decision. This is Astraea's instrument.

Astraea as the goddess of justice is often depicted holding the balance in one hand and the sword in the other. Calderón's *comedia* deals with the two instruments of justice. The Romans, through the rape of the Sabines and the *premática* against women, have tilted the balance towards extreme injustice. And yet, the audience is visually reassured that these extreme actions will be balanced out in the end. A scene depicts the disguised king of the Sabines inspecting the walls of Rome, accompanied by the princess Astraea: "en varonil traje disfrazada, / echada al lado la valiente espada" (p. 1388). In *La vida es sueño*, Rosaura, in a similar *varonil traje*, led Segismundo to become the rightful prince of Poland and bring about a "golden age" of peace and harmony. The mystery of the sword carried by Rosaura underlined her kinship with the goddess of justice. In *El privilegio*, Astraea's sword also points to the actions that will bring justice to the land. It is a *valiente espada*, one that can help only those who esteem valor above all else. Astraea, although apparently in a camp opposed to Coriolano, will help him since he is the epitome of *valor*. This aid will be given indirectly. The princess accompanies Sabino to a spot along the Roman walls, thus enabling the king to witness Roman injustice towards Coriolano. Astraea then departs, allowing the two former enemies to meet alone. As Coriolano approaches, it becomes obvious to Sabino that his enemy has no sword. Coriolano tells the king that he wishes to die: "me arroje a tu acero invicto" (p. 1392). The Sabine, however, praises Coriolano's *valor*, even though it was used to defeat his army. He adds that he knows that Rome has been unjust towards the victorious Coriolano: "tus injusticias he visto" (p. 1392). Rather than running him through with his sword, the king will present it to Coriolano as a gift in hopes that the Roman will help the Sabines conquer the city:

> Y por la espada, me obligo
> ceñirte la que a mi lado
> fué honor del campo sabino.
> Astraea me está esperando,
> mi ejército prevenido
> a mis órdenes aguarda . . .
>
> [p. 1392]

It is significant that the granting of the sword is immediately followed by a mention of Astraea, the goddess of justice. This is followed in turn by a pledge to banish injustice from the city: "Roma sus yerros conozca" (p. 1392). This city has surmounted a first crisis with the heroic help of Coriolano, but now, without him, it must withstand the strength of the vengeful Sabine allied with her exiled but most valiant son. These two warriors are accompanied by Astraea, an emblem of justice. The destruction that precedes the happiest of ages is threatened by this new alliance. The second *jornada* ends with a renewed possibility of *apokatastasis*.

The third *jornada*, by Antonio Coello, depicts the siege of Rome led by King Sabino, Princess Astraea, and Coriolano. The king is described by Coriolano as a "Sabino Marte" (p. 1393), implying that Mars has abandoned his city because true valor is not to be found there, but exists among the Sabines. The princess is addressed by Coriolano as "celestial Astraea" (p. 1393), and is thus equated with the celestial goddess and the zodiacal sign. She no longer waits in the heavens but confronts the corrupt Romans, who are thus threatened with an *apokatastasis*. The third leader, Coriolano, has no epithet. Instead, he speaks to the city. In this apostrophe he evokes images of destruction and reinforces the fear of *apokatastasis*. Inside the city, Coriolano's father, Aurelio, also intones an apostrophe to Rome, suggesting that the city ought to remember its eternal nature and not be overshadowed by the present situation. Aurelio's view of the city's future is thus radically different from that of Coriolano. The son believes that the "funesto día" (p. 1393) will bring about Rome's destruction, while the father places his trust in the eternal nature of the city. These opposing views of Rome are part of the city's mythology. Its inhabitants periodically become fearful that the end of a cycle was at hand and that their period of dominance was over. The Romans assiduously searched for omens that would support or deny this dreaded possibility. In the *Fourth Eclogue*, Virgil asserted that the golden age could return without a prior conflagration. In the *Aeneid*, Venus, Aeneas's mother, complains to Jupiter of her son's future. The father of the gods answers Venus with a prophetic speech. He asserts that the people of Aeneas will eventually build an empire when "Ilia, a royal priestess, shall bear to Mars her two offspring" (p. 261). Romulus will build the city of Rome. As for his descendants and consequently the descendants of Aeneas, Jupiter prophesies: "For these I set neither bounds nor periods of empire; dominion without end have I bestowed" (p. 261). Mircea Eliade explains that "it was not until after the publication of the *Aeneid* that Rome was called *urbs aeterna*. . . . Then arose the hope that Rome could regenerate itself periodically *ad infinitum*. Thus it was, that, liberated from the myths of the twelve eagles and of the ekpyrosis, Rome could increase until, as Virgil foretells, it embraced even the regions 'beyond the paths of the sun and the year.'"[17] Two theories, that of *renovatio* and that of *apokatastasis*, oppose each other through the two apostrophes to Rome uttered by Aurelio and by his son Coriolano.

In order to save Rome from destruction and to implement his notion of regeneration, Aurelio decides to go to the Sabine camp and appeal directly to the enemy. In the meantime, Sabino has conferred equal authority on Coriolano so that the exiled Roman can decide his city's fate (pp. 1396-97). Aurelio must present his arguments to his own son. In the previous act Aurelio served as judge; now he is being judged. The rule of Astraea (justice) is equitable. Aurelio's words echo his apostrophe in that they convey the hope of *renovatio*:

> Roma, fénix sin segundo,
> que hoy, pobre y mísera yace,
> y de sus cenizas nace
> a ser cabeza del mundo.
>
> [p. 1397]

The image of the phoenix, a mythical bird reborn out of its own ashes, is a particularly fitting description of a Rome threatened by *ekpyrosis*. Furthermore, it stresses the role of the city as unique since there is only one phoenix in creation. Indeed, the Arabian bird is as integral a part of the myth of Rome as the tale of Romulus's twelve eagles. Jean Hubaux and Maxime LeRoy present convincing arguments for the relationship of these two birds and their significance in the Roman myth. They stress that both birds are of solar nature and can regenerate themselves through purificatory fire.[18] Although the twelve eagles point to a kind of cyclical pattern that the city must follow, the eagle's nature provides hope for eternal regeneration, since it can purify itself through fire and become young again. The same is true for the phoenix, often used as an emblem for eternity because its apparent death in flames results in its rebirth.[19] Martial compares the phoenix to Rome, since both can undergo *renovatio*. Aurelio is telling his son that Rome has reached the nadir of its existence, the low point in fortune's wheel. It lies in metaphorical ashes like the phoenix. There is no need for *apokatastasis*, since the city can learn from its mistakes and rise from the ashes of corruption and defeat like the phoenix. Aurelio considers that regeneration does not need to be preceded by a true *ekpyrosis*. Rome has the capability of being an *urbs aeterna*.

This view of Rome's history presented by Aurelio to Coriolano is considered by Eliade as a "supreme effort to liberate history from astral destiny or from the law of cosmic cycles."[20] Once the father has presented his optimistic and imperialistic vision, he must convince the son to act in consonance with this view. His attempted persuasion uses two other ideas already presented in *El privilegio*: the notion of Rome as mother and the image of the treacherous child as viper (p. 1397). *El privilegio* does not develop the astral implications of the viper image. Instead, it emphasizes the link between this creature's legend and the myth of Rome as mother. Beryl Rowland shows that the viper "symbolized children plotting against their parents."[21] Aurelio accuses his son of treachery, equating him with the viper. Coriolano, he claims, is plotting to destroy not only his own father, Aurelio, but also his mother, the city of Rome: "Ya que así te persuadieres, / mira que es Roma tu madre, / mira que yo soy tu padre" (p. 1397-98). Coriolano turns his back on his parents and assumes the role of the viper, since he believes that this is his duty. Astraea exclaims, "No he visto valor igual" (p. 1398). Throughout the *comedia*, Coriolano's *valor*, his martial qualities, are never in question. At this point they lack the tempering effect of love and compassion.

A second embassy is sent from Rome. This time it is led by Coriolano's best friend, Enio. He is not able to persuade Coriolano to demonstrate compassion either. As Enio departs, he echoes Aurelio's conception of the exiled Roman as a viper:

> Ese prodigio, ese monstruo,
> esa víbora, ese áspid,
> que nació para romper
> las entrañas de su madre,
> desconsolado me envía.
>
> [p. 1399]

The use of the viper image by Coriolano's father and by his best friend serves to emphasize the precarious balance that has been achieved in the action of the *comedia*. In the first act, the Roman senate issued a *premática* against women. The senators' injustice was equated with the *viboreznos'* murder of their mother. In other words, the senators, as the children of Rome, were seen as destroying the women of the city in their role as mothers. Refusing to change this unjust attitude even when challenged by Rome's greatest hero, the senate exiled Coriolano for his attempt to right a wrong. When the

174   THE RETURN OF ASTRAEA

exiled hero turns against the city, his father and his friend label him a viper. Thus one extreme action leads to another, and an example from the natural world dealing with treachery is first applied to one group and then to its enemy. In this balance of "treachery" we may perceive the goddess Astraea adjusting the scales of justice. Indeed, justice or its absence is a theme that permeates the action of this *comedia*. Coriolano was judged by three men and ordered to leave Rome. Now, he sits in judgment of the city as three different ambassadors plead for his mercy. Two of them, his father and his friend, were judges in Rome. Coriolano rejects their arguments. The third and last ambassador is his beloved Veturia.

In a sudden transformation, Coriolano puts aside his stern and unyielding attitude towards Rome. He responds positively to Veturias's request. Using the power invested in him by the Sabine king, Coriolano pardons the city: "Viva Roma triunfante" (p. 1400). His pardon of Rome is on condition that the women be given back their rights and their freedom. He also demands that they be granted a new privilege: "y por mayor privilegio, / . . . se entregue / todo el honor de los hombres / al poder de las mujeres" (p. 1401). These lines, which reappear virtually unchanged in *Las armas*, constitute a clear and radical statement of the playwrights' attitude towards *pundonor*. Alexander Parker explains: "Only if women rule in the domain of honour will there be the possibility of love, reasonableness and forgiveness ruling in the relations of human beings to each other."[22]

The triumph of Rome has not depended solely on the qualities of Mars. It is true that Coriolano saved the city from the Sabines through his *valor*, the typical martial attribute. But he has had to save the city a second time. At the moment of greatest peril for the city, the women of Rome have been able to elicit from the exiled hero the feminine qualities of love and forgiveness. The valor of Mars has been balanced by the influence of Venus. The offspring of their union is not the treacherous viper but the longed-for Harmonia. Rome has been saved by Coriolano, a man who unites in the self the qualities of Mars and Venus. Such a hero is a true son of Rome. The city is ostensibly ruled by Mars, the father of Romulus, but Rome also owes a debt to Venus, who was Aeneas's mother. Through her prayers, Jupiter awarded Rome dominion without end. What *El privilegio* dramatizes is the shift in the myth of Rome from a city condemned to destruction at the end of a cycle to a realm blessed by the gods as an *urbs aeterna*. *Ekpyrosis* has given way to regeneration since the amiable prayers of Venus have tempered the destructive nature of Mars.

A final balance has been achieved. Astraea has indeed returned.

Her presence need not be feared. No *ekpyrosis* is necessary to bring about a new golden age. Harmony is achieved through the balance between *amor* and *valor*. The Astraea in *El privilegio* is a princess from Chipre. This island, as will become clear in the next chapter, is sacred to Venus. Thus, Astraea has come to guide men to a new age through the unfolding of the qualities of the goddess of love. The women of Rome have saved the world. But in Spain, a 1636 *premática* stands as an example of the rule of Mars and the treachery of the citizens against their own women. If Philip IV is to be the monarch who takes Spain to a new golden age, then he must look to the goddess Astraea and discover in her those qualities of Venus that can help temper himself and his people and thus bring harmony to the land.

El privilegio is an example of a collaborative effort that results in an aesthetically satisfying piece. The play succeeds in presenting a cogent artistic recreation of the myth of Rome as a mirror of the seventeenth-century Spanish Empire. The triumph of love and compassion over cruelty and vengeance and the presence of Astraea as a guide to the hero who will bring a new golden age to his people establish clear parallels between *El privilegio* and *La vida es sueño*. This collaboration should thus not be relegated to the function of mere source for Calderón's later reworking of the Coriolanus theme.

This chapter has stressed the importance of *El privilegio* in an attempt to correct previous neglect. But we cannot move on to Calderón's late Astraea plays without making some reference to *Las armas*. Since Sloman has already discussed most of the changes introduced by Calderón, we will concentrate on those aspects that have escaped critical attention, in particular the myth of Astraea and the myth of Rome.

Two major motifs of *El privilegio* are absent from *Las armas:* the city of Rome as mother and the treacherous offspring as viper. The image of the viper interested Calderón in the years 1635-37. It appears much later, in 1657-58, as a parallel to a contemporary situation. Since *Las armas* was written between these two periods, it is not surprising to discover the absence of the *víbora*. And, since the serpent offspring is closely linked to the image of Rome as a mother in *El privilegio*, this second motif loses importance in *Las armas*. It may also be argued that historical allusions in *Las armas* require the removal of the viper motif.

Juan Eugenio Hartzenbusch believes that *Las armas* was composed in 1652. Most modern critics tend to agree with his analysis, even though some are concerned about the lapse of time between *El privilegio* and *Las armas*. In spite of this, Sloman finds that *Las armas*

"remains close to its model."[23] To support the 1652 dating, Hartzenbusch cites a passage towards the end of the *comedia:*

> Digamos todos, pues todos
> trocamos males a bienes,
> a las plantas de Sabinio,
> Astraea y Coriolano, alegres.[24]
>
> [p. 981]

Hartzenbusch explains: "Aquí el autor, al concluir su obra, dirige
sus respetos á Sabinio, un rey; á Astraea, una reina; y á Coriolano,
un general que merece ser atendido inmediatamente después de los
reyes, un general que *vence* y *perdona.* Creo que estas señas de per-
sonas y hechos corresponden exactamente a Felipe IV, la Reina Mariana, y Don Juan de Austria, despues de la rendición de Barcelona,
que fue seguida de una amnistía."[25] Barcelona fell to the combined
armies of the Marquis of Mortara and don Juan José de Austria on
October 13, 1652. The method used to defeat the city was the same
as Coriolano's strategy to subdue Rome: both leaders surrounded the
city and waited for hunger to weaken the spirit of resistance. The
victor's clemency also reflects Philip IV's mercy towards Barcelona.
As Alexander Parker points out, "The parallel could be pushed further in that the restoration of women's rights in the play, connected
as it is with victory and pardon, might correspond to Philip IV's confirmation of the Catalan *fueros,* in which case the play would have
been written after 3rd January 1653."[26]
The absence of the viper motif may reflect an attitude of concili-
ation. Barcelona was not to be thought of as treacherous, but as fight-
ing for certain rights and privileges. As Parker has warned, *Las armas*
ought not to be interpreted as political allegory since "the correspondences are not exact and since the plot dates from many years earlier."[27] Calderón seldom surrenders to the temptation of political allegory, be it as laudatory propaganda or as satire against the regime.
It is the allusiveness of his *comedias* that attracts the reader or spectator. The relevance of Calderón's images and plots to contemporary
situations captures the attention of the spectator who, in his attempt
to unravel a series of indirect references, enters into an emotional and
intellectual exchange with the dialogic action being presented. Ideas,
images, and concepts lead to contemporary historical events and vice
versa. The play blends with life and elicits response.
If we are to continue the search for certain allusive keys in the
1652-53 *comedia* following Hartzenbusch's suggestions, it might be

that other changes made to the source play are significant. In *El privilegio*, Astraea was the princess of Chipre. In *Las armas* she becomes a Spanish queen. Her new role would make her a more fitting image of Queen Mariana. Sloman points out that Astraea plays a more important role in *Las armas*. In this *comedia*, she falls from her horse and is captured by Coriolano. She tells him that she is one of Astraea's maids and the Roman hero releases her. For Sloman, this serves a double purpose: "Astraea's deliverance by Coriolano provides a motive for her protecting him when he is banished from Rome. At the same time it calls attention again to Coriolano's attitude to women."[28] The scene of Astraea's capture shows at the same time the breakdown of exact historical parallelism and the very allusiveness typical of the texture of Calderón's *comedias*. Following Hartzenbusch, the spectator would see in Coriolano the historical figure of don Juan José de Austria and in Astraea the figure of Queen Mariana of Spain, second wife of Philip IV. Certainly the young soldier never "rescued" the Spanish queen. But what adds an ironic and thoughtful flavor to the incident is the knowledge that Mariana was seeking to destroy don Juan José. He was the only illegitimate son of the king who had been publicly recognized, and Mariana saw him as a threat, not having as yet any male heir with whom to counter his ambitions.[29] That Juan José de Austria would rescue and help a fallen queen would certainly be a most surprising and suggestive episode. Indeed, the conciliatory tone of the *comedia* could include the desire to end all internal strife, including that between the queen and the warrior.

Such a hope is strengthened when later in the play, Coriolano is exiled from Rome and is rescued by Astraea. As opposed to *El privilegio*, where King Sabino wishes to pardon Coriolano, *Las armas* portrays a King Sabinio eager for revenge. Astraea at this point must plead for Coriolano's life. Sloman comments that "Astraea's prevailing upon the King to show mercy foreshadows the achievement of Veturia in Act III."[30] This parallel between Astraea and Veturia in *Las armas* has also been noticed by Melveena McKendrick: "Astraea . . . is extrinsically significant in that she completes the play's dual presentation of feminism: Veturia is the intellectual feminist, Astraea the militant."[31] The two women actually guide and control the action of the play through their guidance of the men at the forefront of the historical situation, King Sabinio and Coriolano. The two women are also representatives of astral and celestial powers. When Sabinio pardons Coriolano through Astraea's intercession, the Roman hero kneels to the goddess of fortune: "Ya no debo / quejarme de ti, fortuna" (p. 968). But King Sabinio tells him that he ought to turn to Astraea and not to Fortuna. Coriolano then addresses the Spanish queen:

> Si al nombre de la deidad
> postrado rendí el obsequio,
> ¿qué haré a la deidad el día
> que obra milagro tan nuevo
> como hacer a un desdichado
> un dichoso, si no puedo
> hacer más que haber traído
> las cadenas a su templo.?
>
> [p. 968]

In *La gran Cenobia* Fortuna was an image of divine providence seen by the ignorant. The truly wise man could envision Astraea, the harmony of creation, in the most confusing and baffling of circumstances. Coriolano's "offering" here is thus to both Fortuna and to Astraea, since they are one and the same goddess. He thanks her for the miracle of saving him, but states that the only offering he has for her temple are the chains he wears. Astraea's reply is in keeping with her role as goddess:

> Que el tiempo me diría el tuyo
> también dije yo, añadiendo
> que fiares de mí; y pues ya
> cumplió su palabra el tiempo,
> también sabré yo cumplir
> la mía, restituyendo
> los puestos y los honores
> que de ingrata te ha depuesto
> tu patria.
>
> [p. 968]

Astraea is the daughter of time ("veritas filia temporis") and it is thus fitting that she speak in terms of *tiempo*. She had asked Coriolano to trust in her, promising that in time they would learn each other's names. And indeed, divine providence has brought them together, and now they will know each other better. Coriolano has already recognized the equation Fortuna-Astraea, and she sees in him a hero who can unfold her truth and justice through time. But a second woman will also have to exercise her influence in order to see that the Romans will be spared and at the same time discover truth. It is a truth of social, political, and astral implications, having to do with women's rights, with a city's search for justice, and with the harmonious influence of the heavens.

Veturia, like Astraea, is more than an ordinary human being. She is an image of a celestial power. As in *El privilegio*, she represents Venus. In *Las armas*, however, this relationship is more explicit. It is the benign influence of the third "star" that guides Coriolano: "de Venus, brillante estrella, pues benigna en mi favor" (p. 941). The heavens have chosen to temper the opposing martial forces through the influence of the planet and goddess Venus. Coriolano responds to Veturia in the same manner as the "Sabino Marte" (p. 971) had responded to Astraea. Harmonia, the offspring of Mars and Venus, comes to a city now ruled by both deities. Explaining his merciful actions to Sabino and Astraea, Coriolano states:

> Que usando de los poderes
> que, como sabinos astros,
> vuestras piedades me ofrecen,
> me he movido a que sus rayos
> hoy alumbren y no quemen;
> y así, en vuestro nombre a Roma
> he perdonado.
>
> [p. 980]

In this passage, the solar rays will not cause the burning of the city but will instead illuminate Rome. This shift in the sun from a destructive to a benefic body coincides with Virgil's transformation of the myth of Rome. Eliade explains that "thus, Virgil, for the last *saeculum*, that of the sun, which was to bring about the combustion of the universe, could substitute the *saeculum* of Apollo, avoiding an *ekpyrosis*."[32]

Rome, in Virgil's new interpretation of history, is given new life by Apollo. At the conclusion of *Las armas*, a similar transformation occurs. Coriolano points to King Sabinio and to Astraea as "sabinos astros" (p. 980) who will not burn Rome, but enlighten her. Sabinio as a solar king is a most appropriate representation for the Spanish monarch. Philip IV, as the fourth of his name, was a figure akin to the sun, the fourth Ptolemaic planet. Instead of an *ekpyrosis*, the sun king will bring light to the empire. This can take place since Astraea stands next to the monarch as another celestial body. She is the zodiacal sign of justice. Her truth is expressed through historical time. And now, her presence on earth indicates the dawn of a new age. With the aid of the benefic influence of Venus, Mars has been tempered and Harmonia can issue forth.

With a few subtle yet masterful strokes and with the assistance of historical circumstances and changing myths, Calderón has transformed the Coriolanus theme into a triumphant yet nostalgic vision of the Spanish Empire. In *El privilegio,* the triumph of Rome contrasted with Spanish failures. While Rome was able to overcome the outcome of an unjust *premática,* Spain had just issued one. The benefic Venus seemed far removed from a nation overwhelmed by foreign wars. But in *Las armas* the tempering influence of the goddess of love reflects Spanish attitudes towards the surrender of Catalonia. More important, Astraea, the regenerative universal power who brings the hope of a new age, is now a Spanish queen. She is wed to Sabinio, the solar monarch Philip IV. Together, with the aid of Coriolano, they save Rome. The survival of the city represents the persistance of the imperial ideal during the Spanish Golden Age.

CHAPTER NINE

The Malefic Astraea

CALDERÓN'S NOSTALGIC STANCE toward the imperial dream as represented by the goddess-queen Astraea in *Las armas de la hermosura* must be balanced by an understanding of his continued "mistreatment" of the heavenly figure in *comedias* that point to the subversion and dissipation of an ideal. We have seen how Astraea, as one of the "maids of autumn," was subjugated by the sorceresses Medea and Circe. In *El mayor encanto, amor,* Ulises emerged triumphant from the snares of a witch who attempted to control him just as she sought to manipulate stars and situations. This apparently wiser Ulises now becomes the protagonist of a one-act play presented at the *Zarzuela* on January 17, 1657.[1] A woman named Astraea has a seemingly minor role in this work, *El golfo de las sirenas*. The *loa* begins by describing the time of year through a lament by the four elements. Earth, water, air, and fire complain of the ravages of winter. Astraea and Sileno are two *villanos* who describe the arrival of newcomers. Astraea relates the effect that these strangers are having on the season. Even though it is the month of January, winter is fleeing in the presence of beauty and spring:

> hermosos coros de Ninfas,
> cuyas diuinas bellezas
> à desagrauiar sin duda
> vienen a la Primauera,
> restituyendo a los campos
> quantos matizes grossera
> de Enero robò la saña.
>
> [p. 495][2]

These nymphs are the ladies of the court accompanying the king and queen. Everett Hesse has pointed out that one of the main purposes of the *loa* is to present a laudatory portrait of the royal family.[3] Sileno describes Philip IV in typical fashion. Since he is the fourth of his name, he is related to the fourth Ptolemaic planet, the sun, who is also the god Apollo (p. 496). Astraea describes Mariana, the second wife of Philip IV. The queen, whose name includes the "Mar" of Marte and the "Ana" of Diana, encompasses two mighty opposites, Mars and Diana, war and peace. The speeches of praise are given by two characters named Sileno and Astraea. Sileno must be the Silenus of mythology, the companion of Dionysus, who represents the power of prophecy. Astraea is also linked to the prophetic through her association with the sibyls. She heralds the return of the golden age. In the *loa*, the transformation of winter into spring is one sign of the dawn of the new epoch, since the happiest of ages was often described as a perpetual spring. Winter's defeat signals the end of the iron age.

In spite of all these laudatory commonplaces, the tone of the *loa* has been described as problematic. The presence of *villanos* in this introductory section, along with their importance in the main body of the work and in the *mogiganga* that follows, has been seen by Thomas O'Connor as undercutting the mythical universe otherwise depicted.[4] And yet, the presentation of Astraea as a *villana* has contemporary sanction and classical precedent. A painting by Salvator Rosa portrays Astraea abiding among the peasants, thus stressing rustic honesty over greed. As Richard Wallace points out, the idea that justice fled to the countryside before leaving earth actually derives from Virgil's *Georgics*.[5] Speaking of the happiness enjoyed by the rustics, the Roman poet claims that "among them, as she quitted the earth, Justice planted her last steps" (vol. 1, p. 149). By having his rustic Astraea hail the Spanish monarchs, Calderón may be incorporating the bucolic view of the golden age into the imperial version of the new epoch. In the *loa* to *El golfo de las sirenas*, the rustics do not necessarily undercut the myth, but make it more vital through a reconciliation of opposites, court and country.

Since the *loa* may be construed as an imperialistic prophecy linked to the Spanish monarchy, the main action of the eclogue could be viewed as a continuation of this laudatory beginning. In *El mayor encanto, amor*, Ulises represented the Spanish king, Philip IV. There the hero was able to overcome his baser nature and triumph over the snares of Circe. The action of *El golfo de las sirenas* also centers around Ulises. It takes place after the Circe episode. Alfeo warns the Greek hero of the perils he will encounter in the land where he has been shipwrecked. Ulises replies that Escila and Caribdis cannot control him since his senses are restrained and guided by prudence. Such a statement could serve a laudatory purpose if the equation Philip IV-

Ulises is preserved in this play, since prudence is a key virtue in a monarch:

>   Siempre los sentidos fueron
>   vassallos de la prudencia,
>   y no tienen contra mi
>   mi vista, ni mi oido fuerça,
>   mas que aquello que yo quiero,
>   que liuianamente tengan.
>
>   [p. 503]

Ulises depicts himself as an ideal hero who, having triumphed over Circe, can now easily control the senses of sight and hearing. These two senses play a prominent role in the work. Escila will tempt Ulises through sight, while Caribdis will utilize hearing in her attempt to destroy the hero. The battle between these two marine deities for control of Ulises recalls the controversy that raged among theatergoers and critics of the epoch as to which was more important in a play, the verbal or the visual. At a time when stage machinery and amazing sets had acquired great popularity at court, a number of poets were reminding the public that the verbal, the poetry, constituted the "soul" of the *comedia*. Scenery and spectacle were merely the "body."[6] In *El golfo de las sirenas*, Ulises must reject the temptations of both senses. This rejection should not be construed as a criticism of all theater, but as a realization of the falseness of the *gran teatro del mundo*. A theatrical controversy has been turned into an attitude towards the world as theater.

Ulises downplays the threat of his enemies. Neither Caribdis's voice nor Escila's beauty can sway him, since they are insubstantial, a part of the world theater. The first he labels the "hija . . . del viento," while the latter is "hija del tiempo" (p. 502). He thus argues that Caribdis's voice cannot sway him since it is mere wind, while Escila's beauty cannot hold him long since it is subject to time. Yet these appellations have deeper significance. The first recalls Queen Semíramis, who is labeled daughter of the air (wind) in the very title of Calderón's two-part tragedy on the subject, *La hija del aire*. The second recalls the motto "veritas filia temporis," which refers to the fact that Astraea as Truth is the daughter of Time (Saturn).[7] Ulises has used these two epithets to downplay his danger, rendering it insubstantial, but each has a greater significance than the hero attaches to it. The "hija del viento [aire]" Semíramis was so persuasive as to become the ruler of a mighty empire. Her voice had a power not so easily dismissed. Indeed, the power of both Escila and Caribdis is clearly portrayed in *El golfo de las sirenas*; Ulises is almost destroyed by them. "Hija del tiempo," on the other hand, points to the resolution of the conflict. Ulises has deceived himself in thinking that he can easily overcome the lure of the senses. Time reveals to him the folly of this attitude. Astraea or truth is unfolded through time.

Ulises does not come upon this truth by himself. He is aided by the rustics Alfeo and Celefa, who help him to bring his senses under control. These *villanos* cleverly utilize the conflict between two opposite forces (Escila-sight and Caribdis-hearing) to neutralize the enemy and save Ulises. They lead him away from the senses and toward the truth of Astraea. There are a number of parallels between *El mayor encanto, amor* and *El golfo de las sirenas*. In both mythological plays Astraea is a seemingly minor figure. A careful examination shows that her role is essential to an understanding of the works. In both plays, Ulises is the hero who arrives at an island and is confronted with danger. The danger takes the form of sensual temptation. Ulises eventually is able to overcome the pull of the senses and save himself. Both *comedias* were performed for the Spanish monarch and contain laudatory passages. Indeed, the king can be equated with the hero Ulises, who becomes an apparently ideal figure by leading his people away from danger to a final harmony akin to the happiest of epochs. Philip IV is thus seen as bringing back that golden age of which Astraea is a symbol. And yet in both plays the figure of Ulises and consequently that of the Spanish monarch is not as flawless as it may appear at first. In *El mayor encanto, amor*, Philip is seen as struggling to rid himself of the influence of a "sorceress" who may stand for his minister Olivares. In *El golfo de las sirenas*, the criticism is more direct. Ulises' boastfulness and initial lack of prudence in spite of his previous experience with Circe make him less than the ideal hero. Through Ulises the play seems to be pointing out that the Spanish monarch has failed to learn the lessons of history. There is still hope though, since truth is unfolded and learned through time: "veritas filia temporis." The Ulises of *El golfo de las sirenas* certainly lacks the heroic grandeur of his predecessor. In *El mayor encanto, amor*, he was shaken from his reliance on Circe by remembrance of Achilles' valor. In the eclogue of 1657, it is the *villanos* who save the Greek hero from the peril he thought he could easily overcome. These peasants share the stage with Ulises, playing tricks and telling jokes. As Thomas O'Connor has pointed out, they actually serve to undercut the mythical ambience of the eclogue. This debunking of myth has a long poetic and pictorial tradition ranging from Góngora's "Hero y Leandro" to Velázquez's "Los Borrachos." Astraea did live among the peasants, but only as a final retreat before departing from earth in order to escape the corruption of men.

Ni amor se libra de amor, a mythological spectacle play presented in 1662, five years after *El golfo de las sirenas,* contains the most clear-cut characterization of an Astraea who stands in contradistinction to the goddess of the golden age. In this *comedia* Calderón alters the myth of Cupid and Psyche by including Astraea as one of the two sisters of the beautiful maiden loved by Cupid. When her two sisters view the magnificent palace where Siquis abides and learn that she has been forbidden to actually see the owner of the sumptuous edifice, they attempt to turn her against this mysterious stranger. Possibly out of ignorance, but more likely out of malice and envy, the sisters advise Siquis to attempt to disobey her beloved by taking in a light in order to gaze at him. Astraea tells Siquis:

> Un fiero encantado monstruo
> es o tu esposo o tu amante,
> porque contenta no estés
> con aquestas vanidades.
>
> [p. 1976]⁸

If this advice is given out of envy, we must conclude that Astraea's characterization stands in opposition to that of the goddess of the golden age. Envy, as we have seen in works such as Lope de Vega's *La Filomena,* is a vice that contrasts with the truthfulness that prevailed in the happiest of ages. It is a fault typical of the iron age. Astraea as the goddess of truth in the very opposite of a woman who exclaims on seeing her sister, "Muriendo de envidia voy" (p. 1949). Astraea's bad counsel in the *comedia* leads to disaster, since Cupid awakens as Siquis brings in a light in order to determine whether he is indeed a monster. When the god of love abandons Siquis, the desperate beauty blames those who were responsible for the bad advice:

> La culpa tuvisteis todos,
> pues contra mi esposo aleves
> os conjurasteis a que era
> un monstruo; y aunque no miente
> la sospecha en que era monstruo,
> en la malicia le ofende,
> pues el bello dios de amor,
> monstruo de todas las gentes,
> fue el que adoré . . .
>
> [p. 1980]

It is possible to translate the conflict between malice and love into astrological terms. A Saturn-Venus opposition often meant delays, oppositions, and tragedies of love.[9] The *malicia* of Astraea recalls the planet Saturn, whose malefic rays were most feared by astrologers. Astraea could very well stand for the powers of Saturn since this god was the ruler of the golden age and thus was closely linked to our goddess. The benefic ruler of the happiest of ages was at the same time the most malefic of planets. Saturn's bipolarity, if extended to Astraea, could explain her *malicia* and *envidia*. In the myth of the four ages of man, Jupiter's role is not necessarily a positive one. He deposes his father Saturn and becomes the leader of the lesser ages. And yet, in astrology, Jupiter is considered the most benefic of planets together with Venus and Sol. The *comedia* includes a reference to Jupiter as "benigno" (p. 1955). But Siquis's fate is not governed by Jupiter. She is under the sway of the malefic Saturn as she listens to her sister's advice. Even the goddess-planet Venus does not appear to be favorable to her at the start, since the people had declared that Siquis's beauty was greater than that of the goddess. Although her physical beauty has been the cause of envy from a sister and from a goddess, it is Siquis's virtue, her soul,[10] that saves her. She proves her love to Cupid by stating that she will not live without him. As she goes to her death, the god of love returns to her and saves her. He states that even Venus has forgiven her. The happy ending represents the triumph of the Celestial Venus or soul[11] over the envy that pervades the iron age and over the malefic rays of the seventh Ptolemaic planet. The malefic Astraea under the rulership of Saturn has been defeated by the power of love, the rule of Venus.

The Saturn-Venus opposition encountered in *Ni amor se libra de amor* becomes a central motif in the next play to be analyzed, *Los tres afectos de amor*. References to oppositions, eclipses, malefic planets, and adverse configurations abound in Calderón's theater. Indeed, the horoscope motif is a recurring element in this playwright's production. But the astrological information provided is often of a general nature. There is seldom enough specific data to provide definitive astral interpretations for the events in a drama. *Los tres afectos de amor,* a mythological spectacle play performed at the Buen Retiro on November 28, 1658, is of particular significance for an understanding of the function of the stars in Calderón's drama since it contains the most specific horoscope found in his *comedias*. The somewhat detailed heavenly configuration may have been incorporated into the play because of the circumstances of its composition and presentation. On November 27, 1657, Felipe Próspero was born. He was the first male heir of Philip IV born to his second wife, Mariana of Austria. The event was particularly dramatic since Mariana almost died in childbirth. Calderón composed several works to commemorate the happy occasion: the *entremés El toreador*[12] and two *comedias, El laurel de Apolo* and *Afectos de odio y amor*. Finally, to celebrate Felipe Próspero's first birthday, Calderón composed *Los tres afectos de amor*, "fiesta a los años del Príncipe nuestro Señor."[13]

Los tres afectos de amor tells of a child who has been born to a king under what appear to be ominous circumstances. The Basilio of *Los tres afectos de amor* is named Seleuco. Like his predecessor, he boasts of his knowledge of astrology, noting that he practices "la judiciaria" (p. 1187).[14] Judicial astrology, the predictive branch of this occult science, was considered suspect during this period.[15] The strong condemnation it received did not prevent the proliferation of treatises on the subject. Many monarchs had their own personal astrologers.[16] It may be that in plays such as *La vida es sueño* and *Los tres afectos de amor*, the sufferings and humiliations endured by the practitioners of this occult science were meant as an admonition to the Spanish king. In any case, the use of astrology was certainly good material for drama. It created suspense and incorporated into the *comedia* a notion akin to the fate that moved classical tragedy. Finally, astrology endowed the action with supreme significance—man and the heavens are at play together.

The Felipe Próspero of this *comedia* is a girl named Rosarda. To avoid the fulfillment of a malefic horoscope, the astrologer-father has locked away the child. Her upbringing is somewhat less austere than that of Segismundo in *La vida es sueño*. Rosarda grows up in an *alcázar* (p. 1185), surrounded by her *damas*. She must not, however, leave the confines of this palace. As Rosarda grows up, she becomes increasingly aware of her lack of freedom. Like Segismundo, she observes the "ave, fiera, pez" (p. 1186) and finds herself "con menos libertad" (p. 1186). Rosarda's lament is interrupted by the entrance of King Seleuco who, having overheard his daughter, finally decides to explain to her the reasons that led him to incarcerate her. The father-son conflict in *La vida es sueño* yields to a more loving father-daughter relationship in this *comedia*. Although there is tension and recrimination, Seleuco is less proud and less inflexible than Basilio, while Rosarda is more understanding and less passionate than Segismundo. In order to explain his apparently cruel behaviour, the king has to convince Rosarda that his actions were based on fear for her safety. It is at this point that *Los tres afectos de amor* presents the omens surrounding Rosarda's birth. The king prefaces these remarks with some words about the events that led to that amazing moment. His happy marriage to Isdaura was strained by the "desconsuelo / de no tener hijos" (p. 1187). This lack led them to pray at the altar of Venus:

Venus (titular diosa
de Chipre, y a cuya estatua
venera ese templo que
sobre la cima descansa
de este monte) . . .
[p. 1187]

Chipre was under Venus's protection since the goddess rose from the sea along its coast. As the princess of Cyprus and as a child born in response to prayers and sacrifices to the tutelary goddess, Rosarda must be considered as ruled by the goddess and planet Venus.

The goddess of love was not the only influence that presided over Rosarda's birth. The first omen perceived by Seleuco was inauspicious. Rosarda's mother died in childbirth:

Naciste tan desde luego
prodigiosa, que hecha humana
víbora, al materno albergue
de las piadosas entrañas
que te hospedaron, pagaste
inculpablemente ingrata,
dando en precio de una vida
una muerte.
[p. 1187]

The comparison between a birth that kills the mother and the viper birth, as has been noted in chapters five and eight, is a recurrent motif in Calderón's *comedias*, and one that reflects the popular belief that this snake was killed by its offspring. The viper image may have been included in *Los tres afectos de amor* as an allusion to a contemporary situation. It was well known that Felipe Próspero's birth had almost caused the death of his mother, Queen Mariana of Austria. Calderón had already alluded to this dramatic moment in the *loa* to *El laurel de Apolo*, composed a few months before:

Y aunque fecunda Lucina
A su horóscopo asistió,
Grosero accidente puso
El alborozo en temor . . .[17]

The *temor* expressed in *El laurel de Apolo* becomes a reality in the fictional world of *Los tres afectos de amor*, where the mother does die at the moment of giving birth. In this *comedia*, the viper image serves to remind the 1658 audience of a tragedy that had been averted the previous year. The fear caused by the threat of death as described in *El laurel de Apolo* was such that it was reflected in the heavens:

> Tanto, que el sol entre nubes
> Como es de las nubes dios,
> Presumimos que llovia,
> Y era que lloraba el sol . . .

The fact that the sun is covered by clouds and appears to rain must mean that Philip IV, the Sun King, cried when thinking that he was going to lose his queen. In *Los tres afectos de amor*, the sun covered by clouds is transformed into a solar eclipse:

> A este primer presagio
> sucedió observar que estaba
> en oposición del sol
> la luna, eclipsando avara
> la misma luz que mendiga.
>   [p. 1187]

In *El laurel de Apolo*, Lucina, the moon in its aspect of goddess of childbirth, presides over the event, and witnesses the *grosero accidente*. Lucina is able to save Mariana from the clutches of death. In *Los tres afectos de amor*, the moon obscures the sun, causing an eclipse, a situation that contrasts with the helpful Lucina of the preceding play. According to the epoch, eclipses often foretold the death of potentates.[18] Calderón follows this astrological belief in both *La vida es sueño* and *Los tres afectos de amor*. In each of these two plays the eclipse signals the death of a queen. Indeed, the eclipse is such a significant celestial event that Basilio uses it in his interpretation of Segismundo's horoscope. Ophiuchus, viper, and eclipse in *La vida es sueño* marked the birth of a figure whose future would be of great consequence: he would either be the perfect prince or the most cruel of kings. At a time when Spain's slow decline was more and more obvious, the birth of Felipe Próspero as heir to the throne must have aroused fears and desires similar to those found in *La vida es sueño*. Describing the mood of the people in 1657 at the time of the prince's birth, Jerónimo de Barrionuevo notes that "los regocijos han sido grandes y cada día serán mayores, y todo esto parece que lo colmara si naciera de veinticinco años y no nos hallara a todos envueltos en tantas guerras y pobrezas como estamos. Dios sobre todo."[19] To national sadness and despair, Calderón may be infusing new hope, with a touch of apocalyptic fear. In Felipe Próspero the nation may find either miraculous hope or damnation. Thus references to viper and eclipse within this context may have served a purpose somewhat distinct from advancing the dramatic action of *Los tres afectos de amor.* However, these allusions kindle interest and emotion in the spectator who, after hopeful and ominous associations, is ready to lend an ear to intricate astrological language. What follows, though brief, is perhaps the most detailed horoscopal reference in Calderón's *comedias:*

> y retrógrado en la casa
> de Venus, Saturno, con
> malévolo aspecto, infausta
> constelación, que me hizo
> de todo punto apurarla . . .
>
> [p. 1187]

The heavenly configuration that concerns Seleuco most is thus the presence of the planet Saturn, retrogrande, in the house of Venus. As Johnstone Parr reminds us, "Saturn was considered by the astrologers to be the most powerful of the malefic planets."[20] Michael Scot, chosen by Dante as one of the "fathers" of astrology, gives a typical assessment of Saturn's influence. Considering this highest of Ptolemaic planets worse than any of the others, he labels it "stella damnabilis, furiosa, odiosa, superba, impia, crudelis, malivola."[21] This attitude towards Saturn prevailed through the Renaissance and beyond. In spite of the Neoplatonic doctrine that proclaimed Saturn the planet of wisdom, astrologers, mythographers, and poets were often of one mind when they considered Saturn the most malefic of planets. In *Los tres afectos de amor,* Calderón follows the naming of this planet with the term *retrógrado.* In astrology this adjective is used "to describe a planet that appears to be moving backwards through the zodiac, from east to west."[22] Such a movement is traditionally interpreted as a debility. Indeed, the negative connotations of retrogradation were well known during this epoch. Marsilio Ficino, for example, wrote a letter to his friend Giovanni Cavalcanti explaining that he was having difficulty solving problems since he was "under the malign influence of my Saturn retrogressing in Leo."[23] In order to present a particularly malefic astrological configuration in *La Dorotea,* Lope de Vega makes use of the two most negative planets and adds the term retrograde: "Y má si tienen a Saturno con Marte retrógrado."[24] When in *Los tres afectos de amor* Seleuco calls attention to a retrograde Saturn, the audience would have been well aware of the ominous nature of the horoscope.

There is a third element mentioned by Seleuco: Saturn is retrograde in the house of Venus. It has been noted that Rosarda in this *comedia* should be associated with Venus since she was born as a result of prayers to this goddess and since she is the heir to the throne of Chipre, an island sacred to Venus, who emerged from the sea at this location. But if the physical "house" of Venus is both Rosarda and Chipre, what is its heavenly house? Venus, according to traditional astrology, has two zodiacal houses, Taurus and Libra. Although Seleuco does not state which of these two abodes holds the seventh planet in Rosarda's horoscope, it is clear from the context that it has to be Libra. The Venus who rises from the sea at Cyprus is the daughter of Uranus, called the Celestial Venus. Her sign is Libra, in contradistinction to the Earthly Venus, whose father is Jupiter and whose sign is Taurus.[25] Seleuco must then be speaking of Libra since it is the sign of the Celestial Venus that rules his island.

Libra, representing the island of Cyprus and Rosarda herself, contains the malefic Saturn with the debility of being retrograde. Saturn in Libra is at its point of exaltation. In astrology, an exaltation is generally positive, since it serves to strengthen the planet's influence. However, an exception is often made in this particular case because "the energy of the planet is exaggerated"[26] and its increase would cause alarm in any astrologer. Seleuco considers Rosarda's horoscope particularly ominous:

> Hallé, digo, que teniendo
> en tu horóscopo contraria
> influencia tu hermosura,
> peligro te amenazaba
> de violenta muerte, siendo
> tu gracia ella y tu desgracia.
> [p. 1188]

The king's interpretation is certainly consonant with traditional astrology, and is clear evidence of Calderón's knowledge of this occult science. Libra, the sign of the Celestial Venus, provides Rosarda with *hermosura*. The presence of the malefic Saturn with exaggerated force through its exaltation and in negative movement, being retrograde, does point to the fact that the girl's beauty could lead to disaster. The *violenta muerte* predicted by Seleuco stems from Saturn, who was often represented with a scythe, and was thus considered the planet of death.[27] The basis for the prediction rests on the enmity between Saturn and Venus, and this was one of the more common oppositions of the epoch. Marsilio Ficino, for example, warns that "the astrologers say that Venus and Saturn are enemies of each other."[28] Lope de Vega, following Ficino, often points in his *comedias* to Saturn as delaying or frustrating love affairs, the business of Venus.[29] What makes

Rosarda's horoscope a particularly ominous one is the technical aspects that increase Saturn's malefic power: its retrogradation and its exaltation.

Having analyzed the horoscope of his daughter, Seleuco decides he will imprison Rosarda from the moment of birth so as to minimize the danger posed by Saturn. This action ironically emphasizes the power of the seventh planet in Rosarda's horoscope. Astrologers agree that its malefic influence often brings with it "great imprisonment."[30] Rosarda, like Segismundo in *La vida es sueño*, suffers incarceration as a result of her horoscope. In both plays the agent who brings about Saturn's influence is the father. The father-son conflict in *La vida es sueño* recalls, as has been previously noted, the Saturn-Jupiter enmity in mythology. Although no such rivalry develops in *Los tres afectos de amor*, Seleuco is here also the agent of Saturn since this planet, according to Guido Bonatti, governs fathers.[31] Furthermore Saturn, being cold and dry, is equated with old age and is often depicted as *senex*. Both Seleuco and Basilio have spent their lives in search of the higher wisdom of the stars, a yearning that Neoplatonists would also associate with Saturn.

Once the children grow up, the fathers—Basilio and Seleuco—begin to reconsider their cruel actions. They come to the tardy realization that a horoscope does not have to be fulfilled; a wise man can triumph over the stars. The ancient saying "Sapiens homo dominatur astris"[32] is echoed in both *comedias* by repentant fathers. In *Los tres afectos de amor*, Seleuco agrees "que no siempre su palabra / cumple el hado, y que el prudente / sobre las estrellas manda" (p. 1188). When Seleuco grants Rosarda *libertad*, he attempts to compensate for her imprisonment by also giving her the freedom to choose between three princes who wish to marry her. The king's reasoning is not entirely without fault: "que no quiero ser en nada / cómplice de tu fortuna" (p. 1188). Seleuco's decision allows him to disclaim any responsibility for what will follow. Since he has concluded that his daughter's horoscope threatens to bring death through her beauty, it follows that one of the suitors is potentially her murderer. In a desperate decision, the king allows Rosarda to freely move to that moment of greatest danger in her life without his counsel. The action of the play will now revolve around Rosarda's future choice, all three suitors attempting to win her favor. While amorous pursuits in the island of Venus reign supreme, the danger of Saturn's malefic influence looms in the background, lending increased tension to the situation.

The three suitors among whom Rosarda must choose her husband are Libio, prince of Gnido; Flavio, prince of Acaya; and Celio,
prince of Rodas. Libio must be Rosarda's choice, since he rules over
Gnido. This location, as Peter Dunn reminds us, is famous in antiquity for possessing a statue of Venus.[33] Her nudity defines her as a
Celestial Venus. Furthermore, Prince Libio's name recalls Libra, the
zodiacal sign ruled by the Celestial Venus. Thus Rosarda ought to
rely on Libio, since both of them are governed by the goddess of love
in her celestial aspect.

This double benefic influence is soon obscured by forces that oppose the future union of these two. A shipwrecked woman emerges
from the ocean and faints at Rosarda's feet. The princess takes this as
an evil omen since the unhappy beauty could be a mirror of what
could happen to her. Rosarda's fear is coupled with compassion. She
leaves the unfortunate lady with Libio, asking him to care for her. As
it turns out, the woman is Ismenia, whom Libio once loved and abandoned. In addition to this thwarted beauty, the first act of *Los tres
afectos de amor* also introduces Anteo, a man whose desire for Rosarda
is frustrated by the king's order that she choose a husband from the
three princes. Anteo, like his mythological namesake, a giant who
was the son of Earth, is a representative of earthly passion. The situation is further complicated by the fact that Anteo despises Libio
since he has been "hechado y desposeído de Famagusta" (p. 1193).
Not only has Libio defeated Anteo in war, but also in love. Anteo lost
Ismenia, who has come to Chipre in search of Libio. The emerging
pattern of amorous difficulties points to Saturn, a planet that causes
delays and frustrations in love. Its malefic influence could lead these
thwarted lovers, Ismenia and Anteo, to seek revenge. The possibility
of violence keeps the horoscope lively in the awareness of the people
as the action focuses on the business of Venus.

During the second act, Ismenia presents herself to Rosarda, in-
venting a tale of woe. The princess of Chipre is happy to receive her.
Gladdened by her reception, Ismenia asks for protection, pretending
to be a Greek maiden named Astraea. She uses the name of the goddess of truth in order to lie about her past. Ismenia-Astraea will not
seek justice, but revenge. She is a "liviana hermosura" (p. 1206)
rather than an image of chastity. This false goddess will exert a negative influence rather than bringing about the harmony that characterized the happiest of ages. In her attempts to destroy Libio and
Rosarda, the children of Venus, Astraea must be seen as governed by
the malefic Saturn as described in Seleuco's horoscope of his daugh-

ter. The Saturn-Venus opposition in this *comedia* will thus be embodied in the conflict between Ismenia and Anteo versus Libio and Rosarda.

Libio's love for Rosarda develops as a reaction to her malefic horoscope. He wishes to link his will and desire to hers in order to save her: "lo imposible de un influjo / que oprimió tu libertad / mi voluntad / movió" (p. 1202). But this *influjo* that is meant to make of Rosarda an unfortunate beauty is already working through Ismenia and Anteo. Alone with Libio, Ismenia explains to him the reasons why she is intent on serving Rosarda:

> que yo,
> ya en su casa, haré que crea,
> si no bastan tus traiciones,
> mis engaños de manera
> que no te quede esperanza.
> [p. 1204]

Ismenia will destroy Libio's chances of being loved by Rosarda through either truth or falsehood. This malefic influence is exercised by Ismenia in Rosarda's own house ("en su casa"). The language makes it clear that Ismenia is intended to represent Saturn positioned in the house of Venus, that is, in Rosarda's own home. Desperate to correct the situation, Libio tries to kidnap Ismenia and send her away. Unfortunately, Anteo appears at this very moment and violence erupts. The king, seeing violence and confusion all around him and fearing the fulfillment of the horoscope, presses Rosarda to make a decision concerning her marriage. Having heard statements condemning Libio, Rosarda wishes to stall for time, and announces that she will go consult the temple of Venus. Ignoring Libio's past mistakes, she promises to marry whichever of the three suitors "tenga en mi servicio hecha / mayor fineza" (p. 1206) by the time she returns.

Rosarda journeys to the temple of a goddess she resembles through her beauty: "Y segunda Venus de Chipre, la hermosa Rosarda" (p. 1208). But she is a Venus under a malefic *influjo*. Although King Seleuco has banished both Anteo and Ismenia from the island, they have not heeded this demand. Ismenia has enlisted Anteo's aid in order to destroy Rosarda's happiness. The thwarted beauty has become envy personified, a "doña Envidia" (p. 1207), as one of the *graciosos* calls her. Envy is a trait contrary to the virtues of the goddess Astraea, and also one of the chief properties of Saturn.[34] Finding the Venus-like Rosarda, Ismenia takes the *carabina* and fires it, proclaiming: "mueran con ella a un tiempo / las esperanza de todos" (p. 1210). True to its reputation, the seventh planet seems to have been the cause of a tragedy of love. The envious and malefic Saturn has exerted its influence through Ismenia-Astraea in order to destroy Venus in her own house, that is, Rosarda in Chipre. Through Rosarda's demise, Ismenia-Saturn also wishes to destroy the aspirations of the three suitors, and in particular those of Libio, who can also be equated with the house of Venus since his name resembles the astrological sign Libra. King Seleuco, hearing of the attempt made on his daughter's life, finds the news a sad confirmation of his interpretation of her horoscope, and goes in search of the dying Rosarda (p. 1210).

At the close of the second act, it appears as if Saturn has prevailed over the benefic influences of Venus. But the last *jornada* belongs to the planet of love. Rosarda, as it turns out, was not even wounded by the *carabina*. It was the horse that was shot, sprinkling its blood on Rosarda. The benefic influences of Venus appear to have tempered the malefic Saturn. But Rosarda is not convinced that the seventh planet is not still exercising its influence on her life. Before the attempt was made on her life, Rosarda had requested a *fineza* from her three suitors. Her imperilled life provided the opportunity for the exhibition of the lovers' qualities. On seeing the attempt on Rosarda, all three suitors reacted differently. Celio pursued the traitors and killed Anteo; Flavio remained with Rosarda in order to help and protect her; while Libio merely fainted. Rosarda finds it difficult to justify marrying the suitor who has done nothing on her behalf. But the third act belongs to Venus. Rosarda, a woman of action, suggests a pilgrimage to the goddess's temple. Only there can the problems of love be resolved.

At the temple, Rosarda asks the goddess to judge which of the three "afectos de amor" ("piedad, desmayo y valor") is the greatest (p. 1220). Venus's choice is also Rosarda's. Libio is judged to be the greatest lover since his feelings were of such intensity as to cause the *desmayo*. The other two suitors each acted out of a single emotion. Celio was led by *valor*, while Flavio experienced *piedad*. Libio explains how these two opposite emotions exploded with such intensity within his psyche as to create the *desmayo* (p. 1216). *Valor* and *piedad* are qualities that can be ascribed to opposing deities, Mars and Venus. Libio's reputation as a warrior is such that he is often equated in the *comedia* with Mars. The mythological love affair between Mars and Venus is translated in *Los tres afectos de amor* into the relationship between Libio and Rosarda. Indeed, Libio himself uses this comparison: "sabe amanecer Marte / al umbral de Venus bella" (p. 1198). The union between Mars and Venus produced an offspring named Harmonia. This harmony is what emerges at the end of *Los tres afectos de amor* with the marriage of Libio and Rosarda. This outer reconciliation of opposites is the result of an inner struggle within Libio. On seeing Rosarda threatened by death, he feels the contrary pull of *valor* (Mars) and *piedad* (Venus). The *desmayo* arises out of his endeavor to balance opposites and represents a most fitting tribute to his name and nature since Libio can be equated with the sign Libra, the balance.

Saturn retrograde has threatened the house of Venus. But the benefic influence of the goddess of love and beauty has proved too powerful. After all, Rosarda is princess of Chipre, an island that has witnessed the birth of Venus. She is defended by Libio, prince of Gnido, a land that harbors the most beautiful statue of the goddess. This prince is judged to be the perfect lover since his extreme emotions towards Rosarda are coupled with inner balance. Indeed, Libio is the balance itself, the sign Libra. As such, he is in sympathy with the Celestial Venus, Rosarda, since this zodiacal sign is also the abode of the goddess of love. The perils of Saturn, expressed by the cruelty of a father who imprisons his own child and by the envy of a thwarted beauty, a false Astraea, have threatened to enact a tragedy of love. Instead, *Los tres afectos de amor* celebrates the triumph of love and harmony in the lands and in the hearts of those ruled by the benefic Venus. Translated into contemporary political terms, the play is not to be interpreted as hailing the birth of Felipe Próspero in the Virgilian manner. The false Astraea in this *comedia* is a malefic force that contrasts with the portrayal of the goddess of the golden age in the *Fourth Eclogue*. In a Spain where poverty and war are the concern of most, it is enough to feel the influence of Venus, a loving and harmonious goddess, and to know that predictions of doom are not always fulfilled.

CHAPTER TEN

Achilles as Astraea

CALDERÓN DE LA BARCA'S final *comedia* dealing with Astraea, *El monstruo de los jardines* (1667), is an important and intriguing piece. Perhaps the disparate elements in this play have constituted a barrier to critical appreciation until recently. In the words of William R. Blue, "This strange combination of palace intrigue, prophecy and love triangles is played out against the mythic background of Achilles' role in the Trojan War."[1] Yet Calderón's careful craftsmanship brings these elements together to create a coherent whole. Blue notes that most of the images of this *comedia* are taken from nature and that the primary ones are the cave and the sea. Angel Valbuena Briones, having compared Calderón's play with Tirso de Molina's *El Aquiles*, also stresses the unity of *El monstruo de los jardines*: "La estructura de *El monstruo de los jardines* es muy superior a la de su antecedente. El autor ha centrado el conflicto de la acción en el problema psicológico de Aquiles que trata de oponerse a su destino sin saber vencerse a sí mismo."[2]

The notions of destiny and of Achilles' psychological problems have been the subject of studies by Alexander Parker and Everett W. Hesse respectively. Analyzing astrological prophecies in Calderón's *comedias*, Parker concludes that "cuando hay profecías astrológicas en los dramas de Calderón, todas se cumplen infaliblemente de la manera revelada, y que Calderón no presenta ningún caso del predominio sobre las estrellas del hombre sabio y prudente, en cuanto esto se refiera a algun decreto celestial revelado en la obra."[3] The one possible exception is *El monstruo de los jardines*, which Parker scrutinizes in order to fit it within this framework. For Hesse, the focus of the action is not in the heavens but in man: "He [Calderón] dramatizes the way in which Aquiles' projection of two personalities, one male, the other female, creates a conflict which delays his sexual and role fulfillment until the protagonist is able to synthesize the disparate elements in his psyche based on a viable philosophy of life."[4] At the beginning of the *comedia*, Aquiles exhibits masculine traits almost exclusively. The feminine side of his personality, the *anima* in Hesse's Jungian analysis, is totally subdued by the *animus*.[5] Aquiles' feminine side eventually emerges in an extreme form—the young hero goes to the palace in feminine attire, disguised as Astraea. The *comedia* dramatizes a conflict between the *animus* and the *anima*. The subsequent harmony can be equated with Aquiles' integration of his personality.

This conflict can be approached from a different perspective, one that will take into account not only the human element studied by Hesse but also the supernatural plane, the notion of destiny which has preoccupied Parker. At the beginning of the play, we witness a pilgrimage to a temple. A song reveals the deities that are to be propitiated: "Venid, venid, zagales, / al templo divino de Venus y Marte" (p. 1986).[6] The goddess of love and the god of strife can be related to Hesse's view of the play as a conflict between the male and female side of Aquiles' personality. But, as we have noted in previous chapters, Mars and Venus are archetypal figures of opposition in an epoch that, according to Robert Grudin, considers "contrariety" one of the major issues of thought.[7] As Ptolemaic planets, these figures are thought to influence human actions. The benefic qualities of Venus temper the malefic rays of Mars. León Hebreo's statement on this subject is typical: "y dicen que Venus corrige con su benigno aspecto toda la malicia de Marte."[8] Furthermore, Venus and Mars embody for Renaissance Platonists a key mystery of the universe, the unlawful union of Mars and Venus, from which issued a daughter named Harmony.

The song about Mars and Venus has alerted us to the mystery to be enacted. The music stands for the harmony that arises from a temple where opposing deities and planets coexist. But the characters in the play ignore the content of the song. As the king leads his daughter upwards towards the temple, he commands, "Ven, pues, porque propicio / por ti Marte responda al sacrificio" (p. 1986). The king makes no reference to Venus. Mars, he hopes, will accept the sacrifice on seeing his beautiful daughter. In other words, Deidamia is taking on the role of Venus. She is becoming the benefic deity or planet that will temper an angry and malicious god.

A second character also ignores the harmonious implications of the song. Ulises calls the people up the mountain:

> Venid todos cantando
> porque admire veloces
> el dios de las batallas nuestras voces;

que si su culto aprecia,
presto de Troya ha de vengarse Grecia.

[p. 1986]

If Mars listens to their voices, Ulises claims, Greece will be able to triumph over Troy. Paradoxically, the beauty of Deidamia and the harmony of the music, qualities of Venus, will move the god to support them in war. Epic and lyric tones are blended in the early scenes of this *comedia*.

When Ulises returns from the mountain, he announces that the god of war has accepted the sacrifice and has uttered a prophecy:

Troya será destruida
y abrasada por los griegos,
si va a su conquista Aquiles,
a ser homicida de Héctor.
Aquiles, monstruo humano
de aquestos montes, en ellos
un risco . . .

[p. 1989]

The prophecy is interrupted by natural portents. Ulises believes that these are brought about by Venus: "(¿quién ignora que sea Venus, / que es afecta a los troyanos?)" (p. 1990). The gods have taken sides. The conflict in the play reflects an epic battle, that between Greece and Troy, which in turn reveals heavenly discord in the opposition between Venus and Mars. The harmony longed for in the song does not exist as yet. The mystery of concord has not been revealed.

From a heavenly "mystery" the prophecy of Ulises turns our attention to an earthly enigma. Aquiles must be found if the Greeks are to succeed. While search parties are dispatched to trap this *monstruo*, Deidamia remains alone with her two maids. Sirene and Cintia sing to entertain their lady, who soon falls asleep. Sirene recalls the sirens, creatures whose song leads men to disaster. Even Ulises, according to myth, has difficulty avoiding their snares. This irresistible song of love belongs to the realm of Venus.[9] Cintia, on the other hand, is another name for Diana, and refers to Mount Cynthus, the place of the goddess's birth. It can be encountered, for example, in Montemayor's *La Diana* as a reference to the goddess Diana.[10] The maids Sirene and Cintia reflect two opposing attitudes as revealed by their link to the two goddesses, Venus and Diana. Indeed, the opposition between Venus, goddess of love, and Diana, goddess of chastity, can be encountered from ancient myth to Renaissance literature. Perhaps the best example is the tragedy of Hippolytus, dramatized by both Euripides and Seneca. This youth's devotion to Diana leads to his demise through the agency of an angry Venus.[11]

In *El monstruo de los jardines*, Deidamia sleeps as both maids sing. Sirene and Cintia can be viewed as opposing impulses within Deidamia. The fact that the lady sleeps while listening to them may reflect a superficial harmony of latent contraries. The ensuing events will bring these opposing forces into conflict. *Concordia* in song, as we have discovered, is not a lasting phenomenon among the mighty opposites that propel the action of this *comedia*. The music is heard by the monster of the prophecy, Aquiles. He emerges from a dark cave in the mountain, where he has lived all his life, and searches for this "nuevo pájaro" (p. 1991) that can sing so well. Meanwhile, Cintia withdraws from Deidamia's presence, since chastity must hide from the coming encounter. Aquiles sees Sirene. Her *canción* moves the human monster towards love. Sirene faints and reveals the now awakened Deidamia. The beauty and the beast gaze at each other, speak, and fall in love. This time it appears as if opposites have a chance of being reconciled. The violence of the "fiero monstruo" (p. 1992), Aquiles, is held in abeyance by the beauty of Deidamia. This dramatic moment recalls Calderón's masterpiece, *La vida es sueño*. Aquiles, a new Segismundo, could very well have uttered here the words of his predecessor on seeing Rosaura: "Tu voz pudo enternecerme, / tu presencia suspenderme." In *El monstruo de los jardines* this dramatic moment is closely tied to the "mystery" that the play enacts. In the attitudes of Aquiles and Deidamia we perceive that the strife of Mars has been tempered by the qualities of Venus. The god of war has succumbed to the goddess of amiability.

Concord is of short duration; mighty opposites appear to prevail in the sublunary realm. The entrance of Lidoro, the prince who is betrothed to Deidamia, introduces the notion of jealousy. Furthermore, Aquiles must escape the search parties. There is even fear of violence in this flight towards safety since Aquiles worries about the *venganzas* (p. 1994) of the deity he has disobeyed by leaving the cave. Aquiles, pressed by his pursuers, invokes Tetis. She appears and leads him away. Amazed at this *prodigio*, all give up their efforts to capture Aquiles.

There is a kind of restoration of order at the end of the first act. But it is an artificial scene based not on the characters' actions but on a *deus ex machina*. The king proclaims, "Si contra oculta deidad / humano poder no basta, / desamparemos el monte" (p. 1996). According to Edgar Wind, the *oculta deidad* or concealed god was a cabalistic term for the Ensoph.[12] More importantly, *oculta deidad* was a key concept in the mysteries that revealed God for the Renaissance Platonists: "'It is written,' [Nicolaus] Cusanus said, 'that God is hidden from the eyes of all sages.' But because the ultimate One is thus invisible, His visible manifestations must be manifold." In *De Visione Dei*, Cusanus adds that "the face is veiled in all faces."[13] In the invisible One, all contraries are united. But the conclusion of the first act of *El monstruo de los jardines*, although alluding to the concealed god of the Platonists who harmonizes opposites, seems to end artificially with a *deus ex machina*, the goddess Tetis. This can be compared to Euripides' imposition of "endings that do not come logically from the conflict but rather are imposed by the playwright for ironic or aesthetic reasons."[14] The goddess artificially creates a brief period of peace, a truce that has fear as its basis. The only reason that the followers of the king do not pursue Aquiles is that he is protected by a powerful force. Indeed, Ulises even proclaims that he will disobey the dictates of the goddess (p. 1996). At the end of the first act, opposition prevails over harmony and strife over love. The influence of Mars persists in spite of the goddess's dictates.

The second act commences by revealing to the spectator the hiding place of the goddess and of the young hero. Their dialogue explains the mysterious actions of the pair. Aquiles is Tetis's son, the result of prince Peleo's lustful violence:

> que embrión de una violencia
> fuiste, porque no te quejes
> de mí, sino de tu estrella;
> pues eres tan desdichado,
> que cuando todos se precian
> que nacieron de un amor,
> naciste tú de una fuerza.
>
> [p. 1999]

Violencia and *fuerza* are key to Aquiles' conception and birth, not *amor*. Thus, the young hero's birth is under the influence of a particular *estrella*, the planet of strife, Mars. As Fritz Saxl states, "The children of Mars are not satisfied with burning, murdering and stealing cattle; true to classical precedent they have added the abduction of women to their duties."[15] Peleo's actions fall under Mars and thus the child's birth is under this planet's influx. The unshakable influence of the fifth Ptolemaic planet is also seen in Tetis's description of events following her rape. First she murdered Peleo. Then she destroyed all buildings in the island and killed all its inhabitants. The only edifice left standing was the "templo de Marte" (p. 1998). Her violent reactions reflect the rule of Mars, as does the fact that his temple was spared. Indeed, the cave where Tetis and Aquiles dwell is directly under Mars's temple. His influence is clearly reflected in the horoscope of Aquiles cast by Tetis:

> y hallé que al tercero lustro
> te amenaza la más fiera
> lid, la más dura batalla,
> la campaña más sangrienta
> de cuantas en sus teatros
> la fortuna representa.
>
> [p. 1998]

Since violence threatened her son, Tetis decided to keep Aquiles safely in the cave. And yet violence was never far removed during those early years of Aquiles' life: the temple of Mars stood directly above the cave. Aquiles grew up a "fiero monstruo" (p. 1992). The events of the day cause Tetis to wonder whether she can indeed foil the horoscope. Mars has now prophesied that Aquiles must be found if the Greeks are to win the Trojan War. The youth is not safe, since others desire to find him and take him to the war.

Aquiles confesses to his mother his passion for Deidamia. Tetis conceives a new plan that can satisfy her son's desires and at the same time conceal him in a more clever fashion. She will have him leave the island of Mars and go to the king's court. Aquiles will be disguised as Astraea, Deidamia's cousin who has perished in a shipwreck on her way to the court. In this manner Aquiles can become intimate with Deidamia without suspicion; no one will think of searching for the hero in the apartments of the ladies of the court. Aquiles will be accepted as Astraea since Deidamia has not seen her cousin for many years. The beauty of youth and the sumptuous dresses and jewels being readied by Tetis will conceal Aquiles' masculinity.

Tetis's scheme to disguise Aquiles in female garb is a central motif in this hero's myth. Apollodorus summarizes the subsequent events: "Thetis, foreseeing that it was fated he should perish if he went to the war, disguised him in female garb and entrusted him as a maiden to Lycomedes. Bred at this court, Achilles had an intrigue with Deidamia, daughter of Lycomedes, and a son Pyrrhus was born to him, who was afterwards called Neoptolemus. But the secret of Achilles was betrayed, and Ulysses, seeking him at the court of Lycomedes, discovered him by the blast of a trumpet. And in that way Achilles went to Troy."[16] Lycomedes' court was on the island of Scyros. Calderón changes the location and makes the king reside at Gnido, a place mentioned repeatedly throughout the *comedia*. Calderón's inspiration for this change was probably Garcilaso de la Vega's *Canción* V, subtitled "Ode ad Florem Gnidi." It has long been argued that in an autobiographical sense, Gnido refers to Nido, a neighborhood in Naples where Violante San Severino, the lady in the poem, lived. However Peter Dunn has demonstrated that this place name has both autobiographical and thematic importance: "The most celebrated of all the ancient statues of the goddess (Venus) was that which has been carved by Praxiteles, rejected by the citizens of Kos, accepted and venerated by the people of Knidos (Cnidus). This Cnidian Venus was well known to sixteenth century writers on antiquity, indeed to anyone who had read as far as the thirty-sixth book of Pliny's *Natural History*. . . . Thus, the Gnidus, Gnido of Garcilaso means Cnidus, the temple of Venus."[17] Indeed, Calderón has used Gnido to refer to Venus in two previous plays discussed in this study, *Ni amor se libra de amor* and *Los tres afectos de amor*.

The island where Aquiles has resided all these years is under the protection of Mars, as evinced by the temple dedicated to him on top of the mountain. His influence is reflected in the violence that has taken place and in the prophecy that Aquiles will be a Greek hero in the Trojan war. Now, Tetis suggests to her son that he move to the court which is in Gnido, a place sacred to Venus. Tetis thus wants to attract the influence of the goddess of love in order to avert or temper a prophecy of war. She has proof that Venus is on her side since the goddess attempted to stop the oracle of Mars. Also, she knows that it would be to Venus's advantage to restrain Aquiles' martial impulses, since the goddess backs the Trojans in the epic war. Tetis also hopes "que sea monstruo en los jardines / el que fue monstruo en las selvas" (p. 2000). The civilizing and harmonizing influence of the court, symbolized by the *jardines*, must replace the wild and chaotic force of the *selva*. But Aquiles is more than a *monstruo*, a composite of different natures that have not been integrated. He is also an undiscovered jewel: "a aqueste bruto diamante / pulir tratéis" (p. 2000). He is a diamond in the rough that must be polished or cut at court through the influence of Venus. The civilizing and tempering effect of the goddess, Tetis hopes, will lead her son away from the dangers of war or Mars.

The change in geography and the hoped-for change in Aquiles' disposition will also be accompanied by an outward metamorphosis. As noted, Aquiles will be disguised as a woman. Up to this point the future hero has been related to Mars. Both oracle and horoscope have shown that the god of strife and violence dominates Aquiles' chart in the same way as he presides over the island's landscape. As the young hero goes to Gnido, the land of Venus, he is dressed as a woman and thinks of love. Thus, the audience may view Aquiles as a Mars disguised as Venus. The opposite figure, a *Venus armata*, was most popular in the Renaissance and was derived from classical models.[18] Calderón may have known Andrea Navagero's poem on the subject, which begins by describing this transformation of the goddess in Sparta and concludes by applying the notion to the poetic voice.[19] Navagero's notion of a Venus disguised as Mars is as startling as Calderón's dramatic presentation of the great Greek hero dressed as a woman. The "incongruity of this simile" (according to Edgar Wind)[20] was a deliberate device in Navagero as it must have been in Calderón. It serves to perplex the beholder or reader and lead him to the Platonic mystery of *discordia concors*. The conjoining of opposites reveals a transcendent unity.

As Aquiles journeys from the *selva* to the *jardín*, from the isle of violence to the court, the audience's attention shifts from the concerns of Mars to those of Venus. As his/her ship enters the port, a trans-elemental image very typical of Calderón's verse compares the *bajel* to a *neblí* flying to its nest: "veloz neblí de las ondas, / el nido del puerto busca" (p. 2005). The pun on Gnido (the court) and nido (the nest) serves to emphasize the importance of a geographical name and recalls Garcilaso's own link between Gnido, the location of Venus's temple, and Nido, a *barrio* in Naples. Aquiles is aware of the importance of geographical shift in terms of personal transformation. Although opposites are warring within his soul, he expresses hope of reconciliation. He recalls Tetis's use of the diamond in the rough to refer to him in the *selva* when he states:

> Hoy de su mina arrancada
> llega tosca piedra inculta
> una alma, a que los crisoles
> del ingenio y la cordura
> con ejemplares la labren,
> y sin castigos la pulan.
>
> [p. 2004]

The hardness of the diamond is often associated with the adamantine qualities of Mars and thus contrasts with the softness of Venus.[21] The beauty of a cut diamond expresses the qualities of Venus that can be found in Mars or Aquiles. The court and Deidamia's love will affect an alchemical transformation within Aquiles. Since he refers to a *crisol*, the perfected stone may be more than a cut diamond. It may be the *lapis* of the alchemists, which according to Jung is a symbol of the integration of the personality.[22]

The name that Achilles assumed at the court of Lycomedes was an obscure mythological fact, one of the questions asked by Emperor Tiberius, according to the historian Suetonius: "His special aim was a knowledge of mythology, which he carried to a silly and laughable extreme; for he used to test even the grammarians . . . by questions something like this: 'Who was Hecuba's mother?' 'What was the name of Achilles among the maidens?'"[23] This particular question could be answered with names such as Cercysera, Issa, and Pyrrha,[24] but never Astraea. Nor does Tirso de Molina use this name in his play *El Aquiles*. This name substitution in *El monstruo de los jardines* recalls *La vida es sueño*, where Rosaura takes the name of Astraea when she goes to Basilio's court. While in Calderón's masterpiece the name evokes the dawn of a golden age of imperial justice, in this late *comedia* the name substitution is closely linked to the mystery of reconciliation of opposites.

Pico della Mirandola "taught how to harmonize extremes, to reconcile the enthusiasm of Plato with the sobriety of Aristotle, the ardour of St. Paul with the calm of St. Peter, the passion of Melpomene with the serenity of Urania, the coldness of justice with the warmth of charity."[25] The final opposition, justice-charity, could be explained in terms of Aquiles' disguise. He has assumed the name of Astraea and is dressed as a woman, desiring love. Astraea is the goddess of justice, while Venus, in one of its higher significations, can stand for charity. Aquiles as Astraea-Venus is thus an icon for the reconciliation of the coldness of justice with the warmth of charity. Sebastian Neumeister comes close to this interpretation when he argues that love in *El monstruo de los jardines* should be construed as a power which determines world history. If Venus is love as charity, then Aquiles as Astraea is the justice of the Last Judgment which comes at the end of the historical process and which leads to a final peace.[26] Although Neumeister's eschatological analysis is valuable, it is difficult to see in the affair between Deidamia and Aquiles the notion of charity or Christian love. Venus in *El monstruo de los jardines* does not represent charity, but the enjoyment of love. What we have in Aquiles' disguise as Venus-Virgo is the opposition between pleasure and justice. Or, to put it in terms of an ever-present conflict in the *comedia*, it is a disguise that reveals the conflict between *el gusto* and *lo justo*.[27] Aquiles is given the choice between personal pleasure (Venus) and martial duties which fall under the realm of Astraea.

Aquiles' disguise as a Venus named Astraea also expresses a conflict within Deidamia's self. The earliest clue of this contrariety is found when Deidamia meets Aquiles. Her maid Sirene, representative of Venus, is present on this occasion since it is a time for the kindling of love. The second maid, Cintia, is absent from the meeting. As a representative of the goddess Diana, she must not be present in a scene that may lead to the loss of chastity. The two maids are aspects of Deidamia's inclinations. Before meeting Aquiles, Deidamia had made statements typical of a *mujer esquiva*:[28]

> sabiendo de mí que tengo
> por natural condición
> tan grande aborrecimiento
> a los hombres . . .
>
> [pp. 1990–91]

These statements also reveal Deidamia as Virgo-Diana, as a person who desires the chaste life in opposition to the cares of marriage. Indeed, Deidamia states that her only *cuidado* before meeting Aquiles had been "Astraea, mi prima" (p. 1991). Although this has been interpreted as a latent lesbianism,[29] we might view it as a desire for pure friendship, a chaste concern which is underscored by the name Astraea, goddess of chastity. After all, through catasterism, the goddess became the zodiacal sign Virgo, the Virgin.

Edgar Wind considers the opposition Venus-Virgo as important as that of Venus-Mars. Like the *Venus armata*, the Venus as Diana, Astraea, or Virgo has classical precedent. In the *Aeneid*, "Venus appears disguised as a nymph Diana, the goddess of love as a devotee of chastity."[30] This semi-chaste, semi-voluptuous figure was popular in the Renaissance as exemplified in the worship of Queen Elizabeth in England as an Astraea and a Venus.[31] Thus, Aquiles combines in his disguise two important Renaissance mysteries: that of Mars-Venus, which reflects his inner struggle, and that of Venus-Astraea, which mirrors Deidamia's internal conflict.

When the disguised Aquiles arrives in Gnido, Deidamia experiences contrary emotions. She accepts the false cousin as "no mi dama / sino mi amiga" (p. 2004). At the same time, she is struck by the beauty of the disguised Aquiles: "En toda mi vida vi / mas peregrina hermosura" (p. 2004). A chaste friendship begins to crumble at the sight of such compelling physical beauty. The disguised Aquiles is certainly a confusing figure not only for Deidamia but for all at Gnido. He is not only a Mars dressed as Venus, but also a Venus named Astraea. This double mystery adds new twists to the palace intrigue and propels the action towards new and surprising situations. Aquiles, a figure who encompasses so many opposites, represents an enigma that must be resolved. The disguised hero tells Deidamia:

Pues si tú dices que estamos
solas, y yo que está aquí
tu amante, bien fácil es
la enigma de descubrir.
[p. 2008]

Although Deidamia unveils the enigma by the beginning of the third act, others must be prevented from discovering this mystery since this seems to be the only way the couple has of seeing each other at will. The enigma also prevents Aquiles from being sent to war. Gnido, the land of Venus, is a perfect location for amorous pursuits. Aquiles plays a double role with Deidamia: "tu dama de día, y de noche / tu galán" (p. 2010). By day Aquiles is Astraea, Deidamia's cousin and a figure who represents chaste friendship. By night, however, the hero becomes the lover, expressing the nature of Venus on shedding his feminine disguise and paradoxically displaying his martial appearance. When Aquiles calls himself a monster, he refers to the multiple facets of his personality. The disguised hero has become a "monstruo de los jardines" (p. 2012) and the garden of the court is the realm of Venus. He thus learns to develop that side of himself that might be labeled feminine. Aquiles learns, for example, the clever language of gallantry: "Hábito de hablar me dió / el hábito de mujer" (p. 2007). As he predicted, the rough and hard stone of his martial disposition is being polished by the courtly environment, the land of Venus. Opposites are coming together to create a fuller person, a shining diamond.

The learning process is not without peril. There is fear of discovery. The tension mounts as Ulises keeps trying to resolve the mystery of Aquiles' whereabouts. He is determined to unravel the riddle posed by the prophecy of Mars. In this, he is aided by kledonomancy, which has been defined as "the listening to stray words and their acceptation as *omina*."[32] In spite of the fact that this type of divination was condemned in treatises such as Pedro Ciruelo's *Reprouación de las supersticiones y hechizerías* (1538), many Golden Age writers incorporate instances of it in their works.[33] Calderón, as we have seen, uses it in *La gran Cenobia*. In *El monstruo de los jardines*, kledonomancy is a recurring phenomenon that keeps Ulises on the verge of discovering Aquiles. For example, when Ulises asks himself at court "¿Dónde está Aquiles?" a voice answers "Aquí" (p. 2004). When he again wonders, "¿Dónde, fortuna, / hallaré a Aquiles?" he hears Deidamia's voice saying "Conmigo" (p. 2006). Although neither voice, that of the *criado* or that of Deidamia, is actually speaking to him, he accepts both as omens.

In addition to this occult art, Ulises utilizes his wit (*ingenio*) and cleverness to solve the riddle of Aquiles' disappearance. He thus exhibits the *sapientia* of the classical hero. According to Ernst Curtius, the Middle Ages and the Renaissance witnessed an interminable debate as to what was the highest virtue in the epic hero, *sapientia* or *fortitudo*.[34] The first was attributed to Ulises, while the latter was examplified by Aquiles. In *El mayor encanto, amor,* the virtues of these two classical heroes are depicted as opposite yet complementary.[35] In *El monstruo de los jardines,* these two figures and their ascribed qualities serve to add one more pair of opposites to the contrariety that creates dramatic tension and suspense. Ulises wishes to combine both of these virtues in his search for Aquiles: "hasta que el valor le encuentre / o el ingenio le descubra" (p. 2004). What we will actually witness is Ulises' *sapientia* in discovering Aquiles through a search for people who exhibit *fortitudo*.

Since kledonomancy has led Ulises to suspect that Aquiles is hiding close to Deidamia, he takes to her apartments a feigned *mercader* so that he can witness the reaction to the merchandise by Deidamia's ladies. This scene, which is reminiscent of the episode of the lover disguised as merchant in *A secreto agravio, secreta venganza,*[36] also centers around jewels. Deidamia's ladies are particularly interested in the *joyas* that the feigned merchant exhibits. It is fitting that the Venus-like Sirene picks a "Cupido de diamantes" (p. 2015). Cintia, representing Diana, chooses a *firmeza*. This jewel symbolizes constancy and is often given as a sacred pledge of marriage.[37] Cintia thus portrays that aspect of Diana-like chastity which finds fulfillment in marital faithfulness and constancy.[38] The two maids reveal the mystery of Deidamia's contrary inclinations. Her nightly meetings with Aquiles in a garden found in Gnido fall under the influence of Venus. On the other hand, her initial chaste friendship with the feigned Astraea had evinced a certain tendency towards Diana's realm. Now Cintia shows Deidamia another road: the chastity of the perfect wife as represented by the *firmeza*. As yet, Deidamia has not opted for Diana's path. She now picks an "áspid de rubíes" (p. 2015), a snake that is often the symbol of poisonous passion.

Ulises is not interested in these selections. He watches Astraea who, instead of admiring the jewelry, makes an atypical choice: "Pues este escudo, este acero / estas plumas y esta espada / tomaré" (p. 2015). Ulises' *sapientia* has led him to prepare a test that will reveal Aquiles through *fortitudo*. The arms donned by the feigned Astraea are symbols of valor, and they point to his/her martial disposition. As the king enters, he is amazed at the sight of Astraea *armata:* "Permite que el verte extrañe / con insignias de Belona / no siendo hermana de Marte" (p. 2016). Contraries are now emerging in unexpected and surprising ways. Calderón has given a new twist to Navagero's astounding depiction of a Venus *armata*. She is now named Astraea, thus evoking Venus's rival, the virgin Diana. The pressure for open conflict and/or resolution mounts. The king announces that Deidamia is to marry Lidoro the next day. A song is heard commemorating the coming event: "Al tálamo casto de virgen esposa" (p. 2016). Deidamia may appear to be the virginal bride who belongs to the realm of Diana, but she has become a passionate woman given to the pleasures of Venus. Neither is the feigned Astraea a representative of Virgo-Diana. Together with Deidamia, the false cousin is under the influence of Venus in a land ruled by the goddess of love. And yet, beneath Astraea's second persona lies one more opposing personality, which Ulises is attempting to bring out.

The clever Ulises now causes martial music to be played. Astraea's reaction serves to confirm Ulises' suspicions since he/she recognizes the sounds as "idioma de la guerra" (p. 2017). Ulises approaches certainty when he realizes that the "voz de Marte . . . sólo en una mujer hizo su efecto" (p. 2017). A third test proves conclusive. Seeing the feigned Astraea deep in thought, Ulises exclaims, "Guárdate, Aquiles que te dan la / muerte" (p. 2019). Astraea reacts as Aquiles would have done, proving to Ulises that his suspicions were correct and that he has solved the *misterio* (p. 1028). He now proceeds to convince Astraea-Aquiles to leave Gnido, realm of Venus, and accept his martial role in the Trojan War. Aquiles, although torn between love and honor, Venus and Mars, agrees to leave for Troy that very night. The young hero realizes that he must accept the role given to him by destiny, *los hados*, (p. 2019). He will shed his feminine attire, symbol of Venus, and assume the tunic of Mars: "Así yo, habiendo dejado / la nupcial ropa de Venus, / solo túnicas de Marte / vestiré" (p. 2020).

Aquiles will leave the dress in the garden, which he no longer views as a "templo / de Amor" (p. 2018). Gnido, the location of the temple of Venus, has now become for Aquiles a temple of *desengaño* (p. 2020). He compares the removal of Venus's adornments, which will remain in the garden, with the serpent's shedding its old skin: "de culebra que renueva / juntas la piel y el aliento" (p. 2020). This is a traditional image of *desengaño*, utilized as a symbol of the man who turns away from the world and prepares to enter, according to St. Augustine, "the strait gate of heaven."[39] This view of the serpent in the play reinforces Neumeister's contention that the *comedia* ought to

be approached through medieval exegesis, which includes allegorical, tropological, and anagogical analysis.[40] Aquiles had previously
succumbed to the serpent's temptation, becoming identified with the
pleasures of the senses. This is represented by Deidamia's asp. Now
he sheds that old skin and returns to God. We have moved from
images of the fall to a symbol of salvation. In the interpretation of the
play as pagan mystery, *desengaño* is also an important consideration.
Aquiles rejects the sensual pleasures of Venus and decides to perform
his allotted duty under Mars. He is no longer engaged in the "refusal
of the call" but accepts what Joseph Campbell labels the "call to adventure," the first step in the hero's monomyth.[41] But Deidamia
seems to be an obstacle in his path. Aquiles hears a "dulce música"
(p. 2021) that calls him back to the realm of love. This is the chant of
Sirena and all the sirens who would impede the hero's progress. The
tension between opposites, from love and war to the physical rivalry
between Aquiles and Deidamia's intended husband Lidoro, now
erupts into violence. The unmasked Aquiles fights for his life as even
the king calls for his death.

At the moment of greatest danger, the goddess Tetis appears and
puts an end to the conflict. Tetis reenacts her role as *deus ex machina*.
This time the peace is not based on fear, but on harmony. Aquiles will
go to war, but he will also marry Deidamia. Mars and Venus join in
this solution that brings about the birth of Harmonia. Tetis now
claims that all danger is over since "Hoy es el día fatal / que amenazó
con agüeros / a Aquiles" (pp. 2021-22).

The crucial battle is over and Aquiles' danger is past. For Parker,
these "palabras tranquilizadoras"[42] do not dupe the public who realize that the horoscope actually foretells a much more violent battle,
the one at Troy. This false solution recalls the false Astraea, another
invention of Tetis. But the goddess's words may simply reflect the
mystery enacted in the *comedia*. Aquiles has passed the crucial test,
that of reconciling opposites within the self. He is no longer a *fiera*,
since love has "civilized" him. He has learned the courtly speech, the
poetry that expresses the beauty of life. He is at home in Gnido, the
realm of Venus. At the same time, Aquiles can accept the influence
of Mars, his call to adventure. Although he removes the dress, he
remains familiar with the feminine side of his nature. The battle of
mighty opposites has been resolved within the self, and Tetis's appearance is but a projection of an inner truth. Her statement that the
greatest danger is over is not misleading since the Trojan war pales
beside the inner struggle that has found a resolution.

Aquiles' disguises have pointed to different aspects of the self that were in need of integration. He now encompasses within himself the strength of Mars and the amiability of Venus. As for Astraea, she is the goddess of truth, and now the hero is true to himself. Furthermore, according to Virgil's *Fourth Eclogue,* the goddess Astraea will return to earth and establish a new golden age. Just before the dawn of this new epoch "a second warfare, too, shall there be, and again shall a great Achilles be sent to Troy" (vol. 1, p. 31).[43] The words of Tetis are not *tranquilizadoras,* but prophetic. Aquiles is Astraea in that he will bring about a new age. If interpreted politically, Astraea can be seen as an imperial goddess, and the words of Tetis might instill new hope in a declining nation. But the play seems to favor a personal interpretation or revelation. Tetis is not merely a *deus ex machina,* but is also that *oculta deidad,* that transcendent power that reconciles opposites within itself. The outward peace established by Tetis among warring factions mirrors the harmony and happiness characteristic of the golden age, a peace that has dawned within Aquiles' integrated self. This is the "mystery" of Aquiles as Astraea, a disguise that has both concealed and revealed the paradox of existence and the wholeness of life.

Conclusion

ONE OF THE MOST COMPELLING DESIRES of traditional societies
is the actualization of the "perfection of beginnings." According to
Mircea Eliade, what took place *in principio* was that "the divine or
semidivine beings were active on earth. . . . Man desires to recover
the active presence of the gods; he also desires to live in the world as
it came from the Creator's hands, fresh, pure and strong."[1] The urge
to travel back to origins, to a time of perfection, to a paradisiacal or
mythological situation, is at the heart of the Astraea myth. Together
with Saturn, she was one of two immortals singled out in Greek and
Roman mythology as having lived on earth during the happiest of
ages. In the pagan and cyclic conception of history, Astraea will return again and again through new golden ages in eternal cycles of
time. Many believed that these paradisiacal epochs would only manifest themselves after a purificatory dissolution of the previous creation. *Ekpyrosis* or destruction by fire was the most common form of
purification. Although Christianity replaced the cyclic with a linear
theory of history, it still held to one final return, the coming of Christ
and the renewal of the universe. It also presented this final age in
apocalyptic terms. Thus, in both the pagan and the Christian conceptions of history, Astraea as an actual goddess or as a symbol of paradise will show herself again to man. In this sense, beginnings can be
equated with endings, and the return of Astraea can be viewed as
satisfying man's nostalgia for the perfection of beginnings. Origins
have been projected into a timeless future.

Astraea as a representative of the nostalgia for beginnings, for
paradise, is only one of the aspects of the goddess that account for
the continued vitality of her image. Her myth also shows a close kinship with humanity. She was the last of the immortals to leave earth
with the corruption that ensued with the ages. She thus endured the
longest in a fallen world. Furthermore, Astraea, according to Virgil's

reinterpretation of the myth, will be the first to return. Many writers, philosophers, and theologians equate their historical period with the iron age, but even during this period of chaos, suffering, and violence, Astraea has not abandoned humanity. Through catasterism the goddess has become the zodiacal sign Virgo or Libra. She waits in the heavens for the moment of return, a time highly feared and desired since it could necessitate an *ekpyrosis* or it could ensue without previous destruction. The proximity of Astraea to humankind, her guiding force, and her nurturing influence as the Virgin with the *spica* can also be seen outside of a historical perspective. Religious beings, according to Eliade, can experience a series of hierophanies, thus bringing the sacred into time.[2] More importantly, they can experience the eternal within their mortal self. This universal experience of religious beings can be found in Christianity through baptism, a sacrament that brings about revival or rebirth. Throughout life, these individuals can culture the fresh, pure, and strong cosmos found in *illud tempus* by somehow opening their mortal frame to the eternal. The inner paradise thus achieved can be equated with Astraea's realm.

Communion with humankind eventually robbed the myth of Astraea of its vitality. Virgil's Messianic Eclogue as reinterpreted by Christian apologists and the transformation of the goddess into an agent of empire, although inspiring some important pieces, led to the trivialization and the desacralization of Astraea. Harry Levin has noted how courtly poets in the Renaissance created a plethora of golden ages through their laudatory verse.[3] Every prince, every nobleman was said to be guided by a goddess who must surely have lost her powers since these human examples were far from embodiments of chastity, justice, and truth. Perhaps the most significant manifestation of this late Astraea is encountered in the age of Elizabeth I. The Virgin Queen as a new Astraea-Virgo became a most apt symbol of English imperial notions, as Frances A. Yates has demonstrated.[4] This was followed by the brief resurgence of Astraea in the France of Henry IV, where the goddess stood for the harmony that would ensue from religious tolerance. Most accounts of the imperial Astraea end here. Yet these late flowerings of the Astraea myth during the sixteenth and the beginnings of the seventeenth centuries should not be taken as final chapters.[5] What this book has documented is perhaps the last great rebirth of Astraea. It may well be that the rivalries between England and Spain and between France and Spain served to revitalize the myth in the Iberian peninsula. But we have noted how the goddess was well known in Spain long before Elizabeth and Henry IV. Spain's imperialist and messianic aspirations were fixed on the goddess Astraea as soon as the country became unified by the Catholic kings.

Astraea's popularity among the Spanish poets contrasts with her neglect in other literary forms. The goddess entered the world of the Spanish *comedia* with the ascension of Philip IV to the throne. In 1622, both Lope de Vega and Villamediana paid tribute to the young monarch by including Astraea in their dramas. However, her glory would have remained far below what she achieved in Italy, France, or England had not Calderón de la Barca introduced Astraea in thirteen of his *comedias*. This study has focused on Calderón's knowledge of and concern with the Astraea myth, showing how the Spanish playwright moved away from the trivial pursuits of panegyrists towards some of the more vital concepts contained in the myth.

The longing for the beginnings of time, for that paradise that reveals not only harmony but also the vitality and force of origins, is a common theme in a number of his plays. At times, the nostalgia is presented as part of the historical process that must lead paradoxically to a future that reveals origins. The return of Astraea in Calderón can be seen as a longing within the human psyche and as an active enterprise of a nation that dreams of universal empire. Fear and desire are the dominant emotions in those that yearn for the mythical epoch yet do not wish for the purification that can precede it. The myth of Rome in *El privilegio de las mujeres* and *Las armas de la hermosura* is equated with contemporary Spain, a declining empire that fears *ekpyrosis* and searches for ways to renew itself. The historical environment of some of these *comedias* points to the corruption, chaos, and violence of an iron age. Witnessing the abuses of power, the poet as panegyrist is transformed into a satirical writer who veils criticism through praise. Astraea is controlled and manipulated by ambitious political figures for the purpose of propaganda in *El mayor encanto, amor* and *Los tres mayores prodigios*. Here, magicians seek to control the heavens in ways that recall certain contemporary situations. In the amazing ups and downs of political careers and warring empires, Fortuna appears to rule. But fortune, we discover, is a nonexistent goddess worshipped by the ignorant. *La gran Cenobia* reveals her heavenly name: Astraea is divine truth unfolded through time.

Those who attain a measure of wisdom in Calderón's theater know that the dictates of providence as written in the heavenly book of stars and constellations will eventually become manifest. However, those who are labeled as *sabios* in these *comedias*, although versed in astrology and other occult arts, exhibit their limitations. Personal and often pessimistic interpretations prevent them from discovering the full meaning of celestial portents, as in the case of Se-leuco in *Los tres afectos de amor*. Desire for power leads some to attempt control over these occult forces. Worse still, pride leads others to be-lieve that they can become co-writers of the cosmic plan. The king in *La vida es sueño* is one such extreme example. As Robert ter Horst puts it, "Basilio thinks that he has eclipsed time as the agent of revelation and yielder of secrets."[6] Although calling himself a *sabio*, Basilio does not represent wisdom. Only those who are able to experience the timeless sacred and unfold the paradise within are truly free to understand, experience, and participate fully in the wondrous uni-versal drama of creation and dissolution. Guided by Rosaura-Astraea, Segismundo becomes the perfect prince, both the apocalyp-tic monster of his father's mistaken horoscope and the promise held by the *nova* in the constellation Serpentarius. The new age dawns when Segismundo pardons his father, thus annulling the apocalyptic predictions, and when he turns away from Rosaura, balancing the scales of justice and affirming chastity as an attribute of the goddess.

Perhaps what is most startling about Calderón's multifaceted and original depiction of Astraea is her humanity. The playwright must have been aware of the myth's uniqueness in its presentation of a goddess particularly close and responsive to the human race. In the *comedias* this proximity is taken to an extreme: Astraea never appears as an actual goddess, but always as a woman. The character named Astraea often exhibits many of the qualities of the deity, but she also possesses typical human weaknesses. Indeed, as a human being As-traea can be controlled by others and by her own passions. As one of the maids of autumn, she can be under the command of the sorcer-esses Medea and Circe. Ismenia, taking the name of Astraea, even becomes a malefic figure. Calderón's "mistreatment" of the heavenly name in his plays points to the subversion and dissipation of the ideal in a corrupt age. Even though the subjected woman reflects the real-ities of an iron age, the portrait of a fallen Astraea can become a most powerful vehicle for the rebirth of the goddess in the most corrupt of epochs. Astraea-Rosaura's fall into Poland can also be interpreted as the fall of the sign Virgo into the world, the infusion of the sacred into the profane. A fallen woman is the vehicle for the merging of sacred and profane time at that point in history when the return of Astraea can signal the actualization of myth, when the active pres-ence of the gods is felt on earth again.

The search for happiness and harmony takes the form of inner transformation and outer warfare in these *comedias*. The priestess As-traea in *La gran Cenobia* guides Decio through reversals of fortune and defeats in battle so as to test his inner qualities and shape a better man, one that can aspire to renew the Roman Empire. In *La vida es sueño*, Segismundo must fight to regain the throne of Poland at the same time that he struggles with his own bestial nature. In *El monstruo de los jardines* Aquiles dressed as Astraea reflects the ancient mystery of *discordia concors*. The hero, before he can act as such, must reconcile the two aspects of his personality symbolized by his two names. In the end, the "hidden god" reveals that the greatest epic conflict is not to be localized at Troy, but has already been fought within Aquiles' own being. Aquiles is Astraea in that he has actualized within himself a paradisiacal situation. Inner harmony is the first step in the transformation of the environment in many of Calderón's plays. The ending of *El monstruo de los jardines* points to Aquiles' future warlike deeds. Although the greek hero will be killed at Troy, the drama does not dwell on a tragic solution. Rather, it presents a joyful conclusion based not only on Aquiles' own transformation, but also on the prophetic implications of Astraea. The audience would recall that in Virgil's *Fourth Eclogue* Aquiles had to engage in warfare previous to the return of the golden age. Calderón's last portrayal of Astraea is not concerned with the profane, fallen, and mistreated woman who struggles to realize her full potential in a corrupt iron age. Rather, he presents a joyful, prophetic, and imperialist goddess who points to personal transformation as the actualization of a golden age within the human heart. For Calderón, the actions of such integrated individuals are truly heroic since they will act with a clear vision of the possibilities inherent in the myth of the return of Astraea.

Notes

CHAPTER ONE

1. Joseph Campbell, *The Masks of God: Oriental Mythology* (New York: Penguin, 1976), p. 117. See also J.L.E. Dreyer, *A History of the Planetary Systems from Thales to Kepler* (Cambridge: Cambridge Univ. Press, 1906), pp. 20-204. Precession is defined as "the continuous shift of the equinoxes backward through the sidereal zodiac, as a result of the slow revolution of the Earth's axis of rotation about the ecliptic pole, itself caused by the gravitational attraction of the Sun and Moon on the Earth's equatorial bulge" (Jean Louis Brau, Helen Weaver, and Allan Edmands, *Larousse Encyclopedia of Astrology* [New York, McGraw-Hill, 1906], p. 225). The precession of the equinoxes led Ptolemy to create a fictitious or tropical zodiac "because from our previous demonstration we observe that their natures, powers and familiarities take their cause from the solstitial and equinoctial starting places, and from no other source. For if other starting places are assumed, we shall either be compelled no longer to use the natures of the signs for prognostications or, if we use them, to be in error, since the spaces of the zodiac which implant their powers in the planets would then pass over to others and become alienated" (*Tetrabiblos*, trans. and ed. F.E. Robbins [Cambridge: Harvard Univ. Press, 1940], pp. 109-11). What Ptolemy means is that, due to this precession, a person born today at the time of the vernal equinox would be Pisces according to the heavenly constellations. For astrological purposes, the tropical zodiac should be utilized. While the constellations slowly shift, the tropical zodiac remains permanently attached to the vernal equinox. Thus a person born today at the time of the spring equinox would be a Pisces if he glanced at the sidereal zodiac, but astrologers would claim he was an Aries, utilizing the tropical zodiac. This permanent zodiac, according to Ptolemy, is based on the "natural" qualities of the signs. Even though Ptolemy established this double system that is still in use today, his observations on the precession of the equinoxes were not as accurate as those of Hipparchus. For a sixteenth-century discussion of precession, see Wayne Shumaker and J.L. Heilbron, *John Dee on Astronomy* (Berkeley: Univ. of California Press, 1978), pp. 78, 228-30. This precession is responsible for the different astrological ages which are also based on the vernal equinox. The age of Aries ended about the time of the birth of Christ. From then on, humanity has been in the age of Pisces and will soon be moving into the age of Aquarius. C.G. Jung finds the notion that the Christian and Piscean ages coincide chronologically to be an interesting phenomenon: "It is therefore only natural that my reflections should gravitate round the symbol of the Fishes, for the Pisces aeon is the synchronistic concomitant of two thousand years

of Christian development" (*Aion: Researches into the Phenomenology of the Self*, trans. R.F.C. Hull, 2d ed. [Princeton: Princeton Univ. Press, 1968], p. ix).

2. The notion of the Great or Platonic year is found in Plato's *Timaeus* and *Politicus*. It is often associated with the precession of the equinoxes, although they are actually two different interpretations of cosmic cycles: "Although there is no statement of the duration of a great year in Plato, it is frequently assumed, on the basis of a passage in his *Republic* VIII.546, that his estimate was 36,000 years. This tradition seems to have been strengthened by the fact that Hipparchus, discoverer of the precession of the equinoxes (Ptolemy VII.i-ii), estimated a precessional period to be 36,000 years. But it is quite clear that there is no connection between Plato's great year and Hipparchus' precessional period" (William Harris Stahl, trans. and ed., Macrobius, *Commentary on the Dream of Scipio* [New York: Columbia Univ. Press. 1952], p. 221).

3. Aratus places *spica* in the Virgin's hand, without specifying which hand. Hipparchus locates *spica* in the left hand, a correction that is included in Germanicus's Latin translation of Aratus's *Phaenomena*.

4. Jean Seznec, *The Survival of the Pagan Gods*, trans. Barbara F. Sessions, (Princeton: Princeton Univ. Press, 1972), p. 38. The other two writers are Eudoxus of Cnidus and Eratosthenes, whose *Catasterismis* standardizes results.

5. A. Bouché-Leclerq, *L'Astrologie grecque* (1899; rpt. Chicago: Bolchazy-Carducci, 1979), p. 62.

6. Cited in Richard Hinkley Allen, *Star Names: Their Lore and Meaning* (1899; rpt. New York: Dover, 1963), p. 462. The Greek poem and an English translation can be found in *Callimachus, Hymns and Epigrams. Lycophron. Aratus* (Cambridge: Harvard Univ. Press, 1955). For this passage see p. 217.

7. William Sale, "The Popularity of Aratus," *Classical Journal* 61 (1966), 162.

8. Renato Poggioli, *The Oaten Flute* (Cambridge: Harvard Univ. Press, 1952).

9. On Aratus's popularity, see William Sale's article cited above; Seznec, *Pagan Gods*, p. 151; and Jean Martin, *Histoire du texte des Phénomènes d'Aratos* (Paris: C. Klincksieck, 1956): "Les témoignages concernant l'histoire antique du texte d'Aratos sont d'une abondance et d'une qualité exceptionelles, tout au moins si on les compare avec les maigres renseignements que l'on rassemble si péniblement sur des oeuvres plus classiques" (p. 9).

10. Sale, "Popularity of Aratus," p. 163.

11. Leonard Barkan, *Nature's Work of Art: The Human Body as Image of the World* (New Haven: Yale Univ. Press, 1975), p. 22.

12. Hesiod, *The Works and Days. Theogony. The Shields of Herakles*, trans. Richard Lattimore (Ann Arbor: Univ. of Michigan Press, 1973), p. 49.

13. Pietro Pucci, *Hesiod and the Language of Poetry* (Baltimore: Johns Hopkins Univ. Press, 1977), p. 53. Pucci distinguishes between *dike* the concept and *Dike* the goddess.

14. Hesiod, *Works and Days*, p. 45.

15. Pucci, *Hesiod and Language*, p. 6. Hesiod lists five generations: 1) the golden race, 2) the silver race, 3) the brazen race, 4) the race of heroes, and 5) the iron age. The sixth age of force is a continuation of the iron age. The fourth race is omitted by most later writers including Aratus and Ovid. Thus, the ages are usually listed as four. Lacking mates, the earlier generations destroy themselves and must be regenerated as inferior races. See J.G. Griffiths, "Did Hesiod Invent the Golden Age?" *JHI* 19 (1958): 19-93.

16. Harry Levin, *The Myth of the Golden Age in the Renaissance* (Oxford: Oxford Univ. Press, 1969), p. 19.

17. Ibid., p. 22.

18. She is also associated with Cybele drawn by lions since the sign Leo precedes

her. Virgo can also be Diana and even Medusa. See Richard Hinckley Allen, *Star Names*, pp. 462-63.

19. Manilius, *Astronomica*, trans. and ed. G.P. Goold (Cambridge: Harvard Univ. Press, 1977), p. 265.

20. Germanicus, *Les Phénomènes d'Aratos*, ed. and trans. André Le Boeuffle (Paris: Societe d'edition "Les Belles Lettres," 1975), p. x.

21. *The Myths of Hyginus*, ed. and trans. Mary Grant. (Lawrence: Univ. of Kansas Press, 1960), p. 215. Hyginus elaborates on the myth of Erigone and Icarius in *Fabulae* 130 (see p. 109). Under the heading of "Mortals who were made Immortal," Hyginus includes the myth of Erigone as Virgo, noting also that Icarius became Arcturus (*Fabulae* 224, p. 159). Virgo-Astraea as Fortuna derived from Eratosthenes is found in at least two commentators of Aratus: Germanicus and Avienius. See *Eratosthenis Catasterismorum Reliquiae* ed. Carolus Robert (1878; rpt. Berlin: Weidmann, 1963), pp. 82-85.

22. Michael C.J. Putnam, *Virgil's Pastoral Art* (Princeton: Princeton Univ. Press, 1970), p. 136.

23. All page references to Virgil's works are from the Loeb Classical Library edition: *Virgil*, 2 vols., ed. and trans. H. Rushton Fairclough, 2d ed., (Cambridge: Harvard Univ. Press., 1934-35).

24. "I suspect that Virgil emphasized Arcadia because he is more interested in the Golden Age than his Greek predecessors. True, the Golden Age and Arcadia are not used together in *Eclogue* 4. But the two concepts are the two sides of the same coin," writes Thomas G. Rosenmeyer in *The Green Cabinet* (Berkeley: Univ. of California Press, 1969), p. 235. Levin, on the other hand, warns: "Arcadia is one myth; the Golden Age is another; and though they have significant linkages, art history does not help by confounding the two" (*Golden Age*, pp. 194-95).

25. Putnam, *Virgil's Pastoral Art*, p. 162.

26. Eleanor Winsor Leach, *Virgil's Eclogues: Landscapes of Experience* (Ithaca: Cornell Univ. Press, 1974), p. 218.

27. Frances A. Yates, *Astraea: The Imperial Theme in the Sixteenth Century* (London: Routledge and Keagan Paul, 1975), p. 33.

28. Putnam, *Virgil's Pastoral Art*, p. 143.

29. Mircea Eliade, *The Myth of the Eternal Return*, trans. Willard R. Trask (Princeton: Princeton Univ. Press, 1954), pp. ix, 81.

30. Eliade speaks of Romulus's eagles (*Eternal Return*, p. 134). Plutarch, on the other hand, emphasizes that the birds are vultures and not eagles: "it preys only upon carrion, and never kills or hunts any living thing: and as for birds, it touches not them, though they are dead, as being of its own species, whereas eagles, owls and hawks mangle and kill their own fellow-creatures. . . . Besides, all other birds are, so to say, never out of our eyes; they let themselves be seen of us continually; but a vulture is a very rare sight . . . their rarity and infrequency has raised a strange opinion in some, that they come to us from some other worlds" (Plutarch, *The Lives of the Noble Grecians and Romans*, trans. John Dryden, rev. Arthur Hugh Clough [New York: Modern Library, 1961], p. 30).

31. Macrobius, *Commentary on the Dream of Scipio*, p. 75.

32. Ibid., pp. 221-22.

33. *"The Republic" of Plato*, ed. and trans. Francis MacDonald Cornford (Oxford: Oxford Univ. Press, 1945), pp. 268-69.

34. On the *yugas* see Joseph Campbell, *The Mythic Image* (Princeton: Princeton Univ. Press, 1974), pp. 141-44; and the *Bhagavad-Gita*, trans. and comp. Maharishi Mahesh Yogi (New York: Penguin, 1969), pp. 251-55.

35. Eliade, *Eternal Return*, p. 87. For the texts of Berossus see Isaac Preston Cory, *Ancient Fragments of the Phoenician, Chaldean, Egyptian, Tyrian, Carthaginian, Indian, Persian and Other Writers* (London: W. Pickering, 1832). Cory includes passages by Berossus contained in the writings of Alexander Polyhistor, Apollodorus, Abydenus, etc. Don Cameron Allen is careful to distinguish Berossus's actual writings from the forged *History of the Chaldeans* published by Nannio de Viterbo during the Renaissance (*Mysteriously Meant* [Baltimore; Johns Hopkins Univ. Press, 1970], p. 61).

36. All page references to this work are from the Loeb Classical Library edition: Seneca, *Naturales Quaestiones*, 2 vols., ed. and trans. Thomas H. Corcoran (Cambridge: Harvard Univ. Press, 1971).

37. All page references to Seneca's plays are from the Loeb Classical Library edition: Seneca, *Tragedies*, 2 vols., ed. and trans. Frank Justus Miller (Cambridge: Harvard Univ. Press, 1917).

38. Domenico Comparetti, *Virgil in the Middle Ages*, trans E.F.M. Benecke (New York: G.E. Stechert, 1929), p. 100.

39. Sabine G. MacCormick, *Art and Ceremony in Late Antiquity* (Berkeley: Univ. of California Press, 1981), p. 210.

40. Poggioli, *Oaten Flute*, p. 18.

41. Ernst H. Kantorowicz, *Laudes Regia: A Study of Liturgical Acclamations and Medieval Ruler Worship.* (Berkeley: Univ. of California Press, 1946), p. 103.

42. Yates, *Astraea*, p. 2.

43. *The Play of Antichrist*, trans. and ed. John Wright (Toronto: Univ. of Toronto Press, 1967).

44. Yates, *Astraea*, pp. 5-7.

45. Ernst Kantorowicz, *Frederick the Second*, trans. E.O. Lorimer, 2d ed. (New York: Frederick Ungar, 1957), p. 686.

46. Norman Cohn, *The Pursuit of the Millennium* (Fairlawn, N.J.: Essential Books, 1957), p. 113.

47. Theodore Otto Wedel, *The Medieval Attitude Toward Astrology* (New Haven: Yale Univ. Press, 1920), p. 68.

48. Ibid., p. 68.

49. Dante Alighieri, *La Divina Commedia*, ed. C.H. Grandgent, rev. Charles S. Singleton (Cambridge: Harvard Univ. Press, 1972), p. 183 (*Inferno* 20. 115-18).

50. E.M. Butler, *The Myth of the Magus*, paperback ed. (Cambridge: Cambridge Univ. Press, 1979), p. 99. Emile Mâle contends that the Erythrean Sibyl was much more popular in representations in the Gothic cathedrals: "She prophesied at the time of the founding of Rome, Achaz, or according to others, Ezekias, being King of Judah. The celebrity of the Sibyl came from a passage in *The City of God*. St. Augustine attributed to her the famous verses on the Day of Judgment" (*The Gothic Image*, trans. Dora Nussey [New York: Harper and Row, 1972], pp. 336-39). But the passage in question in Augustine reveals his doubts as to whether the leading sibyl was the Erythrean or the Cumaean (*The City of God* 28. 23).

51. Dante, *Divina Commedia*, p. 507 (*Purgatorio* 22. 70-72).

52. On Astraea as the blissful and heavenly life see *The Letters of Marsilio Ficino* (London: Shepheard-Walwyn, 1975), vol. 1, p. 147.

53. Don Cameron Allen, *Mysteriously Meant*, pp. 142-48. Among the Renaissance and later commentators of the *Fourth Eclogue* are: Richard Gorraeus (1554), Albericus Gentilis (1603), Guillaume de Oncieu (1620), Huig de Groot (1627), Daniel Heinz (1627), and August Buchner (1682).

54. Levin, *Golden Age*, p. 112. See also Eglal Henien, "Mythes et Mythologie dans

l'Astrée," in *Mythology in French Literature*, ed. Phillip Crant (Columbia: Univ. of South Carolina Press, 1976) pp. 10-16.

55. Elizabeth Armstrong, *Ronsard and the Age of Gold* (Cambridge: Cambridge Univ. Press, 1968), p. 42.

56. Ibid., p. 48. Ronsard relates Astraea to Erigone, calling his beloved "Belle Erigone" (*Les Oeuvres de Pierre de Ronsard*, ed. Isidore Silver [Paris: Marcel Didier, 1966], vol. 2, p. 209).

57. See Myriam Yvonne Jehenson, *The Golden World of the Pastoral* (Ravenna: Longo, 1982).

58. Levin, *Golden Age*, p. 70.

59. All references to *The Tragedy of Titus Andronicus* are from A.M. Witherspoon's edition (New Haven: Yale Univ. Press, 1926). On this play see Yates, *Astraea*, pp. 74-76.

60. Poggioli, *Oaten Flute*, pp. 111-34.

CHAPTER TWO

1. M. Menéndez Pelayo, *Antología de poetas líricos castellanos*, vol. 7 (Madrid: Hernando, 1898), p. xxxvi; Henry W. Sullivan, *Juan del Encina* (Boston: Twayne, 1976), pp. 113, 163. See also Ana M. Rambaldo, ed., Juan del Encina, *Obras completas* (Madrid: Espasa-Calpe, 1978), vol. 1, pp. xxviii-xxxi; Marcial José Bayo, *Virgilio y la pastoral española del Renacimiento* (Madrid: Gredos, 1970), pp. 44-55; and James A. Anderson, *Encina and Virgil* (University, Miss.: Romance Monographs, 1974), pp. 61-76. According to Anderson, "The first question that may occur to one reading Encina's translation for the first time is why he broke from the medieval tradition wherein this eclogue, through Servius' interpretation of it, became the prediction of the birth of Christ (and which made Virgil almost a Christian)" (p. 63). As we have noted, Encina follows the imperial or second tradition that was also popular during the Middle Ages.

2. Juan del Encina, *Obras completas*, ed. Ana M. Rambaldo (Madrid: Espasa-Calpe, 1978), vol. 1, p. 58. All page references to Juan del Encina are from this edition.

3. Marcel Bataillon, *Erasmo y España*, trans. Antonio Alatorre, 2d ed., (Mexico: Fondo de Cultura Económica, 1966), p. 51.

4. Ibid., p. 56. Another reference to Astrea during the reign of the Catholic kings occurs in the *Panegírico a la reina doña Isabel por Diego Guillén de Avila* (Valladolid, 1509; rpt. Madrid: Real Academia Española, 1951): "La virgen Astrea descendió del cielo / de sus compañeras entorno cercada / perdido del todo el viejo recelo."

5. Carlos G. Norena, *Juan Luis Vives* (The Hague: Martinus Nijhoff, 1970), p. 66.

6. Allen, *Mysteriously Meant*, p. 147. Vives was also aware of the astrological importance of Astraea-Virgo since Hyginus was one of his favorite writers.

7. Citations from the Acuña sonnet are from *Varias poesías de Hernando de Acuña* ed. Elena Catena de Vindel (Madrid: CSIC, 1954).

8. John H.R. Polt, "Una fuente del soneto de Acuña 'Al Rey Nuestro Señor,'" *BH* 64 (1962), 226.

9. Ibid., pp. 220-22.

10. Erwin Panofsky, *Problems in Titian* (New York: New York Univ. Press, 1969), p. 86. On Titian's impact on the literature of Spain and his friendship with Charles V see my study "Lope de Vega and Titian," *CL* 30 (1978), 338-52. On Charles V's imperialism see also José Antonio Maravall, *Carlos V y el pensamiento político del Renacimiento* (Madrid: Instituto de Estudios Políticos, 1960).

11. Bernice Hamilton, *Political Thought in Sixteenth Century Spain* (Oxford: Clarendon Press, 1963), pp. 35-41, 96.

12. Joseph R. Jones, ed., Antonio de Guevara, *Una década de Césares* (Chapel Hill: Univ. of North Carolina Press, 1966), p. 36.

13. Joseph R. Jones, *Antonio de Guevara* (Boston: Twayne, 1975), p. 27.

14. Augustin Redondo, *Antonio de Guevara et l'Espagne de son temps* (Geneva: Droz, 1976), p. 581.

15. Yates, *Astraea*, pp. 52-53. In the passage in question Guevara refers to the astrological position of the virgin between Leo and Libra.

16. Antonio de Guevara, *Menosprecio de corte y alabanza de aldea*, ed. M. Martínez de Burgos (Madrid: Espasa-Calpe, 1952), p. 140. Baltasar Gracián in *El criticón* also refers to the present age as an epoch of clay. See M.L. Welles, "The Myth of the Golden Age in Gracián's *El Criticón*," *Hispania* 65 (1982), 388-94. In chapter 16 of the *Menosprecio*, Guevara returns to the theme of the golden age, contrasting it with present corruption: "En aquellos tiempos pasados y en aquellos siglos dorados, en caso de ser uno malo, ni lo ossava ser, ni mucho menos parecer; mas ¡ay dolor! que es venido ya el mundo a tanta disolución y corrupción, que los perdonaríamos si no fuessen desvergonçados" (p. 159). On the relationship between pastoral and golden age in Guevara, see J.M. Aguirre, "Antonio de Guevara's *Corte-Aldea*: A Model for All Seasons," *Neophil* 65 (1981), 536-47. Aguirre states that in Utopia and Arcadia, pain and work are not alien elements, while the golden age is characterized by bliss. They are man's longing for paradise lost.

17. Asunción Rallo, *Antonio de Guevara en su contexto renacentista* (Madrid: Cupsa, 1979), pp. 123-38. Ann E. Wiltrout sees the *Relox* as a more conservative work: "Guevara takes a stance . . . that justifies the imperial expansion resulting from Charles' election as Holy Roman Emperor" (p. 48). Yet, analyzing the *villano del Danubio*, she concludes that "the polemic of conquest, whether European or American, remains unresolved in this narrative" (p. 54). See her perceptive article, *"El villano del Danubio*: Foreign Policy and Literary Structure," *CH* 3 (1981), 47-57.

18. Vasco de Quiroga, for example, contrasts the iron age of Europe with the simplicity of the golden age exemplified by the inhabitants of the New World (Bataillon, *Erasmo y España*, p. 820). Yet the happiness of the golden age reflected in the inhabitants of the New World contrasts with the slavery imposed by the conquerors. Las Casas in his *Apologética historia* speaks of the *libertad natural* of the first epoch, citing Macrobius: "Hobo tanta paz que ninguno se enojaba e hacia mal de otro" (Redondo, *Antonio de Guevara*, p. 580). On the notion of conquest and the rights of the American Indians see also J.A. Fernández Santamaría, *The State, War and Peace: Spanish Political Thought in the Renaissance, 1516-1559* (Cambridge: Cambridge Univ. Press, 1977).

19. Cited in Ronald E. Surtz, *The Birth of a Theater* (Madrid: Castalia, 1979), pp. 121-22.

20. Ibid., p. 122.

21. On Philip's imperialism see J.H. Elliott, *Imperial Spain* (New York: Penguin, 1970), pp. 249-58; and Fernand Braudel, *The Mediterranean and the Mediterranean World in the Age of Philip II*, trans. Sean Reynolds (N.Y.: Harper and Row, 1976), vol. 2, pp. 675-78.

22. Bataillon, *Erasmo y España*, p. 751.

23. On the relationship between Arcadia and the golden age with particular reference to Virgil see Rosenmeyer, *Green Cabinet*, p. 235.

24. Juan Bautista Avalle-Arce, *La novela pastoril española*, 2d ed., (Madrid: Istmo, 1974). "Porque ocurre que este propio complejo—la creencia en un nuevo Edén, en el Siglo de Oro, y todos sus concomitantes—está en trance de agonía para la época de

Balbuena. El mismo no puede dejar de expresar cierta duda al referirse al Siglo de Oro" (p. 211). See also Amadeus Solé-Leris, *The Spanish Pastoral Novel* (Boston: Twayne, 1980), pp. 126-28; and my study "Caves of Fame and Wisdom in the Spanish Pastoral Novel," *SPh* 82 (1985), 332-58.

25. Anthony J. Cascardi, "The Exit from Arcadia: Reevaluation of the Pastoral in Virgil, Garcilaso and Góngora," *JHP* 4 (1980), 121.

26. Gareth A. Davies, "Notes on Some Classical Sources for Garcilaso and Luis de León," *HR* 32 (1964), 202-16. Davies notes that Horace's *Second Epode* was used by both Garcilaso in his *Egloga segunda* and by Luis de León in *Vida retirada*. The purpose of his article is to expand the list of classical sources to include Virgil's *Georgics* II and IV, Seneca's *Hippolytus*, etc.

27. Gareth A. Davies, "Luis de León and a Passage from Seneca's *Hippolytus*," *BHS* 41 (1964), 10-27.

28. *Poesías de Fray Luis de León* ed. P. Angel C. Vega (Madrid: Saeta, 1955), p. 444.

29. Poggioli, *Oaten Flute*, pp. 189, 193.

30. For a list of translators of Virgil see Theodore S. Beardsley, *Hispano-Classical Translations Printed between 1482 and 1699* (Pittsburgh: Duquesne Univ. Press, 1970), p. 156.

31. *Obras completas castellanas de Fray Luis de León*, ed. Félix García (Madrid: Biblioteca de Autores Cristianos, 1959), pp. 1517-18.

32. Ibid., p. 575.

33. Karl A. Kottman, *Law and Apocalypse: The Moral Thought of Luis de León* (The Hague: Martinus Nijhoff, 1972), pp. 79-80.

34. *Poesías de Fray Luis de León*, p. 476.

35. Ibid., p. 36.

36. Américo Castro, *El pensamiento de Cervantes*, ed. Julio Rodríguez Puértolas, 2d ed. (Barcelona: Noguer, 1972), p. 177.

37. All references to *Los trabajos de Persiles y Sigismunda* are from Juan Bautista Avalle-Arce's edition (Madrid: Castalia, 1969).

38. John G. Weiger, *The Individuated Self: Cervantes and the Emergence of the Individual* (Athens, Ohio: Ohio Univ. Press, 1979), p. 85.

39. In *De Trinitate*, Augustine speaks of the "indwelling Teacher" and of interior "illumination," transforming previous Platonic conceptions of the relationship of mind and soul to God. Seventeenth-century English writers such as Henry Vaughan, Thomas Traherne, and John Milton believe that the limitless possibilities of paradise are available to man through his inner journey towards illumination. On this subject see Louis Martz, *The Paradise Within* (New Haven: Yale Univ. Press, 1964).

40. The prophecies of Soldino are addressed to the pilgrims who are journeying to Rome, a place conceived as the seat of Christianity, not as the imperial city. One critic has seen in these prophecies a reminiscence of the *Aeneid*, but does not mention possible parallels with the *Fourth Eclogue* See Alban K. Forcione, *Cervantes' Christian Romance: A Study of the Persiles y Sigismunda* (Princeton: Princeton Univ. Press, 1972), p. 101.

41. Barkan, *Nature's Work of Art*, p. 22.

42. Weiger, *Individuated Self*, pp. 86-87. "In this world- weary soldier who has faithfully served Charles V for many years, we observe the harmonious coexistence of classical antiquity's ideal of moral perfection on earth and the Christian awareness that earthly existence is but a prelude to the life that is to follow" (Forcione, *Christian Romance*, p. 101). Soldino is thus the ideal man who furthers God's purpose through active and contemplative pursuits.

43. Karl Ludwing Selig, "*La Numancia*: A Reconsideration of the Duero Speech," in

Homenaje a William L. Fichter, ed. A. David Kossoff and José Amor y Vázquez (Madrid: Castalia, 1971), 681-85.

44. Miguel de Cervantes y Saavedra, *Obras completas,* ed. Angel Valbuena Prat, 17th ed. (Madrid: Aguilar, 1970), pp. 148-49. All references to *Los tratos de Argel* are from this edition.

45. For the dating of this play see S. Griswold Morley and Courtney Bruerton, *Cronología de las comedias de Lope de Vega* (Madrid: Gredos, 1968), p. 242.

46. Bruce W. Wardropper, "El problema de la responsabilidad en la comedia de capa y espada de Calderón," *Actas del 2 Congreso Internacional de Hispanistas* (Nijmegen: Inst. Español de la Universidad de Nijmega, 1967), pp. 689-94.

47. All page references to *Los embustes de Fabia* are from *Obras de Lope de Vega publicadas por la Real Academia Española,* new edition, ed. Emilio Cotarelo y Mori (Madrid: Revista de Archivos Bibliotecas y Museos, 1918), vol. 5.

48. For the date of this comedia see Morley and Bruerton, *Cronología,* p. 390.

49. M. Menéndez Pelayo, ed., *Obras de Lope de Vega publicadas por la Real Academia Española* (Madrid: Sucesores de Rivadeneyra, 1898), vol. 6, p. cix.

50. Raymond R. MacCurdy, "La tragédie néo-sénéquienne en Espagne," in *Les Tragédies de Sénèque et le théâtre de la Renaissance,* ed. Jean Jacquot, 2d ed. (Paris: Centre National de la Recherche Scientifique, 1973), p. 79.

51. All page references to *Roma abrasada* are from Menéndez Pelayo's edition, vol. 6, cited above.

52. The dating is from Morley and Bruerton, *Cronología,* p. 367.

53. Menéndez Pelayo, ed., *Obras de Lope de Vega,* vol. 9, p. 349.

54. For other examples of Saturn in Lope de Vega, see my study "The Saturn Factor: Examples of Astrological Imagery in Lope de Vega's Works," in *Studies in Honor of Everett W. Hesse,* ed. William C. McCrary and José A. Madrigal (Lincoln, Nebr.: SSSAS, 1981), pp. 63-80.

55. C. Alan Soons, "Augustinian Criticism of the *Comedia* Reconsidered: Lope's *El despertar a quien duerme,*" *REH* 10 (1976), 443-50.

56. On Lope de Vega's astrological expertise see Juan Millé y Giménez, "El horóscopo de Lope de Vega," *Humanidades* 15 (1927), 69-96; Frank G. Halstead, "The Attitude of Lope de Vega toward Astrology and Astronomy," *HR* 7 (1939), 205-19; and Warren T. McCready, "Lope de Vega's Birth Date and Horoscope," *HR* 28 (1960), 313-18.

57. Lope de Vega, *La Arcadia,* ed. Edwin S. Morby (Madrid: Castalia, 1975), p. 399, n. 47. For a description of Erigone-Virgo see Pierre Dinet, *Cinq Livres des Hieroglyphiques* (Paris, 1614), ed. Stephen Orgel (New York: Garland, 1979). Dinet states that since wine was the cause of Icarius's death and Erigone's sadness, the sign Virgo is opposed to drink (Bacchus). He adds that wine is not conducive to chastity, a key quality of this zodiacal sign (pp. 261-62).

58. Lope de Vega, *El peregrino en su patria,* ed. Juan Bautista Avalle-Arce (Madrid: Castalia, 1973), p. 450. See also the edition by Myron A. Peyton (Chapel Hill: Univ. of North Carolina Press, 1971), p. 544. Joaquín de Entrambasaguas mistakes Lope's meaning here and contends he is referring to "los diez últimos días de agosto cuando el signo de Astrea o Virgo, que corresponde a este mes, casi llegaba al final de él, donde comienza el equinoccio." See his "Cronos en el metaforismo de Lope de Vega," in *Estudios sobre Lope de Vega* (Madrid: CSIC, 1947), vol. 1, p. 484.

59. Lope de Vega, *La Arcadia,* p. 399, n. 49.

60. Lope de Vega, *Jerusalén conquistada,* ed. Joaquín de Entrambasaguas (Madrid: CSIC, 1951). All page references are to this edition.

61. Don Cameron Allen, *Mysteriously Meant,* p. 115.

62. G.P. Valeriano Bolzani, *Les Hieroglyphiques*, trans. I. de Montyard, ed. Stephen Orgel (New York: Garland, 1976), p. 795.

63. J.E. Cirlot, *A Dictionary of Symbols*, trans. Jack Sage, 2d ed. (New York: Philosophical Library, 1971), pp. 166-67. Emblems of the period often depict justice in a manner similar to the Tarot. J.E. Boudard, for example, speaks of *Justice humaine* thus: "Les attributs ordinaires de la justice sont les balances et l'épée" (*Iconologie*, ed. Stephen Orgel [New York: Garland, 1976], p. 150). Dinet also speaks of "la balance" as one of justice's symbols in *Cinq Livres des Hieroglyphiques*, p. 694. Some Renaissance manuals of icons and symbols reject sword and balance as the symbols of justice, claiming that they belong to *equité*. It may be that Lope's stress on *igual* stems from this tradition. See Guillaume du Choul, *Discours de la religion des anciens romains illustré* (Lyons, 1556), ed. Stephen Orgel (New York: Garland, 1976), p. 113. On the Tarot see Sallie Nichols, *Jung and the Tarot: An Archetypal Journey* (New York: Samuel Weiser, 1980): "Actually, Justice is related to Libra through her ancestor, Astraea. The latter, daughter of Zeus and Themis, walked on earth during the golden age and had a benign influence on mankind. However, man's subsequent impiety drove the goddess to heaven, for disharmony went against her nature. She was given a fixed place in the heavens as Virgo. The constellation Virgo was later divided to create the astrological signs Virgo and Libra" (p. 160). Actually, the balance emerged from the Scorpion's claws. The Romans claimed to have added Libra to the original signs. See Richard Hinckley Allen, *Star Names*, p. 270; and Bouché Leclerq, *L'Astrologie grecque*, pp. 141-42. Harry Levin does not seem to be aware of the popularity of the image of Astraea holding the scales. Discussing the Terrazzo di Saturno in Vasari's *Ragionamenti*, he states: "Astraea holds an uncharacteristic pair of scales" (*Golden Age*, p. 197).

64. *Obras de Fray Luis de León*, ed. García, p. 1556. Manilius includes similar statements when speaking of Libra and the Ram (*Astronomica*, pp. 59 and 215). Richard Hinckley Allen considers the matter a commonplace (*Star Names*, p. 270).

65. All page references to Lope de Vega's poetry, unless specified, are from *Obras poéticas*, ed. José Manuel Blecua (Barcelona: Planeta, 1969), vol. 1.

66. Joaquín de Entrambasaguas cites verses from the *Isidro* where Astraea is equated with Virgo. The passage tells of the sun's passing from Leo to Virgo-Astraea: "El sol de León saliendo / y entrando en la rubia Astraea" ("Cronos," p. 484).

67. Discussing different *geroglíficos* of justice, Covarrubias mentions the scales: "También lo fué una balança con ésta: *nec huc, nec illuc*. No ha de inclinarse la justicia nunca, siempre ha de estar en fiel." This is the evenhandedness attributed by Lope to the duke. Sebastián de Covarrubias, *Tesoro de la lengua castellana o española*, ed. Martín de Riquer (Barcelona: Horta, 1943), p. 725.

68. As the antithesis of *envidia*, Astraea appears in an epistle, "A don Lorenzo Van der Hamen de León," included in *La Circe*: "que quien la ciencia con envidia agravia / no ha de vivir donde preside Astraea, / ni es justo que una diosa tan gallarda / consienta en Helicón musa tan fea" (p. 1257).

69. Joaquín de Entrambasaguas, "Una guerra literaria del Siglo de Oro," in *Estudios sobre Lope de Vega*, vol. 2, p. 33.

70. Fritz Saxl, "Veritas Filia Temporis," in *Philosophy and History: Essays presented to Ernst Cassirer*, ed. Raymond Klibansky and J.H. Paton (Oxford: Clarendon Press, 1936) pp. 197-222.

71. *Letters of Marsilio Ficino*, vol. 2, p. 28; vol 1. pp. 60, 147. He also speaks of the "one truth, which is the single ray of the one God" (vol. 1, p. 84).

72. Cited in Arthur Henkel and Albrecht Schöne, *Emblemata* (Stuttgart: Metzler, 1976), p. 1816.

73. Erwin Panofsky, *Studies in Iconology* (1939; rpt. New York: Harper and Row, 1962), pp. 70-71. "Rather fitly the renowned ancient poets, when they related the fable that Saturn devoured his own children, under the surface of this rough covering, wished to indicate that everything produced in time, represented by Saturn, was doubtless consumed by it" (Giovanni Boccaccio, *The Fates of Illustrious Men*, trans. Louis Brewer Hall [New York: Frederick Ungar, 1965], p. 6). "Ce qui recoit estre et est produict par le temps, par le mesme est devoré et consommé." (Dinet, *Cinq Livres des Hieroglyphiques*, p. 672).

74. *Letters of Marsilio Ficino*, vol. 1, p. 81.

75. Experiences of light accompanied by a sense of inner peace and an expansion of knowledge have been recorded in individuals and cultures of all epochs. Studying this Mystic Light, Mircea Eliade states: "It reveals the paradox of a mode of existence both in Time and out of Time, a sort of *coincidentia oppositorum*" (*The Two and the One*, trans. J.M. Cohen [Chicago: Univ. of Chicago Press, 1979], p. 72). Time and eternity can be reconciled through this personal experience of the paradise within. It is difficult to say whether Ficino or Lope had such experiences. The writings by both suggest that they were not just imitating previous works or expounding Platonic concepts. Both philosopher and poet express belief in the divine light. It seems probable that Lope, although having faith in the possibility of enlightenment, simply borrowed the terminology from Ficino. The question of Lope's Platonism has not been studied in depth. I would disagree with the view expressed by Dámaso Alonso that Lope utilized Platonic concepts as a reaction to Góngora's *Culteranismo*. See "Un cuarto Lope: Poeta filosófico," in Alonso's *Poesía española* (Madrid: Gredos, 1971), pp. 455-66. As for Lope's mysticism, E. Allison Peers considers him the most unmystical of the religious poets of the golden age in "Mysticism in the Religious Verse of the Golden Age," *BHS* 21 (1944), 217-33.

76. Lope de Vega, *Los pastores de Belén* (Madrid: José Matesanz, 1978). All page references in the text are to this edition.

77. On Lope's concept of the writer or artist as interpreter of history see my study "Pintura y poesía: La presencia de Apeles en el teatro de Lope de Vega," in *Lope de Vega y los orígenes del teatro español*, ed. Manuel Criado de Val (Madrid: Edi-6, 1981). "Los hechos históricos y los personajes que intervienen quedan retratados en los anales de la fama a través de los artistas" (p. 731).

78. Lope de Vega, *El peregrino en su patria*, ed. Avalle-Arce, p. 454.

79. Alan S. Trueblood, *Experience and Artistic Expression in Lope de Vega* (Cambridge: Harvard Univ. Press, 1974), p. 529.

80. Leo Spitzer, *Die Literarisierung des Lebens in Lopes "Dorotea"* (New York: Johnson Reprint Corporation, 1968); Carlos Vossler, *Algunos caracteres de la cultura española*, 3d ed. (Buenos Aires: Espasa-Calpe, 1946), pp. 30-48; William L. Fichter and F. Sánchez Escribano, "The Origin and Character of Lope de Vega's *A mis soledades voy . . .*," *HR* 11 (1943), 304-13; and Alan S. Trueblood, "Lope's 'A mis soledades voy' Reconsidered," in *Homenaje a William Fichter*, pp. 713-24.

81. Vossler speaks of "este diálogo en que se enlaza la persona física, con el yo moral, y la voz del hombre solitario con el mundo, con el tiempo, con la muerte, con la moda, y los íntimos deseos del propio poeta" (*Algunos caracteres*, p. 45).

82. All page references to *La Dorotea* are from Edwin S. Morby's edition (Berkeley: Univ. of California Press, 1968).

83. Carlos Vossler, *Introducción a la literatura española del Siglo de Oro*, 3d ed. (Mexico: Espasa-Calpe, 1961), p. 106.

84. Lope de Vega, *Poesía lírica*, ed. Luis Guarner (Barcelona: Bruguera, 1970), pp. 382-83.

85. Lope's bitterness is emphasized by Juan Manuel Rozas, *Lope de Vega y Felipe IV en el "ciclo de senectute"* (Caceres: Universidad de Extremadura, 1982).

86. Daniel L. Heiple, *Mechanical Imagery in Spanish Golden Age Poetry* (Madrid: José Porrúa Turanzas, 1983), pp. 51-66.

87. Sebastián de Covarrubias, *Emblemas morales*, ed. Carmen Bravo Villasante (Madrid: Fundación Universitaria Española, 1978), fol. 215.

88. Francisco de Villava, *Empresas espirituales y morales* (Baeza: Fernando Díaz de Montoya, 1613), fol. 19.

89. Heiple, *Mechanical Imagery*, p. 56.

90. All textual references are to Baltasar de Vitoria, *Teatro de los dioses de la gentilidad* (Madrid: Impresa Real, 1676).

91. Francisco López de Zárate, *Obras varias*, ed. José Simón Díaz (Madrid: CSIC, 1947), vol. 2, p. 9.

92. López de Zárate, *Obras varias*, vol. 2, pp. 12-15.

93. *Cancionero antequerano*, ed. Dámaso Alonso and Rafael Ferreres (Madrid: CSIC, 1950), pp. 74-75.

94. Ibid., p. 36.

95. Panofsky, *Iconology*, p. 82.

96. Francisco de Quevedo, *Poesía original completa*, ed. Jose Manuel Blecua (Barcelona: Planeta, 1981), pp. 48-49. For a reference to Virgil's *Fourth Eclogue* in Quevedo's prose see *Los sueños*, ed. Julio Cejador y Frauca (Madrid: Espasa-Calpe, 1967), vol. 1, p. 42.

97. Bartolomé Leonardo de Argensola, *Rimas*, ed. José Manuel Blecua (Madrid: Espasa-Calpe, 1974), vol. 2, pp. 145-48.

98. In the poem that follows, the *respuesta* of Argensola to the speaker Alonso de Ezquerra, there is a reference to Astraea as truth exiled: "Antes a la verdad santa enviaron / desterrada" (p. 148).

99. Luis de Góngora, *Sonetos completos*, ed. Birute Ciplijauskaité (Madrid: Castalia, 1969), p. 81.

100. Cited in Antonio Vilanova, "El peregrino de amor en las *Soledades* de Góngora," in *Estudios dedicados a Menéndez Pidal* (Madrid: CSIC, 1952), vol. 3, p. 428.

101. Baltasar Gracián, *El criticón*, ed. M. Romera-Navarro (Philadelphia: Univ. of Pennsylvania Press, 1939-40), vol. 2, p. 200. When speaking about truth in part 3, *crisi* 3, Gracián recalls the myth of Astraea: "Sin duda que allá en aquellos dorados siglos devía parir esta Verdad cada día" (vol. 3, p. 104). On Gracián and the golden age see Welles, "Myth of Golden Age."

102. Theodore L. Kassier, *The Truth Disguised: Allegorical Structure and Technique in Gracián's "El Criticón"* (London: Tamesis, 1976). p. 30. The *isla* can be compared to the "islands of the blessed" described as a golden age since Hesiod's times.

103. Juergen Hahn, *The Origins of the Baroque Concept of Peregrinatio* (Chapel Hill: Univ. of North Carolina Press, 1973), pp. 114-15, 170-71, 172. On nature and language as a source of wonder in Góngora's *Soledades*, see M.J. Woods, *The Poet and the Natural World in the Age of Góngora* (Oxford: Oxford Univ. Press, 1978). For a more general study of wonder see Joseph Anthony Mazzeo, *Renaissance and Seventeenth Century Studies* (New York: Columbia Univ. Press, 1964), especially chapter two.

104. John R. Beverly, *Aspects of Góngora's "Soledades,"* Purdue University Monographs in Romance Languages, vol. 1 (Amsterdam: John Benjamins, 1980), pp. 91, 100.

105. R.O. Jones, "The Poetic Unity of the *Soledades* of Góngora," *BHS* 31 (1954), 189-204.

106. Luis de Góngora y Argote, *Obras completas*, ed. Juan Millé y Giménez and Isabel Millé y Giménez, 5th ed. (Madrid: Aguilar, 1961), p. 700.

107. For a survey of the river speech in Spanish golden age literature see my study "Caves of Fame and Wisdom," cited earlier in this chapter.

108. Dámaso Alonso, *Góngora y el "Polifemo,"* 6th ed. (Madrid: Gredos, 1974), vol. 2, p. 183. The reference is to the 1622 sonnet entitled "De las muertes de don Rodrigo Calderón, del Conde de Villamediana y Conde de Lemos."

109. See, for example, the reference to the *edad de oro* in *Sonetos líricos,* no. 20, pp. 80-81; and the references to Astraea in no. 25, pp. 83-84. All references to Villamediana preceded by *Ob.* are from *Obras de don Juan de Tarsis Conde de Villamediana, y Correo Mayor de su Magestad* (Madrid: María de Quiñones, a costa de Pedro Coello, 1635).

110. Juan Manuel Rozas, ed., Villamediana, *Obras* (Madrid: Castalia, 1969), p. 133. All references to Villamediana, when preceded by *Ro.,* are from this edition.

111. For an instance of Shepherd-King see Marcel Bataillon, "Carlos Quinto Buen Pastor, según Fray Cipriano de Huerga," in Bataillon's *Lección de clásicos españoles* (Madrid: Gredos, 1964), pp. 133-43.

112. Luis Rosales, *El sentimiento del desengaño en la poesía barroca* (Madrid: Cultura Hispánica, 1966), pp. 74, 78.

113. Yates, *Astraea,* p. 210.

114. The Archangel Michael is usually portrayed holding the scales while he judges the souls of the departed. Here, Astraea is in the company of angels, although Michael is not specifically mentioned. See George Ferguson, *Signs and Symbols of Christian Art* (Oxford: Oxford Univ. Press, 1961), p. 180.

CHAPTER THREE

1. Cited in Américo Castro and Hugo Rennert, *Vida de Lope de Vega* (New York: Las Americas, 1968), p. 266.

2. For a discussion of the play see my study "Villamediana's *La gloria de Niquea:* An Alchemical Masque," *JHP* 8 (1984), 209-31; and Surtz, *Birth of Theater,* pp. 123-24. For the source of Villamediana's play see Daniel Eisenberg, *Romances of Chivalry in the Spanish Golden Age* (Newark, Del.: Juan de la Cuesta, 1982), p. 82. For the staging of the play see N.D. Shergold, *A History of the Spanish Stage from Medieval Times until the End of the Seventeenth Century* (Oxford: Clarendon Press, 1967), pp. 264-74.

3. Alonso, *Góngora y el "Polifemo,"* vol. 2, p. 218. Some critics have questioned Villamediana's authorship of this introductory section, ascribing it to Góngora. See Alfonso Reyes, "Góngora y *La gloria de Niquea,"* *RFE* 2 (1915), 274-82.

4. On the different theories concerning Villamediana's relationship with Francisca de Tavora and her liaison with the monarch Philip IV, see Luis Rosales, *Pasión y muerte del Conde de Villamediana* (Madrid: Gredos, 1969).

5. Menéndez Pelayo, ed., *Obras de Lope de Vega,* vol. 4, p. 532. The equation rey-sol was a common one in the drama of the Spanish golden age. On this subject see Angel Valbuena Briones, "Simbolismo: La palabra sol en los textos calderonianos," in his *Perspectiva crítica de los dramas de Calderón* (Madrid: Rialp, 1965), pp. 54-69. The comparison is found with particular frequency in praises of Philip IV since his number was that of the sun's sphere in Ptolemaic terms. Philip soon became known as the *Rey Planeta.* For another instance of Lope de Vega's utilization of this comparison and for its importance in political propaganda see Jonathan Brown and J.H. Elliott, *A Palace for a King* (New Haven: Yale Univ. Press, 1980). Speaking of the Retiro Palace, the authors explain: "The literary celebrations began in style with Lope de Vega's verses in honor of the first *fiesta* held at the new palace, in December 1633. Lope devoted most of his efforts to describ-

ing the appearance of the "royal planet" and the count-duke in equestrian games, where, like the sun and the day, they ran side by side" (p. 229).

6. For a discussion of the importance of the four elements in Villamediana's poetry, see my study "The Four Elements: Key to an Interpretation of Villamediana's Poetry," *HisJ* 4 (1983), 61-79.

7. All page references to *La niñez de San Isidro* and to *La juventud de San Isidro* are from Menéndez Pelayo, ed., *Obras de Lope de Vega*, vol. 4.

8. On the Escorial as the temple of Solomon see Rene Taylor, "Arquitectura y magia: Consideraciones sobre la 'idea' de El Escorial," *Traza y Baza* 6 (1976), 5-62.

9. "No cabe buscar en la obra de Lope un espíritu pacifista. . . . Además sueña con su pueblo el sueño imperial y poco le preocupan las señales de la catástrofe inminente" (Simon A. Vosters, *Lope de Vega y la tradición occidental, parte I* [Madrid: Castalia, 1977], p. 508). The praise of France on the palace's festival stage was common. Another example is found in a 1624 spectacle play by Salas Barbadillo. See Charles V. Aubrun, "Une Comédie de Palais à Madrid, *Vitoria de España y Francia* de Alonso Salas Barbadillo," in *Europaische Hofkultur im 16 und 17 Jahrhundert* (Hamburg: Dr. Ernst Hauswedell & Co., 1979), pp. 287-94. The relationship rey-sol is emphasized in this production.

10. Erich Neumann, *The Great Mother: An Analysis of the Archetype*, trans. Ralph Manheim (Princeton: Princeton Univ. Press, 1972), p. 317.

11. On the significance of the four stones during the Spanish golden age see my study "The Four Elemental Jewels in Calderón's *A secreto agravio secreta venganza*," *BHS* (forthcoming).

12. Recently Angel Valbuena Briones has suggested that *Origen, pérdida y restauración de la Virgen del Sagrario* may be Calderón's earliest play. See his study "La Primera comedia de Calderón," in *Actas del Sexto Congreso Internacional de Hispanistas* (Toronto: Paul Malak and Son, 1980), pp. 753-55.

13. Robert ter Horst, "A New Literary History of Don Pedro Calderón," in *Approaches to the Theater of Calderón*, ed. Michael D. McGaha (Washington: Univ. Press of America, 1982), p. 39

14. James Parr, "An Essay on Critical Method Applied to the Comedia," *Hispania* 57 (1974), 434-44, warns against biographical determinism. Yet there seems to be an obvious connection between Calderón's personal struggle and the conflicts depicted in his *comedias*. Durán characterizes the conflict as follows: "In his action as a disobedient son, he had erred and sinned gravely against his parents and against God. An entire lifetime is not enough to atone for such a sin" (Manuel Durán, "Towards a Psychological Profile of Pedro Calderón de la Barca," in *Approaches to the Theater of Calderón*, p. 21).

15. Alexander A. Parker, "The Father-Son Conflict in the Drama of Calderón," *FMLS* 2 (1966), 99-113.

16. Robert ter Horst *Calderón: The Secular Plays* (Lexington: University Press of Kentucky, 1983), p. 58.

17. Ruth Lee Kennedy, *Studies in Tirso, I: The Dramatist and His Competitors, 1620-1626.* (Chapel Hill: Univ. of North Carolina Press, 1974), p. 72.

18. Durán, "Towards a Psychological Profile," p. 22.

19. Brown and Elliott, *Palace for a King*, pp. 178-92; Simon A. Vosters, *La rendición de Breda en la literatura y el arte de España* (London: Tamesis, 1974); and Everett W. Hesse, "Calderón and Velázquez," *Hispania* 35 (1952), 74-82.

20. Shirley B. Whitaker, "The First Performance of Calderón's *El sitio de Bredá*," *RenQ* 31 (1978), 515-31.

21. Brown and Elliott, *Palace for a King*, p. 182.

22. "On the one hand are Olivares, his family, and dependents; on the other are Philip IV, his family, and retainers. . . . One is immediately struck by the self-assertion implicit in Olivares' allowing his own inner circle to be given a prominence equal to that accorded the king's." (Whitaker, "First Performance," p. 521).

23. Antonio Hurtado de Mendoza, *Obras poéticas*, ed. Rafael Benítez Claros (Madrid: Gráficas Ultra, 1947), vol. 2, p. 14.

24. *El sitio de Bredá: Comedia de Don Pedro Calderón de la Barca* ed. Johanna R. Schrek (The Hague: Publications of the Institute of Hispanic Studies, University of Utrecht, 1957), vv. 35-36. In the *loa* to *Los tres mayores prodigios*, the king is again called "Quarto Planeta de España."

25. Brown and Elliott, *Palace for a King*, p. 230.

26. Durán, "Towards a Psychological Profile," p. 23.

27. N.D. Shergold and J.E. Varey, "Some Early Calderón Dates," *BHS* 38 (1961), p. 278.

28. Richard W. Tyler and Sergio D. Elizondo, *The Characters, Plots and Settings of Calderón's Comedias* (Lincoln, Nebr.: SSSAS, 1981), p. 80.

29. Hildegard Hollmann, "El retrato del tirano Aurelio en *La gran Cenobia*," in *Hacia Calderón: Cuarto Coloquio Anglogermano*, ed. Hans Flasche, Karl-Hermann Körner, and Hans Mattauch (Berlin: Walter de Gruyter, 1979), p. 47.

30. Ludwing Pfandl, *Historia de la literatura nacional española de la Edad de Oro*, trans. Jorge Rubio Balaguer (Barcelona: Sucesores de Juan Gili, 1933), p. 437. "En *La gran Cenobia*, que indudablemente es una de sus obras más absurdas . . ." (Marcelino Menéndez Pelayo, *Calderón y su teatro* [Madrid: A. Perez Dubrull, 1910], p. 360). Not all early accounts were negative. A.F. von Schack calls it one of "las mejores composiciones de Calderón" in *Historia de la literatura y de arte dramática en España*, trans. Eduardo de Mier (Madrid: M. Tello, 1887), vol. 4, p. 385.

31. Angel Valbuena Briones, "El tema de la fortuna en *La gran Cenobia*," in his *Calderón y la comedia nueva* (Madrid: Espasa-Calpe, 1977), pp. 136-46; Jesús Gutiérrez, *La "Fortuna Bifrons" en el teatro del Siglo de Oro* (Santander: Sociedad Menéndez Pelayo, 1975), pp. 283-87; and Juan Manuel Gómez, "A Critical Edition of Pedro Calderón de la Barca's *La Gran Cenobia* with Introduction and Notes" (Ph.D. diss., Univ. of Oregon, 1981).

32. Gutiérrez, *La "Fortuna Bifrons,"* p. 285.

33. Raymond R. MacCurdy, *The Tragic Fall: Don Alvaro de Luna and other Favorites in Spanish Golden Age Drama* (Chapel Hill: Univ. of North Carolina Press, 1978).

34. Gutiérrez, *La "Fortuna Bifrons,"* pp. 283-87.

35. Bouché-Leclerq, *L'Astrologie grecque*, p. 140; *Erathosthenis Catasterismorum Reliquiae*, pp. 84-85. Fortuna seems to have incorporated many of the attributes of other deities during Roman times. See Howard Rollin Patch, "The Tradition of the Goddess Fortuna in Roman Literature and in the Transitional Period," *Smith College Studies in Modern Languages* 3 (1922), 131-235.

36. Yates, *Astraea*, p. 32, n. 5; Valeriano Bolzani, *Les Hieroglyphiques*, p. 795.

37. "y por esta causa creyeron ser dos fortunas, prospera y aduersa: a la prospera la llaman Fortuna buena y a la aduersa Fortuna mala. Y para adorarlas a ambas juntamente, hazían vna estatua con dos caras, la vna blanca, que denotaua la buena, y la otra negra, que denotaua la mala" (Juan Pérez de Moya, *Philosophía secreta* [Madrid: Los Clásicos Olvidados, 1928], pp. 88-91). All page references in the text are to this edition. For a survey of Fortuna in Spain see Otis H. Green, *Spain and the Western Tradition*, vol. 2 (Madison: Univ. of Wisconsin Press, 1968), pp. 283-316.

38. Valbuena Briones, "El tema de la fortuna," p. 138.

39. "Harmonia est discordia concors" (Edgar Wind, *Pagan Mysteries in the Renaissance*, 2nd ed. [New York: W.W. Norton, 1968], p. 86) See also Robert Grudin, *Mighty Opposites: Shakespeare and Renaissance Contrariety* (Berkeley: Univ. of California Press, 1979).

40. All page references to the *Declamación segunda* are to *Obras completas de Bocángel*, ed. Rafael Benítez Claros (Madrid: CSIC, 1946).

41. Astraea as chastity is included in Juvenal's sixth satire, *Against Women*. Bocángel begins the second *declamación* with a quote from Juvenal's tenth satire, *On the vanity of human wishes*. Here the Roman poet states categorically that "If men had any sense, Fortune would not be a goddess. We are the ones who make her so, and give her a place in the heavens" (*The Satire of Juvenal*, trans. and ed. Rolphe Humphries [Bloomington: Indiana Univ. Press, 1958], p. 134).

42. All page references to *La gran Cenobia* are from *Primera parte de comedias de don Pedro Calderón de la Barca*, ed. A. Valbuena Briones (Madrid:CSIC, 1974). On the theory of humors see Donald Bleznick, "La teoría clásica de los humores en los tratados políticos del Siglo de Oro," *Hispano* 2 (1959), 1-9.

43. William C. McCrary, *The Goldfinch and the Hawk: A Study of Lope de Vega's Tragedy, "El caballero de Olmedo,"* 2d ed. (Chapel Hill: Univ. of North Carolina Press, 1968), pp. 117-18. Hildegard Hollman, in "El retrato del tirano Aureliano en *La gran Cenobia*," uses Huarte de San Juan's *Examen de ingenio* to describe Aureliano's condition, but only brings out his imaginative nature (p. 47). Aureliano, like Melibea in the *Celestina* and like Don Quijote, has a choleric disposition. The excessive heat produced by an abundance of this humor leads to melancholy adustion as described by McCrary (p. 115). For a humoral analysis of Melibea see my study "*La Celestina*: An Example of Love Melancholy," *RR* 66 (1975), 288-95. On Don Quijote see Otis H. Green, "El Ingenioso Hidalgo," in Green, *The Literary Mind of Medieval and Renaissance Spain* (Lexington: University Press of Kentucky, 1970), pp. 171-84. See also Daniel L. Heiple, "Renaissance Medical Psychology in *Don Quijote*," *I and L* 2 (1979), 65-72. Other passages in *La gran Cenobia* can also be discussed according to Renaissance medical theories. Aureliano's sleep in the third act, immediately preceding his death, recalls Don Quijote's prolonged sleep before recovering lucidity and dying at the end of the work. As I was completing this study, Teresa Soufas published her important article "Calderón's Melancholy Wife-Murderers," *HR* 52 (1984), 181-203.

44. Francisco Rico, *El pequeño mundo del hombre* (Madrid: Castalia, 1970), p. 249.

45. Richard Hinckley Allen equates Virgo with the "the Singing Sibyl carrying a branch into Hades" (*Star Names*, p. 462).

46. A. Valbuena Briones, "Simbolismo: La caída del caballo," in *Perspectiva crítica de los dramas de Calderón*, pp. 35-53; and Pedro R. León, "El caballo desbocado, símbolo de la pasión desordenada en la obra de Calderón," *RF* 95 (1983), 23-35.

47. On the link between *fortuna* and *mujer* in Spanish poetry see my study "The Four Elements."

48. Juan Boccaccio, *De las ilustres mujeres (Zaragoza, 1494)* (Madrid: Real Academia Española, 1951), fol. CI.

49. Juan de Pineda, *Diálogos familiares de la agricultura cristiana*, ed. P. Juan Meseguer Fernández, vol. 4, in *B.A.E.*, vol. 169 (Madrid, 1964), p. 410.

50. Melveena McKendrick, *Woman and Society in the Spanish Drama of the Golden Age* (Cambridge: Cambridge Univ. Press, 1974), pp. 200-201; Dian Fox, "*El médico de su honra*: Political Considerations," *Hispania* 65 (1982), 36.

51. Daniel L. Heiple, "The Tradition Behind the Punishment of the Rebel Soldier in *La vida es sueño*," *BHS* 50 (1933), 16.

52. On the almond tree see: E. George Erdman, Jr., "Arboreal Figures in the Golden

Age Sonnet," *PMLA* 84 (1969), 587-95; and my studies, "The Flowering Almond Tree: Examples of Tragic Foreshadowing in Golden Age Drama," *REH* 14 (1980), 117-34; and "Los 'naturales secretos' del almendro en el teatro de Calderón," in *Actas del octavo congreso internacional de hispanistas* (forthcoming).

53. Castro, *El pensamiento de Cervantes*, pp. 215-19.

54. Ernst Curtius, *European Literature and the Latin Middle Ages*, trans. Willard R. Trask (New York: Harper and Row, 1973), pp. 170-77.

55. On this subject see C.E. Anibal, "*Voces del cielo*—A note on Mira de Amescua" *RR* 16 (1925), 57-70.

56. See my "Flowering Almond Tree," particularly pp. 124-25.

57. Heiple, ("Punishment of the Rebel Soldier") notes that "the defense of this concept as a principle of justice, as well as the probable source of the Renaissance proverbs, is found in Plutarch's *Life of Romulus*, where he defends the Sabines' punishment of the Roman girl Tarpeia who had betrayed her city to them" (p. 3).

58. Guy Marchant, *The Kalendar and Compost of the Shepherds*, ed. G.C. Heseltine (London: Peter Davies, 1930), p. 143. Robert Fludd also characterizes Mars as hot and dry. These qualities make the planet malicious (Johnstone Parr, *Tamburlaine's Malady and Other Essays on Astrology in Elizabethan Drama* [University, Ala.: Univ. of Alabama Press, 1953], p. 22).

59. "The many Renaissance idylls in which the victorious Venus, having subdued the fearful Mars by love, is seen playing with his armour . . . all celebrate this peaceable hope: that Love is more powerful than Strife; that the god of war is inferior in strength to the goddess of grace and amiability" (Wind, *Pagan Mysteries*, p. 89).

60. Juan Manuel Gómez presents a negative portrayal of Decio. He claims that Decio is guided by his own selfishness and by his love for Cenobia rather than by his concern for Rome ("Critical Edition," pp. 32-35), Yet, we have seen how Decio's motives are not just personal; he thinks of both his personal honor and the welfare of the empire.

61. "Decio al apuñalar a Aureliano no rompe la ley de la lealtad, sino que defiende la autoridad legítima del pueblo ante un gobernante que ha mostrado su poder tiránico y que no atendió a las amonestaciones que se le hicieron" (Valbuena Briones, "El tema de la fortuna," p. 144). Citing Thomas Aquinas and Juan de Mariana, Hollmann shows that Calderón approved of Decio's tyrannicide. He argues that Calderón contrasts the perfect monarch (Decio and Cenobia) with the tyrannical rule of Aureliano, sanctioning his assassination and following accepted authorities on this matter ("El retrato del tirano Aureliano," pp. 53-55). Our study of the play corroborates these viewpoints. There are some critics, however, that do not accept the fact that Calderón sanctioned tyrannicide in this play. See the studies of Dian Fox and Juan Manuel Gómez cited in this chapter.

62. "Bossuet called 'our own ignorance' our inability—as finite beings—to know the mind and the designs of the Infinite" (Green, *Spain and the Western Tradition*, vol. 2, p. 280).

63. Calderón de la Barca, *Obras completas*, ed. Angel Valbuena Prat, 2d ed. (Madrid: Aguilar, 1967), vol. 3, p. 616.

64. Robert L. Fiore, *Drama and Ethos: Natural Law Ethics in Spanish Golden Age Theater* (Lexington: Univ. Press of Kentucky, 1975), p. 63. *No hay más fortuna que Dios*, like *La gran Cenobia*, centers around man's misjudgment of the highest good. Fiore explains: "The error they commit is 'de hacer diosa a la Fortuna, / y no a la Justicia.' Ignorance is the root of this mistake" (p. 75).

CHAPTER FOUR

1. On Astraea in *La vida es sueño*, see Everett W. Hesse, *New Perspectives on Comedia Criticism* (Potomac, Md.: José Porrúa Turanzas, 1980), pp. 108-9 and 141-43; see also my early sketch on this matter: "The Return of Astraea: An Astral-Imperial Myth in Calderón's *La vida es sueño*," in *Calderón de la Barca at the Tercentenary: Comparative Views*, ed. Wendell M. Aycock and Sydney P. Cravens (Lubbock, Tex.: Texas Tech Press, 1982), pp. 135-59.

2. McKendrick, *Woman and Society*, p. 133.

3. Menéndez Pelayo, *Calderón y su teatro*, p. 278.

4. A.E. Sloman, "The Structure of Calderón's *La vida es sueño*," in *Critical Essays on the Theater of Calderón*, ed. Bruce W. Wardropper (New York: New York Univ. Press, 1965), p. 90; E.M. Wilson, "On *La vida es sueño*," and William M. Whitby, "Rosaura's Role in the Structure of *La vida es sueño*," both in *Critical Essays on the Theater of Calderón*; Michele Federico Sciacca, "Verdad y sueño de *La vida es sueño* de Calderón de la Barca," *Clavileño* 1 (1950), 1-9; Harlan G. Sturm, "From Plato's Cave to Segismundo's Prison," *MLN* 89 (1974), 280-89; and Jackson I. Cope, "The Platonic Metamorphoses of Calderón's *La vida es sueño*," *MLN* 86 (1971), 225-41. Cope's article echoes Sloman's conclusion from a Platonic perspective. In the love subplot, Segismundo transcends desire, while in the political action he overcomes the temptation of tyranny.

5. A. Valbuena Prat, *Calderón* (Barcelona: Juventud, 1941); Sloman, "Structure of *La vida es sueño*," p. 100; Vittorio Bodini, *Segni e simboli nella "Vida es sueño"* (Bari: Adriatica, 1968).

6. Eleanor Jean Martin, "Calderón's *La gran Cenobia*: Source Play for *La vida es sueño*," *BCom* 26 (1974), 22-30.

7. Northrop Frye, *Anatomy of Criticism* (Princeton: Princeton Univ. Press, 1971), pp. 137-38.

8. Alexander A. Parker, "Segismundo's Tower: A Calderonian Myth," *BHS* 59 (1982), 248-49.

9. Albert E. Sloman, *The Dramatic Craftsmanship of Calderón* (Oxford: Clarendon Press, 1958), p. 22; and J.A. Van Praag, "Otra vez la fuente de *La vida es sueño*," in *Studia Philologica: Homenaje ofrecido a Dámaso Alonso* (Madrid: Gredos, 1963), vol. 3, pp. 551-62.

10. Everett W. Hesse, "Calderón's Concept of the Perfect Prince in *La vida es sueño*," in *Critical Essays on the Theater of Calderón*, p. 114-33.

11. René Girard, *Violence and the Sacred*, trans. Patrick Gregory (Baltimore: Johns Hopkins Univ. Press, 1977), pp. 56-58.

12. As will be discussed in the next chapter, the viper motif shows that Segismundo may have been illegitimate. To make Segismundo and Rosaura actually brother and sister, one would have to assume that the Clotaldo who left Violante on fathering Rosaura is the same man that committed adultery with Clorilene, Basilio's wife. There is nothing in the play that supports this conclusion. Yet the possibility of the relationship is not ruled out by the prehistory of the *comedia*. On Segismundo and Rosaura as "twins" see Edwin Honig, *Calderón and the Seizures of Honor* (Cambridge: Harvard Univ. Press, 1972), p. 161.

13. Girard, *Violence and the Sacred*, p. 45.

14. All page references to *La puente de Mantible* are from Calderón, *Obras completas*, ed. Valbuena Briones, vol. 2.

15. Clark Colahan and Alfred Rodríguez, "Hércules y Segismundo: Tema y caracter senequistas de *La vida es sueño*," *JHP* 5 (1981), 217.

16. All references to Calderón's masterpiece are from Calderón de la Barca, *La vida es sueño (comedia, auto y loa)*, ed. Enrique Rull (Madrid: Alhambra, 1980).

17. Angel Valbuena Briones, "Simbolismo: La caída del caballo"; Cesáreo Bandera, "El itinerario de Segismundo en *La vida es sueño*," *HR* 35 (1967), 69-84; Margaret S. Maurin, "The Monster, the Sepulcher and the Dark: Related Patterns of Imagery in *La vida es sueño*," *HR* 35 (1967), 161-78.

18. Angel L. Cilveti, *El significado de "La vida es sueño*," (Valencia: Albatros, 1971), pp. 163-72.

19. E.M. Wilson, "The Four Elements in the Imagery of Calderón," *MLR* 31 (1936), 34-47.

20. Rosaura's "fall" into Poland as the sign Astraea-Virgo recalls a similar performance by Leda in Vélez de Guevara's *Virtudes vencen señales*. See Charles Frederick Kirk, "A Critical Edition, with Introduction and Notes, of Vélez de Guevara's *Virtudes vencen señales*" (Ph.D. diss., Ohio State Univ., 1957), p. 33; and Rudolph Schevill, "*Virtudes vencen señales* and *La vida es sueño*," *HR* 1 (1933), 181-95.

21. Cesáreo Bandera, *Mimesis conflictiva* (Madrid: Gredos, 1975), p. 189.

22. Hesse, *New Perspectives*, p. 141.

23. Wind, *Pagan Mysteries*, p. 25.

24. T.E. May, "Brutes and Stars in *La vida es sueño*," in *Hispanic Studies in Honor of Joseph Mason*, ed. Dorothy Atkinson and Anthony Clarke (Oxford: Dolphin, 1972), pp. 167-84.

25. Eliade, *Eternal Return*, pp. 112-15; and Campbell, *Mythic Image*, pp. 141-44.

26. Gabriel Rosado, "Observaciones sobre las fuentes de dos comedias de Lope de Vega: *El esclavo de Roma* y *Lo que ha de ser*," *BCom* 24 (1972), 25-30.

27. Jack Weiner, "Un episodio de la historia rusa visto por autores españoles del Siglo de Oro: El pretendiente Demetrio," *JHP* 2 (1978), 175-201.

28. Robert D.F. Pring-Mill, "La victoria del hado en *La vida es sueño*," in *Hacia Calderón*, ed. Hans Flasche (Berlin: Walter de Gruyter, 1970), pp. 53-70.

29. Plato, *The Republic*, trans. B. Jowett (New York: Random House, 1973), p. 125. See also Francis MacDonald Cornford's translation, cited in chapter one.

30. According to Basilio (vv. 3248-50), Segismundo has been reborn. On this subject see John C. Weiger, "Rebirth in *La vida es sueño*" *RomN* 10 (1968), 119-21.

31. Manilius, *Astronomica*, p. 265.

CHAPTER FIVE

1. Laurens Van der Post, *Jung and the Story of Our Time* (New York: Vintage, 1977), pp. 13-14.

2. By mystery is meant the Renaissance interpretation of the word in its figurative sense as expressed by Plotinus and his followers. The priest Egido da Viterbo summarized its meaning as related to the notion of unveiling hidden truths (Wind, *Pagan Mysteries*, p. 25). We have also noted that Rosaura in *La vida es sueño* refers to her golden sword as a weapon that "encierra *misterios* grandes" (v. 374).

3. Everett W. Hesse, "El motivo del sueño en *La vida es sueño*," *Segismundo* 5-6 (1967), 58. See also his article "Psychic Phenomena in *La vida es sueño*," in *Estudios literarios de hispanistas norteamericanos dedicados a Helmut Hatzfeld con motivo de su 80 aniversario*, ed. Josep M. Sola-Solé, Alessandro Crisafulli, and Bruno Damiani (Barcelona: Hispam, 1974), pp. 275-86.

4. Julian Palley, "'Si fue mi maestro un sueño': Segismundo's Dream," *KRQ* 23 (1976),

151. Another Freudian interpretation is provided by Gisele Feal and Carlos Feal-Deibe, "*La vida es sueño:* De la psicología al mito," *Reflexión* 2, no. 1 (1972), 35-55.

5. On the fulfillment of Basilio's predictions, see Peter N. Dunn, "The Horoscope Motif in *La vida es sueño,*" *Atlante* 1 (1953), 187-201.

6. "Todavía más: el lenguaje común, a imitación del latín de las escuelas y universidades, llegaba a involucrar en la palabra 'Matemático', lo mismo al que se dedicaba a las matemáticas, que al que cultivaba la astronomía y la astrología" (Millé y Giménez, "El horóscopo de Lope de Vega," p. 73).

7. John V. Bryans, *Calderón de la Barca: Imagery, Rhetoric and Drama* (London: Tamesis, 1977). Bryans speaks of the similarity between Segismundo's birth and that of the viper, as expressed in the conceit. He also notes the disparity between human beings and vipers which is also present (p. 104). David Jonathan Hildner, in *Reason and the Passions in the* Comedias *of Calderón,* Purdue University Monographs in Romance Languages, vol. 11 (Amsterdam: John Benjamins, 1982), sees the serpent that begets children that devour it as a universal metaphor in dialectical thinking (p. 4).

8. T.H. White, *The Bestiary: A Book of Beasts* (New York: G.P. Putnam's Sons, 1970), p. 170.

9. Covarrubias, *Tesoro de la lengua,* p. 218. "Julio César Escaligero añade contra el común decir de todos y escribir de sabios, que la víbora no muere cuando pare, ni le roen las entrañas los hijuelos, y que el experimento con una víbora que tuvo enjaulada, y le parió en la jaula, y quedó buena y sana con sus hijuelos" (Pineda, *Diálogos familiares,* vol. 4, p. 13). Similarly, Hernando de Soto in the *Emblemas moralizadas* notes: "De la propiedad de la vívora tratan largamente los naturales, aunque dize Apolonio, que se ha visto lamer y pulir la vívora sus hijuelos, en acabándolos de parir" (ed. Carmen Bravo Villasante [Madrid: Fundación Universitaria Española, 1983], p. 7).

10. Villava, *Empresas espirituales y morales,* p. 49.

11. Lope de Vega, *Poesías líricas,* ed. José F. Montesinos (Madrid: Espasa-Calpe, 1968) vol. 1, pp. 37-38.

12. Don Cameron Allen, *Mysteriously Meant,* p. 112. Ficino's statement is found in his annotations on *Ennead* 5.8. The Renaissance fascination for the primary as closest to divine truth is attested by the popularity of the *Corpus Hermeticum.* On this subject see Frances Yates, *Giordano Bruno and the Hermetic Tradition* (Chicago: Univ. of Chicago Press, 1964), p. 13.

13. *The Hieroglyphics of Horapollo* ed. and trans. George Boas (New York: Phaeton, 1950), p. 98. Other ancient traditions also record the viper anecdote. In an Arab manuscript at the Escorial, we may read: "Al poner los huevos, éstos no tienen salida por lo estrecho de su agujero y se quedan en su vientre hasta que salen las crías, que agujerean el vientre y salen, muriendo la madre al instante" (*Libro de las utilidades de los animales,* ed. and trans. Carmen Ruiz Bravo-Villasante [Madrid: Fundación Universitaria Española, 1980] p. 120).

14. Covarrubias, *Tesoro de la lengua,* p. 218; Villava, *Empresas espirituales y morales,* p. 50; Beryl Rowland, *Animals with Human Faces* (Knoxville: Univ. of Tennessee Press, 1973), p. 158.

15. White, *Bestiary,* p. 170; Rowland, *Animals with Human Faces,* pp. 157, 158.

16. D.W. Robertson, *A Preface to Chaucer* (Princeton: Princeton Univ. Press, 1962), p. 155. For a brief history of the chimera and a different interpretation see Jorge Luis Borges with Margarita Guerrero, *The Book of Imaginary Beings,* rev. and trans. Norman Thomas di Giovanni (New York: E.P. Dutton, 1969), pp. 62-63.

17. Saint Augustine, *The City of God,* trans. Marcus Dods (New York: Modern Library, 1950), pp. 530-31.

236   NOTES TO PAGES 112–116

18. John J. O'Connor, *Amadis de Gaule and Its Influence on Elizabethan Literature* (New Brunswick: Rutgers Univ. Press, 1970), pp. 54, 93. An interesting story concerning the relationship of adultery with abnormal birth is found in the *Caballero del cisne*. When Ysomberta gives birth to seven children, she is afraid: "Ca en este tiempo toda muger que pariese mas de una criatura, era acusada de adulterio e matavan la por ello." To make matters worse, the mother-in-law claims that Ysomberta's offspring were *podencos* and not children (Emeterio Mazorriaga, *La leyenda del caballero del cisne* [Madrid: Victoriano Suarez, 1914], vol. 1, pp. 15-18). On the Endriago see also Juan Manuel Cacho Blecua, *Amadís heroísmo mítico cortesano* (Zaragoza: Cupsa, 1979), pp. 280-86; and John K. Walsh, "The Chivalric Dragon: Hagiographic Parallels in Early Spanish Romances," *BHS* 54 (1977), 189-98. T.E. May, on the other hand, argues that the birth of Segismundo should be considered within a tradition of heroic birth: "Equally, the manner of Segismundo's birth, as that of the *víbora humana del siglo*, could be a good omen, since before Macduff, Julius Caesar himself, like some other great benefactors of the human race, 'was from his mother's womb untimely ripp'd'" ("Brutes and Stars," p. 175). These are indeed *prodigios* similar to the one noted by Basilio. Yet, in the cases of Julius Caesar and Macduff, the image of the viper is absent and we are thus lacking the cruelty and lust they symbolize.

19. Maurin, "The Monster, the Sepulchre and the Dark," pp. 167-78. The term *monstruo* is a common one in Calderón's theater. In the *auto sacramental, La redención de cautivos*, "of all infamous names applied to *la culpa*, that of monster is the one she most resents" (Sister M. Francis de Sales McGarry, *The Allegorical and Metaphorical Language in the Autos Sacramentales of Calderón* [Washington: Catholic Univ. of America, 1937], p. 108). On other uses of the term monster in Calderón see for example: Elenora R. Sabin, "The Identities of the Monster in Calderón's *El mayor monstruo del mundo*," *Hispania* 56 (1973), 269-75; and William R. Blue, "Las imágenes en *El mayor monstruo del mundo* de Calderón de la Barca," *Hispania* 61 (1978), 888-93. For Sabin, the term *monstruo* may refer to jealousy, idolatrous love, fate (the dagger), death (the sea), and the antichrist. Blue relates the viper to "elementos venenosos e innaturales de esta naturaleza circundante" (p. 891).

20. Maurin, "The Monster, the Sepulchre and the Dark," p. 166. In a study of the Sierra Morena episode in *Don Quijote*, Javier Herrero comes closer to our interpretation of the labyrinth. He notes that "lust is the Minotaur which transforms life into a labyrinth" ("Sierra Morena as Labyrinth: From Wilderness to Christian Knighthood," *FMLS* 17 [1981], 56).

22. John Block Friedman, *The Monstrous Races in Medieval Art* (Cambridge: Harvard Univ. Press, 1981), p. 111.

22. All page references to *La devoción de la cruz* are from Calderón, *Obras completas*, ed. Valbuena Briones vol. 1.

23. Honig, *Calderón and the Seizures of Honor*, p. 64.

24. Joseph Campbell, *The Hero with a Thousand Faces*, 2nd ed. (Princeton: Princeton Univ. Press, 1972), p. 15.

25. Ibid., p. 131.

26. Ibid., p. 19.

27. Joseph Campbell, *The Masks of the Gods: Occidental Mythology* (New York: Penguin, 1976), p. 54.

28. Wardropper, "'Apenas llega cuando llega a penas,'" 240-44; Hesse, *New Perspectives*, pp. 84-102; Neumann, *Great Mother*, p. 177.

29. Weiger, "Rebirth," 119-21.

30. Monroe Z. Hafter, *Gracián and Perfection* (Cambridge: Harvard Univ. Press, 1966), p. 51.

31. Everett W. Hesse, "Calderón's Concept of the Perfect Prince in *La vida es sueño*," in *Critical Essays on the Theater of Calderón*, pp. 114-33.

32. Northrop Frye, *The Secular Scripture* (Cambridge: Harvard Univ. Press, 1976), pp. 102, 98. The demonic realm is clearly presented in a number of Calderón's *comedias*. See Susan Fischer, "Calderón's *El mayor encanto, amor* and the Mode of Romance," *Studies in Honor of Everett W. Hesse* pp. 99-112.

33. Bouché-Leclercq, *L'Astrologie Grecque*, p. 399-400.

34. Richard Hinckley Allen, *Star Names*, p. 300. The astronomer cited by Allen is Royal Hill.

35. Ibid., pp. 298-99. Allen cites Novidius in identifying Ophiuchus with St. Paul.

36. Pring-Mill, "La victoria del hado," pp. 53-70.

37. Ervin Brody, "Poland in Calderón's *Life is a Dream*," *Polish Review* 14 (1969), 47. See also Henryk Ziomek, "Historic Implications and Dramatic Influences in Calderón's *Life is a Dream*," *Polish Review* 20 (1975), 11-28; and ter Horst, *Secular Plays*, pp. 216-20.

38. Weiner, "Un episodio de la historia Rusa," pp. 175-201.

39. Brody, "Poland," p. 61.

40. Hana Jechová, "Les motifs polonais ou tchèques dans *La vie est un songe*," *CRCL* 4 (1977), 179-85.

41. R.J.W. Evans, *The Making of the Habsburg Monarch: 1550-1700* (Oxford: Clarendon Press, 1979), p. 32.

42. Jean Charon, *Cosmology*, trans. Patrick Moore (New York: McGraw Hill, 1970), p. 81.

43. Lynn Thorndike, *A History of Magic and Experimental Science*, vol. 6 (New York: Columbia Univ. Press, 1941), p. 68.

44. Angus Armitage, *John Kepler* (London: Faber and Faber, 1966), pp. 97-99. See also Parr, *Tamburlaine's Malady*, p. 71.

45. *Thomas Campanella, An Italian Friar and Second Machiavel. His Advice to the King of Spain for attaining the Universal Monarchy of the World*, trans. E. Chilmead, ed. William Prynne (London: Philemen Stephens, 1660).

46. Max Caspar, *Kepler*, ed. and trans. C. Doris Hellman (New York: Abelard Schuman, 1959), p. 155.

47. Jechová, "Les motifs polonais," p. 184.

48. R.J.W. Evans, *Rudolf II and His World* (Oxford: Clarendon Press, 1973), p. 49.

49. Ludwig Burchard, *Corpus Rubenianum, Portraits*, ed. Frances Huemer (London: Harvey Miller, 1977), pp. 101-2; P. Junquera de Vega and M. Teresa Ruíz Alcón, *Monasterio de las Descalzas Reales. Guía Turística* (Madrid: Patrimonio Nacional, 1961), p. 14.

50. *Archivio di Stato di Firenze*, Mediceo, filza 4959, 4960, *Avvisi* dated 23 July 1633 and 18 February, 1634. I would like to express my appreciation to Professor Shirley Whitaker of the University of North Carolina, Greensboro, for pointing out this information and providing me with copies of the *Avvisi*.

51. Evans, *Rudolf II*, pp. 48, 49.

52. Ibid., p. 49.

53. Miguel de Ferdinandy, *En torno al pensar mítico* (Berlin: Colloquium, 1961); and Parker, "Segismundo's Tower," pp. 247-56.

54. ter Horst, *Secular Plays*, p. 220.

55. Lynn Thorndike, *A History of Magic and Experimental Science*, vol. 7 (New York: Columbia University Press, 1958), p. 28.

56. Evans, *Rudolf II*. "Rudolph himself was highly superstitious by nature: his horoscope had been cast by Nostradamus, and he was disposed to act on all kinds of irrational suggestions. It is likely that part of his 'crisis' in 1600 was due to fears that he

would die before the age of 50. . . . Contemporaries definitely thought that he was under the influence of a prophecy" (p. 279).

57. Caspar, *Kepler,* p. 2.

CHAPTER SIX

1. Wilson, "On *La vida es sueño,*" pp. 87-88. Other critics that agree with Wilson are: Wardropper, "'Apenas llega cuando llega a penas'"; Hesse, "Calderón's Concept of the Perfect Prince"; and Thomas Austin O'Connor, "*La vida es sueño:* A View from Metatheater," *KRQ* 25 (1978), 13-26.

2. Eugenio Suárez-Galbán, "El conflicto de Clotaldo: visión psicológica," *La Torre* 65 (1969), 69-83; Angel L. Cilveti, *El significado de "La vida es sueño,"* p. 132.

3. C.A. Merrick, "Clotaldo's Role in *La vida es sueño,*" *BHS* 50 (1973), 268.

4. Frye, *Secular Scripture,* pp. 127-57. The images of descent associated with the first dream include loss of identity, chaos, darkness, labyrinths, and monsters (pp. 97-126).

5. On the principle of displacement see Frye, *Anatomy of Criticism,* pp. 136-40.

6. Bodini, *Segni e simboli,* p. 117.

7. Merrick, "Clotaldo's Role," p. 260.

8. On the prevalence of trans-elemental imagery in the golden age, see Woods, *Poet and Natural World.*

9. Calderón, *Obras completas,* ed. Valbuena Prat, vol. 3, p. 392.

10. Wilson, "Four Elements," pp. 34-47. According to Wilson, *Aguila* and *Neblí* are the most frequently mentioned birds in this connection.

11. The eagle's flight is narrated in *Hombre pobre todo es trazas.* This bird is significant in the *auto sacramental El águila divina.* It also appears in *Andromeda y Perseo, La redención de cautivos,* and *Los misterios de la misa.*

12. Covarrubias, *Tesoro de la lengua,* p. 56.

13. Rudolf Wittkower, *Allegory and the Migration of Symbols* (London: Thames and Hudson, 1977), pp. 16, 32, 43-44.

14. Maria Elisa Ciavarelli, *El tema de la fuerza de la sangre* (Madrid: José Porrúa Turanzas, 1980), pp. 248-49.

15. Cited in Evans, *Rudolf II,* p. 273.

16. Correspondences and hierarchies are often based on the notion of the Great Chain of Being. See E.M.W. Tillyard, *The Elizabethan World Picture* (London: Chatto and Windas, 1967). Using Raymond de Sebonde's *Natural Theology,* a treasury of commonplaces, Tillyard shows the relationship between the eagle and empire: "Another form of excellence, found in most accounts of the chain of being and certainly connected with it, is that with every class there was a primate. . . .Sebonde speaks of the dolphin among fishes, the eagle among birds, the lion among beasts, the emperor among men" (p. 27).

17. White, *Bestiary,* p. 107.

18. Sebastián de Covarrubias, *Emblemas morales,* ed. Carmen Bravo-Villasante (Madrid: Fundación Universitaria Española, 1970), centuria I, emblema 79.

19. Andrés Ferrer de Valdecebro, *Govierno general, moral y político* (Barcelona, 1696), p. 240.

20. Wayne Shumaker, *The Occult Sciences in the Renaissance* (Berkeley: Univ. of California Press, 1972). Discussing *parabolica similitudo* or figurative analogies, Shumaker shows how "Pico [della Mirandola] comes close to perceiving that all analogical analysis, with which Renaissance thought was permeated, is dangerous" (p. 21).

21. Herbert Friedmann, *A Bestiary for Saint Jerome* (Washington: Smithsonian Institution Press, 1980), p. 214.

22. "significa el magnámimo y generoso que haze poco caso de los denuestos dela gente vil" (Covarrubias, *Tesoro de la lengua*, p. 55); "Generosamente atrevida se opone a los rayos del sol" (Valdecebro, *Govierno general*, p. 64). "Aguila generosa" appears instead of "águila caudalosa" (v. 1038) in the text of *La vida es sueño* found in *Parte treynta de comedias famosas de varios autores* (Zaragoza: Hospital Real y General de Nuestra Señora de Gracia, 1636), p. 141. See note to verse 1038 in Enrique Rull's edition of the play, pp. 166-67.

23. He is described as such by Julian Palley: "In dreams Segismundo would break his bonds, attain the power of the eagle, king of birds, humble his adversaries, kill and rape. The phantasies to which we are given in daydream find concrete form during the Prince's brief period of freedom" ("Segismundo's Dream," p. 153).

24. "La ternura y la fiereza en un solo ser: dos contrarios en un solo sujeto. He aquí la complicación tan grande y tan interesante, que en seguida se nos ocurriría suponerla invención de Góngora. Nada de eso: en realidad, Góngora inventó poco en este punto. Esa complicación, creada por el arte en un alma humana, tiene mas de 2,200 años, por lo menos. Esa coincidencia de contrarios en Polifemo, la hallamos ya en Teócrito" (Alonso, *Góngora y el Polifemo*, vol. 1, pp. 197-98). This passage is cited apropos *La vida es sueño* by Roberto González Echevarría, "El 'monstruo de una especie y otra'; *La vida es sueño*, III, 2, 725," *Co-textes*, no. 3 (1982), pp. 44-56.

25. Javier Herrero, "El volcán en el paraíso: El sistema icónico del teatro de Calderón," *Co-Textes*, no. 3 (1982), p. 81.

26. Bodini, *Segni e simboli*, p. 117.

27. Mark P.O. Morford and Robert J. Lenardon, *Classical Mythology* (New York: David McKay, 1971), p. 33.

28. See my study *Paul Scarron* (New York: Twayne, 1972), p. 140.

29. Diego Saavedra Fajardo, *Idea de un príncipe político cristiano*, ed. Vincente García de Diego (Madrid: La Lectura, 1930), vol. 5, p. 12.

30. John H. Turner, *The Myth of Icarus in Spanish Renaissance Poetry* (London: Tamesis, 1976), p. 43.

31. Cited in Nigel Calder, *The Comet is Coming: The Feverish Legacy of Mr. Halley* (London: Penguin, 1982), pp. 22-23.

32. Theobaldi, *Physiologus*, ed. and trans. P.T. Eden (Leiden: E.J. Brill, 1972), pp. vii, 28-31. The legend of the eagle that renews itself was of classical origin, but became immensely popular during the medieval period. See H.N. Wethered, *The Mind of the Ancient World* (London: Longmans Green, 1937), p. 275.

33. White, *Bestiary*, p. 105.

34. Laura Calvert, *Francisco de Osuna and the Spirit of the Letter* (Chapel Hill: Univ. of North Carolina Press, 1973), p. 62.

35. White, *Bestiary*, p. 105; see also Theobaldi, *Physiologus*, p. 31.

36. White, *Bestiary*, p. 105.

37. By mystical is meant only the infusion of eternal or transcendental values in man. However, it should be noted that numerous mystical writers use the eagle as a symbol of contemplation. See Calvert, *Francisco de Osuna*, pp. 60-63; Gaston Echegoyen, *L'Amour divin: Essais sur les sources de Sainte Therese* (Paris: Féret et fils, 1923), pp. 249-52: "le vol de l'aigle exprime surtout le triomphe de l'ame sur l'instinct" (p. 252). This is precisely Segismundo's triumph.

38. It is not my intent to consider Gnostic influences in Calderón. Myths of life as sleep, anamnesis, or forgetting are common to many systems of belief, as Mircea Eliade

has pointed out in *Myth and Reality,* trans. Willard R. Trask (New York: Harper and Row, 1968), pp. 114-38. Citations of the myth are from this work.

39. Eliade, *Myth and Reality,* p. 129.

40. On the image of the almond tree in Golden Age drama see chapter three, n. 52.

41. Pliny, *Natural History,* trans. and ed. H. Rackham (Cambridge: Harvard Univ. Press, 1945), vol. 4, p. 455.

42. Sloman, "Structure of *La vida es sueño,*" p. 96. Wilson ("On *La vida es sueño*") makes the same point.

43. William M. Whitby, "Rosaura's Role in the Structure of *La vida es sueño,*" in *Critical Essays on the Theater of Calderón,* p. 112.

44. Cohn, *Pursuit of the Millennium,* p. 107; and Kantorowicz, *Frederick the Second,* p. 686.

45. *Escritores místicos españoles,* in *N.B.A.A.,* vol. 16. p. 423.

46. Manilius, *Astronomica,* p. 341.

47. "El águila que lleva a Ganimedes por los ayres, significan la contemplación de las cosas celestiales" (Covarrubias, *Tesoro de la lengua,* p. 55). Covarrubias refers the reader to an emblem by Alciati on this subject.

48. Manilius, *Astronomica,* p. 341.

CHAPTER SEVEN

1. Francisco Ruiz Ramón, *Historia del teatro español,* 3d ed. (Madrid: Cátedra, 1979), vol. 1, p. 239.

2. The second part of *La hija del aire* was published in *Parte quarenta y dos de diferentes autores* (Zaragoza, 1650), where it is attributed to Antonio Enríquez Gómez. Constance Hubbard Rose defends this attribution in "Who Wrote the *segunda parte* of *La hija del aire?*" (*Revue Belge de Philologie et d'Histoire* 54 [1976], 796-822). However, Stephen H. Lipmann has argued for unity in the conception of Semiramis's character. He thus believes that Calderón wrote both *partes.* See his "The Duality and Delusion of Calderón's Semiramis," *BHS* 59 (1982), 42-57. Rose reasserts her attribution to Enríquez Gómez in "Again on the Authorship of the *segunda parte* of *La hija del aire,*" *BHS* 60 (1983), 247-8. Finally, as I was completing this book, Don Cruickshank published an important article that strongly suggests that Calderón is the author of the *segunda parte.* See his "The Second Part of the *La hija del aire,*" *BHS* 61 (1984), 286-94.

3. Theodore W. Jensen, "The Phoenix and Folly in Lope's *La noche de San Juan,*" *FMLS* 16 (1980), 214-23. This essay goes beyond *costumbrismo* to show how it is "thematically and structurally a most complex and beautiful play."

4. Brown and Elliott, *Palace for a King,* p. 230.

5. N.D. Shergold, "The First Performance of Calderón's *El mayor encanto, amor,*" *BHS* 35 (1958), 24-27.

6. Leo Rouanet, "Un autographe inédit de Calderón," *RH* 6 (1899), 196-200.

7. D. J. Gordon and Stephen Orgel, *The Renaissance Imagination* (Berkeley: Univ. of California Press, 1975), pp. 77-101.

8. Kennedy, *Studies in Tirso,* vol. 1, p. 166. This *prólogo* is included in the sixteenth *parte* of Lope's comedias published in 1621.

9. The first act was composed by Antonio Mira de Amescua, the second by Juan Pérez de Montalbán, and the third by Calderón. For the text of this play see *B.A.E.,* vol. 14. On Calderón's refashioning of this source play see Sloman, *Dramatic Craftsmanship,* pp. 128-58.

10. Sloman, *Dramatic Craftsmanship*, pp. 129-30. For a broader interpretation of Ulyses' quest see Fischer, "Mode of Romance."

11. "se abrazará de la virtud; y estando abrazado con ella, volverá Circe desesperada, mesados sus cabellos, y haciendo extremos lastimosos; y viendo a Ulises abrazado de la Virtud, se volverá a él, y le dirá . . ." (from the *memoria* of Cosme Lotti in *B.A.E.*, vol. 7, P. 390).

12. Egla Morales Blouin, *El ciervo y la fuente: Mito y folklore en la lírica tradicional* (Madrid: Studia Humanitatis, 1981).

13. James George Frazer, *The Golden Bough* (New York: MacMillan, 1963), pp. 720-21.

14. All references to *El mayor encanto, amor* are from Calderón, *Obras completas*, ed. Valbuena Briones, vol. 1.

15. Brown and Elliott, *Palace for a King,*, p. 196. Citing a letter from Monanni, they pinpoint the date as Sunday, July 29th. Shergold discusses the date of presentation of *El mayor encanto, amor*: "Unless the news item of 5 July is false, the play was given four performances between 25 June and this date, having previously been prepared for 23 June. A second series of performances ran from 29 July to 3 August" ("First Performance," p. 27).

16. Cited from the *memoria* included in *B.A.E.*, vol. 7, p. 390.

17. Gregorio Marañón, *El Conde-Duque de Olivares*, 5th ed. (Madrid: Espasa-Calpe, 1965), pp. 101, 193.

18. Ibid., p. 196.

19. *La cueva de Meliso*, in *B.A.E.*, vol. 69, 544.

20. Kennedy, *Studies in Tirso*, vol. 1, pp. 205-14.

21. Francisco de Quevedo y Villegas, *La fortuna con seso y la hora de todos* (Madrid: Castalia, 1975), p. 199.

22. Conrad Kent, "Politics in *La hora de todos*," *JHP* 1 (1977), 117.

23. Vitiora, *Teatro de los dioses*. For a discussion of the qualities of the planet Saturn as included in this study see his sixth chapter, "De como Saturno fue tenido por uno de los siete planetas," pp. 19-24.

24. Marchant, *Kalendar and Compost*, p. 141.

25. See my "Saturn Factor," pp. 63-80.

26. Brown and Elliott, *Palace for a King*, p. 228. The writer in question is Andrés de Almansa y Mendoza.

27. Although most modern editions list her name as Libia, the *Segunda parte de las comedias de don Pedro Calderón de la Barca* (Madrid, Pedro Coello, 1637) lists her as Licia. See the facsimile edition prepared by D.W. Cruickshank and J.E. Varey, (Westmead: Gregg International Publishers, 1973), vol. 5, fol. 1. Yet, within the text of the *Segunda parte*, she is named Libia (see fol. 26: "Huye Libia").

28. Astraea and Libia or Licia are not present as characters in Calderón's "source" play, *Polifemo y Circe*. Circe's attendants in that play are Irene and Tisbe. Of the twelve plays in which a character named Astraea appears in Calderón, seven include also a character named Libio or Libia. As noted, Libia together with Astraea appears in *El mayor encanto, amor*, *Los tres mayores prodigios*, and *La hija del aire* II. Libio appears in *La gran Cenobia*, *El monstruo de los jardines*, *Los tres afectos de amor*, and *Ni amor se libra de amor*. However, Libio and Libia are common names in Calderón, appearing in fourteen plays each. Another name that can be significance in our study is Irene. She is the Roman Pax, the sister of Astraea. We have already noted her presence in *La gran Cenobia* and in *Polifemo y Circe*. Irene is a companion to a Libio in *Amado y aborrecido*, *La exaltación de la cruz*, and *La sibila de oriente*.

29. Lope de Vega, *Obras poéticas*, ed. Blecua, p. 279.

30. "To Venus, which is temperate and beneath Mars, were given the next two signs, which are extremely fertile, Libra and Taurus" (Ptolemy, *Tetrabiblos*, p. 81).

31. See, for example, my study "Los excesos de Venus y Marte en *El gallardo español*," in *Cervantes: Su obra y su mundo*, ed. Manuel Criado de Val (Madrid: Edi-6, 1981), pp. 249-60.

32. Parr, *Tamburlaine's Malady*, p. 82.

33. Calderón's martial spirit can be detected in this message. When the uprising in Cataluña took place in 1640, Calderón went to war "en la compañía que levantó y sostuvo Olivares, y su confianza con éste era tal, que el Marqués de Hinojosa, desde Tarragona, le envió para informar verbalmente al ministro del estado de aquel ejército" (Marañón, *El Conde-Duque de Olivares*, p. 151). The apparent friendship between Calderón and Olivares is not reflected in the playwright's works. Marañón comments: "Calderón mejor administrador de su incienso que Lope, apenas lo lanza sobre el Valido" (p. 152). Marañón records only one instance in *Casa con dos puertas* where the *valido* is praised. Here, Calderón refers to king and minister by the mythological names of Alcides and Atlante. The relationship between Calderón and Olivares has not been properly clarified. More work should be done on this topic.

34. Marañón, *El Conde-Duque de Olivares*, p. 244.

35. On the written play as soul see my study "Italian Canvases in Lope de Vega's Comedias," *CH* 2 (1980), 135-42.

36. Brown and Elliott, *Palace for a King*, p. 199. On the early success of the war with France see Francisco Tomás y Valiente et al., *La España de Felipe IV* (Madrid: Espasa-Calpe, 1982), pp. 728-30.

37. Brown and Elliott, *Palace for a King*, p. 204.

38. W.G. Chapman, "Las comedias mitológicas de Calderón," *Revista de Literatura* 5 (1954), 51.

39. A.I. Watson, "Hercules and the Tunic of Shame: Calderón's *Los tres mayores prodigios*," in *Homenaje a William L. Fichter*, ed. A. David Kossoff and José Amor y Vázquez (Madrid: Castalia, 1971), p. 774.

40. Ibid., p. 783.

41. All references to *Los tres mayores prodigios* are from Calderón, *Obras completas*, ed. Valbuena Briones, vol. 1.

42. *Calderón's Comedias*, ed. Cruicksank and Varey, vol. 5, fol. 252.

43. Jessie L. Weston, *From Ritual to Romance* (New York: Doubleday Anchor, 1957), p. 65.

44. Campbell, *Hero with a Thousand Faces*, pp. 318-34.

45. Covarrubias, *Tesoro de la lengua*, p. 941; Michael J.A. Allen, *Marsilio Ficino and the Phaedran Charioteer* (Berkeley: Univ. of California Press, 1981), pp. 194-95.

46. Campbell, *Hero with a Thousand Faces*, p. 116.

47. "La Odisea refiere que las sirenas atraían y perdían a los navegantes y que Ulises, para oir su canto y no perecer, tapó con cera los oidos de sus remeros y ordenó que lo sujetaran al mastil. Para tentarlo, las sirenas prometían el conocimiento de todas las cosas del mundo" (Jorge Luis Borges, "El arte narrativo y la magia," in Borges's *Discusión* [Buenos Aires: Emece, 1964], pp. 84-85. Borges includes in this curious footnote to Jason's adventures many other items concerning the sirens.

48. Vitoria, *Teatro de los dioses*, pp. 247-48. On Proserpine's relation to the summer solstice see my study "Lope de Vega and the Hermetic Tradition: The Case of Dardanio in *La Arcadia*," *RCEH* 7 (1983), 355-56.

49. Benjamin B. Aschom, "The First Builder of Boats in *El burlador de Sevilla*, *HR* 11 (1943), 328-33.

50. Diego Saavedra Fajardo, *Idea de un príncipe político cristiano*, ed. Vicente García de Diego, vol. 3 (Madrid: La Lectura, 1928), p. 188.

51. Kent, "Politics in *La hora de todos*, p. 108.

52. Frank Domínguez, *The Medieval Argonautica* (Potomac, Md.: José Porrúa Turanzas, 1979), p. 112.

53. Pietro Pucci, *The Violence of Pity in Euripedes' Medea* (Ithaca: Cornell Univ. Press, 1980), p. 71. Pucci's statements on *dike* and truth may well apply to Seneca's tragedy and are certainly useful in our interpretation of Calderón's *Los tres mayores prodigios*.

54. Raymond R. MacCurdy, "Notes on the Fateful Curse in Golden Age Drama," *KRQ* 21 (1974), 317-34.

55. Robert B. Tate, "Mythology in Spanish Historiography of the Middle Ages and the Renaissance," *HR* 22 (1954), 1-18.

56. Yates, *Astraea*, p. 23.

57. See my study "The Apples of Colchis: Key to an Interpretation of *La Estrella de Sevilla*," *FMLS* 15 (1979), 1-13.

58. Thomas A. O'Connor, "Hércules y el mito masculino: La posición feminista de *Fieras afemina amor*," in *Estudios sobre el Siglo de Oro en homenaje a Raymond R. MacCurdy*, ed. Angel González, Tamara Holzapfe, and Alfred Rodríguez (Madrid: Catedra, 1983), p. 172.

59. Brown and Elliott, *Palace for a King*, p. 160.

60. Watson, "Hercules and the Tunic of Shame," p. 782.

CHAPTER EIGHT

1. Menéndez Pelayo, *Calderón y su teatro*, p. 376.

2. Alexander A. Parker, "History and Poetry: The Coriolanus Theme in Calderón," in *Hispanic Studies in Honor of I. Gonzalez Llubera* (Oxford: Dolphin, 1959), pp. 216, 217.

3. In Plutarch, Coriolanus's mother feels that the women's plea that the city be spared is deserving of greater fame than the past heroic actions by the Sabine women. They had marched between the army of their people and that of the Romans in order to prevent war between them (Parker, "History and Poetry," pp. 218-19).

4. Ibid., p. 222.

5. Sloman, *Dramatic Craftsmanship*, p. 93.

6. Menéndez Pelayo, *Calderón y su teatro*, p. 377.

7. David G. Lanoue, "Calderón's Late Roman Plays and the Imperial Myth: *Las armas de la hermosura* and *El segundo Scipión*," in *Critical Perspectives on Calderón de la Barca*, ed. Frederick A. de Armas, David M. Gitlitz, and José A. Madrigal (Lincoln, Nebr.: SSSAS, 1981), p. 97.

8. All page references to *El privilegio de las mujeres* are from don Pedro Calderón de la Barca, *Obras completas*, ed. Luis Astrana Marín (Madrid: Aguilar, 1951), vol. 1. The play also appears in *B.A.E.*, vol. 14.

9. "Under Mars is born all thieves and robbers. . . . And he will be rich of other men's goods" (Marchant, *Kalendar and Compost*, pp. 143-44).

10. Fritz Saxl, "The Literary Sources of the Finiguerra Planets," *JWCI* 2 (1938), 72-74. Saxl is discussing a Florentine series of engravings attributed to Finiguerra.

11. Eliade, *Eternal Return*, p. 133.

12. Ibid., p. 124.

13. Gordon, *Renaissance Imagination*, p. 203.

14. Emilio Cotarelo y Mori, *Ensayo sobre la vida y obras de D. Pedro Calderón de la Barca*

(Madrid: Revista de Archivos, Bibliotecas y Museos, 1924), p. 177; Sloman, *Dramatic Craftsmanship*, p. 61.

15. The war with France placed the Spanish empire in a perilous situation. For reflections of this threat in Calderón's theater see the previous chapter. *El privilegio* must have been written in the same period that Calderón also composed *El mayor encanto, amor* and *Los tres mayores prodigios*, the years 1635-36.

16. Some critics disagree with this notion. See, for example, Christiane Faliu-Lacourt, "La madre en la comedia," in *La mujer en el teatro y la novela del siglo XVII* (Toulouse: Université de Toulouse-Le Mirail, 1979), pp. 41-59.

17. Eliade, *Eternal Return*, p. 135.

18. Jean Hubaux and Maxime LeRoy, *Le mythe du phénix dans les littératures grecque et latine* (Paris: E. Droz, 1939), pp. 128-77.

19. Martial, *Epigrams* (5.7), cited in Hubaux and LeRoy, *Le mythe du phénix*, p. 78.

20. Eliade, *Eternal Return*, p. 136.

21. Rowland, *Animals with Human Faces*, p. 158.

22. Parker, "History and Poetry," p. 222.

23. Sloman, *Dramatic Craftsmanship*, p. 61.

24. All page references to *Las armas de la hermosura* are to Calderón, *Obras completas*, ed. Valbuena Briones, vol. 1.

25. Juan Eugenio Hartzenbusch, *Comedias de don Pedro Calderón de la Barca* (Madrid: Hernando, 1926), vol. 4. In *B.A.E.*, vol. 14, p. 677.

26. Parker, "History and Poetry," p. 217.

27. Ibid., p. 217.

28. Sloman, *Dramatic Craftsmanship*, p. 66.

29. On the enmity between Juan José de Austria and Queen Mariana see, for example, R. Trevor Davies, *La decadencia española 1621-1700*, trans. J.M. Garciá de la Mora (Barcelona: Labor, 1969), pp. 126-57.

30. Sloman, *Dramatic Caraftsmanship*, p. 72.

31. McKendrick, *Woman and Society*, p. 186.

32. Eliade, *Eternal Return*, p. 135.

CHAPTER NINE

1. Cotarelo y Mori, *Ensayo sobre la vida y obras de D. Pedro Calderón de la Barca*, p. 305.

2. All page references to the *loa* are from Calderón, *Comedias*, ed. Cruickshank and Varey, vol. 10. This volume is a facsimile of the *Quarta parte de comedias* (Madrid, 1672).

3. Everett W. Hesse, "Court References in Calderón's Zarzuelas," *HR* 15 (1947), 365-77.

4. Thomas O'Connor, "Vraisemblance and Ideological Resistance in Calderón's Piscatory Eclogue, *El golfo de las sirenas*," paper presented at the Simposio de Teatro Internacional Español y Mexicano, held April 4-6, 1984 in San Diego, California, in honor of professor Everett W. Hesse.

5. Richard W. Wallace, "Salvator Rosa's Justice Appearing to the Peasants," *JWCI* 30 (1967), 431-34.

6. Gordon, *Renaissance Imagination*, pp. 77-101; and my study "Italian Canvases in Lope de Vega's *Comedias*."

7. Saxl, "*Veritas Filia Temporis*."

8. All references to *Ni amor se libra de amor* are from Calderón, *Obras completas*, ed. Valbuena Briones, vol. 1.

9. See my "Saturn Factor."

10. "For Psyche in Greek is called the spirit" (Leslie George Whitehead, *Fulgentius the Mythographer* [Columbus, Ohio: Ohio State Univ. Press, 1971], p. 89). On a particular plot derived from this myth see my study *The Invisible Mistress: Aspects of Feminism and Fantasy in the Golden Age* (Charlottesville: Biblioteca Siglo de Oro, 1976), pp. 15-21. Calderón composed two *autos sacramentales* dealing with the myth, where Psyche is the soul.

11. On the myth of the Celestial Venus see Panofsky, *Problems in Titian*, p. 11.

12. Evangelina Rodríguez and Antonio Tordera, *Calderón y la obra corta dramática del siglo XVII* (London: Tamesis, 1983), pp. 152-54.

13. Cotarelo y Mori, *Ensayo sobre la vida y obras de D. Pedro Calderón de la Barca*, pp. 308-9.

14. All references to *Los tres afectos de amor* are from Calderón, *Obras completas*, ed. Valbuena Briones, vol. 1.

15. Pedro Ciruelo, *Reprouación de las supersticiones y hechizerías*, ed. Alva V. Ebersole (Madrid: Albatros-Hispanófila, 1978), p. 57.

16. "Lo cierto es que ningún gobernante del siglo XVI podía permitirse el lujo de dejar de interesarse por conocer su horóscopo, con el fin de sacar partido de sus aspectos favorables y neutralizar los adversos. Se conocen varios horóscopos de Felipe II. . . . Puede además sospecharse que su conocida afición por vestir de negro fue también motivada por consideraciones astrológicas" (Taylor, "Arquitectura y magia," p. 13.

17. All page references to *El laurel de Apolo* are from *Comedias de Don Pedro Calderón de la Barca*, ed. Juan Eugenio Hartzenbusch, in *B.A.E.*, vol. 9 (Madrid: Hernando, 1925).

18. Parr, *Tamburlaine's Malady*, p. 75.

19. Jerónimo de Barrionuevo, *Avisos*, ed. A. Paz y Melia (Madrid: M. Tello, 1892-94), vol. 2, p. 120.

20. Parr, *Tamburlaine's Malady*, p. 26.

21. Cited in Raymond Klibansky, Edwin Panofsky, and Fritz Saxl, *Saturn and Melancholy* (London: Thomas Nelson, 1964), p. 191.

22. *Larousse Encyclopedia of Astrology*, p. 241.

23. *Letters of Marcilio Ficino*, vol. 2, p. 30.

24. Lope de Vega, *La Dorotea*, p. 406.

25. Morford and Lenardon, *Classical Mythology*, p. 98; and Panofsky, *Problems in Titan*, p. 114.

26. On Saturn's exaltation in Libra see Ptolemy, *Tetrabiblos*, p. 89; on the negative connotations of this particular exaltation see *Larousse Encyclopedia of Astrology*, p. 110.

27. For a picture of Saturn holding a scythe see *The Book of Secrets of Albertus Magnus*, ed. Michael R. Best and Frank H. Brightman (Oxford: Oxford Univ. Press, 1973), p. 65.

28. Ficino, *Book of Life*, p. 69.

29. See, for example, *El alcalde mayor* and *El bobo del colegio*, discussed in my "Saturn Factor."

30. Marchant, *Kalendar and Compost*, p. 141.

31. Klibansky et al., *Saturn and Melancholy*, p. 189; Ptolemy, *Tetrabiblos*, p. 241.

32. Klibansky et al., *Saturn and Melancholy*, p. 184. The authors note that the saying is based ultimately on a passage in Pseudo-Ptolemy.

33. Peter N. Dunn, "Garcilaso's Ode *A la flor de Gnido*," *ZRP* 81 (1965), 301-2.

34. Marchant, *Kalendar and Compost*, p. 141; Klibansky et al., *Saturn and Melancholy*, p. 191.

CHAPTER TEN

1. William R. Blue, *The Development of Imagery in Calderón's Comedias* (York, S. C.: Spanish Literature Publications, 1983), p. 172.

2. Valbuena Briones, ed., Calderón, *Obras completas*, vol. 1, p. 1984. On Tirso de Molina's *El Aquiles* see: Everett W. Hesse and William C. McCrary, "The Mars-Venus Struggle in Tirso's *Aquiles*," *BHS* 33 (1956), 138-51; and José A. Madrigal, "La transmutación de Aquiles: De salvaje a heroe (Tirso de Molina, *El Aquiles*)," *Hispano* 77 (1983), 15-26.

3. Alexander A. Parker, "*El monstruo de los jardines* y el concepto calderoniano del destino," in *Hacia Calderón*, p. 94.

4. Everett W. Hesse, "Calderón's *El monstruo de los jardines:* Sex, Sexuality, and Sexual Fulfillment," *RCEH* 5 (19 3), 318.

5. Everett W. Hesse, "Sexual Problems in the Achilles Plays of Tirso and Calderón," *KRQ* 28 (1981), 178.

6. All page references to *El monstruo de los jardines* are from Valbuena Briones's edition, vol 1.

7. Grudin, *Mighty Opposites*, p. 14.

8. Leon Hebreo, *Diálogos de amor*, ed. Eduardo Juliá Martínez, (Madrid: Librería General Victoriano Suárez, 1949), vol. 1, p. 240.

9. The sirens "may well be representations of the inferior forces in woman" (Cirlot, *Dictionary of Symbols*, p. 298).

10. Frederick A. de Armas, "Las tres Dianas de Montemayor," in *Lingüística y educación. Actas del IV congreso internacional de la ALFAL* (Lima: Universidad Nacional Mayor de San Marcos, 1978). One of the three nymphs who guide Felismena to her bath is Cinthia: "Cinthia, posiblemente la misma diosa disfrazada, ha invitado a Felismena a que se bañe con ella y sus ninfas. Este es el mayor honor que se le puede conceder a una mujer, el privilegio de estar presente en el famoso baño de Diana, baño que subraya su castidad en los famosos mitos de Acteón y de Calisto" (pp. 188-89). For Bruno M. Damiani, these three nymphs represent the Three Graces. Such an interpretation does not contradict my own, since Damiani states that they represent Castitas-Pulchritudo-Amor. Cinthia may be Castitas and as such she is related to the goddess Diana. See Bruno M. Damiani, *La Diana of Montemayor as Social and Religious Teaching* (Lexington: Univ. Press of Kentucky, 1983), p. 70.

11. We have discussed previously how Seneca's *Hippolytus* contributed to the myth of the golden age. The Roman playwright, like Calderón, deals with the notion of opposites (Venus-Diana) in a work that evokes the happiest of ages. The relationship between Calderón and Seneca deserves further study. An example of the Venus-Diana opposition in the Renaissance can be found in Boccaccio's *Ninfale Fiesolano* where the conflict has "as its basis the ancient enmity of Venus and Diana" (Daniel J. Donno, introduction to Giovanni Boccaccio, *The Nymph of Fiesole* (New York: Columbia Univ. Press, 1960), p. X.

12. Wind, *Pagan Mysteries*, p. 54. For the importance of *Ein-Sof* in the Kabbalah see Gershom Scholem, *Kabbalah* (New York: New American Library, 1978). Scholem explains that *Ein-Sof* means infinite: "*Ein-Sof* is the absolute perfection in which there are no distinctions and no differentiations, and according to some even no volition. It does not reveal itself in a way that makes knowledge of its nature possible." He adds that this definition led some Kabbalists to the daring conclusion "that only the revealed God can in reality be called 'God', and not the hidden '*deus absconditus*', who cannot be an object of religious thought" (p. 89).

13. Wind, *Pagan Mysteries*, pp. 218-20. For Paul Oskar Kristeller, Nicolaus Cusanus was one of the three great Renaissance Platonists together with Ficino and Pico (*Renaissance Thought and Its Sources* [New York: Columbia Univ. Press, 1979], pp. 57-58).

14. James E. Maraniss, "Euripides and Calderón," in *Calderón de la Barca at the Tercentenary: Comparative Views*, ed. Wendell M. Aycock and Sydney P. Cravens (Lubbock: Texas Tech Press, 1982), p. 161.

15. Saxl, "Literary Sources of the 'Finiguerra Planets,'" p. 73.

16. Apollodorus, *The Library*, ed. James George Frazer (Cambridge: Harvard Univ. Press, 1921), vol. 2, pp. 73-75. The Achilles episode is narrated in 3.13.

17. Dunn, "Garcilaso's Ode *A la flor de Gnido*," pp. 301-2.

18. See, for example, Quintilian, *Institutio oratoria* 2.4; and the *Greek Anthology*, a possible source for Andrea Navagero's poem on the subject. See James Hutton, *The Greek Anthology in Italy to the Year 1800* (Ithaca: Cornell Univ. Press, 1935).

19. *Andrea Navagero Lusus: Text and Translation*, trans. and ed. Alice E. Wilson (Nieuwkoop: B. de Graaf, 1973), poem 42, p. 75.

20. Wind, *Pagan Mysteries*, p. 93.

21. "O crudo, o riguroso, o fiero Marte, / de túnica cubierto de diamante" (Garcilaso de la Vega, *Elegía* II, in *Obras completas*, ed. Elias L. Rivers, [Madrid: Castalia, 1981], p. 250). Rivers notes that these lines have their original inspiration in Homer and Horace.

22. C.G. Jung, *Psychology and Alchemy*, trans. R.P.C. Hull, 2d ed. (Princeton: Princeton Univ. Press, 1968).

23. Suetonius, *The Lives of the Twelve Caesars*, ed. Joseph Gavorse (New York: Modern Library, 1959), p. 160.

24. Apollodorus, *Library*, vol. 2, p. 73.

25. Edgar Wind, "The Four Elements in Raphael's 'Stanza della Segnatura,'" *JWCI* 2 (1938), 78.

26. Sebastian Neumeister, *Mythos und Repräsentation* (Munich: Wilhelm Fink Verlag, 1978), pp. 185-86, 187. At the end of the play, according to Neumeister, Aquiles still must face final victory and death. Troy represents the Last Judgement which leads to the reign of Astraea as *Pax*.

27. Bruce W. Wardropper, "*Fuenteovejuna: El gusto* and *lo justo*," *SPh* 53 (1956), 159-71.

28. On the *mujer esquiva* see McKendrick, *Woman and Society*, pp. 142-73.

29. Hesse, "Sexual Problems," p. 181.

30. Wind, *Pagan Mysteries*, p. 75. "Across his path, amid the forest, came his mother, with a maiden's face and mien, and a maiden's arms" (*Virgil*, ed. and trans. H. Rushton Fairclough, vol. 1, p. 263). Here Aeneas meets Venus in disguise as he reconnoiters the land around Carthage.

31. Yates, *Astraea*, pp. 32, 73-74.

32. Alexander H. Krappe, "Notes on the *voces del cielo*," *RR* 17 (1926), 65.

33. "La tercera especie de agueros y mas vana que las otras; es la que en latin llaman Omen: quiere dezir adeuinar por dichos o hechos que otros los hazen a otro proposito: y los adeuinos los aplican a otro" (Ciruelo, *Reprouación*, p. 63; Anibal, "*Voces del cielo*," pp. 57-70). Anibal finds seven plays by Mira de Amescua where kledonomancy is used. The most extensive use is in *Los lises de Francia*. In "Another Note on the *Voces del cielo*" (*RR* 18 [1927], 246-52), Anibal discusses other works where kledonomancy is found such as *Don Quijote* II, ch. 73, *La Celestina, La lozana andaluza*, etc.

34. Curtius, *European Literature and the Latin Middle Ages*, pp. 170-77.

35. See my study "Metamorphosis in Calderón's *El mayor encanto, amor*," *RomN* 22 (1981), 208-12.

36. See my "Four Elemental Jewels."

37. "L'usage moderne d'offrir un bracelet au moment des fiançailles explique claire-ment le Passage du sens moral de *firmeza* à celui du bijou qui est le symbole d'un engagement sacré" (Jean Sarrailh, "Firmeza," *RFE* 22 [1935], 57).

38. Chastity can be maintained through celibacy or through a faithful marriage. The relationship between constancy, chastity, and the goddess Diana is emphasized in Jorge de Montemayor's *La Diana*. Here the shepherdess Diana cannot enter Felicia's palace since she does not still hold to her first love. On this subject see my study "Las tres Dianas de Montemayor," p. 188.

39. Cited in Hafter, *Gracián and Perfection*, p. 51. For a similar description see White, *Bestiary*, p. 187.

40. Neumeister, *Mythos und Repräsentation*, pp. 165-89. Neumeister refers in his study to the disguise of Aquiles and relates it to Virgil's *Fourth Eclogue*, but does not connect it with the mystery of reconciliation of opposites (see pp. 185-88).

41. Campbell, *Hero with a Thousand Faces*, p. 58.

42. Parker, "El monstruo de los jardines," p. 101.

43. In Neumeister, *Mythos and Repräsentation*, the war at Troy is subjected to exegesis. For him, the Troy of *El monstruo de los jardines* is that second Troy that represents the Last Judgment and the Pax that follows is Astraea's golden age or the Kingdom of God. Neumeister adds that Dante ignored the eschatological interpretation of Astraea (pp. 187-88).

CONCLUSION

1. Eliade, *Sacred and Profane*, p. 92.

2. Ibid., p. 12.

3. Levin, *Golden Age*, p. 112.

4. As I reach the final pages of this book, I would like to express my deep admiration for Frances A. Yates. It was the works of this "sibyline figure," as E.H. Gombrich re-ferred to her (*New York Review of Books*, vol. 30, no. 3 [1983], p. 11), that inspired me to delve into the Astraea myth in Golden Age Spain.

5. A recent book documents the popularity of Astraea in the English Restoration. See Nicholas Jose, *Ideas of the Restoration in English Literature, 1660-71* (Cambridge: Har-vard Univ. Press, 1984), pp. 44-66. Echoes of Astraea and of Virgil's *Fourth Eclogue* con-tinued to be heard beyond the seventeenth century, as exemplified by Alexander Pope's *Messiah*.

6. ter Horst, *Secular Plays*, p. 222.

Bibliographical Note

SINCE MUCH OF THE RESEARCH for this book involved texts outside Calderonian criticism, including numerous studies that are quite removed from Spanish literature, the following bibliographical note can serve to orient the reader to some of the more useful items consulted. The editions and translations listed here are the ones I have used. For example, Jean Seznec's book is not listed in its original French version but in the Princeton paperback that I consulted. Journal abbreviations are taken from the *PMLA* bibliography.

Harry Levin has carefully documented the importance and pervasiveness of the concept of the golden age during the Renaissance, establishing that the panegyrics of courtly poets would locate this happiest of ages in most European courts of the period. *The Myth of the Golden Age in the Renaissance* (Oxford: Oxford Univ. Press, 1969) is thus a starting point for any discussion on the subject. A more specific monograph on this age was written by Elizabeth Armstrong, *Ronsard and the Age of Gold* (Cambridge: Cambridge Univ. Press, 1968). This book owes its inspiration to Frances Yates, *Astraea: The Imperial Theme in the Sixteenth Century* (London: Routledge and Keagan Paul, 1975). Reading it in conjunction with Calderón's *La vida es sueño*, I realized that the cult of Elizabeth I as Astraea, the Virgin Queen, was paralleled in Spain by subtler yet insistent allusions to the return of Astraea during the reign of Philip IV.

Four key studies can serve as guides through classical renditions of the myth of Astraea: Pietro Pucci, *Hesiod and the Language of Poetry* (Baltimore: Johns Hopkins Univ. Press, 1977); William Sale, "The Popularity of Aratus," *Classical Journal* 61 (1966); Michael C.J. Putnam, *Virgil's Pastoral Art* (Princeton: Princeton Univ. Press, 1970); and Eleanor Winsor Leach, *Virgil's Eclogues: Landscapes of Experience* (Ithaca: Cornell Univ. Press, 1974). In addition, Mircea Eliade, *The Myth of the Eternal Return* (Princeton: Princeton Univ. Press, 1954) placed the return of Astraea in the perspective of the cyclic theories of history. This historian of religions describes how it was Virgil's influence that transformed the fear of apocalyptic *ekpyrosis* into the notion of Rome as an *urbs aeterna*, regenerating itself after every cycle. Universal cycles are also discussed in C.G. Jung, *Aion: Researches in the Phenomenology of the Self* (Princeton: Princeton Univ. Press, 1968); and Joseph Campbell, *The Mythic Image* (Princeton: Princeton Univ. Press, 1974). Also useful in this matter is William Harris Stahl, ed. and trans., Macrobius, *Commentary on the Dream of Scipio* (New York: Columbia Univ. Press, 1952).

Since Astraea is associated with the golden age and this epoch is often equated with visions of pastoral, several works on this mode proved most useful: Renato Poggioli, *The Oaten Flute* (Cambridge: Harvard Univ. Press, 1952); Thomas G. Rosenmeyer, *The Green Cabinet* (Berkeley: Univ. of California Press, 1969); Juan Bautista Avalle-Arce, *La novela pastoril española* (Madrid: Istmo, 1974); Manuel José Bayo, *Virgilio y la pastoral española del Renacimiento* (Madrid: Gredos, 1970); and Anthony J. Cascardi, "The Exit from Arcadia: Reevaluation of the Pastoral in Virgil, Garcilaso and Góngora," *JHP* 4 (1980).

A number of general studies on myth proved valuable in this undertaking. They include: Jessie L. Weston, *From Ritual to Romance* (New York: Doubleday Anchor, 1957); Miguel de Ferdinandy, *En torno al pensar mítico* (Berlin: Colloquium, 1961); Joseph Campbell, *The Hero with a Thousand Faces* (Princeton: Princeton Univ. Press, 1968); Erich Neumann, *The Great Mother: An Analysis of the Archetype* (Princeton: Princeton Univ. Press, 1972); Northrop Frye, *The Secular Scripture* (Cambridge: Harvard Univ. Press, 1976); René Girard, *Violence and the Sacred* (Baltimore: Johns Hopkins Univ. Press, 1977); Egla Morales Blouin, *El ciervo y la fuente: Mito y Folklore en la lírica tradicional* (Potomac, Md.: José Porrúa Turanzas, 1981); and Alexander A. Parker, "Segismundo's Tower: A Calderonian Myth," *BHS* 59 (1982).

As important as the deeper structures of myth are the ways in which Greek and Roman deities were viewed by Renaissance and seventeenth-century Christian Western Europeans. Jean Seznec traces the gods' persistent influence in his well-known *Survival of the Pagan Gods* (Princeton: Princeton Univ. Press, 1972). Edgar Wind, *Pagan Mysteries in the Renaissance* 2nd ed. (New York: W.W. Norton, 1968) was most useful in unraveling Calderón's mythical structures. Also of importance were: Don Cameron Allen, *Mysteriously Meant* (Baltimore: Johns Hopkins Univ. Press, 1970); Raymond Klibansky, Erwin Panofsky, and Fritz Saxl, *Saturn and Melancholy* (London: Thomas Nelson, 1964); Erwin Panofsky, *Studies in Iconology* (New York: Harper and Row, 1962); Erwin Panofsky, *Problems in Titian* (New York: New York Univ. Press, 1969); Fritz Saxl, "Veritas Filia Temporis," in *Philosophy and History: Essays Presented to Ernst Cassirer*, ed. Raymond Klibansky and J.H. Paton (Oxford: Clarendon Press, 1936); Rudolf Wittkower, *Allegory and the Migration of Symbols* (London: Thames and Hudson, 1977); and Robert Grudin, *Mighty Opposites: Shakespeare and Renaissance Contrariety* (Berkeley: Univ. of California Press, 1979). Two Spanish mythographers of the sixteenth and seventeenth centuries confirmed the epoch's approaches to myths as described in these modern critical texts: Juan Pérez de Moya, *Philosophía secreta* (Madrid: Clásicos Olvidados, 1928); and Baltasar de Vitoria, *Teatro de los dioses de la gentilidad* (Madrid: Impresa Real, 1676). Emblematic traditions also contribute to the understanding of myths and other systems derived from classical antiquity. I have used in particular two Spanish collections: Sebastián de Covarrubias, *Emblemas morales,* ed. Carmen Bravo Villasante (Madrid: Fundación Universitaria Española, 1978); and Francisco de Villava, *Empresas espirituales y morales* (Baeza: Fernando Díaz de Montoya, 1613).

Astraea's "survival" during the Middle Ages can be gleaned from: Domenico Comparetti, *Virgil in the Middle Ages* (New York: G.E. Stechert, 1929); Ernst Kantorowicz, *Frederick the Second* (New York: Frederick Ungar, 1957); and Norman Cohn, *The Pursuit of the Millennium* (Fairlawn, N.J.: Essential Books, 1957). The popularity of Astraea in Spanish literature of the sixteenth and seventeenth centuries is a topic that needs to be further researched. A few studies have dealt with the notion of the golden age in the period without focusing on Astraea, as for example, Marcia L. Welles, "The Myth of the Golden Age in Gracián's *El Criticón,*" *Hispania* 65 (1982); and J.M. Aguirre, "Antonio de Guevara's *Corte-Aldea:* A Model for All Seasons," *Neophil* 65 (1981). Critical works mentioning Astraea include: John H.R. Polt, "Una fuente del soneto de Acuña 'Al Rey Nuestro Señor,'" *BH* 64 (1962); Juan Manuel Rozas, *Lope de Vega y Felipe IV en el "ciclo de senectute"* (Caceres: Universidad de Extremadura, 1982); Daniel L. Heiple, *Mechanical Imagery in Spanish Golden Age Poetry* (Potomac, Md.: José Porrúa Turanzas, 1983); and C. Alan Soons, "Augustinian Criticism of the *Comedia* Reconsidered: Lope's *El despertar a quien duerme,*" *REH* 10 (1976). Only two studies mention Astraea in Calderón: Sebastian Neumeister, *Mythos und Repräsentation* (Munich: Wilhelm Fink Verlag, 1978); and Everett W. Hesse, *New Perspectives on Comedia Criticism* (Potomac, Md.: José Porrúa Turanzas, 1980).

Since Astraea assumed at times an imperial garb, political theories propounded in Spain during the sixteenth and seventeenth centuries had to be considered. A number of works proved useful: José Antonio Maravall, *Carlos V y el pensamiento político del Renacimiento* (Madrid: Instituto de Estudios Políticos, 1960); Bernice Hamilton, *Political Thought in Sixteenth Century Spain* (Oxford: Clarendon Press, 1963); Marcel Bataillon, *Erasmo y España* (México: Fondo de Cultura Económica, 1966); J.H. Elliott, *Imperial Spain* (New York: Penguin, 1970); Fernand Braudel, *The Mediterranean and the Mediterranean World in the Age of Philip II* (New York: Harper and Row, 1976); and J.A. Fernández Santamaría, *The State, War and Peace: Political Thought in the Renaissance 1516-1559* (Cambridge: Cambridge Univ. Press, 1977). In addition to these background studies, there are several texts that provided vital information for the resolution of certain political problems raised by the presence of Astraea in Calderón's theater. These are: Ervin Brody, "Poland in Calderón's *Life is a Dream,*" *Polish Review* 14 (1969); Jonathan Brown and J.H. Elliott, *A Palace for a King* (New Haven: Yale Univ. Press, 1980); Dian Fox, "*El médico de su honra:* Political Considerations," *Hispania* 65 (1982); Hana Jechova, "Les motifs polonais ou tchèques dans *La vie est un songe,*" *CRCL* 4 (1977); Ruth Lee Kennedy, *Studies in Tirso I: The Dramatist and his Competitors, 1620-1626* (Chapel Hill: Univ. of North Carolina Press, 1974); Conrad Kent, "Politics in *La hora de todos,*" *JHP* 1 (1977); Gregorio Marañón, *El Conde-Duque de Olivares* (Madrid: Espasa-Calpe, 1965); and Jack Weiner, "Un episodio de la historia Rusa visto por autores españoles del Siglo de Oro: El pretendiente Demetrio," *JHP* 2 (1978).

Astraea's survival during the Spanish Golden Age was closely tied to the physical tradition as discussed by Jean Seznec—the goddess is also the zodiacal sign Virgo. Astrology thus plays a crucial role in Calderón's elaboration of the myth. A. Bouché-Leclerq, *L'Astrologie grecque* (1899; rpt. Chicago: Bolchazy-Carducci, 1979) is key to the understanding of the development of western astrology. Theodore Otto Wedel, *The Medieval Attitude Toward Astrology* (New Haven: Yale Univ. Press, 1920) is a clear and erudite presentation of this occult science during the Middle Ages. Don Cameron Allen, *The Star-Crossed Renaissance* (Durham: Duke Univ. Press, 1941) shows the central position of astrology in this period and documents debates over its validity. Wayne Shumaker's *The Occult Sciences in the Renaissance* (Berkeley: Univ. of California Press, 1972) and his *Renaissance Curiosa* (Binghamton: 1982) are most helpful in teaching how to cast and interpret a horoscope. Unfortunately, this cannot be said of J.C. Eade, *The Forgotten Sky: A Guide to Astrology in English Literature* (Oxford: Clarendon Press, 1984). Although the book corrects a number of errors that have been made on astrological interpretations of literature, it tends to lose the reader in technical questions and at times obscures rather than illuminates certain problems. In spite of Earle's criticisms, I prefer Johnstone Parr's *Tamburlaine's Malady and other Essays in Astrology in Elizabethan Drama* (University, Ala.: Univ. of Alabama Press, 1953). Also of interest are two books that deal with the relationship of the cosmos to man: Francisco Rico, *El pequeño mundo del hombre* (Madrid: Castalia, 1970); and Leonard Barkan, *Nature's Work of Art: The Human Body as Image of the World* (New Haven: Yale Univ. Press, 1975). Two reference works are fundamental to the study of astrology in literature: Jean Louis Brau, Helen Weaver, and Allan Edmands, *Larousse Encyclopedia of Astrology* (New York: McGraw-Hill, 1980); and Richard Hinkley Allen, *Star Names: Their Lore and Meaning* (1899; rpt. New York: Dover, 1963).

Although these secondary books are most useful, the study of original astrological texts is not a difficult undertaking. The interested reader may wish to consult the key classical manuals: Ptolemy, *Tetrabiblos*, trans. and ed. F.E. Robbins (Cambridge: Harvard Univ. Press, 1940); and Manilius, *Astronomica*, trans. and ed. G.P. Goold (Cambridge: Harvard Univ. Press, 1977). A popular astrological calendar of the Renaissance was Guy Marchant, *The Kalendar and Compost of the Shepherds*, ed. G.C. Heseltine (London: Peter Davies, 1930). Two Continental seventeenth-century astrological manuals are: Antonio de Nájera, *Suma astrológica y arte para enseñar hazer pronósticos* (Lisbon: P. Alvarez, 1632); and the Comte de Pagan, *L'Astrologie naturelle* (Paris: Antoine de Sommaville, 1659).

There are several articles dedicated to Lope de Vega's interest and use of astrology: Juan Millé y Giménez, "El horóscopo de Lope de Vega," *Humanidades* 15 (1927); Frank G. Halstead, "The Attitude of Lope de Vega Towards Astrology and Astronomy," *HR* 7 (1939); Warren T. McCready, "Lope de Vega's Birth Date and Horoscope," *HR* 28 (1960); and my article "The Saturn Factor: Examples of Astrological Imagery in Lope de Vega's Works," in *Studies in Honor of Everett W. Hesse*, ed. William C. McCrary and Jose A. Madrigal (Lincoln, Nebr.: SSSAS, 1981). There are two key articles on astrology in Calderón: Peter Dunn, "The Horoscope Motif in *La vida es sueño*," *Atlante* 1 (1953); and Alexander A. Parker, "*El monstruo de los jardines* y el concepto calderoniano del destino," in *Hacia Calderón: Cuarto coloquio anglogermano* (Berlin: Walter de Gruyter, 1979). Astrological practices sometimes turned into astral magic. For a discussion of this see, for example, D.P. Walker, *Spiritual and Demonic Magic from Ficino to Campanella* (London: Warburg Institute, 1958); Frances Yates, *Giordano Bruno and the Hermetic Tradition* (Chicago: University of Chicago Press, 1964); Augusta Espantoso Foley, *The Occult Arts and Doctrine in the Theater of Juan Ruiz de Alarcón* (Geneva: Droz, 1972); and R.J.W. Evans, *Rudolf II and his World* (Oxford: Clarendon Press, 1973).

These are some of the works outside the field of Golden Age Spanish drama that I have utilized and that an interested reader may find useful. The debt I have incurred to the many *comediantes* is only insufficiently acknowledged in the footnotes of this book.

Index

Blue, William R., 197
Bocángel y Unzueta, Gabriel, 72–74
Boccaccio, Giovanni, 76
Bodini, Vittorio, 89, 124, 130
Bonatti, Guido, 16, 192
Bouché Leclerq, Auguste, 2, 70, 117
Bovelles, Charles, 23
Braganza, duque de, 39
Brahe, Tycho, 119
Bredá, 67–68
Brindisium, pact of, 7
Brody, Ervin, 118
Brown, Jonathan, 67, 142
Buen Retiro palace, 139–46, 150, 186

Calderón, Rodrigo, 69
Calderón de la Barca, Pedro: *Afectos de odio y amor*, 187; *Amor, honor y poder*, 65–67; *El árbol de mejor fruto*, 68; *Las armas de la hermosura*, 68, 164, 174–80, 181, 214; *A secreto agravio, secreta venganza*, 208; *Los cabellos de Absalón*, 91; *Le devoción de la cruz*, 91, 113–14, 169; *Fieras afemina amor*, 161; *El golfo de las sirenas*, 68, 181–85; *La gran Cenobia*, 37, 68–87, 89–90, 93–96, 101, 129–30, 139, 147, 178, 207, 214–15; *Le hija del aire, II*, 68, 139, 169, 183; *La humildad coronada de las plantas*, 125; *El laurel de Apolo*, 187–89; *La lepra de Constantino*, 68; *El mayor encanto, amor*, 68, 139–49, 151–52, 156, 181–84, 214; *El monstruo de los jardines*, 68, 197–211, 216; *Ni amor se libra de amor*, 68, 185–86, 203; *No hay más fortuna que Dios*, 86; *El nuevo palacio del Retiro*, 142; *El privilegio de las mujeres*, 68, 164–80, 214; *Le puente de Mantible*, 68, 93–96; *El sitio de Bredá*, 67–68; *El toreador*, 187; *Los tres afectos de amor*, 68, 186–96, 203, 215; *Las tres justicias en una*, 91–92; *Los tres mayores prodigios*, 68, 149–63, 214; *La vida es sueño*, 51, 66–68, 74, 88–138, 139, 143, 169–70, 175, 187–89, 192, 200, 205, 215–16; *Yerros de naturaleza y aciertos de la fortuna*, 90–91, 96
Campanella, Tommaso, 119–21
Campbell, Joseph, 114–15, 154, 210
Campo, Jerónimo de, 28
Cancer, 9–10, 14, 97, 145, 155
capa y espada, 34–35
Capricorn, 10
Cascardi, Anthony, 28
Caspar, Max, 119

Cassiopea, 132
Castiglioni, Baldassare, 79
Castro, Américo, 30
catasterism, 20, 37, 39, 70, 213
Catholic Kings, 22–23, 58, 214
Cavalcanti, Giovanni, 190
caves, 30–31, 94, 144, 200. *See also Cueva de Meliso*
Cercysera, 205
Ceres, 5
Cervantes, Miguel de: *Don Quijote*, 30, 79; *La gitanilla*, 30; *La Numancia*, 32; *Persiles y Sigismunda*, 30–31, 52, 59; *Los tratos de Argel*, 32–33
Chapman, W. G., 150
Charlemagne, 15, 93–95, 119
Charles II (king of France), 20
Charles V (Holy Roman Emperor), 24–25, 27, 32, 58, 99, 161
Charles IX (king of France), 18
Charybdes, 183–85
child archetype, 6, 10, 21, 61, 64, 213
Chimera, 112
Chipre. *See* Cyprus
chivalry, 81, 94. *See also* Amadís de Gaula; Villamediana: *La gloria de Niquea*
choleric humor, 74, 83–84, 129–30
Chrysothemis, 5
Cicero, 5, 8–9, 30
Cilveti, Angel, 99, 123
Circe, 139–63, 181–84, 215
Cirlot, Jean, 39
Ciruelo, Pedro, 207
Claudian, 14
Cleopatra, 7
Cnidus, 193, 196, 203–10
Coello y Ochoa, Antonio, 90–92, 164, 171–75
Colahan, Clark, 96
Colchis, 157–58, 163
comets, 132
concorporatio, 15
Constantine (emperor), 14–15, 44
Cope, Jackson, 88
Copernicus, Nicolaus, 118–19
Coriolanus, 164–80
Cotarelo y Mori, Emilio, 168
Covarrubias y Horozco, Sebastián, 47, 58, 110–11, 125, 128–29, 154
Cueva de Meliso, 144
Cumaean Sybil, 6–7, 17, 29, 47, 73, 80
Cupid and Psyche myth, 185–86
Curtius, Ernst, 208

Cusanus, Nicolaus, 201
Cynthia, 199–200, 206
Cyprus, 175–77, 188, 191–96

Daedalus, 131, 159
Dante Alighieri, 16–17, 124, 190
Daphne, 61
Davies, Gareth, 28–29
death, 13, 49–50
deluge, 9–10, 53, 167
Demetrius, 118
desengaño, 44, 55, 75, 209–10
deus ex machina, 200–201, 210–11
diamond, 64, 127, 203, 207–8
Diana, 199, 206–9
Dike, 2–3
Dionysus, 182
discordia concors, 72, 76, 79, 83, 86, 92–93, 136, 204, 211, 216
dolphin, 125
Dominus mundi, 15–16, 24, 58, 157, 161
Donatus, 17
Dryden, John, 20–21
Dunn, Peter, 193, 203
Durán, Manuel, 66–67

eagle: in Rome, 8; in Alonso de Ezquerra, 51; in *La gloria de Niquea*, 60–63, 146; in *La puente de Mantible*, 95; in *La vida es sueño*, 105–6, 115, 123–38; in *El privilegio de las mujeres*, 166, 172
eclipse: in *La vida es sueño*, 106, 115–17, 137; in *Los tres afectos de amor*, 186, 189–90
ekpyrosis, 10–12, 212–14; in *La gloria de Niquea*, 62; in *La gran Cenobia*, 71; in *La vida es sueño*, 97, 106; in *El privilegio de las mujeres*, 167, 172–75; in *Las armas de la hermosura*, 179
elements, four, 61–62, 125, 181–82
Eliade, Mircea, 8–9, 134, 166, 171–73, 179, 212–13
Elizabeth I (of England), 18, 206, 213
Elliott, J. H., 67, 142
Elpis, 4
emblems, 38–39, 47, 50, 58, 110–11, 131
emerald, 64
Encelades, 130
Encina, Juan del, 22–24, 29
Ensoph, 200
Entrambasaguas, Joaquín de, 41
envy, 41, 45, 65, 77, 185–86, 194
equinox, 1, 38, 39, 147, 155. *See also* Ar-

ies; Libra; precession of the equinoxes
Erasmus, 79
Eratosthenes, 5, 70
Erigone, 5, 37–39
Escorial (monastery), 63
estrella de Sevilla, La, 66, 161
Euripides, 200
Europa, 60–62
Evans, R. J. W., 118, 120
exaltation (in astrology), 191
Ezquerra, Alonso de, 50

fateful curse, 160
Fates, 50, 54, 90
father-son conflict, 35–36, 66, 103–4, 187, 192
Felipe Próspero (prince), 186–88, 196
Ferrer de Valdecebro, Andrés, 128–29
Ficino, Marsilio, 17–18, 42–45, 111, 154, 190–91
Fierabrás, 93
Fiore, Robert, 86
fortuna bifrons, 70, 76, 85
Fortune: in Hyginus, 5; in Góngora, 54; in *La gran Cenobia*, 68–87, 214–15; in Eratosthenes, 70; in Seneca, 71–72; in Gabriel de Bocángel y Unzueta, 72–74; in Juvenal, 72; in *Las armas de la hermosura*, 178
Fox, Dian, 77
Francisco Xavier, Saint, 60, 64
Frazer, James, 141
Frederick Barbarossa (emperor), 15
Frederick II, 15–16, 125, 137
Freud, Sigmund, 109
Fronto, Marcus Cornilius, 113
Frye, Northrop, 117, 124
fuerza de la sangre, 127

Galileo Galilei, 118
Ganymede, 138
garamantes, 26
Garcilaso de la Vega, 203–4
Garuda, 125
gens aurea, 6, 107
Germanicus, 5, 7, 8, 70
Geryon, 161
Gibraltar, 161
Girard, René, 91–93
Gnido. *See* Cnidus
Golden Fleece, 151–58. *See also* Aries
Gómez, Manuel, 69